THE BEST
AMERICAN
MAGAZINE
WRITING

2008

THE BEST
AMERICAN
MAGAZINE
WRITING
2008

Compiled by

the American

Society of

Magazine

Editors

Columbia University Press   New York

Columbia University Press
Publishers Since 1893
New York   Chichester, West Sussex
Copyright © 2009 Columbia University Press
All rights reserved

Library of Congress Cataloging-in-Publication Data
ISSN 1541-0978
ISBN 978-0-231-14714-9 (pbk.)

Columbia University Press books are printed on permanent and durable
acid-free paper.
This book is printed on paper with recycled content.
Printed in the United States of America
p 10 9 8 7 6 5 4 3 2 1

References to Internet Web sites (URLs) were accurate at the time of writing.
Neither the author nor Columbia University Press is responsible for URLs
that may have expired or changed since the manuscript was prepared.

Contents

Jacob Weisberg

Introduction

Mine was the family that never threw anything away. This was a luxury permitted by the vast third floor of our shambling house in Chicago, a dusty purgatory where the busted, the superseded, and the seemed-like-a-good-idea-at the-time were sent to sit out the Cold War. These included a sauna salvaged from a failed Michigan motel, a skylit hospice for terminal houseplants, several packed cedar closets, and various crannies devoted to shellac records, typewriter carbons, and reel-to-reel tapes.

There were also magazines, great mounting stacks of them. Though chaotic, these had not been retained indiscriminately. Piled on open shelves were the great journals of my parents' early married years: back numbers of *Harper's*, *Esquire*, *New York*, *Life*, *Look*, the *New York Review of Books*, and *Commentary* chronicling the 1960s and the 1970s. In the twilight of an analogue era incomprehensible to my children, I spent countless afternoons coughing and flipping their pages.

When my mother decided to downsize and completed the North Side's biggest housecleaning since the Great Fire, I rescued a few relics like the *Harper's* issue devoted entirely to Norman Mailer's *Armies of the Night* and the *Esquire* with the cover of Andy Warhol drowning in his tomato soup can. I wish I'd saved more of them because whenever I think about what makes a magazine sing, I drift back to that gray-carpeted attic. That was, I now know, Clay Felker's *New York*, which gave birth to the New Journalism, Willie Morris's *Harper's*, and what must have been a full set of George Lois's *Esquire* covers, currently on view at the Museum of Modern Art. These left me with a feeling for what constitutes a magazine's *moment*, the joyous run one can have when the editor's taste, a culture's preoccupations, and a community of writers and designers come together. The best general-interest periodicals of that era spoke boldly and stylishly amid transformations of politics, art, morality, and manners. They had wide influence and became documents of cultural history. They're just as good if you read them today.

In years since, I've come across other journals that exemplify this kind of achievement: the original *Fortune*, costing a full dollar at the height of the Great Depression and for my money the most beautiful magazine ever produced in the United States; Mencken's *American Mercury*; Ross's *New Yorker*; *The Partisan Review*; and, I'd say, Dwight Macdonald's underappreciated quasi-monthly from the 1940s, *Politics*. From my own conscious lifetime, I'd throw in the vintage *Rolling Stone*, Michael Kinsley's *New Republic* (where I was lucky to get my start), Tina Brown's *New Yorker*, Graydon Carter's *Vanity Fair*, and David Remnick's *New Yorker*.

Others will have their own halls of fame, and I'm happy to play the parlor game anytime. *Spy*? *Ms.*? *The Smart Set*? Adam Moss's *New York* looks to me to be another keeper. But it's important to note that by definition, magazine moments don't last forever—eight years would constitute a very long one. The best writers are lured away, the formula grows familiar, the era's politics take a sharp turn dullward (the late '50s, '70s, and '90s). It can take subscribers a while to notice, but the attentive reader starts to feel he's read this before and, bam, it's over. Sometimes there's a second lease for the same management at the same publication, but more often the opposite occurs. The editor gets too comfortable, hews to formula, and neglects to leave the party while still having fun.

It is tempting to argue that this has been the fate of magazines as a medium, that the age of the greats is over. I would endorse many of the familiar complaints. Not many journals can afford to send writers off on three-month assignment these days. Not many readers have an hour for an article that took three months to write. Photojournalism has lost ground to fashion photography, cultural icons to dismal celebrities. Covers lack guts and imagination. Even the ads have lost their *Mad Men*–era panache.

I think it would be a mistake, though, to write off our era as one of declining craft. As an Internet editor, I have a stake in believing that the freshest work can be found online, and I do think technology and economics point in that direction. But for all our advantages, we websters can't yet do what the magazines in my attic did: hold attention through lengthy narrative, be portable, be beautiful, endure. And when I meet aspiring nonfiction writers, many of the brightest still aspire to the deep-dive, long-form literary journalism of Didion, Mailer, Thompson, and Wolfe.

If you don't harbor that fantasy already, this collection might implant it. "Betrayed," George Packer's account of America's abandonment of its Iraqi translators, was so heartbreaking it was made into a play. Evan Wright's profile of wackadoodle Hollywood-agent-turned-soldier-of-fortune Pat Dollard could be the most epic hatchet job ever executed. Matthew Scully's backhanded tribute to Michael Gerson, his credit-hogging boss in the Bush speechwriting shop, might be the second. Vanessa Grigoriadis's "Everybody Sucks," nails the Gawker phenomenon cold and beats the bloggers at their own game. Reading William Langewiesche's account of how a prison gang called the P.C.C. terrorized Sao Paolo for several days in 2006 intensified my fascinated fear of Brazil. In a more essayistic vein, here are Christopher

Hitchens, Hendrik Hertzberg, Walter Kirn, Kurt Andersen, and Caitlin Flanagan, here at their most urbane and illuminating.

I live in a Manhattan apartment now, with a wife who loves to purge as much as my parents loved to preserve. But I still find it hard to toss old issues of *The New Yorker*, *Vanity Fair*, and *The Atlantic* onto the recycling pile. You never know—a kid might find them someday and get inspired.

Jacob Weisberg is editor-in-chief of The Slate Group and author of *The Bush Tragedy* (Random House, 2008).

Cynthia Leive

Acknowledgments

Every industry has its Big Night. For movie people, there are the Oscars; for music-biz types it's the Grammys; and there's the Air Guitar World Championships if you happen to be a rock lover. For magazine editors, the Big Moment is generally thought to be the National Magazine Awards, the spring evening when we all dress up and try to resemble the glamorous creatures who play us on TV.

Fine. It's a nice night—a great night, actually, even if you're not one of the lucky twenty-five editors who leave Lincoln Center clutching an Alexander Calder–designed "Ellie." But if you ask me, the real highlight of the industry's year comes two months earlier, in the depths of winter, when 292 editors and art directors gather for the judging of those awards, hosted by the American Society of Magazine Editors (ASME). There's no black-tie finery (only the occasional pair of snowboots). No hors d'oeuvres, martinis, or speeches—just three hotel floors' worth of magazine professionals debating what constitutes great reporting, writing, design, and photography. The process takes three full days, and you'd think it would be exhausting, but, like most editors, I always leave that room with my batteries recharged, awed by the great work produced by my colleagues around the country.

The book you are holding in your hands captures much of that greatness: It contains selected finalists and winners of the

2008 National Magazine Awards. Credit for this anthology goes first and foremost to those 292 energetic judges; deep thanks also to Nicholas Lemann, dean of the Columbia University Graduate School of Journalism, cosponsor of the awards, and NMA administrator Robin Blackburn, who organized the 1,964 entries before judging. We are grateful to our book agent, David McCormick of McCormick & Williams, and our publisher, Columbia University Press, for sharing our enthusiasm for magazine journalism. But most of all this book bears the stamp of Marlene Kahan, ASME's executive director, who chose the stories and who is a friend to editors everywhere.

In 2008, as more and more of those editors take their talents online, I can't think of anyone better than Jacob Weisberg to write the introduction to this book. A veteran of *The New Republic* and *Newsweek*, Jacob joined the online magazine *Slate* in 1996 and today—as editor in chief of the Slate Group—proves on a daily basis that high-impact magazine journalism can be found on a laptop as well as on a newsstand. It's no surprise that a story Jacob published—Christopher Hitchens' men's-room musings on Larry Craig—is the first (but surely not last) online piece ever to be collected in one of these volumes.

Enjoy this book. I hope it recharges *your* batteries too.

THE BEST
AMERICAN
MAGAZINE
WRITING

2008

New York

FINALIST—FEATURE
WRITING

After becoming a target of the media-gossip blog Gawker.com, Vanessa Grigoriadis wanted to know more about was behind the must-read site of New York's chattering class. Her article takes readers into the world of Gawker, from its corps of over-worked young bloggers to its founder, the elusive Nick Denton.

Vanessa Grigoriadis

Everybody Sucks

At the risk of sounding like a wounded old-media journalist, let me share a story about my experience with the media-gossip blog Gawker.com, which I, like most journalists who cover stylish topics in New York, have read almost every day for five years. In addition to recently finding attacks on some of my female journalist friends—one of whom was described as slutty and "increasingly sundamaged"; another variously called a "tardblogger," "specialblogger," and "developmentallydisabledblogger"—as well as a friend's peppy little sister, who was put down for wanting to write a "self-actualizing screenplay or book proposal or whatever," I woke up the day after my wedding to find that Gawker had written about me. "The prize," said the Web site, "for the most annoying romance in this week's [*New York Times*] 'Vows' [column] goes to the following couple," and I'll bet you can guess which newly merged partnership that was. It seems that our last names, composed of too many syllables, as well as my alma mater, Wesleyan; the place we fell in love, Burning Man; our mothers' occupations as artists; and my husband's employer, David LaChapelle—in short, the quirky graphed points of my life—added up to an irredeemably idiotic persona (the lesson here, at the least, is that talking to the *Times*'s "Vows" column is a dangerous act of amour propre). Gawker's commenters, the unpaid vigilantes who are taking an increasingly prominent role in the site, heaved insults my way:

"Grigoriadis writes for *New York* magazine. Her last article was entitled, 'You Too Can Be a Celebrity Journalist!' With that kind of work and the newfound fame that comes with a *Times* wedding announcement, she's on the fast track to teaching a class at The Learning Annex."

"Sorry, but I'm obsessed with these two. The last names alone? They have nine vowels between them. And can't you see it when they have their painful hyphenated named children? Does anyone out there know them? Please offer up some stories. Perhaps their trip to Nepal, or her internship with Cindy Sherman. I need more . . ."

"Those two are such easy targets they have to be made up. C'mon, Wesleyan? LaChapelle? The immigrant artist parents? No two people could be that painful."

"Immigrant artist parents=house painters."

Are we ridiculous? Perhaps a little, and I was contemplating this, nervously, when I got a call from my new mother-in-law, who had received the news by way of a Google alert on her son's name. She was mortified, and I=pissed: High-minded citizen journalism, it seems, can also involve insulting people's ethnic backgrounds. I felt terrible about dragging my family into the foul, bloggy sewer of Gawker, one I have increasingly accepted as a normal part of participating in city media. A blog that is read by the vast majority of your colleagues, particularly younger ones, is as powerful a weapon as exists in the working world; that most of the blog is unintelligible except to a certain media class and other types of New York bitches does not diminish its impact on that group.

Like most journalists, I tend to have a defeatist attitude about Gawker, dismissing it as the *Mystery Science Theater 3000* of journalism, or accepting its vague put-downs under the principle that any press is good press. After all, there aren't lots of other news outlets that cover the minutiae of our lives, and we're all happy for any smidge of attention and desperate for its pickups of our stories, which are increasingly essential to getting our work read. The prospect and high probability of revenge makes one think twice about retaliation. Plus, only pansies get upset about Gawker, and no real journalist considers himself a pansy. But there is a cost to this way of thinking, a cost that can be as high as getting mocked on your wedding day.

. . .

Nearly five years ago, in December 2002, Gawker made its debut under the leadership of Nick Denton, the complicated owner of the blog network Gawker Media, and Elizabeth Spiers, a twenty-five-year-old banker turned blogger who was fragile in person but displayed a streak of dark cunning on the page. They didn't exactly invent the blog, but the tone they used for Gawker became the most important stylistic influence on the emerging field of blogging and has turned into the de facto voice of blogs today. Under Spiers's aegis, Gawker was a fun inside look at the media fishbowl by a woman who was, indeed, "snarky" but also seemed to genuinely enjoy both journalism and journalists—Spiers was a gawker at them—and took delight in putting out a sort of industry fanzine or yearbook, for which she was rewarded with fawning newspaper articles casting her as the new Dorothy Parker. Ironically enough, Spiers craved a job at a magazine. She soon left for a position here, at *New York* magazine; two subsequent Gawker editors, Jesse Oxfeld and Jessica Coen, have followed in the past year.

To be enticed, as these writers were, by the credentials extended by an old-media publication is a source of hilarity at the Gawker offices, where, beneath a veneer of self-deprecation, the core belief is that bloggers are cutting-edge journalists—the new "anti-media." No other form has lent itself so perfectly to capturing the current ethos of young New York, which is overwhelmingly tipped toward anger, envy, and resentment at those who control the culture and apartments. "New York is a city for the rich by the rich, and all of us work at the mercy of rich people and their projects," says Choire Sicha, Gawker's top editor (he currently employs a staff of five full-time writers). "If you work at any publication in this town, you work for a millionaire or billionaire. In some ways, that's functional, and it works as a feudal society. But what's happened now, related to that, is that culture has dried up and blown away: The Weimar-resurgence baloney is hideous; the rock-band scene is completely unexciting; the young artists have a little more juice, but they're just bleak intellectual kids; and I am really dissatisfied with young fiction writers." Sicha, a handsome ex–art dealer who spends his downtime gardening on Fire Island, is generally warm and even-tempered, but on this last point, he looks truly disgusted. "Not a week goes by I don't want to quit this job," he says, "because staring at New York this way makes me sick."

It's long been known to magazine journalists that there's an audience out there that's hungry to see the grasping and vainglorious and undeservedly successful ("douchebags" or "asshats," in Gawker parlance) put in the tumbrel and taken to their doom. It's not necessarily a pleasant job, but someone's got to do it. Young writers have always had the option of making their name by meting out character assassinations—I have been guilty of taking this path myself—but Gawker's ad hominem attacks and piss-on-a-baby humor far outstrip even *Spy* magazine's. It's an inevitable consequence of living in today's New York: Youthful anxiety and generational angst about having been completely cheated out of ownership of Manhattan, and only sporadically gaining it in Brooklyn and Queens, has fostered a bloodlust for the heads of the douchebags who stole the city. It's that old story of haves and have-nots, rewritten once again.

Gawker is the finest mechanism to date for satisfying this craving. Two weeks ago, Gawker writer Josh Stein jumped on the four-year-old son of satirist Neal Pollack, calling him a "horror" and "the worst" for providing his father with some cute quips about expensive cheese at a gourmet store. Pollack responded by sending an e-mail blast about his feelings to his friends, but Gawker got hold of the e-mail and relentlessly dug into him again and again. When Pollack first saw the post, "my heart sank to my knees," he says. "Instinctively, and stupidly, I sent out that e-mail, which I should never have done, because it just gave them the satisfaction of knowing that they'd gotten to me. That's all bullies want, really."

A friend of Pollack's later sent him a link to a blog written by a woman who'd dated Stein, which he passed along to me: "It's nice to know that my antagonist is an emotionally manipulative premature ejaculator with a Serge Gainsbourg tattoo on his back," explains Pollack, who'd realized a truth of the bile culture—shame is a weapon.

"Only two of those things are true," jokes Stein. "Look, if I was Neal Pollack, I would be mad too. But when you create a character out of your son, and you develop that character in your prose, that character is open to criticism. I'm actually looking forward to the moment when Neal Pollack is an old person and Elijah Pollack is writing stories about him in a nursing home."

.   .   .

Journalists are both haves and have-nots. They're at the feast, but know they don't really belong—they're fighting for table scraps, essentially—and it could all fall apart at any moment. Success is not solid. That's part of the weird fascination with Gawker, part of why it still works, five years on—it's about the anxiety and class rage of New York's creative underclass. Gawker's social policing and snipe-trading sideshow has been impossible to resist as a kind of moral drama about who deserves success and who doesn't. It supplies a Manhattan version of social justice. In the past couple of years, Gawker has expanded its mission to include celebrity gossip, sacrificing some of its insider voice in the process, but on a most basic level, it remains a blog about being a writer in New York, with all the competition, envy, and self-hate that goes along with the insecurity of that position.

It's not a secret that these are hard times for journalists. In fact, the rise of Gawker over the past half-decade has dovetailed with the general decline of newspaper and magazine publishing, which, like the rest of the publishing industry, has seen revenues stagnate as advertisers are increasingly drawn to the Web. This has made for wholesale changes within magazines, including our own, with Web departments, a few years ago considered a convenient place to dump unimpressive employees, now led by the favored (our own Web site now counts over forty workers). At the same time, the $200,000-a-year print-publishing job, once an attainable goal for those who had climbed near the top of the ladder in editorial departments, has all but disappeared.

Consider the Gawker mind-fuck at a time of rapid deterioration of our industry: Young print journalists are depressed over the state of the industry and their inability to locate challenging work or a job with health insurance. Although the situation may not be as dire as they might imagine—a healthy magazine is constantly on the hunt for young writers, because it wants the fresh take on the world found only in the young, and because young writers tend to be cheap—they need a release, the daily dose of schadenfreude offered by Gawker's gallows humor, its ritualistic flogging of working journalists and relentless cataloguing of the industry's fall (e.g., items like "*New Republic* Page Count Watch"). Though reading Gawker subtly reinforces their misery, they generate an emotional bond and soon begin to tip it with their own inside information (and misinformation, as reserved for their enemies). The system keeps getting stronger, a KGB of media gossip, a complex network of journalist spies and enforcers communicating via e-mail and IM, until Gawker knocks print out of the box. With Gawker, there is now little need for the usual gossip players like the *New York Observer*, vastly diminished in its news-breaking capacity and influence, or even the *New York Post*'s "Page Six," emasculated by the Murdoch hierarchy after the Jared Paul Stern scandal. The panopticon is complete. "Peering into my in-box in the morning is like looking at the id of every journalist in the city," says Gawker writer Emily Gould.

It's almost part of Gawker's business plan to ensure that its young writers, by attracting the attention of those they are sniping at, are able to leap into the waiting arms of the mainstream media before they become too expensive to employ. One afternoon, I meet Gould for tea before her early-evening meeting with an agent for appetizers at Serafina. She has the look of a studious but sexy punk rocker: twenty-six, dirty-blond hair caught in a high ponytail that shakes back and forth like a wagging tail as she speaks, tattoos crawling over a shoulder and back exposed today by a purple-plaid jumper. "I don't even really want to be a writer, but I feel like I don't have a choice," she says quietly. "It's all I've ever known how to do."

Ten or twenty years ago, Gould would have likely emulated Joan Didion, but she is trying to play the blog game now. She means to win, and to grab some attention for herself in the process. This summer, she took some time off in Maine, and before she went posted a picture of herself on Gawker in a bathing suit flipping the bird—"At least I didn't put up the ones of myself in a silver-lamé bikini. That would have been a little much," she says, laughing. She even used to do a lot of TV spots for Gawker, but then got badly beat up by Jimmy Kimmel, who told her on-air (he was subbing for Larry King), "I just want you to think about your life . . . because I would hate to see you arriving in hell and somebody sending a text message saying, 'Guess who's here?'" She was panicked about this at the time, but she's moved past it now. "It's funny," she drawls. "People in publishing treat you like a celebrity when you do this job, but you live in Brooklyn, make $55,000 a year, and don't feel like a celebrity until someone comes up to you on the street and says, 'Buck up, kid. Jimmy Kimmel's an asshole.'"

Though Gould is ruthless in pointing out other writers' shortcomings on Gawker, she is sensitive about her line of work. "In Maine, I was telling the guys I met that I was a yoga teacher," she says. "What am I supposed to say, 'I work for a media-gossip Web site in New York?'" She shakes her head, and the ponytail bops around. "Who knows how this will all play out for me?" she says. "I could be ruining my life."

•   •   •

If there's one person who is most certainly a "have," it's Nick Denton, forty-one, the attractive, upper-class gay Jewish Briton who owns almost all of Gawker Media. He seems to control an entire Soho street, presiding over his empire from his apartment, which is around the corner from the Gawker offices and across the street from his unofficial office, Balthazar (hence his faux IM name on Gawker.com, DarkLordBalthazar). Occasional unpleasantness with employees, who describe him as "less passive-aggressive and more aggressive-aggressive," and rampant speculation as to his skyrocketing net worth fuel his image, and in fact he has a Machiavellian bent. Denton likes to say that his celebrity look-alike is Morrissey, and he does have the same enormous head, but his hair is worn short, at almost the same length as his graying stubble. The pumpkin head bobs over his uniform of hip business casual—collarless navy T-shirt, iPhone in palm, clean dark jeans tapering off to thin-soled shiny black sneakers. He's polite, quiet, and relentlessly confident, an effective, poised leader whose true nature is amoral recklessness, an unrufflable libertarian and libertine. Like Tina Brown, with whom he was intrigued in the past, he's always loved using his position to play-cast a social network with himself at the center. Denton is fond of denying interview requests while secretly helping writers formulate stories about him via off-the-record conversations, then slagging their work later on his blog, calling one journalist who profiled him "about as reliable as a journalist who turns to an Iraqi exile for intelligence on Saddam's hidden nukes." The moment that he told me that he would not conduct an official interview with me, and I said I'd continue reporting without him, was perhaps the only one where I've seen him express emotion. For a split second, he was furious. His eyes flicked back and forth over mine like a metronome, searching for some clue to what I was planning, what angle I might be playing, and he spat out his denial with the intensity of a losing tennis player. "Nick loves press, but only press he can control," says a colleague.

A successful former journalist for the *Financial Times* who never quite became an opinion leader, and the cofounder of two Web 1.0 Internet companies that didn't exactly set Silicon Valley on fire, though one of them was nevertheless reported to have been sold for $50 million to Israeli venture capitalists, Denton has been jubilant over the success of Gawker, taking on the self-image of a maverick who has thumbed his nose at both of his former industries. Like most journalists trained in the British system, Denton does not believe in privacy for public figures, nor really for anyone else (except himself, apparently). "Everyone suspects Nick's motives, and he has defiantly lower print standards than any of us," says Sicha. "I'll tell him, 'That guy's gay,' or 'That guy's having an affair,' and he'll say, 'Then write that.' Well, I haven't slept with the guy, so I don't want to go to court over that. Nick communicates such things intentionally to us, to continually erode our standards." According to a post by another Gawker writer, one day Denton harangued Gawker's editors about being too mean on the site; a few minutes later, he began suggesting ideas for posts, like "Who's shorter in real life than you'd think they'd be? Who has dandruff?" "Does Nick believe in quality, or does Nick believe in respecting other people's idea of quality he doesn't believe in?" Sicha muses. "He has to believe not just in page views. But I don't know how exactly."

Of all the ways in which Gawker is antithetical to journalistic ethics—it's self-referential, judgmental, ad hominem, and resolutely against effecting change in the world—it pushes its writers to be honest in a way that's not always found in print publications. Little is repressed; the id, and everything else, is part of the discourse (including exhibition and narcissism). Even the Gawker office, a kind of journalistic boiler room, can serve as a metaphor for transparency, open for anyone to see, operating behind a plate-glass window in a Crosby Street storefront. Some of Denton's bloggers are onboard with this mission: "Quite frankly, fuck discretion," writes Moe Tkacik, a former newspaper reporter, on Denton's newest site, Jezebel. "Discretion is how I didn't figure out how to come until I was twenty-four years old; discretion is why women's magazine editors persist in treating their fellow humans like total shit; and when you've spent a career trying to catch others in their own indiscretions, discretion just feels a little dishonest and superior."

It's a good trick, taking the one thing that journalists have in the world—honesty—from them, and setting up Gawker.com to instill fear of being caught in their foibles. It's what someone would do if they were trying to usurp an industry, which is exactly what Denton has always wanted (do not, however, buy Gawker's tepid new book, *The Gawker Guide to Conquering All Media*, and think you will find genuine tips on how to do this yourself, as none are forthcoming). These days, Gawker is merely the flagship property of a Gawker Media empire, one Denton likes to compare to Condé Nast. Employees have started talking about his blogs as "magazines," and the company as a "stable of magazines." All fourteen Gawker blogs maintain standards of stratospherically higher writing quality than other Web sites in this LOLcat era, displaying their wares on sites with hilarious, deadpan names: Fleshbot (porn), Jalopnik (cars), Gizmodo (gadgets), and Kotaku (games); an early name for Gawker was "YouNork." Half of Denton's sites are modeled on Gawker's model of pairing a mannered gossip column with the industry of a given city, including Wonkette (D.C. politics), Defamer (Hollywood), Valleywag (Silicon Valley), and the new, excellent Jezebel (women's magazines and fashion). Denton is only intermittently involved in content and gives free rein to his editors to attack anyone they'd like (only ex-employees get a pass).

Denton's most successful blogs are, unsurprisingly, Gizmodo and Kotaku, at about 11 and 4 million visits per week. Or, to use the preferred metric, which has the benefit of being a higher number, the two blogs receive about 12 and 5 million "page views" per week, which is the number of times each visitor clicks on any blog page. Page views are very important: Advertisers usually pay for online ads in a unit of 1,000 ad impressions, and the number of page views a Web site receives have become like points for content-driven Internet properties, a way to keep score on competitors. Gawker nearly doubled in size last year, but the rate slowed to perhaps 30 percent last year, and the site now does about 2.5 million page views per week. For years, Denton told colleagues that there was no money to be made in blogs, even providing such a quotation to the *New York Times*. He didn't see the advantage in talking it up. Today, Gawker Media has approximately one hundred employees and contractors. "Nick made us all join Facebook," says Sicha. "I think he came to the office one day and couldn't recognize anybody—'Which one are you?'" Very few Web sites provide their traffic information, but Denton has chosen to do so with a link on his home page: No one can accuse him of not keeping his business transparent, at least superficially. Brightly colored traffic graphs provide the curious the illusion of being able to figure out his earnings, but without knowing the percentage of ad inventory sold across all blogs, it's impossible to generate more than a back-of-the-envelope guess of $10 to $12 million in revenue annually if most of his blogs sell ads at the industry standard.

"How many page views are you getting?" That's Denton's favorite question to ask fellow Internet entrepreneurs at a party.

•   •   •

Denton's place is one of the great Manhattan apartments for a party, a cavernous loft that seems to be decorated only in titanium and suede in a Soho building whose other tenants include Kelly Ripa and Harvey Weinstein. Sometimes he throws open his doors to everyone in town, on Halloween and during the holiday season, but more often he plays host to a select group of entrepreneurs and writers.

Over the summer, at the tail end of a cocktail hour, he's cleaning up the wrappers of White Castle hamburgers he provided as hors d'oeuvre. "I had a book party for Rebecca Mead at the New York Public Library last week, and they gouged me on the catering," he says, pursing his lips slightly. "These were so cheap!" Denton's boyfriend, a lovely African American artist, begins to get ready for their next stop of the evening, a going-away party for Gawker Media managing editor Lockhart Steele, leaving to build his own blog network with Denton joining an angel investment round. "Are there going to be a lot of bloggers there?" his boyfriend asks, and Denton nods. He sighs.

At Steele's party, at a dirty bar on Clinton Street, a white limousine with the license plate FILTHYNY rolls by as dozens of bloggers spill onto the sidewalk, surreptitiously drinking beers until a couple of cops begin handing out tickets. Everyone has a

slightly hunted look, born of spending all day at a computer
with a gun to their heads: Most bloggers in Denton's network
work under the most severe deadlines imaginable, with many
contracted to write twelve posts per day. At the same time, they
are unbelievably fulfilled: Bloggers get to experience the fantastic feeling of looking at everything in the world and then having
everyone look at them through their blog, of being both subject
and object, voyeur and voyeurant. To get more of that feeling,
some bloggers—if we were a blog, we'd tell you who—are in the
bathroom snorting cocaine, or Adderall, the ADHD drug popular among college kids on finals week, the constant use of which
is one of the only ways a blogger can write that much ("We're a
drug ring, not a bunch of bloggers," one Gawker Media employee tells me cheerily). Pinched nerves, carpal tunnel, swollen
feet—it's all part of the dastardly job, which at the top level can
involve editing one post every fifteen minutes for nine hours a
day, scanning 500 Web sites via RSS for news every half-hour,
and on "off-hours" keeping up with the news to prepare for tomorrow.

The Gawker.com editors stand mostly to the side, in a cool-kid
clique. Although they may in some sense be outsiders with their
noses pressed to the glass, horrified by a world of New York that
doesn't quite want to have them as members, in the bubble of
blogs, they're the elite, especially because lots of smaller bloggers' traffic relies on "link-whoring" (i.e., Gawker editors being
solicited for links by smaller sites). Sicha leans against the back
of a parked car, tanned and lean, his jeans slung low enough to
reveal the waistband of his underwear, talking to Alex Balk, a
former copywriter who tweaks Denton's desire for lowbrow
posts that generate page views by dialoguing with a character
known as "My Cock" (his bitterness conceals an emo side: Balk's
previous blog was named after a line from a Leonard Cohen
song). One Gawker Media videographer, widely known in the
office as the guy who had sex after-hours on the office couch,

lurches around in tight white jeans. "I was talking to this writer from *Elle Girl*, and then she said, 'I heard you're a crack whore but really good in bed,'" he tells a Gawker ad-sales guy, who snickers.

A Town Car pulls to the curb: It's the most famous journalist in the city, Julia Allison.

"Don't write about her, don't feed into it," two female bloggers beg me, stepping out of Allison's way as she approaches.

Allison is what Denton likes to call a "Gawker celebrity": Like all editors of gossip publications, he enjoys thinking of himself as a star-maker and lays claim to creating the personalities that he promotes, much in the way that some writers of the *New York Post*'s "Page Six" have always said they made Paris Hilton. But, like Paris, Allison is quite complicit in her star-making process— although she would never admit it, because that would ruin her image. She is pretty, though she looks even better on your computer screen because she chooses her outfits explicitly for the cameras: Her look is southern deb or, more precisely, an actress playing a southern deb—a polka-dot Nanette Lepore suit with no blouse underneath, a string of her grandmother's pearls, thickly applied lavender lipstick, and five-inch white platform shoes. "I'm just a small yappy dog Nick finds amusing," says Allison later, in a deep voice that projects across the room. "He's a godlike figure at the center of his universe," she says on another occasion. "The godfather! First he started a company, and now it's a culture."

A recent Georgetown University grad who moved to New York to become Candace Bushnell, Allison had a little-read dating column in *AM New York*—and a list of paramours that included former Tennessee congressman Harold Ford Jr.—when she decided to change her focus. She grabbed Denton's eye by showing up at one of his Halloween parties in a bustier made entirely of Trojan Magnum XL condom wrappers and developed a sophisticated Web site ("I dated a computer-science guy!"). She link-whored herself to Gawker on a daily basis, even if it meant sharing videos of herself in a white bikini riding a horse. "Freelancers are like the migrant workers of publishing—when I heard that Tom Wolfe makes $6 a word, I was like, 'Whoa,'" says Allison. "I figure if you make yourself a marquee name, you can't be replaced."

Soon, Allison landed a column in *Time Out*, where she was popular for her ability to get her stories linked on Gawker. Gawker was free advertising, after all: "*Time Out New York* dating columnist Julia Allison tackles the age-old dilemma faced by men around the world: How do you trick a chick into bed? Jules' advice: Be cheesy, surround yourself with hot ass, and buy her greasy food. (Not recommended: Yelling, 'Now suck my cock.')" Next, she was hired by *Star* magazine as an editor-at-large. She doesn't actually write anything, though. Her job is to go on TV and pretend that she works at *Star*.

· · ·

The value of Allison to Denton is not only tits=page views: It's also her popularity with Gawker's commenters, the largely anonymous readers whose responses to Gawker's posts are included on every item page. Commenters are the mob sneering at the tumbrels as they pass by—their comments are sometimes hilarious but always cruel and vicious, an echo chamber of Gawker's meanness. Gawker editors let them know their place by introducing "Commenter Executions," by which they banned a few of the lamest commenters each week (e.g., "Crime: on certain days, comments on every single post—yet says nothing"). But now Denton—impressed by the microblogging capabilities of current Silicon Valley darling Facebook and crushing on its founder, young Harvard dropout Mark Zuckerberg—wants to make more of them. He spent most of the summer working with developers on new software that tailors Gawker's page to the specific commenter who visits it. In fact, he'd love to see a site where half the page is taken up with comments.

"Gawker comments, long an embarrassment, frankly, now represent one of the strongest aspects of the site," he wrote recently (in Gawker's comments!). "They reintroduce an element of anarchy, which was in danger of otherwise being lost, as the site became more professional. I *want* secrets to be exposed, memos leaked, spy photos published, arguments to fly." Noah Robischon, Gawker's new managing editor, adds, "There are no immediate plans to reward commenters, but it is a natural way for us to scout for talent. I wouldn't be surprised if commenters who are promoted regularly end up as paid contributors." But are commenters even close to being in the loop? Last week, Denton tried to get them to step up: "Okay, how about a comment from someone who was actually at the Mediabistro party? Facts, please, people." But no one, of course, could answer such a thing—the best they could do is snipe: "Who would admit to this [being at the party], even under the cloak of i-anonymity?" sneered one.

The success of the comments has even made Denton rethink the compensation he pays his bloggers, the cows he has to pay for milk. Gawker as an automated message board, with commenters generating exponentially greater numbers of page views as they click all over the site to see reactions to their comments, could be the dream. There would then be no editors to pay, even at the rates he has to shell out. Until recently, most Gawker bloggers were paid a flat rate of twelve dollars per post for twelve posts a day, with quarterly bonuses adding to the bottom line; these bonuses could be used to buy equity in the company, which took two years to vest. Now, Denton is moving to a pay-for-performance system. He has always tracked the page views of each individual Gawker Media writer, thinking of them like stocks in a portfolio, with whoever generates the most page views as his favorite. If each writer was only as valuable as the page views he drew, then why shouldn't Denton pay him accordingly?

Balk, the site's primary troublemaker, quickly posted an item on Gawker about this change with the slug "Like Rain on Your Wedding Day, Except for Instead of Rain It's Knives." Denton wasn't amused. "Your item makes the argument for performance pay even stronger," he responded in the post's comments. "This awesomely self-indulgent post—of interest to you, me, and you, and me—will struggle to get 1,000 views. Which, under the new and improved pay system, Balk, will not even buy you a minute on your bourbon drip." (Balk gave notice two weeks later.)

Denton is a visionary tech geek, so it's not surprising that he would be fascinated by such new applications, but his relentless focus on page views may be evidence of restlessness, or even an existential crisis: Now that he's making money, really coining it, he knows he may have reached the top. There is a rush on advertising on the Web now, with TNS Media Intelligence reports showing that online advertising was up 17.7 percent for the first half of 2007, while print and TV were in decline. But in its current form, it's not going to solve the publishing crisis, online or off.

In fact, even Gawker.com has become boring to Denton, because it doesn't get the number of page views of his more popular sites. There were probably only going to be a few big Web companies anyway, as well as Google, and even though he still entertained the notion of holding onto his blogs for posterity, word had started to leak out of his talk about selling them down the road. Eventually, New York media would be like the New York film business—there would still be a lot of work, but except for some small independents, all the platforms would be owned elsewhere, operated out of office parks in San Jose, California. Possibly, Denton is holding onto Gawker.com as a kind of hobby, partly for the fun of having a catalogue of the decline of New York print publishing, an entire history of the fall. His roots are in journalism, and he undoubtedly enjoys the notoriety that Gawker brings—he's running one of the best circuses in the city. But a business model is a business model, and increasingly, in the media business, it's hard to find one. Maybe New York was done as a media town.

.   .   .

On a chilly evening in September, Gould and I went out for sushi. She traipsed down Prince Street in a tight electric-blue shirt, the same color as her fingernail polish, and white knee-high boots she had polished up for the fall season. She had just been at her shrink's, where she says she spends all her time talking about Gawker—"It's just such a weird cross between being an artist and working in a sweatshop," she'd said earlier. She tucked her hair behind her ears and sighed. "Plus I have gotten so much flak over the past year, from everyone from random people who e-mail me that I'm a bitch and a cunt, to my family, to Jimmy Kimmel calling me the devil—to my boyfriend of six years, when we broke up and I was moving my dishes out of his apartment, asking, 'Why did you write that post about that Stevie Nicks song? Now it's obvious to everyone that you were having an affair with your co-worker.'" She shot me a lopsided smile.

I asked her how she felt about the upcoming changes in comments and pay at Gawker. "I can't have feelings about that kind of thing," she said. "It's kind of like you're in jail and you have feelings about the color they paint the walls." Gould published a book last spring, and wasn't sure if she should write another. "At the end of the day, your ideas in a book have less impact than if you had summed them up in two paragraphs on the most widely read blog at the most-read time of the day, so why'd you spend two years on it?" she said, delicately picking up a piece of toro.

"But there's other ways to get noticed than the Internet, right?" She laughed bitterly. "There's always TV."

Recently, she'd bonded with Julia Allison—the two went to a psychic in Staten Island together, driving in a Mercedes convertible Allison had borrowed (though the guy who owned it didn't really know she had borrowed it), booming the stereo and singing along to the lyrics of Prince's "Pussy Control." The psychic told Allison that she had to be more "real" and Gould that she was on the road to love—but then she was not, so that was all a waste of time. But at least she decided Allison was cool. "It's not like Julia keeps her enemies close and her friends closer," said Gould. "She doesn't even make a distinction between the two."

In an insult culture, shamelessness is a crucial attribute, was part of the point. Last week at Gawker's book party, Allison appeared in a particularly revealing top and told me, "I figure if people look at my cleavage they won't listen to my words," then winked. She and Gould were both wearing polka-dots, not on purpose, and they cavorted in their outfits for a photographer, slinging their arms around Allison's boyfriend, even though Gould was sure to overdramatically grimace in some of the pictures.

By Gawker's rules, Allison seemed to be winning the game. Still, the question remained: Could you be successful in New York without becoming a—well, a douchebag? It was something that Gould would have to ponder.

National Geographic

WINNER—REPORTING

Combining exhaustive on-the-ground reporting with meticulous research and analysis, reporter Peter Hessler tells the dramatic story about the economic forces that are transforming China almost overnight.

Peter Hessler

China's Instant Cities

How Boss Wang and Boss Gao Became the Lords of the (Bra) Rings

At 2:30 in the afternoon, the bosses began designing the factory. The three-story building they had rented was perfectly empty: white walls, bare floors, a front door without a lock. You could come or go; everything in the Lishui Economic Development Zone shared that openness. Neighboring buildings were also empty shells, and they flanked a dirt road that pointed toward an unfinished highway. Blank silver billboards reflected the sky, advertising nothing but late October sunlight.

Wang Aiguo and Gao Xiaomeng had driven the 80 miles from Wenzhou, a city on China's southeastern coast. They were family—uncle and nephew—and they had come to Lishui to start a new business. "This whole area just opened up," Boss Gao explained, when I met him at the factory gate. "Wenzhou used to be this way, but now it's quite expensive, especially for a small company. It's better to be in a place like this."

On the first floor, we were joined by a contractor and his assistant. There was no architect, no draftsman; nobody had brought a ruler or a plumb line. Instead, Boss Gao began by handing out 555-brand cigarettes. He was thirty-three years old, with a sharp crewcut and a nervous air that intensified whenever his uncle was around. After everybody lit up, the young man reached into his shoulder bag for a pen and a scrap of paper.

First, he sketched the room's exterior walls. Then he started designing; every pen stroke represented a wall to be installed, and the factory began to take shape before our eyes. He drew two lines in the southwest corner: a future machine room. Next to that, a chemist's laboratory, followed by a storeroom and a secondary machine room. Boss Wang, the uncle, studied the page and said, "We don't need this room."

They conferred and then scratched it out. In twenty-seven minutes, they had finished designing the ground floor, and we went upstairs. More cigarettes. Boss Gao flipped over the paper.

"This is too small for an office."

"Put the wall here instead. That's big enough."

"Can you build another wall here?"

In twenty-three minutes, they designed an office, a hallway, and three living rooms for factory managers. On the top floor, the workers' dormitories required another fourteen minutes. All told, they had mapped out a 21,500-square-foot factory, from bottom to top, in one hour and four minutes. Boss Gao handed the scrap of paper to the contractor. The man asked when they wanted the estimate.

"How about this afternoon?"

The contractor looked at his watch. It was 3:48 P.M.

"I can't do it that fast!"

"Well, then tell me early in the morning."

They discussed materials—paint, cement, cinder blocks. "We want the ten-dollar doors," Boss Wang told the contractor, who was a Lishui native. "And don't try to make money by getting cheaper materials—do a good job now, and we'll hire you again. That's how we make money in Wenzhou. Do you understand?"

A Sea of Commodities

The Wenzhou airport bookstore stocks a volume titled, *Actually, You Don't Understand the Wenzhou People.* It shares a shelf with *The Feared Wenzhou People, The Collected Secrets of How Wenzhou People Make Money,* and *The Jews of the East: The Commercial Stories of Fifty Wenzhou Businessmen.* For the Chinese, this part of Zhejiang Province has become a source of fascination, and the local press contributes to the legend. Recently, Wenzhou's *Fortune Weekly* conducted a survey of local millionaires. One question was: If forced to choose between your business and your family, which would it be? Of the respondents, 60 percent chose business, and 20 percent chose family. The other 20 percent couldn't make up their minds.

From the beginning, an element of desperation helped create the Wenzhou business tradition. The region has little arable soil, and the mountainous landscape made for bad roads to the interior. With few options, Wenzhou natives turned to the sea, developing a strong trading culture by the end of the Ming dynasty, in the seventeenth century. But they lost their edge after 1949, when the communists came to power and cut off overseas trade links, as well as most private entrepreneurship. Even in the early 1980s, when Deng Xiaoping's free-market reforms began to take hold, Wenzhou started with distinct disadvantages. Residents lacked the education of people in Beijing, and they didn't attract the foreign investment of Shanghai. When the government established the first Special Economic Zone, whose trade and tax privileges were designed to spur growth, they chose Shenzhen, which is near Hong Kong.

But Wenzhou had the priceless capital of native instinct. Families opened tiny workshops, often with fewer than a dozen workers, and they produced simple goods. Over time, workshops blossomed into full-scale factories, and Wenzhou came to dominate certain low-tech industries. Today, one-quarter of all shoes bought in China come from Wenzhou. The city makes 70 percent of the world's cigarette lighters. Over 90 percent of Wenzhou's economy is private.

The Wenzhou Model, as it became known, spread throughout southern Zhejiang Province. Although nearly 80 percent of all Zhejiang entrepreneurs have a formal education of only eight years or less, the province has become the richest in China by most measures. The per capita incomes for both rural and urban residents are the highest of any Chinese province (this excludes specially administered cities such as Shanghai and Beijing). Zhejiang reflects China's economic miracle: a poor, overwhelmingly rural nation that has somehow become the world's most vibrant factory center.

Over the course of a year, I traveled repeatedly to Zhejiang, every time renting a car in Wenzhou and driving into the province. In the same way that a pilgrim treks across Spain, stopping at the shrines of obscure saints, I passed the birthplaces of products that are usually taken for granted. From the airport, driving south along the coast, I started with hinges—a stretch of road where the vast majority of billboards advertised every possible variation of the piece of metal used to swing a door. A mile later, the ads shifted to electric plugs and adapters. Then I reached a neighborhood of electric switches, followed by fluorescent lightbulbs, then faucets.

Deeper in the province, the shrines became more elaborate. At Qiaotou, I stopped to admire the twenty-foot-high silver statue of a button with wings that had been erected by the town elders. Qiaotou's population is only 64,000, but 380 local factories produce more than 70 percent of the buttons for clothes made in China. In Wuyi, I asked some bystanders what the local product was. A man reached into his pocket and pulled out three playing cards—queens, all of them. The city manufactures more than one billion decks a year. Datang township makes one-third of the world's socks. Songxia produces 350 million umbrellas every year. Table tennis paddles come from Shangguan; Fenshui turns out pens; Xiaxie does jungle gyms. Forty percent of the world's neckties are made in Shengzhou.

Everything is sold in a town called Yiwu. For the Zhejiang pilgrim, that's the promised land—Yiwu's slogan is "a sea of commodities, a paradise for shoppers." Yiwu is in the middle of nowhere, a hundred miles from the coast, but traders come from all over the world to buy goods in bulk. There's a scarf district, a plastic bag market, an avenue where every shop sells elastic. If you're burned out on buttons, take a stroll down Binwang Zipper Professional Street. The China Yiwu International Trade City, a local mall, has more than 30,000 stalls—if you spend one minute at each shop, eight hours a day, you'll leave two months later. Yiwu attracts so many Middle Eastern traders that one neighborhood has become home to twenty-three large Arabic restaurants, as well as a Lebanese bakery. I ate dinner at Arbeer, a Kurdish joint, with a trader from northern Iraq. He was buying blue jeans and electric lamps.

In the past, Lishui was the only major Zhejiang city that wasn't on the pilgrim's route. It's high in the mountains, where the Ou River runs too shallow for big boats; one local described it as the Tibet of Zhejiang. That was an oxymoron—the Alaska of New Jersey—but he made his point: In an industrial landscape, Lishui was the final frontier. It was the poorest city in China's richest province, but the new highway was almost finished, and investors were moving in fast.

The Memory of Liu Hongwei

Three months after designing the factory, Boss Gao and Boss Wang tested the equipment. Since my first visit, they had poached half a dozen skilled workers from another factory in southern China, and an assembly line had been installed. The fifty-foot-long machine lurked sullenly in the corner room, six tons of steel painted sea green.

The thing rumbled when the head technician threw the switch. Gas burners hummed beneath blue flames; a stainless steel belt lurched forward. The digital console tracked the rising temperature: 200 degrees Celsius (390°F), 300 degrees (570°F), 400 (750°F). It hit 474 (885°F), then dropped. They needed to reach 500 (930°F) before production could begin.

"Maybe it's because it's colder here than in Guangdong," the technician said. His name was Luo Shouyun, but everybody called him Mechanic Luo. He put on a pair of fireproof gloves and tried to open the door to one of the machine's ovens. But the handle melted off in his hand; he dropped it, cursing. The red-hot piece of metal lay on the floor, hissing like an angry snake.

"*Mei shir*," Boss Wang said. "No problem."

Mechanic Luo fiddled with the control box. He theorized that the natural gas canisters might be too cold. The men adjusted the valves and began to rock the massive metal tubes. The temperature didn't rise. They shook the tubes harder; nothing happened. Somebody went to get a stepladder and boiling water.

Boss Gao looked even more skittish than usual; he'd never installed such a big assembly line. More than a decade ago, he had started his first workshop in the outskirts of Wenzhou. With his parents and two sisters, he produced the fabric that lines the waist of cheap trousers. Initially, profits were 50 percent, and the workshop steadily expanded. But the neighborhood became home to more than twenty other companies making trouser lining, and the margins dropped until Boss Gao finally quit. "It used to be that you'd try to find a product that nobody else was making," he explained. "But now everything is already being made by somebody in China."

That's one weakness of the Wenzhou Model. Entrepreneurs produce goods that require little capital and low technology, which makes it easy for neighbors to jump in. Boss Wang, the uncle, had slipped into the same pattern. Previously, he had manufactured the steel underwire for women's brassieres, and his profits had dropped steadily. When the two men joined forces, they decided to continue manufacturing underwire, but their goal was to find a more profitable main product.

Fortunately, the average bra is composed of twelve separate components. In a figurative sense, the men began their quest at the bottom, with the underwire, and worked their way up. They thought about thread; they looked at lace; they considered the clasp. But when they reached the top, where tiny 0- and 8-shaped rings adjust the bra straps, they found what they were looking for.

A bra ring consists of steel coated with high-gloss nylon, requiring a specialized manufacturing process. The key equipment is a computer-regulated assembly line, divided into three separate stages, each of which heats the object to over 500 degrees Celsius. Originally, Europeans produced the rings, but by the early 1990s Taiwan dominated the market. In the middle of that decade, a mainland Chinese company called Daming imported an assembly line.

After its arrival on the mainland, where production costs are much cheaper, "the Machine" essentially minted money. The boss got rich, and then a worker named Liu Hongwei got an idea. Despite his lack of formal education, Liu was a skilled mechanic, who worked closely with the Machine. Meticulously, he memorized the assembly line, piece by piece, and in secret he sketched out blueprints. When the plans were complete, he contacted a second boss at a company called Shangang Keji, in the city of Shantou.

In 1998, Boss Number Two hired Liu and took the blueprints to Qingsui Machinery Manufacture Company, in Guangzhou, which custom-built the assembly line. Initially, the new Machine didn't work—nobody's memory is perfect, after all—but two months of adjustments solved the problems. Shangang Keji began producing bra rings, but then Liu found Boss Number Three, at a company called Jinde. Every time Liu jumped, he demanded money for his blueprints and expertise; some believe he made as much as $20,000.

Without knowing it, the man was following a path blazed by other societies that had also experienced sudden manufacturing booms. In 1810, a wealthy American named Francis Cabot Lowell traveled to England, where he used his connections to tour the world's premier textile mills. British law forbade the export of machinery or blueprints, but Lowell had an excellent memory. He returned to the United States, where, in the words of his business partner, he reinvented the Cartwright loom. Lowell became an American hero, with a Massachusetts factory town named in his honor.

Nearly two centuries later, Liu Hongwei's luck ran out when he tried to switch to Boss Number Four. According to a former coworker, Number Three put a $12,000 bounty on Liu's head, and he fled. "I know that Jinde was looking for him, and they were angry," said Gu Hong, a Qingsui business manager who had helped custom-build the Machine. "He disappeared."

The industry, though, had already been changed. In the five years after Liu's reinvention, the bra-ring price dropped by 60 percent. Today, more than twenty Chinese companies manufacture the object, and the Machine is available to anybody with $65,000. Previously, all major manufacturers had been concentrated in the south, but now Boss Gao and Boss Wang hoped to be the first to make rings in Zhejiang.

On the day they tested the Machine, the temperature refused to budge, and the men took turns standing on the stepladder and dumping buckets of boiling water over the gas canisters.

Half an hour later, steam filled the room, and they had discovered a new axiom: Pouring boiling water on natural gas canisters has no effect on the production of bra rings.

After four hours of testing, they gave up. In the end, Mechanic Luo disassembled the Machine, replaced a key part, and moved the burners closer to the assembly line. It took nearly two weeks. Some sections of the Machine had to be jury-rigged with plywood and string; they never reattached the melted handle. "The blueprints still aren't very good," Mechanic Luo explained. Years ago, he had worked alongside Liu Hongwei, and he said the same things about the technology thief that I heard from others. Liu was tall, devious, and from Sichuan Province. People speculated that Liu wasn't his real name, and they had never met his wife or child. Nobody had any idea where the man had gone.

Moving Mountains

The government motto of the Lishui Economic Development Zone is "Each person does the work of two; two days' work is done in one." The slogan may be too modest. From 2000 to 2005, the city's population went from 160,000 to 250,000, and the local government invested 8.8 billion dollars in infrastructure for the region it administers. During those five years, infrastructure investment was five times the amount spent in the previous half century. In money terms, what was once fifty days' work is now done in one.

For the past three decades, China's economy has averaged nearly 10 percent annual growth. The economy is fueled by the largest migration the world has ever seen: An estimated 140 million rural Chinese have already left their homes, and another 45 million are expected to join the urban workforce in the next five years. Most have gone to factory towns along the coast, but in recent years migrants have been drawn increasingly to cities in the interior, where there's less competition for jobs.

Such cities must expand and attract industry on their own, because the central government no longer provides the funding and guidance of the old planned economy. One common strategy is to establish a factory zone: Clear out land, sell it at reduced rates, and give investors tax breaks. In 2002, Lishui began construction of a factory zone, which consists of a 5.6-square-mile plot to the south of the city proper. By 2006, nearly 200 plants had started production, attracting 30,000 migrant workers.

This early growth had been guided by Wang Lijiong, the forty-eight-year-old director of the development zone. As a young man, Wang's first job had been in a dynamite factory, and then he spent five years driving a tank for the People's Liberation Army. Upon leaving the military, he worked in a state-owned bank, and then he began to rise through the government bureaucracy. He is friendly and open—qualities unusual for a Chinese official. He told me that he still draws inspiration from his military experience. "In a tank, you go directly at your goal," he said. "You need the spirit of persistence."

Lishui's zone occupies what was previously rugged farmland. Director Wang told me that approximately one thousand peasants had been relocated, as well as exactly 108 separate mountains and hills. He said, simply, "We lowered the higher places and raised the lower places." During one of my earlier trips to Lishui, I had watched a higher place get lowered. There were thirty dump trucks and eleven Caterpillar excavators; workers had just packed the hillside with 9.9 tons of dynamite. Eventually, this site would become home to a half dozen chemical factories.

A worker noticed me and walked over. In each hand, he carried a cheap plastic shopping bag filled with explosive. He set the bags on the ground and said, "Will you take my little brother to New York?"

Having lived as a foreigner in China for a decade, I was accustomed to non sequitur conversations, but that opener left me speechless. Anyway, I couldn't take my eyes off those plastic bags. The man smiled and said, "I'm joking. But he really wants to go to America."

He introduced me to Mu Shiyou, who was in charge of detonation. Mu and I walked to the base of the doomed hill, where a tangle of wires connected to the packed dynamite. He spliced the wires to a single line and payed it out as we walked away. All vehicles and workers had been evacuated; it was so quiet that I could hear birds overhead.

The detonator box had two switches labeled "Charge" and "Explode." We stood behind the treaded wheels of a parked Caterpillar. A command crackled over Mu's walkie-talkie: "Charge!"

He hit the switch and said, "Get out there where you can see it better!" A countdown, another command ("Explode!"), and he flipped the second switch. For the briefest instant, before there was any sound, a web of electricity flickered across the hillside, like lightning come to earth.

Willing to Eat Bitterness

On February 6, half a month after testing the Machine, Boss Wang officially opened the factory by igniting two boxes of fireworks. According to the lunar calendar, it was the eighth day of the new year, and a feng shui expert had advised the owners to take advantage of eight, a lucky number in China.

Like most Wenzhou businessmen, Boss Wang was deeply superstitious. He had a high-pitched voice and a slight stutter; his eyelids fluttered rapidly when he spoke. He was forty years old, and in the past he had always manufactured parts of objects: pieces of piping, pieces of bicycle bells, pieces of brassieres. In hindsight, he wished that as a young man he had gone into the shoe business. "I have some regrets," he told me, because a number of his boyhood friends had become shoe-factory millionaires. Even in the new Lishui factory zone, where virtually everything was still under construction, the grass was already greener next door. Boss Wang's neighbor was Geley Electrical Co., whose owner had started as a lowly button manufacturer in Qiaotou before moving on to bigger and better things. Now Geley employed hundreds of workers, and the new factory produced three-dollar plastic electric outlets that were marketed proudly as the Jane Eyre model.

Boss Wang and Boss Gao gave their company the English name Lishui Yashun Underdress Fittings Industry Co., Ltd. Branding was instant: For less than $800, a Wenzhou designer created a logo, sample books, Web site, and business cards. Everything was hot pink; the Web site and sample books featured photographs of sultry foreign women wearing bras. The men's business cards bore the logo:

I wondered if the design represented a bird in flight, or maybe a heart, or perhaps a pair of—

"I don't know what it's supposed to be," Boss Wang admitted. "It doesn't matter, as long as it looks good. The designer probably took it from some other company."

Three days after setting off the fireworks, Boss Wang posted a handwritten job notice on the factory gate:

1. Ages 18 to 35, middle-school education
2. Good health, good quality
3. Attentive to hygiene, willing to eat bitterness and work hard.

All across the Lishui development zone, young people wandered in packs, reading the factory signs that had been posted at the end of the New Year holiday. At the local job fair, migrants gazed up at a digital board with listings so terse they read like code:

"Cashiers, women, 1.66 meters [5.4 feet] or taller"
"Willing to eat bitterness and work hard, 25 to 45 yuan a day, male, middle school"
"Male workers 35 yuan, female workers 25 yuan"
"Average workers, people from Jiangxi and Sichuan need not apply."

There were no euphemisms, no apologies. If a company preferred its women to be tall, they asked for tall women. If they had a prejudice against a certain region, tough luck. At a factory called Jinchao, the guard turned away all applicants from Guizhou, the poorest province in China. When I asked the manager why, he said, "Around here, a lot of the petty criminals are from Guizhou." At Yashun, Boss Gao's father handled the hiring, and I sat in on a job interview in which he asked an applicant how old she was. The woman said, "Do you mean my real age, or the age that's on my identity card?" She explained that seven years ago, when she had first left home, she'd forged the ID because she'd been so young. The man offered her a job; he told me that a woman like that must really enjoy working.

In China, minimum wage varies by region, and Lishui's is about forty cents an hour. Yashun offered jobs at the lowest rate, but applicants poured in; there was no shortage of unskilled labor. Boss Gao's father kept a pile of bra rings on his desk, to show what the factory produced. On the second day, after the workers' list was full, he told an applicant that her name would be on the backup sheet.

"Just switch my name with somebody else's," she said.

"I can't do that. We already have enough. We have nineteen."

The woman had short-cropped hair and lively eyes; her identity card said she was seventeen. She leaned close to the desk and fiddled nervously with the bra rings, as if they were pieces in a game she was determined to win.

"Just change a name," she said. "Why does it matter?"

"I can't do that."

"I would have come yesterday if I'd known."

"I'll make sure you're first on the second list. See, I even wrote 'good girl' next to your name."

But the woman wouldn't give up. At last, after ten minutes of pleading, he added her name—but then the Wenzhou superstition struck. "Now it's *ershi*," he said. "Twenty. That's a bad-sounding number—too much like *esi*, starving to death. So I'll have to add another."

The woman thanked him and headed toward the door.

"But if the boss says twenty-one is too many, then it'll have to be nineteen," he warned her.

The woman walked back to the desk. "Move my name up the list."

Five minutes later, her name was squarely in the middle of the sheet. When she finally left, the man shook his head admiringly. He said, "That girl knows how to get things done."

Later they realized that she had used her older sister's identity card. The girl who got things done, it turned out, was barely fifteen years old.

Even the Fountains Make Music

The first time I visited the factory, the road in front was dirt, and the development zone's billboards were mostly blank. By my second visit, six weeks later, the Yintai real estate company had posted an advertisement. The road was being paved during my third trip. On the fourth, I saw a woman drive the front left wheel of her Honda into an open manhole. The manhole covers were installed by my fifth visit. A medical clinic appeared before the sixth trip. Sidewalks and streetlights by the seventh. Trees and bus stops by the eighth.

Factory production didn't wait for finished infrastructure, and neither did daily life. In a Chinese development zone, construction sites are essentially public space, and the factory's street hosted all sorts of makeshift entertainment. One week, a traditional Wu opera troupe erected a stage in the middle of the road; later, a traveling carnival set up shop. Every month, the local government parked a truck at an intersection, unfurled a white screen, and showed a free double feature. Nearby, a real estate company used its construction site to sponsor the Harmonious Sound Workers' Karaoke Contest. Representatives from local factories competed, and over 12,000 workers came to watch. The winner was a security guard from a plant that made down blankets and clothing. He sang a popular love song—"A Woman's Heart."

One week, the Red Star Acrobatic and Artistic Troupe came to town. Their battered truck had side panels that unfolded to reveal a marquee with photographs of half-dressed women, along with bright slogans (Passion! Perfection!). The truck's body converted into a box office; they pitched a tent in back. Admission was sixty cents, and 160 people bought tickets—almost all men. Troupe members sang songs and performed skits; one man acted out the heartbreaking story of a migrant imprisoned for theft. Another man popped his shoulder out of its socket and writhed on stage while his brother took up a collection. At the end, a woman stripped.

It was all illegal. Nude shows are banned in China, and the troupe wasn't registered; no one even had a driver's license. They were an extended family from Henan Province, bouncing their way south—in succession, they'd been kicked out of Nanjing, Hangzhou, and Yongkang. When I asked Liu Changfu, the troupe leader, why they included nudity, he said, "Before people buy tickets, they often ask if we have some 'open entertainment.' We need to be able to say yes.'" The task of stripping fell to the wife of the most distant cousin. Liu told me they were profitable as long as they kept moving, and there was always another half-built development zone down the road.

Lishui depended as much on construction sites as did the itinerant entertainers. Chinese cities aren't allowed to raise funds through municipal bonds or sharp tax increases, so they turn to real estate. Legally, all land belongs to the nation, but local governments can approve the sale of land-use rights—the closest thing to private ownership. Cities acquire suburban land from peasants at artificially low set rates, approve it for development, and sell for a profit on the open market. Across China, an estimated 40 to 60 percent of local government revenue is acquired in this way.

New apartment complexes were rising all around Lishui, and one of the biggest was the Jiangbin development. Formerly, the 16.5 acres had belonged to the village of Xiahe, but in 2000 the city government bought the land-use rights for one million dollars. Three years later, Lishui flipped the land to Yintai Real Estate for 37 million dollars. Given that corruption is endemic in Chinese real estate, the actual price may have been even higher.

In such an environment, everybody gambles on growth. Most of the city's massive investment in infrastructure had been borrowed from state-owned banks, which also loaned money to the developers—Yintai had borrowed over 28 million dollars for its Jiangbin venture. If the real estate market went cold, the whole system was in trouble, and the central government had recently instituted new laws intended to slow down such expansions. But the money kept pouring in—during the past five years, the average price of a Lishui apartment had risen sixfold.

On paper, it looked untenable, but the Chinese economic and social environment is unlike anything else in the world. Real estate laws are skewed in the government's favor, and migration and the export economy create a constant demand for expanding cities. After the hard times of the twentieth century, the average citizen is willing to tolerate unfairness as long as his living standard improves. In Jiangbin, I met Zhang Qiaoping, whose family had formerly farmed one-third of an acre on the site. The government paid him $15,000 for a plot of land that was worth at least $200,000. Zhang wasn't happy, but he hadn't protested; instead, he invested in a small shop next to the site. Most customers were construction workers. There wasn't much money trickling down to the lowest levels, but Zhang had tapped into enough to support his family.

Some peasants even made it to the top. Yintai is owned by the Ji family, whose patriarch had been a farmer before engaging in small-scale construction work in the 1980s. Eventually, he expanded into real estate, and now his three sons help manage the company. I met the youngest, Ji Shengjun, at the nightclub he owns. Flanked by his bodyguard, the twenty-six-year-old was drinking Matisse scotch mixed with green tea, and listening patiently to the entreaties of a pretty young woman. Ji wore Prada trousers and a Versace shirt; his Piaget watch had cost $10,000. He told me that Yintai expected to profit 19 million dollars from Jiangbin. The apartment complex would feature a musical fountain bigger than a football field. The pretty young woman was begging Ji to help her acquire a visa to Portugal.

A Negotiated Child

Much of China's economy depends on peasants who have left the land, and that was also true at the Yashun factory. Boss Wang and Boss Gao come from rice-growing families; Mechanic Luo was born on a cotton plot. A former orange grower worked the metal punch machine, and the chemist had grown up with tea, tobacco, and peanuts. The assembly-line women knew wheat and soybeans. The accountant came from pear country.

Despite their varied rural backgrounds, now everybody concentrated on the production of exactly two things: underwire and bra rings that weigh half a gram each.

Even the bosses were willing to work like peasants—every day, the men spent long hours on the factory floor. Each had invested his life savings in the business—cash—and only Boss Gao had borrowed a little from the bank. There was no management board, no investment schedule, no business plan. They began production without a single guaranteed customer. Throughout March and April, Boss Wang traveled to bra assembly plants, bearing gifts: Chunghwa cigarettes, Wuliangye alcohol, yellow croaker fish (a Wenzhou favorite). But potential customers were slow to make orders, and by summer the factory had over one million bra rings in storage. They laid off most unskilled workers and slashed the technicians' salaries in half.

Initially, the bosses had moved with remarkable speed, but now they paid for the lack of a system. Such institutional weaknesses are becoming more apparent in Chinese businesses because of the increasingly competitive environment. And the nation's next desired economic stage—innovative products and the creation of international brands—will require more creativity and logical organization.

At Yashun, only Boss Gao had as much as a trade-school education, and Mechanic Luo, the most important employee, hadn't finished elementary school. When he began working full-time at the age of fourteen, he was nearly illiterate, but he enrolled in night classes in Shenzhen. Such courses are common in Chinese boomtowns, and Luo eventually received his high school certification. He also acquired technical skills that allowed him to work with the Machine, and over the years he had been poached three times from bra-ring jobs. Along the way, his salary had risen to $760 a month, a high wage in China. As is common in the cutthroat factory world, he left every job without notice.

Each time, he simply asked for a few days' vacation, changed his cell phone number, and never returned.

When Yashun struggled, the bosses cut Mechanic Luo's salary in half, and then they stopped paying him at all. Perversely, this reflected his value—he was the only person who understood the Machine. During a crisis, small Chinese factories sometimes withhold salaries, because workers won't leave when they're owed money. Everything came to a head in July, when Mechanic Luo's wife was about to give birth. She was in his hometown in Hubei Province, and he told me that this would be their second child.

The bosses refused to grant leave. On July 27, the baby was delivered by C-section, and Mechanic Luo told the bosses that he absolutely needed to return, to help his wife recover from surgery. Finally, they agreed, but they balked on paying the back salary. That evening, when I took Mechanic Luo out for a celebratory dinner, negotiations were still in progress. In the end, the bosses paid one-third of what they owed him, and he promised to return within a week.

Later, the mother and baby traveled twenty-one hours by bus to Lishui. They shared the factory dorm room with Mechanic Luo, who proudly introduced me. I asked how the child's brother was doing; I assumed he was still in the village with his grandparents. But the man's face fell, and I feared that something terrible had happened.

"This is actually our first child," he said, dropping his voice. "When Boss Wang and Boss Gao hired me, I told them I already had a son, so I could ask for a higher salary. I didn't want to lie to you, but they were around when we were talking."

After two months, his wife took the baby back to her home province of Guizhou. At the Guiyang rail station, two women approached and offered her a ride. They led her to a minivan that contained two men. After they left the city, she noticed a strong chemical smell and felt disoriented. The next thing she knew, they had robbed her of $120 in cash, her cell phone, and her earrings. Afterward, the baby was unusually sleepy, and the mother called Mechanic Luo in a panic. He told her to wash the child immediately. Since then, the baby had seemed healthy. Not yet four months old, he'd lived in a factory, served as a pawn in salary negotiations, and been drugged and robbed. Mechanic Luo had named him Wen, "cultured," because he dreamed of his son becoming an educated man.

A Difference of Three Dollars

The fifteen-year-old at the factory had dropped out of school after the seventh grade because her family needed money. Nobody at the factory seemed to mind that she had initially used her older sister's name. In China, where the legal working age is sixteen, it's common for workers to register with false IDs. In fact, the sister ended up working there, too, as did the father. Their name was Tao, and they had migrated from Anhui Province. Unlike most workers, they lived in a rented room nearby instead of the factory dorm. During the summer months, when the plant verged on failure, the Taos were rarely called in to work. But then Boss Wang's courtship of customers finally began to pay off. By August, the factory had five steady buyers. In September, eleven months after the factory had been designed, it turned its first monthly profit. By October, business was good, and the Taos were working long hours every day.

The older sister sorted bra rings on the Machine's assembly line, while the fifteen-year-old, whose name was Yufeng, handled underwire. She placed the curved wires onto a spring that was sent into an industrial heater. The job paid by the piece, and on a good day Yufeng could finish 30,000 wires, for a wage of $7.50. She was quick, reliable, and completely self-possessed. She talked back to Boss Wang like nobody else. One evening, when a coworker celebrated her sixteenth birthday, Yufeng used the occasion to bully her foreman into drinking shots. Chugging Sprite to his Double Deer beer, the girl was relentless. "Drink! Drink! Drink!" she shouted, turning to me and the other men at the table. "Toast him! I want to get him drunk so I won't have to work hard tomorrow!"

Yufeng, like her sister, gave all her earnings to the parents. Her dream was to open a shoe factory someday; she told me that if she became successful, she'd build a three-story home in her grandparents' village. When I asked about the grandparents, the girl's eyes filled with tears, and then I didn't ask about that anymore.

By November, the Machine was turning out 100,000 rings daily, and the bosses had installed a bigger assembly line for underwire. But like everybody in Lishui, they had gambled on rapid growth, hoping to expand to sixty workers by the end of the first year. In fact, they had only twenty, and the building was three times bigger than necessary. "It's still too early," Boss Wang grumbled, when I asked about Lishui's development. "If we have to get a part, or do anything related to machinery, we have to go all the way to Wenzhou."

That month, the bosses decided to relocate the factory. The decision was instant; there was no consultation with Mechanic Luo or anybody else. Boss Gao found two available buildings in the marshlands north of Wenzhou, and then they consulted the feng shui expert. His advice was unequivocal: November 28 was also the eighth day of the lunar month, and you can't do better than double eights.

Most workers decided to move with the factory, but the Taos' situation was complicated. The mother ran a small dry goods stand nearby, and the youngest son was enrolled in a local middle school. If the father and daughters kept their jobs, the family would be divided. At the factory, the decision became a topic of daily discussion.

"You should be independent by now," Mechanic Luo said to Yufeng, one day at lunch.

"You don't have a bank account, do you?"

"No," she said.

"You're still giving all your money to your parents!"

"They need my help."

"It helps more if you learn to be independent."

The man scoffed that he had first left home with only six dollars in his pocket. The way he told it, Yufeng was just another overprotected fifteen-year-old working fifty hours a week on an assembly line. But the father refused to leave the decision to his daughters. He insisted they would leave together—but only if the salary was renegotiated.

The night before the move, the bosses finally offered a raise. The father asked for more; the bosses dragged their heels. No one was willing to meet directly, so Mechanic Luo carried messages back and forth. At eight o'clock, he visited the Taos' mud-walled room. The girls went outside; the men lit West Lake cigarettes. The father said, "I'm not willing to move unless they make it worth my while."

"I know," Mechanic Luo said. "And I don't want to train new workers."

The mother said, "Maybe we should just send them to work in a shoe factory."

"Don't talk about that yet," the father said. "We need to figure this out first."

He demanded the same wage for everybody: a guaranteed 127 dollars a month, plus overtime, and six dollars in living expenses. Mechanic Luo returned to the bosses, who cut the expenses in half—a difference of three dollars. The father didn't reply, and that offer was still on the table when the night ended.

Good Days Ahead

That fall, Lishui applied to add another 13.5 square miles to the development zone. The expansion would require an investment of almost 900 million dollars, most of which would come from bank loans. They planned to double the city's population by 2020. With energy demands rising, the Tankeng Dam was being constructed in the mountains south of Lishui. In preparation, 50,000 people were being relocated from ten towns and eighty villages. I had watched the final evacuation of Beishan, the largest town, on October 25 of 2005—an auspicious date according to the feng shui experts. There were good days for everything, even abandoning your hometown. Families packed flatbed trucks full of furniture; they unloaded in eight new resettlement communities that had yet to be finished. In Youzhou, Chen Qiaomei told me she'd had trouble finding her apartment, which had no windows yet. "They all look the same!" she said.

When I talked about Lishui's factory zone expansion plans with Director Wang, he acknowledged that approval for such projects was becoming more difficult. The central government feared a real estate bubble, but he remained confident. "We're applying to develop an area where the land isn't good for farming," he explained.

On his office wall hung a map of the proposed expansion—future roads, industrial blocks, waterworks. "We'll have to move more than 400 mountains and hills," he said. He invited me to return in January, when his boy would be home for vacation. The son of the former tank driver was at the University of Auckland, studying international finance.

Factory Ghosts

They moved the bra-ring factory in one day. The bosses hired a forklift, four flatbed trucks, and seven laborers. Mechanic Luo disassembled the Machine into three parts; the finished bra rings were packed into ninety-four boxes. They removed everything of value, even the carpet and the lightbulbs. A year earlier, they had ordered ten-dollar doors, and now they took them off the hinges.

At three o'clock, the Tao sisters showed up with their bags packed. Their father, it turned out, had found a better-paying job for himself at a nearby factory that produced synthetic leather. He had arranged it days ago, in secret; the insistence on staying with his daughters turned out to be a negotiating ploy. There weren't any tears at the factory gate. The last thing the father said was, "You need to dress warmly. It's going to get cold, and you'll get sick if you're not careful. If you're sick, you'll have to spend money on medicine. So dress warmly, OK? Goodbye."

Two days later, I drove to the development zone, past rows of finished billboards: Amway, Haishun Steel Structure, Fengchang Steel Hooks. The former Yashun factory was unlocked. Inside, bra rings were strewed everywhere—bent rings, dirty rings, broken rings. There were crumpled cigarette packages and used rolls of tape. An empty diaper bag. A wall calendar frozen at November 22. A good luck charm with Mao Zedong's face on one side and a bodhisattva on the other. And throughout the dormitories, on the white plaster walls, graffiti had accumulated over the months. Next to his bed, one worker had listed numbers: winning lottery combinations. Another had inscribed, "Find success immediately." Others wrote:

"Reflect on the past, consider the future."

"Pass every day happily! A new day begins from right now!"

"Face the future directly."

"Leave the world."

"A person can become successful anywhere; I swear I won't return home until I am famous."

A cold wind blew against the windows. Outside, I heard neighboring plants—the rattle of glassmaking, the rumble of plastic molds, the pneumatic hiss of water heaters being produced. But there wasn't a single human sound, only the silent voices on the walls of the abandoned factory.

The Atlantic

"Present at the Creation," is a devastating deconstruction of the public persona crafted by former chief White House speechwriter Michael Gerson and a critical look at the gullibility of leading journalists who bought into the myth.

Matthew Scully

Present at
the Creation

Michael J. Gerson, my former speechwriting colleague in the Bush White House, is a talented fellow with a first-rate mind and serious purposes—all of which we can expect to see in his new book, *Heroic Conservatism*. But reading a few insider stories in the first chapter of the book, which his publisher has sent out for publicity, I was not surprised to find that the personal heroics begin early.

By page 3, a "solemn quiet" has fallen over the Oval Office, and we have one of those crossroads moments that come in every White House memoir. Large and consequential matters were in the balance, "the keepers of the budget" were about to crush the hopes of millions, only truth well spoken could save the day, and guess who had the courage to speak it? The conviction and idealism of his words were so characteristic that, in Mike's telling of the story, President Bush declared, "That's Gerson being Gerson!"

The president's little tribute, however, would much better describe what happened after this incident, when the story of "Gerson being Gerson" found its way into a Washington Whispers item by a friend of Mike's at *U.S. News & World Report*. *Someone* had to tell the reporter about this inspiring moment, and I have a feeling it wasn't the keepers of the budget. It was always like this, working with Mike. No good deed went unreported, and many things that never happened were reported as fact. For all of our chief speechwriter's finer qualities, the firm adherence to factual narrative is not a strong point. He has chosen the perfect title for his book, because in his telling of a White House story, things often sound a lot more heroic than they actually were.

This tendency to rearrange and romanticize events could be observed in the scores of media profiles and other articles that Mike sat for over the years. When he resigned in June 2006, *USA Today* remembered "the man whose words helped steady the nation" after 9/11—meaning Mike, not President Bush. It was Michael Gerson, said the *Washington Post*, who "crafted the two speeches after the September 11, 2001, attacks that will probably be recorded as Bush's signal moments of national leadership: the service at the Washington National Cathedral and the address to Congress." He "filled George Bush's mouth with golden phrases," said the *Times* of London. In numerous profiles, Mike was the "conscience of the White House" and answered also to "moral compass for the Bush presidency."

In a January 2006 piece, the *Atlanta Journal-Constitution* gave the standard portrait:

> A devout Christian known to lead fellow staffers in prayer, Gerson is what colleagues call a writer's writer, a big-picture thinker with an instinct for the broad sweep of history who melds the mind of a policy wonk with the heart of a poet.

He is surely the only member of our presidential speechwriting fraternity as celebrated for his moral example as for his literary inspirations. A couple of years ago, *Time* magazine even named the "President's Spiritual Scribe" one of the "25 most influential evangelicals" in America, placing Mike in the company of Billy Graham.

"Leading staffers in prayer" might not have been a bad idea, but in our White House speechwriting office it never happened—unless it was the practice to get the morning oblations out of the way before I showed up. Yet even to point out such errors was futile: the "spiritual scribe" served some larger purpose for the media, as a character of their own invention as much as of his own, and attempts at correction only intruded on a private and mutually satisfying arrangement.

My favorite example came in a piece by Bob Woodward and two other *Washington Post* reporters. The writer's writer and the reporter's reporter spent a lot of time together, and whatever Bob got out of the deal you could always find Mike's reward in print. There had been a September 13, 2001, Oval Office meeting attended by adviser Karen Hughes and three speechwriters—Mike, John McConnell, and me. Early in the meeting President Bush said to us, "We're at war"—an exact quote, and not the sort of moment easily forgotten. In the *Washington Post* account, however, the rest of us have vanished, and the president declares, "Mike, we're at war."

One word, and history is changed. And not only have colleagues been cleared out, but the attention of Woodward's readers isn't even on the president anymore. Things like this happened all the time with Mike—crowded rooms and collaborative efforts gave way, in the retelling, to the self-involved spectacle of one.

Then there was Mike's *Newsweek* account last year of the high drama he experienced trying to get into Washington on September 11, while "my evacuated staff" near the White House was doing, well, whatever. (That would be us, his colleagues, who contributed the sole line in that evening's address, drafted by Karen Hughes, that anyone remembers: "We will make no distinction between the terrorists who committed these acts and those who harbor them.") Mike never made it into town that day, but that doesn't prevent him, in his own version, from staying at the center of events—a position from which even the president, as Mike put it in *Newsweek*, looked "stiff and small."

"Gerson is a 'planner,' not a 'plunger,'" a 2005 *National Journal* profile noted, "meaning that he makes a meticulous outline, which he consults during the writing process." This is true, and equal care and intensity went into crafting the Gerson image. Colleagues were not in the outline, nor were the normal standards of discretion in White House speechwriting. People have a way of disappearing in Mike's stories. The artful shaping of narrative and editing out of inconvenient detail was never confined to the speechwriting. (The phrase *pulling a Gerson*, as I recently heard it used around the West Wing, does not refer to graceful writing.) And though in *Heroic Conservatism* Mike has doubtless offered a kind word or two for speechwriting colleagues, no man I have ever encountered was truer to the saying that, in Washington, one should never take friendship personally.

Woodward's trilogy about the Bush years is a tale of speechwriting glory that Mike himself could hardly improve upon. Remember those powerful and moving addresses the president gave after September 11? According to Woodward's *State of Denial*, Mike wrote all of those speeches by himself—and if there were other speechwriters, well, they must not have made it back from the evacuation:

> Gerson, a 40-year-old evangelical Christian who had majored in theology at evangelist Billy Graham's alma mater, Wheaton College in Wheaton, Illinois, had written all of Bush's memorable post-9/11 speeches, including the one he gave at Washington's National Cathedral on September 14, 2001—"This conflict has begun on the timing and terms of others. It will end in a way, and at an hour of our choosing"—as well as his remarks before a joint session of Congress on September 20, 2001: "Americans should not expect one battle but a lengthy campaign." Gerson had written Bush's 2002 State

of the Union speech identifying Iraq, Iran and North Korea as an "Axis of Evil" connecting terrorism with weapons of mass destruction, and had also come up with the intellectual and historical roots for Bush's "preemption" doctrine speech, delivered at West Point in June 2002—"The war on terrorism will not be won on the defensive."

How do I break the news to Bob Woodward that his high-placed source wrote not a single one of the lines quoted above, at best a third of any of the speeches he mentions, and that the National Cathedral address was half-written before Mike even entered the room?

Without fear of contradiction—because it's all in the presidential records—I can report here that Michael Gerson never wrote a single speech by himself for President Bush. From beginning to end, every notable speech, and a huge proportion of the rest, was written by a team of speechwriters, working in the same office and on the same computer. Few lines of note were written by Mike, and none at all that come to mind from the post-9/11 addresses—not even "axis of evil."

He allowed false assumptions, and also encouraged them. Among chummy reporters, he created a fictionalized, "Mike, we're at war" version of presidential speechwriting, casting himself in a grand and solitary role. The narrative that Mike Gerson presented to the world is a story of extravagant falsehood. He has been held up for us in six years' worth of coddling profiles as the great, inspiring, and idealistic exception of the Bush White House. In reality, Mike's conduct is just the most familiar and depressing of Washington stories—a history of self-seeking and media manipulation that is only more distasteful for being cast in such lofty terms.

There are rewards for such behavior, and in Mike's case the Washington establishment has raised him up as one of its own—a status complete with a columnist's perch at the *Washington*

Post. There is a downside, too, measured in the lost esteem of friends and in the tainting of real gifts and achievements. At his best, Mike is a serious man, with an active Christian faith that could be seen in his work as an adviser in the president's program for helping AIDS and malaria victims in Africa—a vital contribution and well deserving of praise. Yet being a part of such efforts was never reward enough for Mike, and there was always more to the story, always an angle.

Merriman Smith, a White House correspondent from the 1940s to the 1960s, wrote in his book *A President Is Many Men* of Clark Clifford at the beginning of his career as a figure of renown in Washington. After the special counsel settled into his White House office, Smith wrote, "word passed that Clifford had become one of the top idea men for Mr. Truman." He "attracted a steady flow of reporters and photographers," and soon tested the patience of colleagues. "During one week when Clifford was featured in several big national magazines, a White House old-timer wisecracked, 'What the hell is going on—Clark Clifford Week?'"

For us, it was always Mike Gerson Week, with the difference that the self-publicizing was accompanied by pretense. And nobody outside the speechwriting department ever seemed to wonder what the hell was going on.

Power and Piety

Like so much else, it started with Karl Rove. Karl understood, after the misfortunes of the 1996 Dole campaign, that the party would need a "different kind of Republican" and a different kind of speechwriter to go with him. In his engaging book about the 2000 campaign, Stuart Stevens, a Bush media adviser, describes "compassionate conservatism" as a matter of having to "face reality" and recalls the meeting in which Karl explained how it would work. Every big Republican idea—the Laffer Curve, the Gingrich revolution—is first scrawled out on a napkin, and in Stuart's telling of the story there's one for compassionate conservatism, too. He and Karl were at an Austin coffee shop in April 1999, and Karl laid out the logic of Bush II:

> "He's a different kind of Republican. Compassionate conservatism." Karl scribbled on a napkin. He was drawing little boxes—one was labeled BUSH, another BIG STATE GUV. He made COMPASSIONATE CONSERVATISM a big box that overlapped the others. This was what Lee Atwater would have called "the ditch we're going to die in." If compassionate conservatism "worked," the campaign worked.

To keep the campaign on the high road, Karl turned to Mike in early 1999. At the time a senior editor at *U.S. News*, Mike had been a ghostwriter for Charles Colson, the evangelical founder of Prison Fellowship Ministries, and a speechwriter for Senator Dan Coats of Indiana and for the Dole campaign. He had a reputation for religious conviction, and the *National Journal* profile describes his first encounter with Bush as "the calling of the apostle."

My own, less providential summons came in a phone call from Mike in late April 1999: Would I be interested in moving to Texas? I was just then starting a book, but the offer made a lot of sense. Among other reasons, I was quite fond of Mike, whom I had first met on the Dole campaign, and figured it would be great fun to work with him. Our previous joint effort had been to finish a book proposal that Mike had begun for Senator Coats—the work was to be called *Power and Piety*—and, oddly enough, it hadn't gone well at all. Seeing the two of us sitting all afternoon on January 23, 1997, staring at the blank computer screen in my apartment, you'd never have guessed we were destined for future collaborations, and on works even more powerful and pious. But I found Mike to be hilarious company, a side that doesn't really come out in the profiles. When White House staff secretary Harriet Miers decreed in 2003 that we were using too many contractions in speeches—getting just a little too informal and "unpresidential"—Mike forwarded the e-mail to John McConnell and me with a note saying that if we ever again quoted Todd Beamer, one of the heroes of Flight 93, be sure to make it: "Let us roll."

John completed the speechwriting department in Austin, arriving on January 2, 2000. He and I had become friends while working for Vice President Dan Quayle. It was John who strolled into my office one day in 1992, looked over a speech on the "cultural elite" theme that was getting great play in those days, and penciled in one of the more notable lines of that pre-compassionate-conservative era: "I wear their scorn as a badge of honor." In the small universe of speechwriters in Washington, we both wound up working for the Dole campaign. For all the praise that speeches by our "different kind of Republican" received in 2000—for a new tone, so refreshing compared with that of our previous standard-bearer—somehow no one ever noticed that the different kind of speechwriters were three of the same guys who had written for Dole in '96. (And when you look at some of that stuff written for Senator Dole—"There are those who seek to focus on what divides us ... I prefer to focus on what unites us"—it has a familiar ring.)

Unlike the directionless Dole campaign, Bush 2000 was a sharp, disciplined operation. And a case could be made that we three overdid things a bit, with occasionally grandiose rhetoric and a tendency to preen. In speechwriting, the game was always "big ball," and Mike had a particular knack for it. I used to kid him that I could guess the direction of his outline for any given speech on the compassionate-conservative theme, because the Gerson formula never varied: We begin with great and inexorable "callings" of history, then move on to hard moral "duties" and "nonnegotiable demands" of conscience, proceeding through the bramble patch of "temptations"—not to be merely avoided but *"actively confronted"*—arriving in due course at the solution, and with that the "confident hope" of a better day. Mike's conceptual architecture was always indispensable, with a kind of thematic big-think that was beyond my reach.

John, a Yale-educated attorney, brought a more grounded and mature tone to the writing, and usually kept us from going overboard. Often in Bush speeches you will find one slightly overstated sentence followed by another of elegant understatement, as in a 2002 address to the German parliament: "Those who despise human freedom will attack it on every continent. Those who seek missiles and terrible weapons are also familiar with the map of Europe." The first is Mike and the second is John. In John's hands, moral and religious ideas also had a more solid feel—more in the tone, for example, of the remarks that he and I wrote for delivery after the execution of Timothy McVeigh:

> This morning, the United States of America carried out the severest sentence for the gravest of crimes. The victims of the Oklahoma City bombing have been given not vengeance, but justice. And one young man met the fate he chose for himself six years ago. . . . Under the laws of our country, the matter is concluded. . . . May God in his mercy grant peace to all; to the lives that were taken six years ago, to the lives that go on, and to the life that ended today.

As a general rule in Bush speeches, if the writing is graceful, judicious, and understated, and makes you think about the subject at hand instead of anyone's particular craftsmanship or religiosity—there's a better-than-even chance that it is by John McConnell. John is always the first to deflect attention elsewhere, a reflex of modesty and good manners that Mike and I witnessed many times. The truth of the matter is that of the three of us, John is by far the man most like Bush himself in his personal rectitude and goodness of heart, and these qualities shine through in all our best work for the president.

'The Sirens of Baghdad Are Quiet'

In Austin and in Washington, we wrote speeches together on a single computer, in office conditions that John described as resembling the "back room of a cheap restaurant." And though the rhetoric of President Bush has been praised for its "high seriousness," it wasn't that way in the drafting.

It was a rare day when Karl Rove, Josh Bolten, Dan Bartlett, or someone else didn't open the door to see what we were all howling about, or to add to the fun with their own routines and Hill Country antics. Even on the dreariest days—slogging through a tax, education, or Chamber of Commerce speech—Mike and John and I endlessly entertained one another, with all the running jokes and gags you'd expect three guys in a room to develop. Education speeches in particular— with their endlessly complicated programs and slightly puffed- up theories, none of which we could ever explain quite to the satisfaction of our policy people—were always good for a laugh. As John observed in late 2003, around draft twenty in the typically chaotic revising of an education speech, "We've taken the country to war with less hassle than this."

We once wrote, "This nation will prepare. We will not live in fear. We choose to fight them there, so we don't have to fight them here," only to read it aloud and realize it sounded less like Winston Churchill than Dr. Seuss. When one of us offered up a bad idea, we'd all laugh—the offender as much as the other two—and then launch into extended parodies of similarly pompous sentiments that could be added to the speech. When one writer was "on," the teasing took the form of exaggerated deference. With enough prodding, John would favor us with one of his impersonations—a repertoire ranging from a very impressive Harry Truman to the "Matt Foley" motivational-speaker character of the late Chris Farley. This may not sound like much, but for three guys working up the presidential turkey-pardon remarks for the fourth year in a row, it's Vegas material.

Some moments seem ludicrous only in retrospect, as when we wrote the speech that Bush would give on the deck of the USS *Abraham Lincoln*, on May 1, 2003—remembered now for the "Mission Accomplished" banner. As usual, Mike had come in with a grand, historic vision for the effort—along with a literary antecedent to imitate. This was another habit of his, and with each speech you could always predict which models he would turn to. When it was a speech on race, in would come Mike with a sheaf of heavily underlined Martin Luther King Jr. speeches. For speeches on poverty, it was time for more compassionate-conservative fervor, drawn secondhand from the addresses of Robert F. Kennedy. For updates on the war against terrorism, we could expect to see Mike's well-worn copies of JFK and FDR speeches plopped on the table for instruction, and for imitation that when unchecked (as in the second inaugural) could slip perilously close to copying.

In writing the *Abraham Lincoln* speech, this habit of historical reenactment spelled trouble. As John and I sat down to get started, in marched Mike with a muffin in one hand and Douglas MacArthur's "the guns are silent" speech—delivered on the deck of the USS *Missouri* at the end of World War II—in the other. And this time Mike had worked up his own memorable variation: "The sirens of Baghdad are quiet. The desert has returned to silence. The Battle of Iraq is over, and the United States and our allies have prevailed." Much as I'd like to record that I had the good sense to object, I think I even added my own touches to the glory of the moment. The honored role here in averting rhetorical disaster was assumed by Donald Rumsfeld, who expressed alarm at this overreach, and by Karen Hughes, who often checked our more blustery outbursts. "These are beautiful sentences," she wrote on draft three, "but may overstate the case—there is still shooting going on."

Every time, line by line, the three of us talked the speeches through, taking turns at the keyboard and generally agreeing when one of us had come up with the right thought, sentence, or edit. For important speeches, we spent hours on a single paragraph, and in a day got through maybe 500 words of a 3,800-word effort. In that room, at least, vanity was kept under close guard, and, if only to break the silence, you had to be willing to offer up thoughts and phrases that might fall flat. In even the most unusable line or unformed thought, there might be some little glimmer of a better idea to move the work forward.

Mike's outlines were always sound and sometimes inspired—although after a while we started doing the outlines together as well. And in both cases these consisted mostly of placeholders to capture the shape of a thought. For a crucial section in remarks written for Bush during the Florida recount, the notes read:

> At some point, something becomes something. And something becomes something. Loser becomes sore loser. Justified case becomes. At some point the voting must end . . . rule of law, not endless lawsuits. Call for recount, search for new results. Endless litigation. Ballot boxes and courts. War of words, something of lawyers.

When we sat down together this became: "At some point, we must have an end. At some point, the counting of votes must stop, and the votes must count. At some point, the law must prevail, and the lawyers must go home."

'A Unique (and Enjoyable) Working Relationship'

The wonderful thing was how we tended to draw out each other's strengths and check each other's faults—somehow each recognizing, for all our differences in style and temperament, the same standard of polished but conversational rhetoric. The method was really a kind of-writing and editing all at once, with the further advantage of speaking the words as they naturally came to mind before they were written on the screen. It had a way of keeping things on track.

A reporter from the *New York Times Magazine* spent some time with the three of us during the writing of the joint-session speech of September 20, 2001, and gave an accurate account of how it came together:

> Gerson, Scully and McConnell began on the Taliban. Scully started: "We're not deceived by their pretenses to piety." Gerson wrote: "They're the heirs of all the murderous ideologies of the 20th century. By sacrificing human life to serve their radical visions, by abandoning every value except the will to power, they follow in the path of Fascism and Nazism and imperial Communism." Scully added, "And they will follow that path all the way to where it ends." They paused. Where would it end? They didn't know. But there were plenty of ready-made phrases around. McConnell threw out five or six, like crumbs from his pocket. They liked the idea of predicting the end of the Taliban's reign of terror. "You know, history's unmarked grave," McConnell said. The group bounced the phrase around until McConnell came up with: "It will end in discarded lies." Gerson liked that, too. So the line read, "history's unmarked grave of discarded lies."

On September 13, 2001, when we sat down to begin that address, all we had on the screen were a few notes, such as:

> Darkness. Light . . . harm/evil . . . challenge . . . enemy . . . defeat and destroy. Eyes open . . . alerted. We've been a continent shielded by oceans. Carnage known only in Civil War.

> Foe: Political ideology, not a religion. Our view of the world—'challenge we did not ask for in a world we did not make.' People turn to America. Much grief but many questions. Who is the enemy?

It was in a shorthand that only we could understand, each phrase a reminder of themes that we three—along with National Security Council speechwriter John Gibson, who always helped with foreign-policy addresses—had talked through with the president, Condoleezza Rice, Hughes, Rove, and others.

Above all, we shared a respect and affectionate regard for George W., the straight-up guy we'd come to know in Austin. Though our rhetoric did have a way of overdoing the drama sometimes, none of that was ever to be confused with the personal qualities of the man we served, who in the opinion of those who worked there was the actual conscience of the White House. I have never encountered a politician less impressed with himself. There was no surer way to get a laugh out of Bush than with some personally grandiose sentiment, or even an excessive use of "I." He paused once during the rehearsal of a speech when we'd gone overboard with the global- freedom- agenda rhetoric: "What is this stuff? I sound like Spartacus or someone." A similarly overwrought speech inspired him to rise and read it aloud with the exaggerated solemnity of Edward Everett Hale or some other nineteenth- century orator, to laughter all around. Modesty is a very becoming quality in people of his standing. There are CEOs and Washington bureau chiefs who carry themselves with a greater sense of their own importance than this president of the United States ever has.

After one of our "death marches"—John's term for writing a State of the Union address—Mike said that it was a rare thing in life when you can spend nine days in the same room working with the same people and drive in on the morning of the tenth day still looking forward to it. He put it even better in late 2003 when I was thinking about moving along:

> I hope you will think about the timing. This [2004] election will be important to the direction of the country, and our contribution will be made mainly from the State of the Union in January to the convention speech this summer. After that point, the themes are pretty much set, the huge speeches given. In this period, John and I will need your help. We have established a unique (and enjoyable) working relationship, and, frankly, I don't want to face this last major challenge without your help, and without your company. We are talking about a little over half a year—and after four years, I hope that isn't too much to ask. I can't set your course, but I think this is important, and I know it is important to me.

We knew the feeling, John and I. It extended outward, too, in a sense of daily camaraderie with all the others on staff who invariably contributed ideas, lines, edits, and other touches essential to the work.

'The Fine China'

So it was a perplexing experience to read press accounts of Bush speeches that left the distinct impression that they were the work of just one man.

I first noticed the problem in Austin, when we were sitting together at the shared laptop and Bush would call. Just like that, the fellowship of the moment vanished, and one heard the singular instead of the plural: "Yes, Governor, I'm working on it now . . . Mm hmm . . . Mm hmm . . . I can have it done by then, yes . . . I've got some lines here I think you'll like."

When speeches by the three of us were particularly good, Mike attended meetings about them by himself, and then reassembled the team for even minor revisions, no matter how late the hour. When speeches by the three of us were more pedestrian, he made sure that his name disappeared from the draft. Reporters came and went at campaign headquarters, the drawn shades on Mike's interior window signaling their presence and discouraging introductions. The three of us ran into E. J. Dionne of the *Washington Post* in Philadelphia during convention week, and Mike's collaborators on the convention address rated an awkward, "Oh, and these guys are, uh, writers for the campaign."

Likewise, the only time Mike ever appeared disturbed by the approach of public attention was during the preparation of the *New York Times* magazine account of the making of the joint-session speech, when the magazine's fact-checkers started calling to confirm such details as who wrote what. Fact-checkers of tomorrow will find somewhere in the presidential archives a frantic e-mail from Mike in which a colleague was ordered not to take any further calls from *Times* fact-checkers.

Mike once said to us, in passing, "You guys had your administration"—meaning Bush-Quayle—and this seemed to explain his program for Bush 2000. Even during the campaign, he had apparently kept our colleagues—who all had better things to think about, anyway—unsure about how speeches got written. However things worked, they worked, and that was what mattered. Mike attended senior staff meetings, and what went on there could be glimpsed in a cover note he sent his superiors that found its way to us. We had just spent hours working up some humor for the 2000 convention speech. Mike sent the material along to senior staff, with a reminder to be lenient in judgment, since "it's not easy to write jokes sitting alone in a room."

In a rapture of self-congratulation following coverage of one or another campaign speech in 2000, he actually told us that Bush and the senior staff viewed his contributions, well, *differ-*

ently from ours: "I think they look at my writing as the fine china, to be taken out on special occasions." What to say when a friend and colleague lays that one on you?

Maybe you have brushed up against such people in your own workplace. If so, you know that it is a peculiar vice, this kind of credit hounding. One is left almost disoriented by the gall of it. It was amazing that a friend could carry on like this in full view and still act as if nothing were out of order. The sheer pettiness of such conduct served to repel corrective action, because who wants to be drawn into little games of guile and manipulation? Mostly, though, I felt so embarrassed for Mike that it was just too unpleasant to bring up. Besides, for President Bush, we writers were always "the troika," "the lads," "the team," and sometimes even "the A-team." He knew how the work got done, and his good opinion was sufficient.

The problem did come up a few times in plain words, however, and Mike's reactions could be even more jarring than his dreamy self-regard when left unchallenged. I think particularly of the 2000 convention address, the "crafting" of which became a staple of early Gerson profiles and, even before the speech was delivered, inspired an Associated Press piece titled "The Craftsman Behind George Bush's Acceptance Speech." For more than a week Mike was gone from our midst, working alone to compose the address ("with a rollerball pen on yellow legal pads," as the AP described it) in the private apartment of the governor's father at his presidential library, at Texas A&M University. After months of joint authorship, it was time to lay out the fine china, and convention delegates were going to see the complete set.

But the muse had somehow missed the appointment in College Station, and what Mike came back with was an outline—clever, ambitious, and usable, as always, but in the way of actual writing no more than a bundle of overwrought phrases and brittle loftyisms. Among the highlights were the "heat and hate and horror" of war and the "whisper of duty above the shout of fear." America's greatest generation was passing away, "and they left our country a 'golden legend to her people.'" Now "the rising generations of this country have their own appointment with greatness," and "after eight years in the wilderness, we can see the promised land." "My generation has stumbled, but I believe we can soar."

Of these lines—delicate pieces of the fine china—"appointment with greatness" actually made it into the final speech, having survived eighteen drafts collaboratively written. I happened to be sitting at Mike's laptop when it came time for us to send the very last draft to senior staff, and Mike, noticing that I had cc'd John and myself, stopped me: "Don't do that! You can print copies from here!" I said, "Michael, *why* can't I copy John and me?" This brought a frantic admission: "Because they don't know you're involved!" "And why is it a secret that we're doing this together?" Because it was all very confidential, Mike explained as he rushed off—senior staff didn't want anything leaking out. This performance was repeated at the White House, when Mike insisted that the usual author identifications not appear on drafts going to the president, or pouted when our department secretary put all three names there anyway. He seemed to think this was standard practice—just "the way it's done" in Washington.

'The Solitude of Writing'

I have never cared much for the first inaugural address, though I reviewed it extensively with Mike, and the first 200 or so words are not his work at all. John had no part in the effort, and it shows in passages that manage to be derivative, simple, and wordy all at the same time—doubtless a product of the wearisome calculation and "performing writer" routine that went into its production.

There is a line in the speech that goes, "Sometimes in life we are called to do great things. But as a saint of our times has said, every day we are called to do small things with great love." While Mike was drafting the speech, I was somewhere on the outskirts of Tar Heel, North Carolina, researching my book *Dominion*. As we were editing the speech by phone—Mike in the transition office in Washington, me in a parked rental car by a factory farm—we were interrupted by a call from my old friend Jay Heiler, a political consultant in Arizona. Jay suggested the Mother Teresa quote. I wrote it down, hit "Flash," and passed the quote on to Mike, who immediately found a place for it in the inaugural. In a Gerson profile in *USA Today*, these lovely words of the saint—called in from Phoenix via a hog farm in North Carolina—became further evidence of the man's near-mystical spirituality: He had a special devotion to Mother Teresa. "A favorite Gerson icon, she surfaces again in Bush's inaugural."

Another line in that speech reminds us, "No insignificant person was ever born." David Kusnet, a former Clinton speechwriter, offered it as evidence in the *New Republic* that "Gerson's eloquence made the president seem compassionate, conciliatory, and conservative, all at the same time." The line is actually from a column I did for the *Wall Street Journal* after the death of former Pennsylvania Governor Robert Casey, my onetime employer, and in the inaugural was offered as a little tribute to a great man. A simple line, but Mike liked it enough to accept praise for the sentence, and he uses it again, without quotation marks, in the first chapter of *Heroic Conservatism*.

The only time our chief speechwriter was ever heard to say things like "I didn't write that" or "That was John's idea" or "I got that from Karen" was in the case of our more pedestrian efforts together. And then suddenly we'd find ourselves singled out for special attention, lavished with explicit recognition in mentions to the president or in e-mails that made sure everyone understood that this latest offering from the speechwriting shop was not to be confused with the fine china.

Perhaps you have read that Mike wrote some of the most memorable post-9/11 addresses in longhand, sitting by himself in a Starbucks. His colleagues heard that rumor as well, and in the profiles it became as much a part of the persona as Left Bank cafés to Sartre or London pubs to Shakespeare. The *New Yorker*'s profile came with a playful sketch of Mike dressed as Cyrano de Bergerac, quill in hand, Starbucks cup next to the ink bottle. Starbucks was "where he frequently writes speeches," noted the magazine. As *USA Today* captured the scene, "He chews up uni-ball pens by the packet, scribbling out Bush's most acclaimed speeches in longhand on a yellow legal pad. He sometimes takes days to produce a first draft. And he does some of his best writing in the nearest Starbucks." In a Fox News "Power Player of the Week" send-off after Mike had announced his resignation, Chris Wallace explained in the closing shot: "If you're wondering about all those legal pads on Gerson's desk, in this age of computers, he liked to write the first draft of presidential speeches by longhand."

My most vivid memory of Mike at Starbucks is one I have labored in vain to shake. We were working on a State of the Union address in John's office when suddenly Mike was called away for an unspecified appointment, leaving us to "keep going." We learned only later, from a chance conversation with his secretary, where he had gone, and it was a piece of Washington self-promotion for the ages: At the precise moment when the State of the Union address was being *drafted* at the White House by John and me, Mike was off pretending to *craft* the State of the Union in longhand for the benefit of a reporter.

He yearned for escape sometimes and preferred the "buzz" of the coffee shop to the "solitude" of his White House office, Mike explained in a 2002 ABC News *Nightline* segment, "Up Close: Michael Gerson." This is a lengthy discourse on the craft of speechwriting (and indeed on how speechwriting "cultivates a sense of humility," as Mike told *Nightline*) that happily I missed at the time and only came upon recently. To fully appreciate the dramatic tension here, just remember that as a matter of undeniable fact—entered in the permanent records of the United States, which will include more than 10,000 different speech drafts saved on the computer we shared—every major Bush speech of the first term was written from start to finish in the office of John McConnell, by the good old team.

During the *Nightline* interview, we hear the voice of President Bush at the National Cathedral saying: "We are here in the middle hour of our grief," "This conflict was begun on the timing and terms of others. It will end in a way, and at an hour, of our choosing," and other lovely and powerful lines written in my presence by John. And then we hear the guest explain how he himself wrote them:

NIGHTLINE: When you're writing a speech, how do you find the words that fit the man?

GERSON: For me, it is a, you know, process of drafting, redrafting, and reading aloud . . .

NIGHTLINE: How do you, physically, write a speech? I mean, are you working at a computer keyboard, or what do you do?

GERSON: Well, actually, when I'm working on the initial phases of a speech, it's hard to work in my windowless basement office at the White House. I actually like to work with people around.

NIGHTLINE: But you have an office in the West Wing, which is pretty good real estate.

GERSON: I do. It is—it's nice, and I'm glad to be there. But the fact is that I, in that stage of writing, I'll often go to a Starbucks or some other place

> to put together ideas. I guess in some ways it
> breaks the solitude of writing to be around a
> buzz of people. And I'll do that on notepads
> and put together my ideas. And then, at some
> stage, you do, you know, go to a computer
> screen.

Notice how the comfortable use of personal pronouns—*I* go to Starbucks, *I* make notes—suddenly shifts into generality in the description of actual speechwriting: "You do, you know, go to a computer screen." For, of course, the computer screen to which he returned from Starbucks every time was John's computer screen, in the office where we were working—probably even during this interview—and where others had written the very passages that *Nightline* played in the background. Reading the transcript, I found myself almost rooting for Mike to get out of there *fast*, without having to come clean with the whole miserable tale.

Printing the Legend

Once you gain a reputation in Washington, things have a nice way of falling into place, in a print-the-legend fashion. John and I had the experience of working on the president's eulogy for Ronald Reagan, and about midway through the effort getting an e-mailed "bulletin" from a Washington news service called the Frontrunner: "Gerson Writing Reagan Eulogy for Bush." It cited a *Los Angeles Times* story that provided some further details: "The eulogy is being prepared by Bush's chief speechwriter, Michael Gerson, who also wrote the president's moving speech for a memorial service in the same cathedral after the Sept. 11 terrorist attacks." The three of us spent two of our best days laboring over a speech delivered on Goree Island in West Africa, only to have the *New Yorker* pronounce it "perhaps Gerson's most extraordinary speech."

It was the same story with "axis of evil": assumptions casually made and casually left uncorrected. And the most absurd thing about the episode, the sole occasion when credit snatching ever came up for public discussion, was that our colleague David Frum took the rap. David is a highly conscientious person, a gentleman, and, as the most accomplished author on our staff, hardly in need of exaggerating his achievements. Yet during that whole business, as another writer's name started appearing in newspapers, now suddenly it was our chief speechwriter who was alarmed by an unseemly display of self-publicizing. The studio makeup scarcely washed away from "Up Close: Michael Gerson," he let it be known that he did not approve: "Senior White House staff," reported the *Daily Telegraph*, "have sharply criticised Mr. Frum in private for taking the credit for crafting the phrase instead of allowing it to be attributed to President Bush. Mr. Gerson, in particular, is understood to have been annoyed by the disclosure."

What actually happened is that David came up with the phrase "axis of hatred" and e-mailed it, along with some other lines, to John, Mike, and me. We copied the material into the jumble of onscreen notes we kept beneath our working texts. Mike thought we should use the phrase, and we added it to the text. I said, "I hate *hatred*"—which brought to mind the ineffectual "forces of hatred" favored by Clinton speechwriters—and proposed going with evil instead, since we were already confronting *evildoers, wickedness,* and the like. It was agreed—"States like these, and their terrorist allies, constitute an axis of evil, arming to threaten the peace of the world"—and we moved on.

For a time, I congratulated myself on at least preventing the even more melodramatic "axis of hatred" from marching into history—though, looking back, I suppose "axis of evil" was a case of how the very intensity of these speeches could sometimes give events a false momentum and fill the air with needless drama. Good phrase or bad, however, that's how it got in there.

It was not added by Mike—though he assured the *New Yorker*, "Evil exists, and it has to be confronted."

Great works carried out collaboratively make for an undeniably less interesting story than the solitary genius scribbling away. If you write profiles, or submit to them, it complicates things. And when we are given credit for things we didn't do, or feel tempted to grab at undeserved acclaim, we show what we are made of.

I think of our White House colleague Peter Wehner, who once picked up a magazine and was mortified to find himself improperly credited with writing parts of the National Cathedral address. With unhesitating honesty, he e-mailed me to say, "As a rule, I don't think speechwriters should claim credit for this or that speech. . . . And while it's nice for folks to implicitly ascribe beautiful words to me, they were someone else's (yours, or John's, or Mike's), and I'm sorry it happened. . . . I've already dropped John & Mike a note." But this gracious example, so characteristic of Pete Wehner, never caught on. For all of Mike's moralizing on grander matters, he just never understood that a modest round of merited applause is worth far more than a standing ovation undeserved.

Harder to explain than one man's foolish vanity is the gullibility of those who indulged him. Mike had the benefit, I suppose, of presenting an easy positive story to reporters generally hostile to President Bush. If only to keep up appearances or reward a faithful source, reporters had to find a happier angle on the administration. They needed something nice to say, and some color to go with it, and why not start with the bookish evangelical?

After a while, Gerson profiles took on an interchangeable quality, as if mere parts of the same tedious tract, and lost in the haze of sanctimony were the real qualities of the man I know—especially Mike's ability to spot the very kind of pretension that filled his own press coverage. It was the Nixon speechwriter William Safire who, in his enduring 1975 book, *Before the Fall*, captured the false note heard throughout the whole self-indulgent exercise. By adopting a certain tone and manner, Safire observed,

> the writer thereby not only buttresses his reputation for having a passion for anonymity but gains fame. This is known as ostentatious self-effacement, and it works its oily way far more effectively than less subtle forms of self-aggrandizement.

The 'Contributor'

The worst of my former colleague's conduct was not mere vanity, however. It was not even the pettiness and selfishness, or the casual treatment of the trust of friends. The real offense was to the president. And the most appalling part of the story is that such behavior could continue even in the weeks after 9/11—no "new normal" in the speechwriting department. Indeed, there was actually a commemorative edition of the joint-session speech sold in bookstores under the title *Our Mission and Our Moment*. It is still being sold by Amazon as a work "by Mike Gerson." But at least George W. Bush isn't overlooked entirely. He gets some of the credit too—as a "contributor."

As it happens, that title line in the joint-session speech—"We have found our mission and our moment"—was inspired by my observation of the contributor's conduct in the days after 9/11, by the way he carried himself and the things he said to us. He was not a "president stiff and small," as Mike described him in *Newsweek*, and the clear, manful, and gracious tone that comes across in all of those post-9/11 speeches was not some invention of the speechwriters.

Six years later, with all that has gone wrong in Iraq, I know one is now supposed to sigh with regret at how mistaken we all were about Bush in those days, how foolish of us to think the man had greatness in him. As Jonathan Rauch reflected a year ago in these pages, Americans "thought they saw a Churchill," but all that's gone and now we know better. And yet I think I recognize greatness when it steps before me, and the sight of George W. Bush in those days left an impression that has never worn off.

It was apparent when he stood on the ruins of the World Trade Center, and again in his "I'm a loving guy" moment in the Oval Office. And we speechwriters saw his qualities of character just as vividly when the cameras were withdrawn. In hundreds of pre-9/11 speeches, we had been straining for the unforgettable turn of phrase, the noble sentiment, the heroic gesture. Now, nobility and heroism were actually on display, and it turned out he could do it without us.

The National Cathedral and joint-session speeches marked a clean break in our rhetoric, a casting-off of the fine china and the stuff of Starbucks. No more stilted generational summonses, no more made-up "callings." Here, finally, was the real thing—a real calling with real heroism—and the words we found for all of this could have been written for that man and no other.

Some of the most moving lines in the joint-session address were just slightly polished versions of what Bush himself had told us: "Tonight we are a country awakened to danger and called to defend freedom. Our grief has turned to anger, and anger to resolution. . . . We will not tire, we will not falter, and we will not fail." As John, Karl, and I watched from the side of the House floor that night, it was a case of presidential speechwriting working exactly as it should, with the words spoken by the very man who inspired them.

That's where presidential speechwriters belong—off to the side, where even the best there ever was, Ted Sorensen, was always content to stay. Speechwriting is a job with many privileges, but also its own rules, temptations, and demands of conscience, obvious and nonnegotiable. The work has rewards enough without each speechwriter stepping forward to give his or her name its own permanent shine in history.

In times of trial—of historic drama and of true presidential greatness, as after 9/11—it adds nothing useful for a speechwriter to be endlessly holding forth on the craft and performing for television crews. It only diminishes the moment and the achievement. In the presidency of George W. Bush, these achievements were the finest we ever shared, all of us together. And they require no embellishment or shading of truth.

The New Yorker

FINALIST—REPORTING

Jane Mayer weaves together history, analysis, and detailed reporting to produce one of the most powerful accounts yet written of C.I.A. interrogation in the post-9/11 era.

Jane Mayer

The Black Sites

In March, Mariane Pearl, the widow of the murdered *Wall Street Journal* reporter Daniel Pearl, received a phone call from Alberto Gonzales, the attorney general. At the time, Gonzales's role in the controversial dismissal of eight United States attorneys had just been exposed, and the story was becoming a scandal in Washington. Gonzales informed Pearl that the Justice Department was about to announce some good news: a terrorist in U.S. custody—Khalid Sheikh Mohammed, the Al Qaeda leader who was the primary architect of the September 11th attacks—had confessed to killing her husband. (Pearl was abducted and beheaded five and a half years ago in Pakistan, by unidentified Islamic militants.) The administration planned to release a transcript in which Mohammed boasted, "I decapitated with my blessed right hand the head of the American Jew Daniel Pearl in the city of Karachi, Pakistan. For those who would like to confirm, there are pictures of me on the Internet holding his head."

Pearl was taken aback. In 2003, she had received a call from Condoleezza Rice, who was then President Bush's national security adviser, informing her of the same news. But Rice's revelation had been secret. Gonzales's announcement seemed like a publicity stunt. Pearl asked him if he had proof that Mohammed's confession was truthful; Gonzales claimed to have corroborating evidence but wouldn't share it. "It's not enough for officials to call me and say they believe it," Pearl said. "You need evidence." (Gonzales did not respond to requests for comment.)

The circumstances surrounding the confession of Mohammed, whom law-enforcement officials refer to as K.S.M., were perplexing. He had no lawyer. After his capture in Pakistan, in March of 2003, the Central Intelligence Agency had detained him in undisclosed locations for more than two years; last fall, he was transferred to military custody in Guantánamo Bay, Cuba. There were no named witnesses to his initial confession, and no solid information about what form of interrogation might have prodded him to talk, although reports had been published, in the *Times* and elsewhere, suggesting that C.I.A. officers had tortured him. At a hearing held at Guantánamo, Mohammed said that his testimony was freely given, but he also indicated that he had been abused by the C.I.A. (The Pentagon had classified as "top secret" a statement he had written detailing the alleged mistreatment.) And although Mohammed said that there were photographs confirming his guilt, U.S. authorities had found none. Instead, they had a copy of the video that had been released on the Internet, which showed the killer's arms but offered no other clues to his identity.

Further confusing matters, a Pakistani named Ahmed Omar Saeed Sheikh had already been convicted of the abduction and murder, in 2002. A British-educated terrorist who had a history of staging kidnappings, he had been sentenced to death in Pakistan for the crime. But the Pakistani government, not known for its leniency, had stayed his execution. Indeed, hearings on the matter had been delayed a remarkable number of times—at least thirty—possibly because of his reported ties to the Pakistani intelligence service, which may have helped free him after he was imprisoned for terrorist activities in India. Mohammed's confession would delay the execution further, since, under Pakistani law, any new evidence is grounds for appeal.

A surprising number of people close to the case are dubious of Mohammed's confession. A longtime friend of Pearl's, the former *Journal* reporter Asra Nomani, said, "The release of the confession came right in the midst of the U.S. attorney scandal. There was a drumbeat for Gonzales's resignation. It seemed like a calculated strategy to change the subject. Why now? They'd had the confession for years." Mariane and Daniel Pearl were staying in Nomani's Karachi house at the time of his murder, and Nomani has followed the case meticulously; this fall, she plans to teach a course on the topic at Georgetown University. She said, "I don't think this confession resolves the case. You can't have justice from one person's confession, especially under such unusual circumstances. To me, it's not convincing." She added, "I called all the investigators. They weren't just skeptical—they didn't believe it."

Special Agent Randall Bennett, the head of security for the U.S. consulate in Karachi when Pearl was killed—and whose lead role investigating the murder was featured in the recent film *A Mighty Heart*—said that he has interviewed all the convicted accomplices who are now in custody in Pakistan, and that none of them named Mohammed as playing a role. "K.S.M.'s name never came up," he said. Robert Baer, a former C.I.A. officer, said, "My old colleagues say with 100 percent certainty that it was not K.S.M. who killed Pearl." A government official involved in the case said, "The fear is that K.S.M. is covering up for others, and that these people will be released." And Judea Pearl, Daniel's father, said, "Something is fishy. There are a lot of unanswered questions. K.S.M. can say he killed Jesus—he has nothing to lose."

Mariane Pearl, who is relying on the Bush administration to bring justice in her husband's case, spoke carefully about the investigation. "You need a procedure that will get the truth," she said. "An intelligence agency is not supposed to be above the law."

•   •   •

Mohammed's interrogation was part of a secret C.I.A. program, initiated after September 11th, in which terrorist suspects such as Mohammed were detained in "black sites"—secret prisons outside the United States—and subjected to unusually harsh treatment. The program was effectively suspended last fall, when President Bush announced that he was emptying the C.I.A.'s prisons and transferring the detainees to military custody in Guantánamo. This move followed a Supreme Court ruling, *Hamdan v. Rumsfeld*, which found that all detainees—including those held by the C.I.A.—had to be treated in a manner consistent with the Geneva Conventions. These treaties, adopted in 1949, bar cruel treatment, degradation, and torture. In late July, the White House issued an executive order promising that the C.I.A. would adjust its methods in order to meet the Geneva standards. At the same time, Bush's order pointedly did not disavow the use of "enhanced interrogation techniques" that would likely be found illegal if used by officials inside the United States. The executive order means that the agency can once again hold foreign terror suspects indefinitely, and without charges, in black sites, without notifying their families or local authorities, or offering access to legal counsel.

The C.I.A.'s director, General Michael Hayden, has said that the program, which is designed to extract intelligence from suspects quickly, is an "irreplaceable" tool for combating terrorism. And President Bush has said that "this program has given us information that has saved innocent lives, by helping us stop new attacks." He claims that it has contributed to the disruption of at least ten serious Al Qaeda plots since September 11th, three of them inside the United States.

According to the Bush administration, Mohammed divulged information of tremendous value during his detention. He is said to have helped point the way to the capture of Hambali, the Indonesian terrorist responsible for the 2002 bombings of night clubs in Bali. He also provided information on an Al Qaeda leader in England. Michael Sheehan, a former counterterrorism official at the State Department, said, "K.S.M. is the poster boy for using tough but legal tactics. He's the reason these techniques exist. You can save lives with the kind of information he could give up." Yet Mohammed's confessions may also have muddled some key investigations. Perhaps under duress, he claimed involvement in thirty-one criminal plots—an improbable number, even for a high-level terrorist. Critics say that Mohammed's case illustrates the cost of the C.I.A.'s desire for swift intelligence. Colonel Dwight Sullivan, the top defense lawyer at the Pentagon's Office of Military Commissions, which is expected eventually to try Mohammed for war crimes, called his serial confessions "a textbook example of why we shouldn't allow coercive methods."

The Bush administration has gone to great lengths to keep secret the treatment of the hundred or so "high-value detainees" whom the C.I.A. has confined, at one point or another, since September 11th. The program has been extraordinarily "compartmentalized," in the nomenclature of the intelligence world. By design, there has been virtually no access for outsiders to the C.I.A.'s prisoners. The utter isolation of these detainees has been described as essential to America's national security. The Justice Department argued this point explicitly last November, in the case of a Baltimore-area resident named Majid Khan, who was held for more than three years by the C.I.A. Khan, the government said, had to be prohibited from access to a lawyer specifically because he might describe the "alternative interrogation methods" that the agency had used when questioning him. These methods amounted to a state secret, the government argued, and disclosure of them could "reasonably be expected to cause extremely grave damage." (The case has not yet been decided.)

Given this level of secrecy, the public and all but a few members of Congress who have been sworn to silence have had to take on faith President Bush's assurances that the C.I.A.'s internment program has been humane and legal, and has yielded crucial intelligence. Representative Alcee Hastings, a Democratic member of the House Select Committee on Intelligence, said, "We talk to the authorities about these detainees, but, of course, they're not going to come out and tell us that they beat the living daylights out of someone." He recalled learning in 2003 that Mohammed had been captured. "It was good news," he said. "So I tried to find out: Where is this guy? And how is he being treated?" For more than three years, Hastings said, "I could never pinpoint anything." Finally, he received some classified briefings on the Mohammed interrogation. Hastings said that he "can't go into details" about what he found out, but, speaking of Mohammed's treatment, he said that even if it wasn't torture, as the administration claims, "it ain't right, either. Something went wrong."

•   •   •

Since the drafting of the Geneva Conventions, the International Committee of the Red Cross has played a special role in safeguarding the rights of prisoners of war. For decades, governments have allowed officials from the organization to report on the treatment of detainees, to insure that standards set by international treaties are being maintained. The Red Cross, however, was unable to get access to the C.I.A.'s prisoners for five years. Finally, last year, Red Cross officials were allowed to interview fifteen detainees, after they had been transferred to Guantánamo. One of the prisoners was Khalid Sheikh Mohammed. What the Red Cross learned has been kept from the public. The committee believes that its continued access to prisoners worldwide is contingent upon confidentiality, and therefore it addresses violations privately with the authorities directly responsible for prisoner treatment and detention. For this reason, Simon Schorno, a Red Cross spokesman in Washington, said, "The I.C.R.C. does not comment on its findings publicly. Its work is confidential."

The public-affairs office at the C.I.A. and officials at the congressional intelligence-oversight committees would not even acknowledge the existence of the report. Among the few people who are believed to have seen it are Condoleezza Rice, now the secretary of state; Stephen Hadley, the national security adviser; John Bellinger III, the secretary of state's legal adviser; Hayden; and John Rizzo, the agency's acting general counsel. Some members of the Senate and House intelligence-oversight committees are also believed to have had limited access to the report.

Confidentiality may be particularly stringent in this case. Congressional and other Washington sources familiar with the report said that it harshly criticized the C.I.A.'s practices. One of the sources said that the Red Cross described the agency's detention and interrogation methods as tantamount to torture, and declared that American officials responsible for the abusive treatment could have committed serious crimes. The source said the report warned that these officials may have committed "grave breaches" of the Geneva Conventions, and may have violated the U.S. Torture Act, which Congress passed in 1994. The conclusions of the Red Cross, which is known for its credibility and caution, could have potentially devastating legal ramifications.

Concern about the legality of the C.I.A.'s program reached a previously unreported breaking point last week when Senator

Ron Wyden, a Democrat on the intelligence committee, quietly put a "hold" on the confirmation of John Rizzo, who as acting general counsel was deeply involved in establishing the agency's interrogation and detention policies. Wyden's maneuver essentially stops the nomination from going forward. "I question if there's been adequate legal oversight," Wyden told me. He said that after studying a classified addendum to President Bush's new executive order, which specifies permissible treatment of detainees, "I am not convinced that all of these techniques are either effective or legal. I don't want to see well-intentioned C.I.A. officers breaking the law because of shaky legal guidance."

A former C.I.A. officer, who supports the agency's detention and interrogation policies, said he worried that, if the full story of the C.I.A. program ever surfaced, agency personnel could face criminal prosecution. Within the agency, he said, there is a "high level of anxiety about political retribution" for the interrogation program. If congressional hearings begin, he said, "several guys expect to be thrown under the bus." He noted that a number of C.I.A. officers have taken out professional liability insurance, to help with potential legal fees.

Paul Gimigliano, a spokesman for the C.I.A., denied any legal impropriety, stressing that "the agency's terrorist-detention program has been implemented lawfully. And torture is illegal under U.S. law. The people who have been part of this important effort are well-trained, seasoned professionals." This spring, the Associated Press published an article quoting the chairman of the House Intelligence Committee, Silvestre Reyes, who said that Hayden, the C.I.A. director, "vehemently denied" the Red Cross's conclusions. A U.S. official dismissed the Red Cross report as a mere compilation of allegations made by terrorists. And Robert Grenier, a former head of the C.I.A.'s Counterterrorism Center, said that "the C.I.A.'s interrogations were nothing like Abu Ghraib or Guantánamo. They were very, very regimented. Very meticulous." He said, "The program is very careful. It's completely legal."

Accurately or not, Bush administration officials have described the prisoner abuses at Abu Ghraib and Guantánamo as the unauthorized actions of ill-trained personnel, eleven of whom have been convicted of crimes. By contrast, the treatment of high-value detainees has been directly, and repeatedly, approved by President Bush. The program is monitored closely by C.I.A. lawyers, and supervised by the agency's director and his subordinates at the Counterterrorism Center. While Mohammed was being held by the agency, detailed dossiers on the treatment of detainees were regularly available to the former C.I.A. director George Tenet, according to informed sources inside and outside the agency. Through a spokesperson, Tenet denied making day-to-day decisions about the treatment of individual detainees. But, according to a former agency official, "Every single plan is drawn up by interrogators, and then submitted for approval to the highest possible level—meaning the director of the C.I.A. Any change in the plan—even if an extra day of a certain treatment was added—was signed off by the C.I.A. director."

●　　　●　　　●

On September 17, 2001, President Bush signed a secret presidential finding authorizing the C.I.A. to create paramilitary teams to hunt, capture, detain, or kill designated terrorists almost anywhere in the world. Yet the C.I.A. had virtually no trained interrogators. A former C.I.A. officer involved in fighting terrorism said that, at first, the agency was crippled by its lack of expertise. "It began right away, in Afghanistan, on the fly," he recalled. "They invented the program of interrogation with people who had no understanding of Al Qaeda or the Arab world." The former officer said that the pressure from the White

House, in particular from Vice President Dick Cheney, was intense: "They were pushing us: 'Get information! Do *not* let us get hit again!'" In the scramble, he said, he searched the C.I.A.'s archives, to see what interrogation techniques had worked in the past. He was particularly impressed with the Phoenix Program, from the Vietnam War. Critics, including military historians, have described it as a program of state-sanctioned torture and murder. A Pentagon-contract study found that, between 1970 and 1971, 97 percent of the Vietcong targeted by the Phoenix Program were of negligible importance. But, after September 11th, some C.I.A. officials viewed the program as a useful model. A. B. Krongard, who was the executive director of the C.I.A. from 2001 to 2004, said that the agency turned to "everyone we could, including our friends in Arab cultures," for interrogation advice, among them those in Egypt, Jordan, and Saudi Arabia, all of which the State Department regularly criticizes for human-rights abuses.

The C.I.A. knew even less about running prisons than it did about hostile interrogations. Tyler Drumheller, a former chief of European operations at the C.I.A., and the author of a recent book, *On the Brink: How the White House Compromised U.S. Intelligence*, said, "The agency had no experience in detention. Never. But they insisted on arresting and detaining people in this program. It was a mistake, in my opinion. You can't mix intelligence and police work. But the White House was really pushing. They wanted *someone* to do it. So the C.I.A. said, 'We'll try.' George Tenet came out of politics, not intelligence. His whole modus operandi was to please the principal. We got stuck with all sorts of things. This is really the legacy of a director who never said no to anybody."

Many officials inside the C.I.A. had misgivings. "A lot of us knew this would be a can of worms," the former officer said. "We warned them, It's going to become an atrocious mess." The problem from the start, he said, was that no one had thought through what he called "the disposal plan." He continued, "What are you going to *do* with these people? The utility of someone like K.S.M. is, at most, six months to a year. You exhaust them. Then what? It would have been better if we had executed them."

The C.I.A. program's first important detainee was Abu Zubaydah, a top Al Qaeda operative, who was captured by Pakistani forces in March of 2002. Lacking in-house specialists on interrogation, the agency hired a group of outside contractors, who implemented a regime of techniques that one well-informed former adviser to the American intelligence community described as "a *Clockwork Orange* kind of approach." The experts were retired military psychologists, and their backgrounds were in training Special Forces soldiers how to survive torture, should they ever be captured by enemy states. The program, known as SERE—an acronym for Survival, Evasion, Resistance, and Escape—was created at the end of the Korean War. It subjected trainees to simulated torture, including waterboarding (simulated drowning), sleep deprivation, isolation, exposure to temperature extremes, enclosure in tiny spaces, bombardment with agonizing sounds, and religious and sexual humiliation. The SERE program was designed strictly for defense against torture regimes, but the C.I.A.'s new team used its expertise to help interrogators inflict abuse. "They were very arrogant, and pro-torture," a European official knowledgeable about the program said. "They sought to render the detainees vulnerable—to break down all of their senses. It takes a psychologist trained in this to understand these rupturing experiences."

The use of psychologists was also considered a way for C.I.A. officials to skirt measures such as the Convention Against Torture. The former adviser to the intelligence community said, "Clearly, some senior people felt they needed a theory to justify what they were doing. You can't just say, 'We want to do what Egypt's doing.' When the lawyers asked what their basis was, they could say, 'We have Ph.D.s who have these theories.'" He said that, inside the C.I.A., where a number of scientists work, there was strong internal opposition to the new techniques. "Behavioral scientists said, 'Don't even think about this!' They thought officers could be prosecuted."

Nevertheless, the SERE experts' theories were apparently put into practice with Zubaydah's interrogation. Zubaydah told the Red Cross that he was not only waterboarded, as has been previously reported; he was also kept for a prolonged period in a cage, known as a "dog box," which was so small that he could not stand. According to an eyewitness, one psychologist advising on the treatment of Zubaydah, James Mitchell, argued that he needed to be reduced to a state of "learned helplessness." (Mitchell disputes this characterization.)

Steve Kleinman, a reserve Air Force colonel and an experienced interrogator who has known Mitchell professionally for years, said that "learned helplessness was his whole paradigm." Mitchell, he said, "draws a diagram showing what he says is the whole cycle. It starts with isolation. Then they eliminate the prisoners' ability to forecast the future—when their next meal is, when they can go to the bathroom. It creates dread and dependency. It was the K.G.B. model. But the K.G.B. used it to get people who had turned against the state to confess falsely. The K.G.B. wasn't after intelligence."

As the C.I.A. captured and interrogated other Al Qaeda figures, it established a protocol of psychological coercion. The program tied together many strands of the agency's secret history of Cold War–era experiments in behavioral science. (In June, the C.I.A. declassified long-held secret documents known as the Family Jewels, which shed light on C.I.A. drug experiments on rats and monkeys, and on the infamous case of Frank R. Olson, an agency employee who leaped to his death from a hotel window in 1953, nine days after he was unwittingly drugged with LSD.) The C.I.A.'s most useful research focused on the surprisingly powerful effects of psychological manipulations, such as extreme sensory deprivation. According to Alfred McCoy, a history professor at the University of Wisconsin, in Madison, who has written a history of the C.I.A.'s experiments in coercing subjects, the agency learned that "if subjects are confined without light, odors, sound, or any fixed references of time and place, very deep breakdowns can be provoked."

Agency scientists found that in just a few hours some subjects suspended in water tanks—or confined in isolated rooms wearing blacked-out goggles and earmuffs—regressed to semipsychotic states. Moreover, McCoy said, detainees become so desperate for human interaction that "they bond with the interrogator like a father, or like a drowning man having a lifesaver thrown at him. If you deprive people of all their senses, they'll turn to you like their daddy." McCoy added that "after the Cold War we put away those tools. There was bipartisan reform. We backed away from those dark days. Then, under the pressure of the war on terror, they didn't just bring back the old psychological techniques—they perfected them."

The C.I.A.'s interrogation program is remarkable for its mechanistic aura. "It's one of the most sophisticated, refined programs of torture ever," an outside expert familiar with the protocol said. "At every stage, there was a rigid attention to detail. Procedure was adhered to almost to the letter. There was top-down quality control, and such a set routine that you get to the point where you know what each detainee is going to say, because you've heard it before. It was almost automated. People were utterly dehumanized. People fell apart. It was the intentional and systematic infliction of great suffering masquerading as a legal process. It is just chilling."

·　　·　　·

The U.S. government first began tracking Khalid Sheikh Mohammed in 1993, shortly after his nephew Ramzi Yousef blew a gaping hole in the World Trade Center. Mohammed, officials learned, had transferred money to Yousef. Mohammed, born in either 1964 or 1965, was raised in a religious Sunni Muslim family in Kuwait, where his family had migrated from the Baluchistan region of Pakistan. In the mid-eighties, he was trained as a mechanical engineer in the U.S., attending two colleges in North Carolina.

As a teenager, Mohammed had been drawn to militant, and increasingly violent, Muslim causes. He joined the Muslim Brotherhood at the age of sixteen, and, after his graduation from North Carolina Agricultural and Technical State University, in Greensboro—where he was remembered as a class clown, but religious enough to forgo meat when eating at Burger King—he signed on with the anti-Soviet jihad in Afghanistan, receiving military training and establishing ties with Islamist terrorists. By all accounts, his animus toward the U.S. was rooted in a hatred of Israel.

In 1994, Mohammed, who was impressed by Yousef's notoriety after the first World Trade Center bombing, joined him in scheming to blow up twelve U.S. jumbo jets over two days. The so-called Bojinka plot was disrupted in 1995, when Philippine police broke into an apartment that Yousef and other terrorists were sharing in Manila, which was filled with bomb-making materials. At the time of the raid, Mohammed was working in Doha, Qatar, at a government job. The following year, he narrowly escaped capture by F.B.I. officers and slipped into the global jihadist network, where he eventually joined forces with Osama bin Laden, in Afghanistan. Along the way, he married and had children.

Many journalistic accounts have presented Mohammed as a charismatic, swashbuckling figure: in the Philippines, he was said to have flown a helicopter close enough to a girlfriend's office window so that she could see him; in Pakistan, he supposedly posed as an anonymous bystander and gave interviews to news reporters about his nephew's arrest. Neither story is true. But Mohammed did seem to enjoy taunting authorities after the September 11th attacks, which, in his eventual confession, he claimed to have orchestrated "from A to Z." In April 2002, Mohammed arranged to be interviewed on Al Jazeera by its London bureau chief, Yosri Fouda, and took personal credit for the atrocities. "I am the head of the Al Qaeda military committee," he said. "And yes, we did it." Fouda, who conducted the interview at an Al Qaeda safe house in Karachi, said that he was astounded not only by Mohammed's boasting but also by his seeming imperviousness to the danger of being caught. Mohammed permitted Al Jazeera to reveal that he was hiding out in the Karachi area. When Fouda left the apartment, Mohammed, apparently unarmed, walked him downstairs and out into the street.

In the early months of 2003, U.S. authorities reportedly paid a $25 million reward for information that led to Mohammed's arrest. U.S. officials closed in on him, at 4 A.M. on March 1, waking him up in a borrowed apartment in Rawalpindi, Pakistan. The officials hung back as Pakistani authorities handcuffed and hooded him, and took him to a safe house. Reportedly, for the first two days, Mohammed robotically recited Koranic verses and refused to divulge much more than his name. A videotape obtained by *60 Minutes* shows Mohammed at the end of this episode, complaining of a head cold; an American voice can be heard in the background. This was the last image of Mohammed to be seen by the public. By March 4, he was in C.I.A. custody.

Captured along with Mohammed, according to some accounts, was a letter from bin Laden, which may have led officials to think that he knew where the Al Qaeda founder was hiding. If Mohammed did have this crucial information, it was time sensitive—bin Laden never stayed in one place for long—and officials needed to extract it quickly. At the time, many American intelligence officials still feared a "second wave" of Al Qaeda attacks, ratcheting the pressure further.

According to George Tenet's recent memoir, *At the Center of the Storm*, Mohammed told his captors that he wouldn't talk until he was given a lawyer in New York, where he assumed he would be taken. (He had been indicted there in connection with the Bojinka plot.) Tenet writes, "Had that happened, I am confident that we would have obtained none of the information he had in his head about imminent threats against the American people." Opponents of the C.I.A.'s approach, however, note that Ramzi Yousef gave a voluminous confession after being read his Miranda rights. "These guys are egomaniacs," a former federal prosecutor said. "They *love* to talk!"

．　　　．　　　．

A complete picture of Mohammed's time in secret detention remains elusive. But a partial narrative has emerged through interviews with European and American sources in intelligence, government, and legal circles, as well as with former detainees who have been released from C.I.A. custody. People familiar with Mohammed's allegations about his interrogation, and interrogations of other high-value detainees, describe the accounts as remarkably consistent.

Soon after Mohammed's arrest, sources say, his American captors told him, "We're not going to kill you. But we're going to take you to the very brink of your death and back." He was first taken to a secret U.S.-run prison in Afghanistan. According to a Human Rights Watch report released two years ago, there was a C.I.A.-affiliated black site in Afghanistan by 2002: an underground prison near Kabul International Airport. Distinctive for its absolute lack of light, it was referred to by detainees as the Dark Prison. Another detention facility was reportedly a former brick factory, just north of Kabul, known as the Salt Pit. The latter became infamous for the 2002 death of a detainee, reportedly from hypothermia, after prison officials stripped him naked and chained him to the floor of his concrete cell, in freezing temperatures.

In all likelihood, Mohammed was transported from Pakistan to one of the Afghan sites by a team of black-masked commandos attached to the C.I.A.'s paramilitary Special Activities Division. According to a report adopted in June by the Parliamentary Assembly of the Council of Europe, titled "Secret Detentions and Illegal Transfers of Detainees," detainees were "taken to their cells by strong people who wore black outfits, masks that covered their whole faces, and dark visors over their eyes." (Some personnel reportedly wore black clothes made from specially woven synthetic fabric that couldn't be ripped or torn.) A former member of a C.I.A. transport team has described the "takeout" of prisoners as a carefully choreographed twenty-minute routine, during which a suspect was hog-tied, stripped naked, photographed, hooded, sedated with anal suppositories, placed in diapers, and transported by plane to a secret location.

A person involved in the Council of Europe inquiry, referring to cavity searches and the frequent use of suppositories during the takeout of detainees, likened the treatment to "sodomy." He said, "It was used to absolutely strip the detainee of any dignity. It breaks down someone's sense of impenetrability. The interrogation became a process not just of getting information but of utterly subordinating the detainee through humiliation." The former C.I.A. officer confirmed that the agency frequently photographed the prisoners naked, "because it's demoralizing." The person involved in the Council of Europe inquiry said that photos were also part of the C.I.A.'s quality-control process. They were passed back to case officers for review.

A secret government document, dated December 10, 2002, detailing "SERE Interrogation Standard Operating Procedure," outlines the advantages of stripping detainees. "In addition to degradation of the detainee, stripping can be used to demonstrate the omnipotence of the captor or to debilitate the detainee." The document advises interrogators to "tear clothing from detainees by firmly pulling downward against buttoned buttons and seams. Tearing motions shall be downward to prevent pulling the detainee off balance." The memo also advocates the "Shoulder Slap," "Stomach Slap," "Hooding," "Manhandling," "Walling," and a variety of "Stress Positions," including one called "Worship the Gods."

In the process of being transported, C.I.A. detainees such as Mohammed were screened by medical experts, who checked their vital signs, took blood samples, and marked a chart with a diagram of a human body, noting scars, wounds, and other imperfections. As the person involved in the Council of Europe inquiry put it, "It's like when you hire a motor vehicle, circling where the scratches are on the rearview mirror. Each detainee was continually assessed, physically and psychologically."

According to sources, Mohammed said that, while in C.I.A. custody, he was placed in his own cell, where he remained naked for several days. He was questioned by an unusual number of female handlers, perhaps as an additional humiliation. He has alleged that he was attached to a dog leash, and yanked in such a way that he was propelled into the walls of his cell. Sources say that he also claimed to have been suspended from the ceiling by his arms, his toes barely touching the ground. The pressure on his wrists evidently became exceedingly painful.

Ramzi Kassem, who teaches at Yale Law School, said that a Yemeni client of his, Sanad al-Kazimi, who is now in Guantánamo, alleged that he had received similar treatment in the Dark Prison, the facility near Kabul. Kazimi claimed to have been suspended by his arms for long periods, causing his legs to swell painfully. "It's so traumatic, he can barely speak of it," Kassem said. "He breaks down in tears." Kazimi also claimed that, while hanging, he was beaten with electric cables.

According to sources familiar with interrogation techniques, the hanging position is designed, in part, to prevent detainees from being able to sleep. The former C.I.A. officer, who is knowledgeable about the interrogation program, explained that "sleep deprivation works. Your electrolyte balance changes. You lose all balance and ability to think rationally. Stuff comes out." Sleep deprivation has been recognized as an effective form of coercion since the Middle Ages, when it was called *tormentum insomniae*. It was also recognized for decades in the United States as an illegal form of torture. An American Bar Association report, published in 1930, which was cited in a later U.S. Supreme Court decision, said, "It has been known since 1500 at least that deprivation of sleep is the most effective torture and certain to produce any confession desired."

Under President Bush's new executive order, C.I.A. detainees must receive the "basic necessities of life, including adequate food and water, shelter from the elements, necessary clothing, protection from extremes of heat and cold, and essential medical care." Sleep, according to the order, is not among the basic necessities.

In addition to keeping a prisoner awake, the simple act of remaining upright can over time cause significant pain. McCoy, the historian, noted that "longtime standing" was a common K.G.B. interrogation technique. In his 2006 book, *A Question of Torture*, he writes that the Soviets found that making a victim stand for eighteen to twenty-four hours can produce "excruciating pain, as ankles double in size, skin becomes tense and intensely painful, blisters erupt oozing watery serum, heart rates soar, kidneys shut down, and delusions deepen."

Mohammed is said to have described being chained naked to a metal ring in his cell wall for prolonged periods in a painful crouch. (Several other detainees who say that they were confined in the Dark Prison have described identical treatment.) He also claimed that he was kept alternately in suffocating heat and in a painfully cold room, where he was doused with ice water. The practice, which can cause hypothermia, violates the Geneva Conventions, and President Bush's new executive order arguably bans it.

Some detainees held by the C.I.A. claimed that their cells were bombarded with deafening sound twenty-fours hours a day for weeks, and even months. One detainee, Binyam Mohamed, who is now in Guantánamo, told his lawyer, Clive Stafford Smith, that speakers blared music into his cell while he was handcuffed. Detainees recalled the sound as ranging from ghoulish laughter, "like the soundtrack from a horror film," to ear-splitting rap anthems. Stafford Smith said that his client found the psychological torture more intolerable than the physical abuse that he said he had been previously subjected to in Morocco, where, he said, local intelligence agents had sliced him with a razor blade. "The C.I.A. worked people day and night for months," Stafford Smith quoted Binyam Mohamed as saying. "Plenty lost their minds. I could hear people knocking their heads against the walls and doors, screaming their heads off."

Professor Kassem said his Yemeni client, Kazimi, had told him that, during his incarceration in the Dark Prison, he attempted suicide three times, by ramming his head into the walls. "He did it until he lost consciousness," Kassem said. "Then they stitched him back up. So he did it again. The next time, he woke up, he was chained, and they'd given him tranquillizers. He asked to go to the bathroom, and then he did it again." This last time, Kazimi was given more tranquillizers, and chained in a more confining manner.

The case of Khaled el-Masri, another detainee, has received wide attention. He is the German car salesman whom the C.I.A. captured in 2003 and dispatched to Afghanistan, based on erroneous intelligence; he was released in 2004, and Condoleezza Rice reportedly conceded the mistake to the German chancellor. Masri is considered one of the more credible sources on the black-site program, because Germany has confirmed that he has no connections to terrorism. He has also described inmates bashing their heads against the walls. Much of his account appeared on the front page of the *Times*. But, during a visit to America last fall, he became tearful as he recalled the plight of a Tanzanian in a neighboring cell. The man seemed "psychologically at the end," he said. "I could hear him ramming his head against the wall in despair. I tried to calm him down. I asked the doctor, 'Will you take care of this human being?'" But the doctor, whom Masri described as American, refused to help. Masri also said that he was told that guards had "locked the Tanzanian in a suitcase for long periods of time—a foul-smelling suitcase that made him vomit." (Masri did not witness such abuse.)

Masri described his prison in Afghanistan as a filthy hole, with walls scribbled on in Pashtun and Arabic. He was given no bed, only a coarse blanket on the floor. At night, it was too cold to sleep. He said, "The water was putrid. If you took a sip, you could taste it for hours. You could smell a foul smell from it three meters away." The Salt Pit, he said, "was managed and run by the Americans. It was not a secret. They introduced themselves as Americans." He added, "When anything came up, they said they couldn't make a decision. They said, 'We will have to pass it on to Washington.'" The interrogation room at the Salt Pit, he said, was overseen by a half-dozen English-speaking masked men, who shoved him and shouted at him, saying, "You're in a country where there's no rule of law. You might be buried here."

According to two former C.I.A. officers, an interrogator of Mohammed told them that the Pakistani was kept in a cell over which a sign was placed: "The Proud Murderer of 3,000 Americans." (Another source calls this apocryphal.) One of these former officers defends the C.I.A.'s program by noting that "there was absolutely nothing done to K.S.M. that wasn't done to the interrogators themselves"—a reference to SERE-like training.

Yet the Red Cross report emphasizes that it was the simultaneous use of several techniques for extended periods that made the treatment "especially abusive." Senator Carl Levin, the chairman of the Senate Armed Services Committee, who has been a prominent critic of the administration's embrace of harsh interrogation techniques, said that, particularly with sensory deprivation, "there's a point where it's torture. You can put someone in a refrigerator and it's torture. Everything is a matter of degree."

.　　　.　　　.

One day, Mohammed was apparently transferred to a specially designated prison for high-value detainees in Poland. Such transfers were so secretive, according to the report by the Council of Europe, that the C.I.A. filed dummy flight plans, indicating that the planes were heading elsewhere. Once Polish air space was entered, the Polish aviation authority would secretly shepherd the flight, leaving no public documentation. The Council of Europe report notes that the Polish authorities would file a one-way flight plan out of the country, creating a false paper trail. (The Polish government has strongly denied that any black sites were established in the country.)

No more than a dozen high-value detainees were held at the Polish black site, and none have been released from government custody; accordingly, no firsthand accounts of conditions there have emerged. But, according to well-informed sources, it was a far more high-tech facility than the prisons in Afghanistan. The cells had hydraulic doors and air-conditioning. Multiple cameras in each cell provided video surveillance of the detainees. In some ways, the circumstances were better: the detainees were given bottled water. Without confirming the existence of any black sites, Robert Grenier, the former C.I.A. counterterrorism chief, said, "The agency's techniques became less aggressive as they learned the art of interrogation," which, he added, "*is* an art."

Mohammed was kept in a prolonged state of sensory deprivation, during which every point of reference was erased. The Council on Europe's report describes a four-month isolation regime as typical. The prisoners had no exposure to natural light, making it impossible for them to tell if it was night or day. They interacted only with masked, silent guards. (A detainee held at what was most likely an Eastern European black site, Mohammed al-Asad, told me that white noise was piped in constantly, although during electrical outages he could hear people crying.) According to a source familiar with the Red Cross report, Khalid Sheikh Mohammed claimed that he was shackled and kept naked, except for a pair of goggles and earmuffs. (Some prisoners were kept naked for as long as forty days.) He had no idea where he was, although, at one point, he apparently glimpsed Polish writing on a water bottle.

In the C.I.A.'s program, meals were delivered sporadically, to insure that the prisoners remained temporally disoriented. The food was largely tasteless, and barely enough to live on. Mohammed, who upon his capture in Rawalpindi was photographed looking flabby and unkempt, was now described as being slim. Experts on the C.I.A. program say that the administering of food is part of its psychological arsenal. Sometimes portions were smaller than the day before, for no apparent reason. "It was all part of the conditioning," the person involved in the Council of Europe inquiry said. "It's all calibrated to develop dependency."

The inquiry source said that most of the Poland detainees were waterboarded, including Mohammed. According to the sources familiar with the Red Cross report, Mohammed claimed to have been waterboarded five times. Two former C.I.A. officers who are friends with one of Mohammed's interrogators called this bravado, insisting that he was waterboarded only once.

According to one of the officers, Mohammed needed only to be shown the drowning equipment again before he "broke."

"Waterboarding works," the former officer said. "Drowning is a baseline fear. So is falling. People dream about it. It's human nature. Suffocation is a very scary thing. When you're waterboarded, you're inverted, so it exacerbates the fear. It's not painful, but it scares the shit out of you." (The former officer was waterboarded himself in a training course.) Mohammed, he claimed, "didn't resist. He sang right away. He cracked real quick." He said, "A lot of them want to talk. Their egos are unimaginable. K.S.M. was just a little doughboy. He couldn't stand toe to toe and fight it out."

The former officer said that the C.I.A. kept a doctor standing by during interrogations. He insisted that the method was safe and effective, but said that it could cause lasting psychic damage to the interrogators. During interrogations, the former agency official said, officers worked in teams, watching each other behind two-way mirrors. Even with this group support, the friend said, Mohammed's interrogator "has horrible nightmares." He went on, "When you cross over that line of darkness, it's hard to come back. You lose your soul. You can do your best to justify it, but it's well outside the norm. You can't go to that dark a place without it changing you." He said of his friend, "He's a good guy. It really haunts him. You are inflicting something really evil and horrible on somebody."

Among the few C.I.A. officials who knew the details of the detention and interrogation program, there was a tense debate about where to draw the line in terms of treatment. John Brennan, Tenet's former chief of staff, said, "It all comes down to individual moral barometers." Waterboarding, in particular, troubled many officials, from both a moral and a legal perspective. Until 2002, when Bush administration lawyers asserted that waterboarding was a permissible interrogation technique for "enemy combatants," it was classified as a form of torture, and treated as a serious criminal offense. American soldiers were court-martialed for waterboarding captives as recently as the Vietnam War.

A C.I.A. source said that Mohammed was subjected to waterboarding only after interrogators determined that he was hiding information from them. But Mohammed has apparently said that, even after he started cooperating, he was waterboarded. Footnotes to the 9/11 Commission report indicate that by April 17, 2003—a month and a half after he was captured—Mohammed had already started providing substantial information on Al Qaeda. Nonetheless, according to the person involved in the Council of Europe inquiry, he was kept in isolation for years. During this time, Mohammed supplied intelligence on the history of the September 11th plot, and on the structure and operations of Al Qaeda. He also described plots still in a preliminary phase of development, such as a plan to bomb targets on America's West Coast.

Ultimately, however, Mohammed claimed responsibility for so many crimes that his testimony became to seem inherently dubious. In addition to confessing to the Pearl murder, he said that he had hatched plans to assassinate President Clinton, President Carter, and Pope John Paul II. Bruce Riedel, who was a C.I.A. analyst for twenty-nine years, and who now works at the Brookings Institution, said, "It's difficult to give credence to any particular area of this large a charge sheet that he confessed to, considering the situation he found himself in. K.S.M. has no prospect of ever seeing freedom again, so his only gratification in life is to portray himself as the James Bond of jihadism."

· · ·

By 2004, there were growing calls within the C.I.A. to transfer to military custody the high-value detainees who had told interrogators what they knew, and to afford them some kind of due process. But Donald Rumsfeld, then the defense secretary, who had been heavily criticized for the abusive conditions at military prisons such as Abu Ghraib and Guantánamo, refused to take on the agency's detainees, a former top C.I.A. official said. "Rumsfeld's attitude was, *You've* got a real problem." Rumsfeld, the official said, "was the third most powerful person in the U.S. government, but he only looked out for the interests of his department—not the whole administration." (A spokesperson for Rumsfeld said that he had no comment.)

C.I.A. officials were stymied until the Supreme Court's Hamdan ruling, which prompted the administration to send what it said were its last high-value detainees to Cuba. Robert Grenier, like many people in the C.I.A., was relieved. "There has to be some sense of due process," he said. "We can't just make people disappear." Still, he added, "The most important source of intelligence we had after 9/11 came from the interrogations of high-value detainees." And he said that Mohammed was "the most valuable of the high-value detainees, because he had operational knowledge." He went on, "I can respect people who oppose aggressive interrogations, but they should admit that their principles may be putting American lives at risk."

Yet Philip Zelikow, the executive director of the 9/11 Commission and later the State Department's top counselor, under Rice, is not convinced that eliciting information from detainees justifies "physical torment." After leaving the government last year, he gave a speech in Houston, in which he said, "The question would not be, Did you get information that proved useful? Instead it would be, Did you get information that could have been usefully gained only from these methods?" He concluded, "My own view is that the cool, carefully considered, methodical, prolonged, and repeated subjection of captives to physical torment, and the accompanying psychological terror, is immoral."

Without more transparency, the value of the C.I.A.'s interrogation and detention program is impossible to evaluate. Setting aside the moral, ethical, and legal issues, even supporters, such as John Brennan, acknowledge that much of the information that coercion produces is unreliable. As he put it, "All these methods produced useful information, but there was also a lot that was bogus." When pressed, one former top agency official estimated that "90 percent of the information was unreliable." Cables carrying Mohammed's interrogation transcripts back to Washington reportedly were prefaced with the warning that "the detainee has been known to withhold information or deliberately mislead." Mohammed, like virtually all the top Al Qaeda prisoners held by the C.I.A., has claimed that, while under coercion, he lied to please his captors.

In theory, a military commission could sort out which parts of Mohammed's confession are true and which are lies, and obtain a conviction. Colonel Morris D. Davis, the chief prosecutor at the Office of Military Commissions, said that he expects to bring charges against Mohammed "in a number of months." He added, "I'd be shocked if the defense didn't try to make K.S.M.'s treatment a problem for me, but I don't think it will be insurmountable."

Critics of the administration fear that the unorthodox nature of the C.I.A.'s interrogation and detention program will make it impossible to prosecute the entire top echelon of Al Qacda leaders in captivity. Already, according to the *Wall Street Journal*, credible allegations of torture have caused a Marine Corps prosecutor reluctantly to decline to bring charges against Mohamedou Ould Slahi, an alleged Al Qaeda leader held in Guantánamo. Bruce Riedel, the former C.I.A. analyst, asked, "What are you going to do with K.S.M. in the long run? It's a very good question. I don't think anyone has an answer. If you took him to any real American court, I think any judge would say there is no admissible evidence. It would be thrown out."

The problems with Mohammed's coerced confessions are especially glaring in the Daniel Pearl case. It may be that Mohammed killed Pearl, but contradictory evidence and opinion continue to surface. Yosri Fouda, the Al Jazeera reporter who interviewed Mohammed in Karachi, said that although Mohammed handed him a package of propaganda items, including an unedited video of the Pearl murder, he never identified himself as playing a role in the killing, which occurred in the same city just two months earlier. And a federal official involved in Mohammed's case said, "He has no history of killing with his own hands, although he's proved happy to commit mass murder from afar." Al Qaeda's leadership had increasingly focused on symbolic political targets. "For him, it's not personal," the official said. "It's business."

Ordinarily, the U.S. legal system is known for resolving such mysteries with painstaking care. But the C.I.A.'s secret interrogation program, Senator Levin said, has undermined the public's trust in American justice, both here and abroad. "A guy as dangerous as K.S.M. is, and half the world wonders if they can believe him—is that what we want?" he asked. "Statements that can't be believed, because people think they rely on torture?"

Asra Nomani, the Pearls' friend, said of the Mohammed confession, "I'm not interested in unfair justice, even for bad people." She went on, "Danny was such a person of conscience. I don't think he would have wanted all of this dirty business. I don't think he would have wanted someone being tortured. He would have been repulsed. This is the kind of story that Danny would have investigated. He really believed in American principles."

The Nation

Starting with a hunch, Joshua Kors discovered that Jon Town, a Purple Heart–winning army specialist seriously injured in Iraq, was one of 22,500 veterans denied medical and disability benefits. Reform followed, and the affected vets received back benefits.

Joshua Kors

Specialist Town Takes His Case to Washington

On April 9, Spc. Jon Town was featured on the cover of *The Nation*, in an article that told how he was wounded in Iraq, won a Purple Heart, and was then denied all disability and medical benefits. Town's doctor had concluded that his headaches and hearing loss were not caused by the 107-millimeter rocket that knocked him unconscious but by a psychological condition, "personality disorder," a preexisting illness for which one cannot collect disability pay or receive medical care.

Soon Town became a national figure, the human face of the 22,500 soldiers discharged with personality disorder in the past six years. His story was picked up by the *Army Times*, Washington Post Radio, and ABC News's Bob Woodruff. It was dramatized in a May episode of NBC's *Law & Order*. And rock star Dave Matthews began discussing Town's plight at every stop in his spring concert series.

Further investigation by *The Nation* has uncovered more than a dozen cases like Town's from bases across the country. All of the soldiers interviewed passed the rigorous health screening given recruits before being accepted into the army. All were deemed physically and psychologically fit in a second screening as well, before being deployed to Iraq, and served honorably there in combat. None of the soldiers interviewed during this eleven-month investigation had a documented history of psychological problems.

Yet after they returned from Iraq wounded and sought treatment, each was diagnosed with a preexisting personality disorder, then denied benefits. As in Town's case, army doctors determined that the soldiers' ailments were preexisting without interviewing friends, family, or fellow soldiers who knew them before they were wounded in combat.

In this article you will hear from army doctors who say wounded soldiers are routinely misdiagnosed. One says he was pressured by superiors to diagnose personality disorder in cases where soldiers were physically wounded or suffering from post–traumatic stress disorder (PTSD).

Maj. Gen. Gale Pollock, acting surgeon general of the army, was briefed on the problems with the army's personality disorder discharges. Instead of correcting cases like Town's, she buried them. The surgeon general released a series of memos filled with fabrications. Pollock then informed wounded soldiers that their cases had been thoroughly reviewed by an independent panel of health experts when in fact no such review was conducted.

"This is not the way the government ought to work. It's not the way they should be responding to veterans," says Representative Bob Filner, chair of the House Committee on Veterans' Affairs. He first heard Town's story in April and began working soon afterward to bring the soldier to Washington. There Town would get his chance to tell Congress everything: about his diagnosis, his discharge, and the work of Surgeon General Pollock.

'Thoroughly Evaluated and Reviewed'

Andrew Pogany, an investigator for the soldiers' rights group Veterans for America, has been looking into personality disorder discharges for two years. The discharge, officially known as

Regulation 635-200, Chapter 5-13, is simply a loophole, he says, to dismiss wounded soldiers without providing them benefits. Pogany says Town's case is a textbook example of how Chapter 5-13 is being applied. Town had no history of psychological problems and had served seven years, winning a dozen medals, before being discharged with a personality disorder.

The investigator was so disturbed by the army's use of 5-13 discharges that he brought his research to Pollock. In late October 2006, he and Steve Robinson, Veterans for America's director of veterans affairs, met with Pollock and presented her with a stack of personality disorder cases, including Town's. The surgeon general promised a thorough review.

On March 23, five months after her meeting with Pogany, Pollock released her findings. Her office had "thoughtfully and thoroughly" reviewed the personality disorder cases and determined that all of the soldiers, including Town, had been properly diagnosed. Pollock commended the doctors who diagnosed personality disorder for their excellent work.

Four days later the military followed up with a press release, this one signed by Lieut. Col. Bob Tallman, the army's chief of public affairs. Tallman's memo provided further detail on Pollock's review. A panel of behavioral health experts had reviewed the personality disorder cases, Tallman wrote, and they didn't stop at the stack of cases presented to the surgeon general. They "thoroughly evaluated and reviewed" all the Chapter 5-13s from the past four years at Fort Carson, where Specialist Town had been based, and determined that all of those cases had been properly diagnosed as well.

There was a glaring problem with Pollock's review. In the five months she spent "thoughtfully and thoroughly" reviewing the cases, her office did not interview anyone, not even the soldiers whose cases they were reviewing.

Asked how he could call the surgeon general's review "thorough" when no soldiers were interviewed, Tallman said he could not. "Let me be honest with you," he said. "I know nothing about this memo and little to nothing about the review." Tallman said the memo bearing his name was actually ghostwritten by Pollock's office. The lieutenant colonel added that as far as he knew, Pollock conducted no review at all.

Pollock's office quickly admitted that it had ghostwritten the Tallman memo but assured veterans' groups that the surgeon general had indeed conducted a review. In an e-mail Pollock's chief spokeswoman, Cynthia Vaughan, explained that the surgeon general did not want to interview soldiers because she felt they had no medically valid information to share. "Calling a soldier who underwent a 5-13 Chapter in 2003 and asking him (in 2007) to recall his mental condition in 2003 does not hold medical validity," Vaughan wrote.

That statement angered many soldiers, including Jon Town. "You'd think I'd remember, even today, if I had headaches and hearing loss before the rocket attack," he says. The surgeon general tried to quell veterans' groups by emphasizing that, as stated in the March memos, the comprehensive review was conducted by a panel of health experts and that those experts "did not provide the initial evaluations." This wasn't a case of one doctor reviewing his own work, the surgeon general said.

Both of those assurances crumbled on May 4, when *Army Times* reporter Kelly Kennedy revealed that in fact there was only one reviewer: Col. Steven Knorr. Knorr was a strange choice to be the sole reviewer. He was far from an objective observer. As chief of Fort Carson's Behavioral Health unit, Knorr had overseen all the original diagnoses and, in his capacity as a psychiatrist, also diagnosed several soldiers with personality disorder.

Months earlier Knorr had spoken out in defense of the army's practice of not interviewing soldiers' family or friends before labeling their condition "preexisting." Unlike his staff, he said, family members are not trained to recognize signs of personality disorder, so speaking to them would be of limited value. "The soldier's perception and their parents' perception is that they were fine. But maybe they didn't or weren't able to see that wasn't the case."

In the same interview, published in *The Nation*, Knorr said there was a simple reason why in so many cases the lifelong condition of personality disorder isn't apparent until after troops serve in Iraq. Traumatic experiences, he said, can trigger a condition that has lain dormant for years. "[Troops] may have done fine in high school and before, but it comes out during the stress of service," he said. Knorr's assertion was a sharp break from the accepted medical understanding of personality disorder and provoked a flood of angry letters from psychiatrists and veterans' leaders.

Veterans were further agitated by a vivid profile of Knorr, by NPR's Daniel Zwerdling broadcast in late May. Zwerdling details a memo written by Knorr in which he advises his doctors that trying to save every soldier is a "mistake." "We can't fix every Soldier," the memo states. "We have to hold Soldiers accountable for their behavior. Everyone in life beyond babies, the insane, and the demented and mentally retarded have to be held accountable for what they do in life."

Knorr's memo, which he posted on his office's bulletin board, warns his doctors not to take soldiers' descriptions of their ailments at face value. "We're not naïve, and shouldn't automatically believe everything Soldiers tell us," the colonel writes. Knorr also urges his doctors to discharge troubled soldiers quickly—as he puts it, "Get rid of dead wood."

"That memo made me sick," says Russell Terry, founder of the Iraq War Veterans Organization. "It's incomprehensible that [Pollock] would choose him to lead the review." Terry says that if she had wanted to do a real review, the surgeon general could have organized a panel of impartial medical experts. "By having Knorr review his own stuff, there's no outside opinion, no one to uncover the misdiagnoses—no one to object."

The surgeon general declined to be interviewed. But in a recent statement, Pollock defended her office's review and showed continued support for Knorr, calling him an "appropriate" choice to spearhead the review.

By May the army had a nascent PR nightmare on its hands. The story of Pollock, Knorr and the "thoughtful and thorough" five-month review had been picked up by news talk programs on NPR, Washington Post Radio, and ABC News. To stem the tide, officials at Fort Carson did something odd: They released a new memo stating that fifty-six soldiers discharged from Fort Carson with personality disorder actually had PTSD.

It was a stunning admission. As soon as they released it, officials tried to downplay it. Col. John Cho, former commander of Fort Carson's hospital, quickly submitted a second statement, saying that the first memo was not an admission of guilt. Soldiers suffering from PTSD could be rightfully discharged with personality disorder if they had that condition too and their PTSD was not "severe," he said. But Army Regulation 40-501, Chapter 3-33, is clear. It states that if a soldier is suffering from PTSD, he must be discharged by a medical board, which can provide him the lifetime of disability and medical benefits denied soldiers discharged with personality disorder.

Fort Carson officials provided an unintentionally comic coda to their admission when they insisted that all fifty-six cases were properly diagnosed, shortly after Cho admitted in writing that his office could find only fifty-two of them. Base officials said the remaining four cases had been lost or misplaced. They could not explain how they knew those cases were properly diagnosed when they couldn't be found. "It's incredible when you think about it," says Pogany. "They're doing everything they can to cover this up—and doing a lousy job of it."

On May 16, army officials clarified: The four-year review of personality disorder cases trumpeted in the Tallman memo never occurred.

'I Refused to Diagnose as They Wanted'

By the time Dr. Michael Chen stepped down, he had been serving the army for more than thirty years. The psychiatrist had treated soldiers at several bases and looked forward to continuing his work at a new installation after being transferred.

Chen's enthusiasm was short-lived. Soon he began clashing with his superiors. "I refused to diagnose as they wanted," he says. "They wanted the diagnoses to be personality disorder, instead of PTSD." The psychiatrist says the soldiers he saw weren't suffering from preexisting conditions; they had PTSD and traumatic brain injury (TBI). Chen says he relayed this information to his colonel, to no avail. "The establishment wants to hear what the establishment wants to hear."

Chen is not the doctor's real name. Because he fears retribution from the army, the psychiatrist agreed to speak only if his name and base were not revealed. He says he wasn't the only doctor pressured to misdiagnose: Other psychiatrists were pressed as well, resulting in numerous fraudulent diagnoses of personality disorder. "I've seen that story happen hundreds of times," he says.

While serving at the army hospital, Chen did diagnose personality disorder. But eventually the absurdity of the recommended diagnoses proved too much. The psychiatrist recalls one soldier who returned from Iraq with a massive hunk of his right calf missing. "They thought he had personality disorder," Chen says, the anger in his voice suddenly palpable. "Imagine: You get your leg blown off, you get a Purple Heart and now they say it's from personality disorder. It's absurd." Frustrated, the psychiatrist approached the commanding general of the hospital.

Chen says he met with the official numerous times. But the pressure to misdiagnose continued.

"It's just criminal," he says. The doctor says that at his base wounded soldiers were treated like broken appliances: When they no longer functioned, the command simply wanted to "throw them out" with a preexisting condition. "And it's appalling to me that my colleagues would go along with it."

The psychiatrist says he doesn't blame the commanding general for the pressure on him and other doctors to misdiagnose soldiers. Their meetings made it clear that the general was simply taking orders from "high up on the food chain." In some sense, says the doctor, that was to be expected, because with personality disorder, there's so much money at stake. *The Nation* reported in April that the military is saving $12.5 billion in disability and medical care by discharging soldiers under Chapter 5-13, a figure drawn from a recent Harvard study by Professor Linda Bilmes. Chen believes $12.5 billion is a gross underestimate—that from what he's seen at his medical center, if all the wounded soldiers returning from Iraq were properly diagnosed, the long-term cost of benefits would be exponentially larger.

As it was, says Chen, the medical ethic at the army hospital followed the guidelines of the Knorr memo, which urged doctors not to take soldiers' descriptions of their ailments at face value. The psychiatrist's own approach was radically different. "If a soldier said he had PTSD, I wrote up 'PTSD.' Finally I was told I couldn't see any more soldiers because I diagnosed PTSD too much." Chen left the hospital soon after. Today he treats patients at a nonmilitary facility.

Dr. Brian Harrison still works for the military. Like Dr. Chen, his years as an army psychiatrist have been contentious. Harrison says that at his medical center, "there has been a tradition of 'underdiagnosing.'" That means soldiers with PTSD don't always receive that diagnosis. And their health isn't always the top concern. Foremost on the command's mind, says Harrison, is getting soldiers back to Iraq. He says doctors at his base understand that when wounded soldiers seek treatment from them, their job is to get the soldiers back to the battlefield, even if they are traumatized. The psychiatrist quotes his hospital's chief of Behavioral Health as saying, "If they're not suicidal or homicidal, they're fit to go back." If they don't meet that standard, the doctors are to get rid of them fast. Wounded soldiers are "seen as damaged merchandise," Harrison says. "The command wants people like that out of their hair, out of their way."

Harrison is also a pseudonym. The doctor says he is speaking out in violation of an e-mail from his superiors ordering psychiatrists at his facility not to talk to the media. If he gives his name, he says, he could be fired.

The doctor says he has never been pressured to misdiagnose. The biggest challenge he has faced is making a correct diagnosis, given the brevity of his appointments. Until recently, he was allowed to meet with soldiers for an hour. But now, he says, the chief of his department has pressed him to cut his evaluation time to half an hour and make future appointments between fifteen and thirty minutes. "I can't do an evaluation in half an hour," says the psychiatrist. "To properly diagnose a soldier, you need at least an hour." Like Chen, Harrison doesn't blame his department's chief, noting that there's pressure on him from his superiors—"the money managers," Harrison calls them. "Those jackasses—they don't have any clinical experience, they've never worked with soldiers, and they don't care."

The bitterness in his voice is broken suddenly with a warm laugh. "Maybe I'm just old-fashioned," says the elderly doctor. Harrison has been practicing psychiatry for almost forty years and still insists on some decidedly "old-fashioned" techniques, like interviewing soldiers' families when diagnosing a preexisting condition to see whether the soldiers' troubles existed before joining the service. Other doctors at the army hospital "don't make any effort to do that," he says. "And they don't have time to. They're busy herding people through."

Surgeon General Pollock declined to comment on Chen's and Harrisón's allegations. In a statement, she says she is disturbed by the idea that "individuals [are] pressuring providers to falsify diagnoses. . . . Such conduct, of course, would be totally unacceptable." Pollock advises doctors who feel under pressure to diagnose personality disorder to contact the Inspector General. She asks soldiers who feel they have been misdiagnosed to approach her directly. Due to "my concern over these issues, they may provide their information to me and I will have the staff review their records."

Flying Blind

In May, before most in Washington had even heard of Chapter 5-13, Senator Kit Bond was studying the discharge—and calling for its abolition. "You have 22,000 soldiers who passed through all the tests required to send them to Iraq, and they came back and were diagnosed with a preexisting condition? It just doesn't compute. We need to fix the system," he says. "They ought not have the 5-13 as an easy way to put these soldiers out." As the system is now, the senator says, some of the cases he's seen "just scream out to me: 'This person was railroaded.'"

The Republican from Missouri helped put together a coalition of thirty-one senators spanning the political spectrum, from Hillary Clinton to Joseph Lieberman to fellow conservative Elizabeth Dole. In June they wrote a letter to Defense Secretary Robert Gates requesting that he investigate the 5-13 discharge process. Bond also cowrote a defense authorization amendment with Senator Barack Obama and others that would put a temporary freeze on all personality disorder discharges. The amendment has been referred to the Armed Services Committee.

The past year has exposed several problems in the way we're treating veterans, says Bond. "And this 5-13 seems to be a major part of the problem."

By July the Senate wasn't the only organization in Washington concerned about personality disorder. The Department of Veterans Affairs was worried too. "We wanted to prioritize injured [Iraq War] veterans. We want to provide a seamless transition" from the army, says a top VA official. But with these personality disorder discharges, "you have people now falling through the cracks." The official, who demanded anonymity because he had not received clearance to speak, says the problem with phony discharges like personality disorder is that they short-circuit the VA's Red Flag system.

The Red Flag system is an informal name for the VA's method of identifying the most wounded soldiers. The agency does this, explains the official, by keeping its eye on the army's medical board hearings, where wounded soldiers are supposed to go before their discharge. The board evaluates injured soldiers and gives them a disability rating. Under the Red Flag system, those who leave the army's medical board hearings with a high disability rating are flagged and targeted for immediate medical care.

But soldiers discharged with personality disorder are denied the opportunity to see a medical board and thus don't get a disability rating. As a result, they fly under the VA's radar. Those who need immediate medical care get dumped into the stack of 800,000 cases currently waiting to be processed by the VA. For the VA to function, says the official, the army has to pass wounded soldiers through its medical boards. Otherwise, the agency is flying blind.

·　　　·　　　·

Jon Town knows firsthand the price of that blindness. He submitted an application for VA medical care shortly before leaving the army. Seven months later he was still waiting for his first doctor's appointment.

Without medical treatment, Town struggled alone with deafness, memory loss, insomnia and a headache that was still raging three years after the rocket attack. The specialist tried to take a few jobs, but each time he was fired after his health proved too much of an issue. His wife, Kristy, had to keep the family of four afloat with her minimum-wage job on the assembly line at Filtech, an oil-filter manufacturer in their hometown of Findlay, Ohio. Soon the family was teetering on the verge of bankruptcy. In May, the phone company shut off their service because the Towns couldn't pay their bill.

The media took note. In April came the *Nation* article, followed by the *Law & Order* episode, which introduced Town's story to 9 million viewers. When musician Dave Matthews saw the article and began discussing it in concerts, his enraged fans took up a collection for Town, which raised $3,000. The guitarist followed up by posting a petition on his Web site, urging Congress to hold hearings on personality disorder. Within weeks the petition was signed by 23,000 people.

"There are times when an injustice is so clear, it's not a matter of opinion," says Matthews. "Nobody would argue that what's happening to Jon Town is right. And to think that it's happening over and over again . . . it's just astounding. It's a crime against these young people that's so profound—and it's happening right now. I had to ask myself, 'Does America think this is OK?'" People won't think it's OK once they learn what's going on, says Matthews. "We can fix this catastrophe. It's just a matter of getting people to know about it."

Soon *Nation* readers, NBC viewers, and Matthews fans were reaching out to Town en masse: e-mails, phone calls, small personal checks. The local chapter of Veterans of Foreign Wars organized a motorcycle ride to honor his service. A veteran from

Boston offered Town his disability pay until the specialist could secure his own.

Strangely enough, Town's big break came not from Matthews, NBC, or even Senator Bond but from Lou Wilin, a reporter at the *Findlay Courier,* Town's hometown paper (circulation 23,000). After reading Town's story in *The Nation,* Wilin wrote a profile of the soldier, which ran in the newspaper's April 16 edition. The article caught the eye of an admiral in the VA who happens to live a few miles east of Findlay. The admiral flagged Town's case, kicked it to the Cleveland VA, which passed it to the Dayton VA, where case manager Janine Wert was ready to take action. Wert received Town's case the morning of April 19 and had the soldier in her office before the end of lunch. She listened to his story and cried.

"His childhood, high school, and military history—none of it supports a personality disorder. When you're a teenager, there are certain things that pop up that are vividly obvious, red flags for personality disorder. Those aren't present in Jon's history," says Wert, a social worker with a master's degree in mental health. Wert says Town's PTSD and TBI symptoms were obvious from their first meeting. She was struck by the absurdity of the army's diagnosis. "I have never in my life heard of personality disorder causing deafness," says the counselor.

Wert arranged an immediate doctor's appointment for Town and scheduled an evaluation by a VA medical board. On June 11 the VA ruled that Town was in fact wounded in combat. The agency declared him 100 percent disabled.

Town's VA rating guaranteed him disability and medical benefits for the rest of his life. The VA also provided the disability pay that Town should have received in the months following his discharge. On June 25, just weeks after his family's phone had been shut off, the specialist received a check for $20,000.

"I almost started to cry," says Town. "They were ready to repossess everything. And now I knew we weren't going to lose our cars to bankruptcy, that we'd have food on the table for years to come. . . . There isn't a word for what I was feeling."

The diagnosis was a remarkable victory for the Town family—and a pointed defeat for the army, which to this day insists that Town was not wounded in combat and that his health problems stem from a personality disorder. He still has not received any of the benefits owed him by the army.

"This is a scandal," Representative Filner said in May. And members of his VA Committee would be interested in pursuing it, "but right now, they just don't know anything about it." With the uproar about Town, Filner saw an opportunity to change that. On July 12 he announced that his committee would hold a hearing on personality disorder. To do it right, he said, "we definitely want to hear from soldiers."

Filner had a particular soldier in mind.

'This Would Be Wrong'

July 25. By 10 A.M., it's standing room only at the Cannon House Office Building, the hearing room swimming with men in uniform, veterans with camouflage accessories, protesters in bright pink sporting handwritten placards demanding justice for soldiers. A row of photographers crouch beside the CBS News camera; reporters for ABC News, NPR, and the *New York Times* have set up shop behind the soldier at the witness desk.

Not surprisingly, Town didn't sleep the night before. His headache is still raging; his eyes look a bit bloodshot. But his blond bangs are combed, and his favorite red-striped Old Navy shirt is gone, as is the brown ball cap and reflective sunglasses, replaced with a well-pressed navy suit and crimson tie. Town holds his dog tags in his hand and rubs them nervously between his thumb and forefinger as he looks up at the committee, his voice defiant and jittery.

"I want to state that I did not have a personality disorder before I went into the army, as they have stated in my paperwork. I did not suffer severe nonstop headaches. I did not have memory loss. I did not have endless, sleepless nights. I have post-traumatic stress disorder and traumatic brain injury now due to the injuries I received in the war, for which I received a Purple Heart," he says. "I shouldn't be labeled for the rest of my life with a personality disorder, and neither should my fellow soldiers who also incorrectly received this stigma."

Filner looks down at the specialist with paternal eyes. When the applause dies down he says, "Thank you, Mr. Town. You did not sign up to have to do this. But you are helping a lot of people, and we thank you for your courage."

Two hours later Surgeon General Pollock's psychological consultant, Col. Bruce Crow, sits at the witness desk. Pollock herself was called to testify; her name appeared on the original witness list. But today she's nowhere to be found, a fact that angers several of the congressmen. Speaking in her stead, Crow says, "Questions have been raised about whether army psychiatrists and psychologists are misdiagnosing soldiers with personality disorder instead of correctly diagnosing PTSD or traumatic brain injury." If they are misdiagnosing soldiers, says Crow, "this would be wrong."

Pollock's consultant says that the surgeon general is reviewing the cases of 295 soldiers discharged with personality disorder. Pollock will conduct the review, says Crow, by having "a team of senior mental health providers" look over the soldiers' paperwork.

Filner shakes his head, baffled. "The first panel shocked me," says Filner, referring to Town's testimony. "You guys shocked me even more." The allegation "that there's a systematic and policy-driven misdiagnosis of PTSD as personality disorder to get rid of soldiers early, to prevent any expenditures in the future, which were calculated in the billions of dollars . . . it's a pretty serious allegation." Crow looks back at Filner. He says nothing. "And if you think that we're going to believe an evaluation of 295 cases, whichever ones you happen to pick—that we're going to believe what you say—I'll tell you now, I'm not going to believe it. So why bother?" says the chairman. "Let's have an independent evaluation."

When the hearing ends, Crow exits. Several congressmen walk toward the gallery to shake Town's hand. The hearing went well, says the soldier. He was glad to hear support on both sides of the aisle for the Bond/Obama amendment to freeze 5-13 discharges and its companion legislation in the House, HR 3167, put forward by Congressman Phil Hare and others.

Now that Town has gotten his VA benefits, his eye has turned toward the national issue of 5-13 discharges. That is where there's a lot of work left to be done, he says. Town points out that still today, not a single person has been held responsible for the 5-13 discharges—not Surgeon General Pollock, not Colonel Knorr, not even the army psychologist who diagnosed his personality disorder, Dr. Mark Wexler.

And there hasn't been any effort to go back through the files and find the thousands of Jon Towns who are struggling right now without benefits or the media spotlight. "The army needs to go back and find these guys," says the specialist. "They need to show up and say, 'We apologize—and we're here to rectify the situation.'"

Until that happens, he says, his work is not done.

Vanity Fair

FINALIST—REPORTING

This richly detailed dispatch examines how a disciplined criminal force reached beyond the prisons and the shantytowns to paralyze Brazil's largest city, then receded into the shadows— waiting to avenge the next police action or perceived insult.

William Langewiesche

City of Fear

For seven days last May the city of São Paulo, Brazil, teetered on the edge of a feral zone where governments barely reach and countries lose their meaning. That zone is a wilderness inhabited already by large populations worldwide, but officially denied and rarely described. It is not a throwback to the Dark Ages, but an evolution toward something new—a companion to globalization, and an element in a fundamental reordering that may gradually render national boundaries obsolete. It is most obvious in the narco-lands of Colombia and Mexico, in the fractured swaths of Africa, in parts of Pakistan and Afghanistan, in much of Iraq. But it also exists beneath the surface in places where governments are believed to govern and countries still seem to be strong.

Certainly Brazil qualifies. And São Paulo is not some flimsy town. Though it suffers from violent crime and shoddy streets, it is the largest metropolis in South America, home to 20 million people, a global business and banking center, and the capital of Brazil's wealthiest and most powerful state. From its center of luxurious condominiums and office towers, it spreads across 3,000 square miles, sprouting tall apartment buildings for as far as the eye can see. It has a problem with shantytowns and slums, the favelas which ring the city with illegal constructions and millions upon millions of the ultra-poor. But most of the favelas lie on the periphery, so far beyond view that for the upper and middle classes they can almost be ignored. And look on the bright side: back toward the center, São Paulo has a great university, beautiful garden restaurants, and Japanese food that puts New York's to shame.

But then, suddenly, on the afternoon of Friday, May 12, 2006, São Paulo came under a violent and coordinated attack. The attackers moved on foot, and by car and motorbike. They were not rioters, revolutionaries, or the graduates of terrorist camps. They were anonymous young men and women, dressed in ordinary clothes, unidentifiable in advance, and indistinguishable afterward. Wielding pistols, automatic rifles, and firebombs, they emerged from within the city, struck fast, and vanished on the spot. Their acts were criminal, but the attackers did not loot, rob, or steal. They burned buses, banks, and public buildings, and went hard after the forces of order— gunning down the police in their neighborhood posts, in their homes, and on the streets. The police shot back and killed some people, but the others did not stop. They were like ghosts. On an animated plot of São Paulo their presence would have seemed like pinpoint flashes of light sparkling at random far and wide. The sparkling was slow, but word spread quickly, and traffic snarled as citizens tried to rush home. After they settled behind locked doors, they did not dare to venture out. Restaurants and shops were closed. The boulevards lay lit and abandoned. On television came news that the attacks were the work of a prison gang, half forgotten but widely known, called Primeiro Comando da Capital, or P.C.C., the First Command of the Capital. Across the state seventy-three prisons rose in synchronous rebellion. This caused less concern than one might expect, in part because prison riots are common in Brazil, and are routinely if sometimes brutally contained. But the attacks against the city were something else, and the government had no idea how to respond.

. . .

State authorities claimed that the situation was under control, but television showed that it was not. In fact, the authorities were barricaded inside their headquarters watching the same broadcast scenes. Some of the replays were set to music. The attacks continued in irregular waves, without discernible patterns. Through Friday night and across the weekend the police reeled backward, abandoning their posts, only to be ambushed in the open. The police in São Paulo are despised for corruption and brutality, but they do loosely stand for law and order, and it was shocking to see them in retreat. Over the first two days more than forty police officers and prison guards were killed, and also one of the firemen responding to the flames. For every agent killed, several others were wounded. Passersby died, caught in the crossfire. The national government offered to send in the army, but for political reasons the state refused. It was Sunday now, and Mother's Day. I later heard the recording of a cell-phone call in which a woman who had just torched a bus complained that a service station had sold her adulterated gasoline that did not burn hot enough. Who can you trust? The city huddled through the third night. On Monday morning, after a period of calm, people summoned the courage to return to work, in the hope that the trouble was over. But at midday the attacks resumed, and people again fled for their homes, creating one of the greatest traffic jams in São Paulo's great traffic-jam history.

Then, as abruptly as they had started, on Monday night the attacks suddenly stopped. It was widely assumed that the state had caved in and made concessions. And in fact the state had tried. Halfway through the weekend, having realized that they lacked the ability to restore order, the authorities bitterly concluded that they would have to negotiate—but with whom and about what? The P.C.C. is an immense and secretive network of semi-autonomous cells, and is shapeless by design. It includes 90 percent of São Paulo's 140,000 inmates, and at least as many people in the slums. The authorities knew that its leaders were angry about a certain transfer of prisoners that had just taken place, but this was not something the government could survive undoing, and in any case the P.C.C. had made no such demand. Indeed, it was making no demands at all. The gang's top man was being held in solitary confinement at a maximum-security prison 350 miles west of the city. He was a career criminal named Marcos Camacho, or Marcola, who was said to be intelligent and a careful student of Sun Tzu's classic text, *The Art of War*. Now thirty-nine, he had spent half of his life in prison and was serving a long sentence for armed robbery and kidnapping. On Sunday, May 14, with the attacks ongoing, a police airplane flew four envoys from São Paulo to see him and negotiate a peace. Typically, Marcola denied any knowledge of the attacks and refused to get involved. He would not even use a proffered cell phone to quash a rumor of his demise, though he finally did allow another prisoner to make the call. After several hours the envoys flew home.

The day after the attacks suddenly stopped, word spread through São Paulo that the state had agreed to provide the P.C.C. with sixty flat-screen televisions for enhanced viewing of the upcoming World Cup soccer matches. A prison official later told me that the televisions in question already belonged to the P.C.C., that they were part of a hijacked load, and that the P.C.C. had wanted—and now received—the right to bring them in as a jailhouse boast. And okay, in Brazil soccer really does matter. But no such petty purpose can explain an assault on an entire city, nor can superficial political theories, of which there are several. Clearly, something much larger was going on. What is certain is that the assault was a demonstration of strength, an act of self-affirmation, and a measured blow against the rule of law. Some of the attacks were so brazen as to be nearly suicidal. The point being made was not that they could be carried out, but that they could be sustained. The lack of serious demands added a vicious twist. It denied the government the power even to concede, and allowed the P.C.C. to script the drama from beginning to end. Moreover, because the P.C.C. leaders were already in prison, they had little to fear of punishment. They could taunt the state from within the very walls it had built to contain them. Ah, the art of war.

A lawyer I spoke to called the asymmetry outrageously unfair. She said, "They can send people to kill the police, but the police can't do the same to them, because they are under state protection!" The police in particular felt the frustration. Able to identify only the occasional culprit, and ordered by their superiors nonetheless to get tough, they struck back with masked death squads and uniformed agents against the residents of the slums. Brazilian law officially precludes capital punishment. But by the end of the week, when the actions ceased, the police had killed at least 450 people, many with execution-style shots to the head. The state disputed the numbers and came up with a hundred or so dead, most of them killed while resisting arrest. In a traumatized city where many people had condoned the police actions, only the most credulous could believe such unbelievable claims. The state was making a show of its fictions. It is a fact of history that the pretense of governing endures even as government disappears.

Big Jelly and Little Cesar

Brazil. The World Cup. The P.C.C. was a soccer team at the start. It was founded in a São Paulo state prison in the summer of 1993 by eight players, seven of whom have since died. The prison sits in the city of Taubaté, off the road to Rio de Janeiro.

At the time it was a punishment unit, where troublemakers went for stints of solitary confinement before being returned to larger prisons elsewhere in the state. Conditions there were atrocious. The prisoners lived locked alone into 160 dark and putrid cells, surviving on filthy slops, defecating into holes they could not flush, and subject to beatings by the guards. They were released into the yards only every few days, and in groups of merely five. Some committed suicide. Most, however, were tough, and managed not only to remain vital but also to communicate fully from cell to cell. In 1993, when they lobbied the warden for a soccer tournament, he decided to let them form teams. It is unclear how exactly they proceeded, given that they remained locked in their cells and could not assemble to practice. Through the jailhouse telegraph they gave their teams names in anticipation of battle. Several included the word "Command" for the swagger, but the P.C.C. outdid all the others by calling itself "First," and staking claim to the "Capital." In light of subsequent events, the name may sound like a warning. The warden himself was eventually murdered by the monster he had created. But the Primeiro Comando da Capital was born wanting just to play soccer.

The games were held in an enclosed yard, without spectators or guards. The P.C.C. won a few matches, became its cellblock champion, and prepared to play a rival team from another part of the prison. During the run-up to the game, the competition got out of hand when the boasts turned to taunts, and the taunts became threats. Each team vowed to drink the other team's blood. The captain of the P.C.C. was a killer from the lowest of São Paulo's slums, a physically powerful man named Geleião (Big Jelly), who had grown up in the gutter, and was now thirty-five. His sidekick was a natural-born fighter named Césinha (Little Cesar), five years younger, who had a reputation for bravery and was to serve as the P.C.C.'s chief executioner over the decade to come. Césinha had been raised in a middle-class family, but even as a child had idealized crime, and at the age of twelve had killed for the first time.

On the day of the match, August 31, 1993, the two teams moved together down a hallway toward the prison yard. The details remain obscure, but it seems that the guards were nowhere to be seen, and that the last P.C.C. player closed a barred door behind them to ensure privacy. Just before they got to the yard, Geleião made the first move. He grabbed an opposing player, and with a single ferocious twist killed the man by snapping his neck. Césinha and the others sprang forward, and with bare hands and shivs took another four lives. There is no evidence that they enjoyed the killing. They inhabited a violent world and had responded necessarily to insults they believed it would have been dangerous to leave unanswered. In doing so they had also condemned themselves to lives of unending vigilance and strength, since every one of the dead men had family or friends who might try to take revenge. Afterward, they swore a public vow of mutual defense. Through the telegraph they declared, "We are united forever now. Whatever happens to one happens to all. We will never betray each other. We are brothers for life." That simple vow proved impossible to follow, but it established a principle from which all else evolved, and among the prisoners of São Paulo it resonated loudly.

The Mark of the P.C.C.

The prisons of São Paulo were falling apart under the loads they had to bear. The most notorious of them was a decrepit facility named Carandiru, which dated from 1956 and was the largest in Brazil. It stood inside the São Paulo city limits in an industrial neighborhood on the north side of town, surrounded by high gray walls and accessed through a single heavy gate. It contained nine cellblocks, each five stories tall, and by the early 1990s held more than 7,000 inmates, nearly twice the intended capacity. On

October 2, 1992—eleven months before the P.C.C.'s bloody birth in Taubaté—it was the scene of a massacre by the police, who while suppressing a rebellion in its Cellblock Nine had killed 111 prisoners, and wounded 130 others. To carry this out the police had fired merely 515 rounds—a record of efficiency reflecting the fact that most of the shooting had been done at point-blank range on prisoners who had already surrendered and were cowering in their cells.

In the background was a crime rate in São Paulo that was among the highest in the world, and the fact that even as the city was remaking itself into a center of global business it was being transformed into an archipelago of innumerable little fortresses where a large population of the fortunate lived and worked in near-total isolation from the poor. The two transformations were related. It was not only that the poor were being abandoned by government but that the very need for government was being questioned by the elites. Armored cars, private guards, helicopters, and business jets. Walls and high-voltage fences. Cheap labor, filthy rivers, and private schools. Tax evasion. Yes, and the fullness of long-distance communication. Within the limits of comfort, global capital seemed to be seeking places where laws were almost a charade, and in São Paulo it was demonstrating that the connection that mattered was neither to the street nor to the state. For better or worse the pattern was driven by trends larger than Brazil. For better or worse national policies were helpless to stop it. No insight was required to understand that crime was a symptom of poverty and alienation. But these were problems that government programs could barely address, let alone solve, and so, predictably, in the 1990s, authorities in São Paulo started cracking down and getting tough on crime. Fading states are not without power. Arrests and convictions soared, and sentences grew longer. It was a popular policy in São Paulo, where people assumed that their streets would grow safer, as if crime were a finite problem, and violence was a predilection of some certain percentage of the population. Recently I met an anthropologist with a different view, who told me that after a talk she gave in São Paulo she encountered a businessman who was very mad. He said, "Don't talk to me about projects in the slums. What we need now is an even harder line." The previous week in his new armored car he had been robbed and shot in the arm when he had pushed the wrong button and rolled down a window instead of sounding an alarm. Oh, and she knew of another driver who had kept his windows closed in a similar circumstance, but while yanking out a pistol just to be safe had shot himself in the leg. Was this the fate of São Paulo? All that is certain about the get-tough campaign is that in the 1990s the state's prisons could not handle the surge, and that Carandiru, for one, was overwhelmed.

$\bullet \qquad \bullet \qquad \bullet$

Carandiru had at most 100 guards for its inmate population of 7,000, a ratio approximately one-tenth that of San Quentin. Though the guards circulated throughout the prison, for the most part the prisoners were left alone to sort things out for themselves. To some degree they did. A medical doctor named Drauzio Varella, who for thirteen years volunteered his services every Monday there, told me that Carandiru offered proof that people are not rats. Varella is a man of extraordinary talents, a renowned oncologist and writer, who published a memoir of Carandiru and in recent years has produced a series of popular television documentaries on subjects of health. We walked together through an impoverished area near the city's center, stopping every few minutes for strangers who approached to say hello or complain of their ailments. In the intervals we talked. Varella said, "Rats who are overcrowded become violent. There have been experiments in the United States to show it. But Carandiru showed that people in those same conditions will organize, and establish rules for their survival. The rules in Carandiru evolved as the prison grew more crowded. They were not written down, but were passed on as understandings. For instance, you had to wash. Every day. And during meal delivery you could not stay in the hallways. For hygiene. Inside the cells, when people were eating, you could not use the toilet. You could not spit. You could not cough. You could not pick your teeth."

And these were mere manners. More serious restrictions applied to the regular weekend visits by family and friends, when concerns greater than health were at play. Since 1984 the right to such visits has included the right to have sex. Space for these "intimate visits" is not officially provided, but is arranged nonetheless by the inmates. Varella was struck by the system in Carandiru. He said, "Some of the cellblocks had more than a thousand prisoners. Five, six guys per cell. Can you imagine women coming to such a place to have sex with their men? But it was the most respectful thing. The couples went up the stairs. While they climbed on one side, on the other side men came down to receive their own visitors. When a woman passed as she climbed, these prisoners averted their gazes—aggressively. Usually they looked at the walls. And then there was the scene upstairs. Men without visitors were not allowed to descend, but had to leave their cells and stand in the halls. As the couples walked along the halls, all these men looked at the ground. You could track the progress of the couples by watching the heads go down. And so the couple entered a cell. If there were two or three guys getting intimate visits, they made a timetable between them. Each couple was allowed one hour alone. And after one hour, they had to go out. I was so impressed that it was possible in Carandiru for these men to organize in such a way. But, you know, anarchy does not endure in human affairs. And there is no empty space for power in prison."

I said, "There is no empty space for power in the world."
He laughed. "Yes, in the world."

.   .   .

The first rule was the need to pay debts. The deal-making was
pervasive. Prisoners decided between them who would sleep
where. The best cells were considered owned, and were bought
and sold and rented. The main business, however, was in drugs.
The principal drug was cocaine, which people injected into their
veins, or smoked in the form of crack. The price was twice that
of the street. Varella said, "The law was very strict. If you didn't
pay, you died. Because if I sold you crack and you didn't pay me
back, if I did nothing, nobody else would pay me, either. And
I had to pay my supplier, because he had to pay his own supplier. So I had to kill you. This usually happened on Mondays,
because the sellers gave the weekends for families to bring
money."

In each cellblock the acknowledged boss, according to Varella, was the chief of the inmate janitors, known as the Cleaner.
Varella said, "If you wanted to kill me, you had to talk to him
first. You had to go to the Cleaner and say, 'I have to kill Drauzio
Varella.'

" 'Okay, why?'

" 'Because back in the neighborhood he raped my sister-in-law.'

" 'Do you have any evidence?'

" 'I have a police report of the rape.'

" 'So bring it to me.' "

Varella went on with his story. He said, "The Cleaners were
the judges of the cellblocks. Very smart guys. Silent. They knew
how to listen. Very calmly. They would talk economically. They
were interesting types. Usually they were not physically strong.
Sometimes they were very small guys. But strength had no role

at Carandiru, because people had to sleep. And if you gather twenty guys, even Mike Tyson wouldn't stand a chance. So you would bring your evidence to the Cleaner, and he would read it and say, 'Okay, you can kill Varella. But I'll tell you which day.' Not just any day, because it might conflict with other plans, like a drug deal, another killing, or an attempted escape. The Cleaner would say, 'Okay, you can do it on Friday morning.' And then you really had to follow through. If you went back to the Cleaner and said, 'I thought a little bit more, and I decided after all that I don't need to do this,' then you were not a serious guy. You would have to leave the cellblock, ask the guards to transfer you, because the Cleaner would never again allow you to share the space with him."

Varella's affection for Carandiru was unabashed and clear: he had been seduced by the humanity residing there. He was also an embellisher, an artist with a poetic South American mind, who had experienced Carandiru subjectively and now remembered it through the constructs of his writing. This was obvious, and he pretended nothing else. His descriptions of the prison were matters of the heart as well as the mind. But he was not, as some people claim dismissively, an apologist for the men who were being held there, or for the society they had built. After all, he was a doctor too and squarely confronted the horrors. Man-on-man rapes. Thoughtless wars over turf. Unprovoked murders. Sadistic cruelties of the worst kind. Suicide. Many of the inmates lived in desperation or denial. Crack was an epidemic, and intravenous cocaine nearly as bad. Seventeen percent of the prisoners had H.I.V. or full-blown aids. Sixty percent of them had hepatitis C. Varella tested a group of eighty transvestites for H.I.V. and found that 78 percent were positive; among those who had been in prison six years or more, the rate was 100 percent. And they were doing this to themselves. Anarchy does not endure in human affairs, but Carandiru had rules that were clearly inadequate.

Varella saw the worst of it because one of his duties was to inspect the dead. He said, "That is a very disgusting experience, to see these guys stabbed and covered in blood. Full of holes from different-sized knives. And it was very common. Sometimes I'd have two or three or five bodies at a time. And then one day it got even worse. I think this was around 1995. A man was killed, and when I turned his body over, his head flopped to the side. He was nearly decapitated. It was clear that this had been done after his death. When people are killed, they fight and scream and try to escape. They all do. No one could have made such a full clean cut on someone struggling like that. And so I said, 'What savagery is it to do this to anyone?'

"A guard said, 'This is the P.C.C.'s mark.'

"And I said, 'What is the P.C.C.?'

"The guard said, 'It's a small group of guys who are very cruel and are trying to impose themselves by violence.'"

Cell-Phone Swarm

Geleião and Césinha had arrived from Taubaté. Under their leadership at Carandiru the P.C.C. expanded into the narcotics trade. Though it was ruthless, it was also judicious and cool. It murdered spectacularly, but only in calculation of need. What it had that the competing factions lacked was discipline. The discipline was based on a moral code that enhanced the existing prison rules and included an insistence on better living conditions and prisoners' rights. The P.C.C. was a criminal gang but also a political force—albeit an absurdly self-righteous one. Prisoners were attracted to the group because it brought order to their lives and gave them purpose, protection, and power. There were obligations. P.C.C. followers lived by its laws under penalty of death. Those who formally joined became "Brothers" for life. They were initiated with a baptism involving water, and had to sign a sixteen-point manifesto that still serves as the P.C.C.'s constitution. The sixteenth point was a declaration of the group's intent. It stated, "No one can stop our struggle, because the seed of the Command has spread throughout the prison system of the state, and we are also succeeding in establishing ourselves on the outside. . . . We will revolutionize the country from inside the prisons, and our strong arm will be the Terror of the powerful." For the initiates, there was no possibility afterward of backing out. They had to pay monthly dues and share their windfall profits. They were given a voice in weekly meetings, but once a decision was made, they had to carry out orders.

The seed was spread as the prison administrators transferred the members around. Those transfers were routine and in no sense a recognition of the P.C.C.'s strength. Indeed, the administrators insisted on seeing the new brotherhood as just another jailhouse gang, and would have scoffed at any suggestion that it required special care. When questioned by the press, government officials denied the group's existence. The secretary of prisons refused to acknowledge it even internally, behind closed doors. After a fight with a rival gang in Carandiru toward the end of 1995, Geleião and Césinha were shipped to prisons in other states—respectively, Paraná and Mato Grosso—with no warning to the authorities there. They were gone for a few years and took the opportunity to plant the group beyond São Paulo. After the two men incited some prison rebellions in those states, local officials irritably shipped them home. During their absence, and with their approval, control of the group in Carandiru had shifted to two senior members of the group, named Sombra and Blindado. They in turn were befriended by Marcola, who heads the P.C.C. today. Marcola was a childhood friend of Césinha's. He had been in Taubaté at the gang's formation, though as a player on another team, and had observed the P.C.C. from the outside for a while before joining. He was more business-minded than the others and was seen to be the smartest of the bunch; he soon assumed the position of the leadership's adviser.

The subsequent twists are too intricate to follow. The P.C.C. was not as coherent as it pretended to be. It suffered from internal power struggles, and for a while took to extorting money from other prisoners—a serious violation of its own creed that might have doomed the group, had Geleião not intervened. But the P.C.C. was remarkably self-corrective. It put Blindado and Sombra to death, and having made that point continued to grow.

•　　　•　　　•

Though the gang was funded by criminal ventures, including the narcotics trade, its motivation was never primarily greed. Even today the leaders show little sign of personal wealth, and though some must profit from their positions, they do not seem to use the group's resources as their own. Marcola supports a girlfriend in middle-class style but himself lives a life that is famously austere. Still, there were perks from early on. Amid the general squalor of the prisons, full members were provided with immaculate quarters in special P.C.C. sections, where the cells were freshly painted white, hung with art and illustrations, and well stocked with food and drink, magazines, books, and eventually TVs. The advantages of the group's discipline were felt elsewhere as well. Excluding the killings carried out by the P.C.C. itself, murders started declining if for no other reason than that rivals were being crushed. Rape was effectively outlawed. And pressure was being applied against the use of injected drugs and crack cocaine—both seen by the P.C.C. as corrosive to its power. H.I.V. rates began to drop. This happened even as the state continued to overcrowd the prisons, increasing the population by 800 inmates a month, and measurably aiding the P.C.C. in its rise to power.

Further aid was provided by globalization. Under pressure from international lenders, and burdened by state-owned industries it could no longer sustain, Brazil had opened itself to global capital and was pursuing a policy of economic liberalization. In 1997 it deregulated and privatized telecommunications. The result was an explosion of networks as multinational companies rushed in to compete for the business. Until then cell-phone coverage in São Paulo had been spotty, but within two years the gaps had been filled, and prices had begun to come down. Particularly around the prisons, the usage was high, and the companies responded by building more capacity. According to one official I spoke to, the government was not aware of the pattern at the time, but, later, when it was and requested that the companies shut down their services within reception range of the prison walls, the companies resisted, as they resist today, in the name of the greater good provided by a truly free market. Be that as it may, the P.C.C. stood at the forefront of telecommunications. The phones it used were smuggled into the prisons, along with a flood of cards containing hijacked numbers. The system was sophisticated and was built by corrupted technicians. It relied on several dozen "centrals," which functioned as cell-phone forwarders through which conference calls could be made.

Starting around 1999, the conference calls were made twice a day. Typically they consisted of the most senior leadership connecting with the top men in each of the prisons—thirty or forty at a time—and because of the large numbers, the calls required discipline and practice. Each call began with a social round, reaffirming the P.C.C.'s integrity and goals. Good morning, Brother. How are you today? Now, tell us if you've run into problems, and what we can do to help. The first order of business pertained to the details of prison life—inedible food here, an abusive guard there, the rough treatment of visiting families everywhere. The second order of business pertained to business itself, to challenges or opportunities in the drug trade, to punishments that had to be meted out, and to budgets. On whatever subject, solutions were openly discussed (and opinions were sometimes polled) before the ranking member made a decision and moved the conversation on.

.   .   .

The P.C.C. was ignorant and cruel, but it was also proving itself to be extraordinarily adept. At a point when greed and overextension might have caused a more rigid organization to break apart, the P.C.C. gained the strength to take on the state. The cell phones lay at the heart of that process. They allowed the P.C.C. to transcend the pettiness of location, to rise even above prison walls, and to operate without restraint in an ethereal world of communication. The group began to reshape itself, away from its original pyramid design, and toward a structure of semi-autonomous cells which was so fluid and complex that it could not be pinned down. A young prosecutor near Taubaté showed me a map of the connections that his office had made. It was based on intercepted calls and was plotted with the same investigative-analysis software used by the U.S. military in Iraq. I mentioned to the prosecutor that his map looked like those purporting to chart the insurgency in Anbar Province—a web of lines so chaotic that no useful pattern results. The prosecutor nodded glumly and said, "What in God's name is happening in Iraq?"

I held up my hands in surrender. "This P.C.C. structure, do you think it was intended?"

"No, look at it—how could this be planned? It was built of nothing but relations that multiplied."

It was built of conversation. It was financed by crime. It was too loose to be steered tightly, but it had the innate ability to swarm. It offered proof that people are not rats, because they organize in ways that change with the times. By 2001 even the government had to recognize the P.C.C.'s power. The recognition went public on the morning of February 18, when Carandiru and twenty-eight other prisons rose in simultaneous revolt—an action of unexpected scale, now known as the "Mega-Rebellion," whose immediate cause was the transfer of 10 P.C.C. leaders to Taubaté. All for ten and ten for all. More profoundly, the time had come for the P.C.C. to demonstrate its strength. For reference, the 9/11 attacks on the United States lay seven months ahead. Because 2/18 was a Sunday, the prisons were filled with visiting families and friends. Prison tradition precluded trouble on visitors' days, but the P.C.C. saw the advantage to be gained, and it took 7,000 people hostage behind the barricades. To the state the message was Fuck you and checkmate. Some of the hostages felt betrayed, but most accepted the logic of the game: their presence could keep the police at bay and would prevent the massacre of their beloved men. The P.C.C. had an elegant touch. When given the chance to leave, most hostages chose to stay. The rebellious prisons were hardly calm: sixteen prisoners were murdered by fellow inmates who took this opportunity to settle accounts. But the state was indeed thrown into doubt, and it reacted with uncommon caution. When the police were sent in they killed only four men, and probably in genuine self-defense. They moved so slowly that after two days it was the P.C.C. and not the state that restored order in most of the prisons.

Afterward, the authorities took credit for themselves and publicly proclaimed that they would not tolerate this gang. But within the privacy of the prisons they had to cede ground. The P.C.C. did not expect the state to disappear; it accepted that the government controlled the police, the courts, and the prison perimeters, and it required that the government provide health care, food, and blankets. But beyond such basics, it pushed to create prisons where the state could barely function. The authorities pushed back, as authorities do. Carandiru was a symbol for much that had gone wrong, and in September 2002 it was emptied and slated for demolition. It was replaced with new, smaller prisons, in the hope that smaller populations could be controlled more easily. The prison administration transferred some leaders and swept the cellblocks, confiscating weapons and cell phones. None of this mattered. The P.C.C. continued to grow. And so, after a while, with an election coming, officials simply declared that victory had been won. Your taxes at work. Mission Accomplished. Thanks to good government, the citizens of São Paulo could again sleep soundly.

Carandiru Rules

But many citizens already did sleep soundly—and all the more so because they had invested in private guards and fortifications, using some of the money they saved by evading taxes. Out in the city's favelas, the state's claims provoked laughter. The favelas are among the wildest slums in the world—places where the police are vigorously despised, and where it is good government, and not the P.C.C., that seems to have been dismantled. In 1998, there were no murders in the wealthy Jardins neighborhood, while in the shantytown of Jardim Ângela, there were nearly 200. The P.C.C.'s growth in the favelas was typically unplanned. It proceeded spottily as drug purchases were made to supply the prison market, members came home after serving their time, P.C.C. families sought assistance and protection, and independent criminals saw advantages that the affiliation might provide. Residents had never encountered such a group before. These Brothers who did not mess around, these sons who had become such serious men. Initially the P.C.C. treated its favela crews as subsidiaries whose function was to support its prison agenda, but later, as it reshaped itself around cell-phone communications, the distinction dissolved, and the leaders discovered that they could direct an outside empire from inside the prisons' walls. Marcola in particular had the imagination and strength to do it. He led a coup in 2002, put a bounty on the heads of Geleião and Césinha, and, having assumed the top position, aggressively expanded the P.C.C. not only to the 90 percent point in the inmate population but also to a position of such strength that it could dominate millions in the city's unruly slums.

Elsewhere in São Paulo the domination is still poorly understood. After the attacks last May, newspapers worldwide reflected the confusion when they reported that the mysterious attackers were inmates who had been released on leave for the Mother's Day weekend. They were not. They were city residents, low-level P.C.C. operatives, some with debts to repay. Following the destruction of New York's World Trade Center, the P.C.C. started calling such people "bin Ladens." In May they were indeed terrorists for a few days, but so politically hollow that even social reformers in middle-class São Paulo insist that the rhetoric of the P.C.C. is a sham. The unanimity of opinion is striking. Apparently there are a few old-fashioned Marxists who proclaim that the P.C.C. is the vanguard—at last!—of the long-awaited revolution. But outside the favelas I myself have not met a single person in São Paulo who doesn't dismiss the P.C.C. as merely criminal.

•   •   •

Across the city's divide and inside the favelas, opinions are more ambivalent. People do not deny that the P.C.C. is a ruthless criminal enterprise occupied primarily with the narcotics trade. But they acknowledge its positive effects as well, not only in the prisons and for prisoners' families, but in the communities at large, where the gang, however selfishly, has provided for a crude new order one step up from the chaos that preceded its arrival. People understand the context too. Over beers in a favela I met a community leader and former armed robber who went by the name Marcos and was certainly no apologist for the P.C.C., but who tried to give me the view from the slums. He said, "We have all this information now—the TV, the Internet—so we've become more aware of what's happening in the world, and in this city. Whether it's soap opera or not, we see how the rich live. We also see how the TV lies. It shows a Brazil in which everything is perfect—the houses, the neighborhoods, the families. The poor look happy, like the Carnaval. But the reality in most of São Paulo is murder, violence, and drugs."

I said, "It seems like there are two realities here, Marcos. Because the rich can hide from you, and as far as I can tell, in São Paulo they hide pretty well."

He reminded me of the May attacks. "All their walls and armored cars won't solve the problem for them. They should start paying attention to the entire city. If they dropped the walls, they'd have to."

"But Brazil is moving in the opposite direction."

"Yeah, it is. And the candidate for governor says, If I get elected I'm going to build five new prisons and add 30,000 people. Well, if he's got the money to do that, why doesn't he put it into the schools, or into programs that help the people—into avoiding having 30,000 new prisoners?"

I answered, "Because it would be more expensive. Because it would require more time. Because the taxpayers don't pay taxes. Because they wouldn't support the programs if they did. Because the programs might help a little, but wouldn't help enough. Because it would be hard to measure results. Because the government is not trusted. Because Brazil has to pay back its international loans."

He said, "Okay, so the P.C.C. has come along."

I asked him for details. He said, "First, it looks after the prisoners' families by making sure they have enough to eat, and running a weekend bus service to the prisons for free. But it also helps ordinary people who have nothing to do with crime. If they go to the P.C.C. and mention their needs, usually they will be provided with the basic things, like food baskets, or medications, or maybe some material for patching their roofs. A lot of the older people are afraid of the P.C.C. and stay away. But the young ones will turn to anyone who can help."

I said, "I spoke to a prosecutor yesterday who denies absolutely that this happens. He says that the P.C.C. only looks after itself."

"The guy you spoke to yesterday, he's part of the government. He'll never admit that the P.C.C. is playing a role. But we live here, and we know." Others sitting with us chimed in to agree. Marcos said, "But the most important thing that the P.C.C. provides is not charity but rules. Like if you're someplace where there's about to be a fight with guns, and suddenly the P.C.C. arrives, people immediately calm down. Anyone who violates the rules they impose is going to have to answer for it."

"What are these rules?"

"Basic rules that we all agree with. For instance, not to look at another man's wife, not to rape, not to steal from the poor, not to steal from the little businesses here, not to inform on people, not to get in an argument and just take out your gun and kill someone. The rules aren't written down, but we all know what they are. What's wrong and what's right. Even the top drug dealers don't dare be arrogant the way they were. They have to be humble, because even if they're not P.C.C., they have to answer to the P.C.C. That goes for all of us now. You can't kill someone just because he did something you don't like. You have to go to the P.C.C. and explain why he has to die, and they will talk to the guy and decide on the punishment."

I said, "Carandiru rules."

Marcos had been a prisoner there. He said, "Like that. And the murder rate has dropped way off. A few years ago we had lots of killings here, and now things are much safer. The government goes around claiming credit because of its security policies, and programs like bringing in water and closing the bars earlier at night, but the truth is that the killings have slowed because the P.C.C. has arrived. See, murder was mostly a favela crime. Look at the rest of São Paulo, where the P.C.C. doesn't have much interest, in the better parts of town. There they have lots of police, but kidnapping, robbery, and theft keep goingup—understand?"

•   •   •

He called the P.C.C. a "parallel government," but "proto-government" might be a better term, since the P.C.C.'s rule is exceedingly crude. Either way, the credit given to it for improvements seems nearly universal in the favelas. In another such neighborhood I met a young woman who for years had "walked" with the P.C.C. without becoming a full member, and whose name I cannot use, because she had turned against the group and was trying at some risk to disengage. Even she, who was otherwise skeptical, appreciated the gang's effect on civic order. She said, "There used to be a dealer here who tried to dominate the area, and would not share the business at all. When the Brothers came, they threw him out. Actually, they caught him and were going to kill him, but he escaped and ran away. But they don't use violence cheaply. Every Wednesday they get together and talk about all the events of the week, and they really try to find ways to avoid having to kill people for what they've done wrong. And things are much better now in the favela. It used to be that you didn't dare go out on the streets late at night. You couldn't enjoy yourself. You couldn't go dancing. You had to stay home and stay inside. It used to be there was a lot of gunfire. Exchanges of gunfire. That doesn't happen so much anymore."

She was sitting on her bed in her little dark hole of a window-less two-room cinder-block home. She laughed when I asked her if the police at the district station could offer any protection. Only if you have money, she said, then just maybe they will protect you. But no no, if you go to the station or contact them in any way, they will make you wait for hours, make your life hard, treat you like a criminal. They care only about extorting money from drug dealers on the streets. So, no, not the police, not me, not ever. She had a friend who was pregnant and who phoned them after her husband beat her, and they said, Are you sure you really want to file a complaint, because if you do you'll be waiting for hours just to fill out the report, and then it'll be days before we'll get around to calling your husband in.

I said, "Why didn't she go to the P.C.C.?"

"If she had gone to the Brothers they would have been quick. But then her husband would have been in real trouble. They would either have expelled him from the neighborhood or warned him and given him another chance. But that would have been the last chance." She laughed again. "And she was in love."

.   .   .

Several nights later on the far side of the city I met with the leader of a P.C.C. cell, a "pilot" in the parlance of the gang, in reference to the responsibilities of command. He controlled five municipalities, where perhaps a half-million people live. The encounter was difficult to arrange. It took place in a slum where police death squads had been active in May, in a small house crammed with beds and used as a crash pad for P.C.C. soldiers. The neighbors had been warned to stay off the streets, and for several blocks P.C.C. sentries had been posted; they stood against walls and in the darkness of doorways, with no weapons in sight. My intermediary seemed nervous, but then he got stoned. We waited inside the house by a window without glass that overlooked a favela valley. The night was hot. P.C.C. soldiers milled about, drinking beer that we had brought. Some sat in chairs. They were mostly silent. One mentioned that he had just escaped from prison by buying the paperwork to order his release.

When the pilot walked in, everyone stood up. He was a tall, heavyset man in his late twenties, and completely unsmiling. Despite the heat, he wore a sweater and a heavy wool cap. He sat and we talked, but the conversation was sparse. He made claims about the P.C.C. that were transparently false. He said, "The Command has a vision of progress not only inside the prisons but outside in society. Not everyone who joins is a criminal. We also have good lawyers, and lots of upper-class people and intellectuals."

"Why would upper-class people get so involved?"

"Because they have revolutionary minds."

"So the Command is a revolutionary movement?"

"Yes."

"Okay, so jump ahead and tell me what you are fighting toward. Let's say you win your revolution and take power. What kind of Brazil do you want to build then?"

A smile flickered across his lips. He said, "We do not think about winning. We rebel against the government more to give a response now than with a vision of the future in mind."

That part at least seemed honest. But then he said, "In all the attacks against the police last May, we didn't kill a single innocent man. Everyone who was killed deserved to die for what he had done. The action was carefully planned."

"And perfectly executed."

"We respect the police who do their job correctly. We can accept it if they come to us after we have committed a crime. But the police who come and just humiliate the people, mistreat them, beat them up—those police will be stopped."

"What about the police who came in here afterward and killed so many innocent people? Since the P.C.C. provoked those killings, wasn't it your duty to fight back at that time? To defend the people?"

"The fault is with the media. Since it shows the Command in such a negative light, we have to stay quiet and hidden. And that's why it's difficult for us to protect society."

And so it went for an hour or more. From his position of authority, the pilot expected his words to be accepted at face value. He was a politician practicing spin. He was proto-presidential. Certain topics remained off limits to me. When I followed general questions about P.C.C. dues—its primitive form of taxation—by asking where the money ends up, my intermediary fluttered in his marijuana haze and apologized on my behalf. The pilot said, "It's a sensitive subject." He let the moment pass. When he frowned he was the picture of magisterial calm. He was strangely pompous, it now seemed to me. He was positively governmental.

The Feral Zones

The P.C.C. brought order to the prisons and slums, but showed itself to be lower than animalistic. It perfected a form of murder by which those whom it condemned to die were forced through threat of torture to commit suicide. In 2005, during a two-day riot that gutted a prison in a town called Venceslau, it invaded a protective-custody section, decapitated five of its enemies, mounted the heads on poles to wave before TV cameras, and, it is alleged, then placed one on the ground for a game of P.C.C. soccer. The P.C.C. was feral and twisted, but so what—it existed. The state secretary of prison administration at the time was a Japanese Brazilian named Nagashi Furukawa, who had arrived as a reformer and for five years had tried to apply the principles of good government, one of which is the need to be realistic. Furukawa despised the P.C.C., but he had formally recognized its power, and, having accepted a permanent withdrawal of guards from the cellblocks and yards in most prisons, he had tried to manage the inmate populations through the sole use of

P.C.C. intermediaries. For a while the prisons had been calm, but now riots were again on the rise, and the P.C.C. was becoming insatiable in its demands. By the end of 2005, Furukawa was at a loss. He tried to isolate Marcola and his nine top "generals" in a distant prison—a move that only demonstrated the lack of good choices. In January the police arrested thirty heavily armed P.C.C. commandos who were poised to mount a raid of liberation. After the arrests Furukawa continued to take the threat seriously. Hoping to throw the P.C.C. off balance, he transferred Marcola and his men to a maximum-security prison in Avaré, close to São Paulo.

From there in February, March, and April, the P.C.C. leaders increased the pressure, issuing a string of demands so evidently superficial that they could be seen only as a mockery of the state or an insult to the reforms of Furukawa. They asked for the right to bring in those famous hijacked flat-screen TVs, for changes in the color of the prison uniform from yellow to gray, for longer intimate visits, for better cigarettes. In the past Furukawa might have arranged for such inconsequentials, but he could not now appear to be giving in. Over the first four months of 2006 he faced fourteen prison riots. At the end of April, the police intercepted another P.C.C. raiding party, this one intent on hitting Avaré. Word arrived that the P.C.C. was going to demand an end to R.D.D., Regime Disciplinar Diferenciado, a new and more intensive system of solitary confinement. Word arrived that it was planning another Mega-Rebellion, perhaps for Mother's Day, Sunday, May 14. Word arrived that there might be some sort of attacks against the city.

Furukawa made a last-ditch effort to gain control. On Thursday, May 11, guards seized the top P.C.C. leaders in every prison in the state and sent them off—765 in all—to the newly rebuilt and temporarily empty prison in Venceslau. Furukawa recently explained the plan to me as if he still thought it could have worked. The idea was to disassemble the gang by interrupting its communications and isolating its best men in a truly clean, cell-phone-free facility, where the guards would not be corrupt, and a special unit of nearly one hundred equally honest policemen would scrutinize every visitor, deter all smuggling, and somehow keep the P.C.C. lawyers from passing messages and commands. Naturally, nothing of the sort happened. The police unit never materialized—despite Furukawa's pleas to the governor to issue the necessary orders—and Venceslau today is a prison like any other.

That outcome was so predictable even last May that on the most practical level the P.C.C. hardly needed to respond. But more was at stake than just business or prisoners' rights. The chosen 765 were not merely the gang's elite but the very representatives and intermediaries whose recognition by the state had helped to sustain the P.C.C.'s authority in the prisons. Yes, they could be replaced by new P.C.C. intermediaries—and they immediately were—but the transfer of the 765 was an assault on recognition itself, and a betrayal of the established lines of communication. Furukawa was not thinking in those terms, but to the P.C.C. he seemed to be cheating. The P.C.C. felt further insulted when it obtained an illegal recording of secret testimony in the Brazilian congress in which the transfer was discussed as if the gang could so easily be manipulated and denied. But the P.C.C. had a plan in place. On Friday, May 12, one day after the transfer occurred, Marcola is believed to have ordered the attacks.

· · ·

It was not a war but a struggle which neither side could win, difficult though this was for government officials to accept. For the P.C.C., calling off the attacks made sense once it had made a show of itself. The P.C.C. really had no larger point to make. Nor really did the state. The rule of law? Marcola was returned to R.D.D. confinement in Bernardes. Most of the chosen 765 remained at Venceslau, where they soon resumed business. Once the police death squads finished killing the wrong people in the slums, São Paulo got back to its normal, strange existence. Furukawa was replaced by a prison stalwart whose vision of the future was a memory of the past. According to Furukawa, the new secretary accused him of corruption. To me, in turn, Furukawa accused the new secretary of the same. The new secretary set up a group to study privatizing the system, perhaps by calling in one of the multinational prison companies that offer to step in now where governments have failed. In July and again in August, the P.C.C. mounted small versions of the May attacks, killing eight off-duty prison guards, bombing government buildings, shooting at the police, and burning buses. A reporter for Globo television was kidnapped, and was released two days later, but only after the network aired a P.C.C. video in which an armed and hooded man read a statement denouncing prison conditions and vowing vengeance. Through the fall and into the winter, prison riots continued, as did occasional bus burnings— though these may have been the work of imitators and independents. Government officials were warned of a possible shift toward the kidnapping of their families. Marcola went on a hunger strike for weeks in protest of the R.D.D. The P.C.C. issued a long manifesto, threatening the city with more attacks, and warning that a grand reckoning would arrive on a day it called "the Day of the Roses." The date was not specified, but there was no reason to doubt that escalations were being planned. After Christmas similar attacks were mounted against Rio de Janeiro, ordered from within the prisons by local gangs and coordinated by cell phone. International tourism was affected. In January 2007, Brazilian president Luiz Inácio Lula da Silva said this was "terrorism, and must be dealt with by the strong hand of the Brazilian state." He soon announced that he was sending in the army, navy, and air force to protect the beloved city. Also, a federal security force would be deployed along the Rio de Janeiro state borders to keep out weapons, drugs, and criminals. The gestures were empty, but governments are condemned to govern.

In São Paulo, I spoke to a prosecutor engaged in tracking the P.C.C.'s finances. He said, "If we can succeed in this matter, we can stop the P.C.C."

I was skeptical. "And if you don't succeed?"

"We have to succeed."

"But if you don't, what happens then?"

"We don't have another plan. We have only one plan, and that is to eliminate this P.C.C. The state cannot stand to live with such a group. It is impossible."

"I'm asking you a primitive question, but why? Why can't the state stand to live with this group?"

"It is very damaging to society as a whole. The absolute lack of control that the state has over the prisons. People see this. They know this."

The lack of control is much larger than that. It extends to the favelas and, more important, to the office towers where global money flows. People see this, or they should. São Paulo is not alone. Consider all the other Third World cities, consider Moscow, consider L.A. The P.C.C. is just another inhabitant of the growing feral zones. I said, "But isn't it possible that this is a level of chaos that São Paulo can continue to live with? With all its fortifications and armored cars? Doing business with the world?"

He said, "We've got to fear what we do not know. They grew up under our noses without us seeing them. And we are still in the dark. We don't know what's coming in the future. It is simply unacceptable that a criminal gang can order attacks against security agents, against judges, that it can attack financial institutions, that it can bring the transport system to a halt. What is a state if it cannot keep this from happening?"

Atlanta

WINNER—FEATURE WRITING

Without a trace of false sentimentality, Paige Williams tells the tale of a teenager who survived a war, lost her entire family, fled two continents and wound up in Atlanta, where she is helped to find a bright future by an unlikely network of "angels," including a middle class family and an indefatigable immigration attorney.

Paige Williams

"You Have Thousands of Angels Around You"

Part 1

She got off the plane from Paris with nothing more than a couple of small bags. The bags had been packed for days as she waited for Eddie, a stranger who had approached her out of nowhere to say he knew all about her problems and could help. For $155 Eddie had given her a passport in the name of Marie-Therese Ekwa, age twenty-four, from Verviers, Belgium. This young woman, however, was seventeen, and her journey had not started in Paris, and she had never been to Belgium.

It was just before five in the afternoon. Detroit. September 4, 2001.

The airport agent looked at the passport and asked her to state her business. She spoke very little English and did not understand.

Français?

Oui.

She wore her long hair in braids and had on a T-shirt and pants. She stood five-foot-ten and carried her slender height gracefully, almost gliding. Despite the long flight, she had not slept but rather spent the transatlantic journey in conversation with herself: Where am I going? What am I doing? Have I done the right thing?

In an office, an agent asked questions in English and a translator repeated them in French.

Why are you going to Canada?

For my brother's wedding, she answered. Her Northwest Airlines ticket showed Montreal as the final destination. The flight would depart at 9:05.

Where are you from? Where do you live?

She gave an address in Brussels, telling the agents she had lived there eleven years and was a Belgian citizen. I was born in Cameroon but went to Belgium to live with my parents, she explained. They are dead now. I live with my boyfriend. He is a student.

Prove you're Belgian. You don't have other identification?

I lost my bag in Paris, she said.

What is your brother's phone number in Montreal? We'll call him.

I don't know.

Where is the dress you'll wear to this wedding?

My brother will buy it for me when I get there. He is a Canadian citizen and has been living in Canada for twelve years.

By now she should have been making her way to gate C26, where her plane would board, but the questioning went on. Finally the translator said: "Look, we've tested your passport and we know it's a fake. You need to tell us now—what is the truth?"

It was late and she had run out of stories. This business about her brother's wedding, this had come from nowhere. She had not been prepared for an interrogation—she thought she would simply switch from one plane to another and wind up in Canada, where they spoke her language and where Eddie would meet her. Now, the only story that mattered was the one she most hated to tell.

"Tu comprends ce que je t'ai dit?" the agent asked. Do you understand what I've said to you?

"Oui."

"Do you have any questions?"

"No."

"Are you willing to answer my questions at this time?"

"Yes."

"Do you swear and affirm that all the statements you are about to make are true and complete?"

"Yes."

The time would soon come and go to board Flight 3468.

"What is your full and correct name?"

"Siyomvo, Cynthia."

"What is your date and place of birth?"

"September 29, 1983. Kayanza, Burundi."

"Are any of your immediate relatives living in the United States? Father? Mother? Brother? Sister?"

"No."

"Have you ever been arrested or convicted of a crime anywhere in the world?"

"No."

"Have you ever been in prison in any country in the world?"

"No."

"How long were you planning on staying in Canada?"

"I was going to ask for asylum in Canada."

"Do you have any family in Canada?"

"No."

"Where is your mother and father at the moment?"

"They are deceased."

"Do you have a fear of returning to your home country?"

"Yes."

"Will you be harmed if you are returned to your home country?"

"Yes."

"Do you have anything to add to this statement?"

"I would just like for the United States to take care of me."

● ● ●

Remove everything, they said.

Cynthia's wrist felt strange now, bare. She had not taken her bracelets off since the day her brother, Franck, gave them to her. They were made of tiny blue strung beads and she wore them as a pair on her left wrist. She could not remember exactly when or why Franck gave her the bracelets or even whether he gave them to her before or after their parents died. At the time, the bracelets had meant little to her, but they meant quite a bit to her now that she had nothing from home—not a photograph, letter, or keepsake, no evidence that she or her family even existed. As she had grown older and taller, the bracelets tightened on her wrist. It would take a contortionist feat to get them off, and she begged the jailer not to make her do it. But Cynthia was an official U.S. alien now and those were the rules. One bracelet broke. The other they bagged with the rest of her personal effects. Nearly starving had been hard; running had, too, and seeing so much death. But in some ways this felt even worse, being stripped and searched and locked in a cell.

After three days the door opened and they put her on a plane and flew her south, away from any possibility of Canada and who, or what, might have been waiting for her there. Another contortionist feat and she got her remaining bracelet back on as she moved once again into the unknown.

From Hartsfield International Airport, they drove her down past Fayetteville, past Peachtree City, to the Georgia Baptist Children's Home in Meansville. A country town, population 192. A home full of other children in her situation— unaccompanied, undocumented—but from Honduras, Guatemala, and Mexico, as well as China, some trafficked to work illegally in the garment industry or as sex slaves. An official in Detroit had wondered whether the fellow Eddie, whom eventually they had learned about, hadn't been planning something similar for Cynthia. "You're lucky *we* got you," one of the INS people had told her.

Set on a hundred acres, the home looked like a college campus or some kind of summer camp and certainly like no refugee camp Cynthia had ever seen: tidy residential cottages, a school, a gymnasium, a chapel, ball fields, ponds. No one spoke her language, but she understood by everyone's tone and gestures that they meant her no harm. Every morning before class, they gathered to worship and sing. Obviously these were people who believed in God. For the moment, she was safe. The world, increasingly less so. Several days later, as she watched the events of 9/11 unfold on television, Cynthia stared at the falling and burning buildings and the parade of stunned faces, wondering what to make of this nation's grief.

·   ·   ·

In her West Peachtree Street law office, Sue Colussy, director of immigration services at Catholic Social Services, got a phone call from an Atlanta-based INS agent named Irene Holth. "I've got this kid who's about to age out," Holth told Colussy, "and I don't want her going to detention."

Colussy quickly understood the girl's asylum case to be unusual for a couple of reasons. First, she came from Burundi. So few Burundians sought protection in the United States that the nationality hardly even registered on statistical reports and usually wound up lumped into the category of Central Africa. Half of America had never even heard of Burundi. It sounded a little like that fictional country Eddie Murphy came from in *Coming to America*, his royal path scattered with rose petals. But no paths were scattered with rose petals in Burundi, the most densely populated country in Africa and one of the poorest, tensest places on earth.

About the size of Maryland, with 6 million inhabitants, Burundi lay wedged between Zaire and Lake Tanganyika to the west and southwest, Tanzania to the south and east, and the similarly diminutive Rwanda to the north, in the Great Lakes region. About 250,000 people lived in the capital, Bujumbura, but the second largest town had only 15,000 residents. Others lived not so much in towns or villages as on hills, on family plots where they grew their own food. Churches and schools usually stood alone in the countryside. Commercial districts, if they could be called that, and if there were any, consisted of a few houses used as government buildings or shops. Everyone spoke Kirundi, and the educated also spoke French, but most were not educated; most could not even read.

As in Rwanda, the primary ethnic groups were Hutu, traditionally farmers, and Tutsi, aristocratic cattle herders. The Hutu overwhelmingly outnumbered the Tutsi at 85 percent yet held none of the power. When the Hutu tried to gain power in 1972, the Tutsi-led army put them down with such gruesome violence—a genocide that killed as many as 150,000—that no one would ever forget. When a Hutu finally became president, in 1993, he lasted barely a hundred days.

The conditions for conflict had simmered for centuries, but, Sue Colussy knew, this latest civil war had been going on since late 1993, nearly eight years of fighting there in that lush, mountainous nation of coffee plantations and banana groves. When it started, Cynthia Siyomvo would have been a schoolgirl who had just turned ten. Rwanda's genocidal horrors of April 1994 would have been six months away. Rwanda would eventually draw the world's attention and regret, while comparatively few knew that a similarly medieval war had been waged in Burundi with barely a western finger lifted in aid. It was all very simple and complicated and interconnected, the situation in Burundi and Rwanda. "If Rwanda sneezes, Burundi gets a cold," or so the paraphrased saying went. Colussy had worked with refugees from all over the world but amid the massacres of the nineties saw hardly any Burundians and Rwandans, because so few survivors were able to get out.

Catholic Social Services, soon to be renamed Catholic Charities of the Archdiocese of Atlanta, had been around for fifty years and offered, among other things, legal aid to the poor. Its immigration division had existed for thirty years. Colussy had been there twenty-two. She and her handful of bi- and trilingual attorneys worked out of basement offices just down from the North Avenue MARTA station. Colussy's office faced the street, and if she had time to look up from her work she might see passing heads, or daylight. She could have chosen the big money of a private practice but preferred to be here, in the world of Hail Marys and sliding scales. And she wasn't even Catholic. She wasn't even particularly—what was the term? Warm and fuzzy. But so what? Just because she wasn't the type to sit you down and hand you a lollipop didn't mean Sue Colussy wasn't your truest ally or your best hope. She had trained half the immigration lawyers in this city. Her staff kept 2,000 or more immigration cases going at a time, at least 10 percent of them asylum cases, such nightmarish stories you'd wish to go back to a time when you never knew about them. People like Colussy made it their business to know about them. Your huddled masses didn't come to Catholic Social Services for warm and fuzzy. They wanted a better life. They wanted *life.*

Cops and shelters and hospitals and clients and former clients and INS agents passed Colussy's name on so quickly—uttered almost as one word, suecolussy—that some misheard and showed up in search of "Sister Lucy." Hundreds of those who had survived homeland brutalities only to face Atlanta's particularly tough immigration court would tell people, "I owe Sue Colussy my life." Even other lawyers revered her. "She should be sainted," as Charles Kuck once put it. Kuck in 1990 turned his entire private practice to immigration law. He went on to become managing partner of Kuck Casablanca, the largest immigration-only law firm in the Southeast; by 2007, he'd be president of the American Immigration Lawyers Association. He and Colussy operated at different points on the fee scale but shared reasons for choosing immigration. They enjoyed the increasingly complex puzzle of U.S. immigration law and a role in making a difference in someone's life.

The work allowed them to witness with regularity the resilience of men, women, and children whose lives were desperate and endangered enough to compel them to stow away in ships, or sneak across guarded borders, or risk sharky seas on makeshift rafts, or simply board a plane on faith. "Lazy people don't walk across the desert," Kuck liked to say. "This country attracts the best and the brightest. We attract the *spirited* people from around the world. People don't come here for welfare benefits—they don't get any. They come here to change their lives."

And increasing thousands were coming to Atlanta. The 1996 Olympics anchored the city in the global consciousness and brought international newcomers in ever-larger numbers. As thirteen counties experienced a triple-digit population increase, the metro area was seeing a 49 percent increase in the number of foreign-born residents. Mexicans held the lead with more than 182,000, followed by Indians, Koreans, Jamaicans, Vietnamese, and Chinese. But the city also had Brazilians, Colombians, Germans, Nigerians, Guatemalans, Australians, Russians, Bosnians, Cubans, Romanians, Ukrainians, Filipinos, Pakistanis, Haitians, Iranians, and Cambodians, among many others. More were immigrating from Latin America, Central America, and Asia than anywhere else. Only 30 percent came from Africa. There were Western Africans, including Nigerians, Liberians, and Ghanians, and Eastern Africans (Ethiopians and Kenyans), and about a thousand North Africans, from Egypt, yet few Central Africans.

But now here was this kid from Burundi. Sue Colussy knew that Cynthia's most pressing problem had been her unlawful arrival, but added to that now was a ticking clock. In two weeks, Cynthia would turn eighteen—adulthood in the eyes of the court. Too old for a group home, too old for foster care. Without a sponsor or asylum, which would take months to secure if it could be secured at all, Cynthia, who by all evidence had never done anything wrong, would be reintroduced—indefinitely—to a necessary ugliness of the immigration flow: adult lockup. Jail.

.   •   •

Grace Uwimfura, a Catholic Social Services caseworker, occasionally translated for Sue Colussy. Soft-spoken, with a brilliant smile that transformed her face into the shape of a heart, Grace wore a gold locket whose contents were between her and the Lord.

Grace enjoyed working for Colussy—she admired her style. Colussy pushed hard but was forthright and fair, always listening closely and peering through her rimless glasses. Sue Colussy seemed to understand that most of her clients came with nothing—no money for lawyers and no country to return to. Grace had come to Atlanta under similar circumstances herself, from Rwanda, with her three youngest children and with every intention of also getting her two war-orphaned nephews out of a refugee camp in Kenya. As a ward of the United Nations, she had come fully documented and rubber-stamped by the U.S. government; in June 1996—two years after the epic genocide that killed 800,000 Rwandans in just 100 days, Grace's husband included—Grace and the children had stepped off a plane in Atlanta and into the security of completed paperwork and the embrace of Saint Lawrence Catholic Church of Lawrenceville. They had been living amid the filth and starvation of refugee camps, but now the people of Saint Lawrence, with help from World Relief, were settling them into an apartment carefully furnished and stocked, down to the medicine cabinet. "They don't even know me, they've never even seen my face," Grace thought, "and they're treating me like a human." She had lost her husband and country—her very identity, except as a mother and a Christian. Before she boarded the plane to America, she had prayed, "God, wherever you send me, just be there before I arrive." And there were the people of Saint Lawrence.

They came to her home and taught her English. They drove her to the grocery store and taught her how to shop. They helped her find a job and took turns driving her there. While she worked, they babysat her youngest children in shifts. They taught her to drive. They found her a car. Grace knew some immigrants came to the United States with the dream that life would be perfect, that everything would flower, only to arrive and feel overwhelmed by a language they did not speak, laws and customs they couldn't understand, and a dizzying abundance of human diversity and commerce. Grace felt like a newborn, but the people of Saint Lawrence spared her some of the loneliness and bewilderment of starting a new life.

And they did not stop there. Saint Lawrence helped get her nephews out of Kenya, and now these boys, her slain brother's children, were Grace's children, too. All the school-age kids were enrolled now and thriving. In time, they had moved into a nice two-story home open and full of life. Dinner conversation might start in Kirundi and wind up in French or Swahili or English. Grace never put the topic of their difficult past off limits but chose not to dwell on it. Wars between Hutu and Tutsi—so ridiculous. Were they all not black? Did they not eat the same food and speak the same language? If you are born into a family where a Hutu and a Tutsi married, how can you differentiate? One is your mother, one is your father. You love your mother, you love your father.

And what good would it do to talk about those who had murdered her husband? To be angry all the time? What could she do about it, get a gun and go kill . . . whom? She would not even know where to seek her revenge. And if she did, what then? She would go to jail because she killed somebody who killed somebody who killed somebody. The children did not need to see anger. If mom is angry, they will feel the need to join her in her anger. The children took their cues from her, parroted her. If she prepared them with peace and love, educated them in courage and forgiveness, then the world could use them.

With Americans, the genocide was almost impossible to discuss. If you have not been through war, you cannot understand war. War is like a tornado. One moment you have your life and the next moment everything explodes. When war starts, you cannot sit down at a computer and type something in and say, "Okay the war has started now, let me see where I can go." You don't even have time to pack. You just grab your children and run to the next place you think will be safe. You hope to keep your mind. In war, the mind comes and goes. Sometimes you even think, Oh my God, did this happen? Was my husband really killed? And where is he now? In a grave? Eaten by dogs?

What is it like to be in a war?

"It is beyond," Grace said when she had no words. "It is beyond."

"I am not a politician, I am just a mother," she had decided. "The peace comes from me. I have created peace for myself and for the ones who belong to me—*that* is what I am in charge of. The future of the world, no. My children, yes."

Cynthia was the same age as Grace's son Oliver. The girl's mother would have wanted her to be cared for, protected. It was important to treat Cynthia gently, to build trust.

During their first translation, even when addressing her in Kirundi, Grace could barely get a word out of her. "Oh my God, she is measuring her words," Grace thought. "She is afraid."

"She's just shy," someone suggested later.

"If you were in her situation, that is the attitude you would have, too," Grace said. "This girl, she is seventeen. Her life is in danger. She is by herself—no family. She does not know what is going on, what is going to happen."

As Colussy got to work on Cynthia's asylum application, Catholic Social Services e-mailed hundreds of contacts, looking for a sponsor. "If they don't find someone soon," Grace told herself, "I will talk to my priest and we will save her life before she turns eighteen." At home in Lawrenceville, she gathered her large family and said, "We have to pray."

•   •   •

In a borrowed office near Chastain Park, Reid Preston Mizell stared at her computer screen, absorbed in a struggle to come up with a business plan for what one day would be Tula Communications. A marketing veteran, she had headed U.S. operations for Lang Associates, a Canadian firm, and, partly because she earned a year of her Georgia State MBA from École Superior de Commerce de Paris, she had served on the staff of Atlanta's Olympics bid committee.

After the '96 Olympics, she had moved with her husband, Robert, an architect, and their three children to Sydney, where she ran Lang's operations before the 2000 Games. But now they were back in Buckhead, in the Roxboro Drive house that Robert designed, and Reid was figuring out her future. On September 30, 2001, she and Robert would celebrate their twenty- third wedding anniversary. Their kids were doing well: Callie, twenty-two, was finishing a biology degree at Georgia State; Sara, seventeen, had just started her senior year of high school; Jackson, fifteen, was a sophomore at a boarding school in New Hampshire. Now seemed like a good time, and yet the worst time, to be thinking of starting her own firm—Robert had decided to go out on his own, too. Their friends thought they were nuts to make such huge leaps at the same time.

Reid had made bold moves before, though. In the mid-eighties, despite an abundance of private schools, she cofounded Atlanta International School, a 4K–12 International Baccalaureate academy dedicated to bilingual education, whole-child development, and diversity. She was a brand-new mother at the time but already knew she wanted her children to grow up open to other cultures and to all the world had to offer.

Reid herself, a native Alabaman, came from such a family. Her father, an IBM executive, moved the family all over the country. No matter where they lived, the Prestons maintained an open-house policy. If business contacts came from overseas, Reid's parents insisted on putting them up. As a child, Reid would come home to find the house filled with the conversation of Brits, Belgians, Italians. Her father stoked her intellectual curiosity as much as her teachers did. If Reid hadn't read the daily newspaper, she was not allowed to sit at the dinner table with the grown-ups. If she asked a question about something, her father would supplement his answer by buying Reid a book about it and expecting her to read it. Her father was a man hungry to know the world, a man at home in the world; Reid shared that attitude and wanted her children to have it, too.

A devout member of the Cathedral of Saint Philip in Buckhead, she also believed—strongly—in the Episcopal Church's tenet that its members had a responsibility to participate in missions of justice, compassion, and reconciliation in the world, that everyone must play a part.

As she sat staring at her computer, an e-mail appeared from a friend at Saint Philip, a man Reid knew volunteered at Catholic Social Services.

"Reid," the note said, "you speak French, don't you?"

.   .   .

"Oh my God, she's Sara's age," Reid thought as she read the e-mail about Cynthia.

She picked up the phone and called Donna Dunson, head of upper school at Atlanta International School, and asked, "What can we do?" Dunson went to AIS admissions director Aileen Williams, who offered to bring Cynthia into AIS on full scholarship.

Driving home, Reid thought, "Okay the scholarship is a huge help, but who's going to sponsor her?" Then, sitting at a red light, she just started laughing. The clarity of the moment struck her.

The Mizells had room in their home. Most of them spoke French. Of all the schools in metro Atlanta, the Mizells had helped start the one that would best serve someone like Cynthia. Sara was her age—they could be classmates. Reid thought, "Obviously, I'm part of somebody's plan here."

At home, she called a family meeting with Robert, Sara, and Callie. They rang Jackson in New Hampshire to talk about offering this young woman a home. Could it work? They had the space, but would a teenager from Burundi feel comfortable with a white family in Buckhead? Would she have emotional problems, given all that she had been through? What *had* she been through? And say she had coped well, as some war survivors miraculously did, wouldn't she be terribly behind in school? AIS students routinely learned several languages, including English, but Cynthia had been educated in the refugee camps of wartime Africa, and sporadically at that.

"If we do this, the burden will be on you," Reid told Sara, who was only weeks into her senior year. "You're her age. You're going to have to go to school with her every day. This is going to intrude on your life the most on a day-to-day basis."

"I understand that," Sara said.

"Let's go meet her," Reid said. "If you feel you don't want to do it, no judgment. We'll just say no."

Reid and Sara drove to Meansville on September 28, twenty-four days after Cynthia arrived in the United States and one day before her eighteenth birthday. When the INS agent introduced Cynthia to the Mizells, Cynthia began crying, and then Reid began crying, and then the INS agent began crying, and then Sara rolled her eyes and took Cynthia by the hand.

"*Bon alors, on va parler,*" she said. Come on, let's go talk.

Sitting on a garden bench, Sara explained in French all about her family and their house and her school—that many students there were learning to speak English and that Cynthia could, too. Merci, Cynthia kept saying, and *je ne le crois pas*—I can't believe it.

When they walked back over to Reid and the agent, Sara whispered to her mother, "Let's do this."

Reid looked at the agent and said, "Okay."

·   ·   ·

Okay. One word and everything changed.

Let's do this.

Okay.

Or was it more than one word?

Look, I've got this kid . . .

Reid, you speak French, don't you?

Let's do this.

Okay.

The e-mail from Catholic Social Services had gone out to hundreds who had forwarded it to hundreds, and out of the silence one responded, like an answer to an SOS.

Day after day, Grace had signed onto her e-mail at work, hoping for good news about Cynthia. With one day left on the ticking clock, a colleague stopped by her cubicle and grinned: "Have you opened your e-mail yet?"

"No!"

"Yes!"

The staff and residents of the children's home celebrated Cynthia's birthday a day early with a cake and gifts. Cynthia had never had a birthday cake before. The next day, when she arrived in Buckhead, the Mizells were waiting with a birthday cake of their own.

Part 2

Here is your room, here is your bathroom, here is your closet.

The house was modern, multistoried, airy as a lodge, with a stone fireplace and leather sofas and broad windows overlooking a deeply wooded lot that glowed a thousand shades of green.

Here is the newspaper, the stereo, the television. Here is Baxter the cat. Here is the kitchen—please eat a lot. Here is your house key. This is your home.

Cynthia's room lay at the top of a short flight of steps. It held a brass bed with fresh linens, and a desk. The picture windows faced the lush, peaceful leafiness of the forested yard. With the blinds open it was like living in a tree house.

They showed her where to put her things and invited her to their table. As she sat quietly and took it all in, they cooked for her and talked to her and went about their gregarious Mizell ways. On this day eighteen years ago Cynthia had been born in Kayanza, Burundi, up in the mountainous north, near Rwanda; born into a family of two parents and an older brother: Paul, Marie, Franck—gone now, all. And here she was in Buckhead, Atlanta, Georgia, United States, North America, 7,700 miles from where she started, with a family called Mizell giving her anything she needed, feeding her birthday cake.

That was Saturday. On Monday, she went to school.

Despite her unusual history, admissions tests showed her to be especially skilled in math and science. Right away, AIS customized a curriculum that allowed Cynthia to take her classes in French and move into the mainstream as she learned English. An unusual approach, but it could work.

And Cynthia was clearly determined to make it work. AIS turned out kids who went on to the Ivies, and from the start Cynthia matched them in determination, always with her face in a book or working with an after-school tutor. In class, she responded respectfully to teachers and classmates alike as if reared by parents who had emphasized the importance of good manners. Beyond that, she said little, as if still in survival mode: watching, waiting. Teachers wondered whether her seriousness was simply her demeanor or rather a manifestation of deep sadness. How overwhelming it must be, Dunson and others thought, to come not just to a new school, which is stressful enough for a teenager, but also to a new family and an entirely new world. Cynthia had left an impoverished country of 6 million for a superpower of 278 million. In Burundi, her life expectancy would have topped out at age forty-seven; by coming to America, she effectively doubled it. She had left a country where only 35 percent of the population could read for one where 97 percent could. Burundians had 440,000 radios; Americans had 575 million. The United States had nearly 15,000 airports; Burundi had four. She had left a country where a conversation with the wrong person could get her killed for a place where absolute strangers were going to all ends to help her.

In ESOL (English for Speakers of Other Languages), Shanta Kalyanasundaram's students happened to be studying human rights. Kalyanasundaram wondered whether she should change the subject matter for Cynthia's benefit but decided against it. For days, they discussed child soldiers, Amnesty International, the meaning of life, the concept of man's inhumanity to man, Cynthia riveted. She also showed a particular interest in natural disasters—earthquakes, volcanic eruptions. When Kalyanasundaram commented on the instability of Earth during a discussion on tectonic plates, Cynthia looked up from her textbook as if in alarm and Kalyanasundaram thought, "Oh no, have I said something wrong?" She reminded Kalyanasundaram, who is South African–Indian, of other African students she had known—resilient, determined. The Mozambique children she had known had walked through land mines to save themselves, and lost limbs, yet were the most positive, productive people she knew. "They work and work and work," Kalyanasundaram thought. Cynthia proved herself no different. She needed none of the usual reminders and constant affirmation. "Her whole aim in life is to get on with it," Kalyanasundaram thought. "To move on."

At home, as the weeks passed, Cynthia answered politely when spoken to but volunteered nothing more. She seldom made eye contact. She moved through her budding world as if on untested ice. "She knows what it's like to have everything taken from her," Reid thought. If Cynthia had any scars, and surely she must, she kept them to herself. "What she's been through could freeze a person," Sara thought. "How is it humanly possible to have been through what she's been through and not be paralyzed and afraid all the time? How do you ever start to trust people? How do you ever start to relax?" Some of Sara's friends had been more emotionally damaged by bad breakups, it seemed. "If she's damaged, she doesn't let it hold her back," Sara decided.

Yet when months had passed and Cynthia had barely ventured a smile, Reid asked Grace, "What can I do? What can I do for her?"

"It's a new family to her, a new culture," Grace said. "She has to learn. Even though I am basically from her country, I am new to her life, too. She's in between. Life is not just what you eat."

If Cynthia opened up, it was with Grace; her questions betrayed her worry. Will I get asylum? How long will it take? If I don't get asylum, will they send me back to Burundi? Is it improper to watch television with the Mizells after dinner? Cynthia still did not know whether she had been adopted or was living with the Mizells only until she got her papers, or what. She mastered the remote control and the smorgasbord of channels faster than she could figure out even the most basic things. How to greet people, for instance. Burundians kissed three times in greeting, left cheek to right cheek to left. In Atlanta, people said hello with hugs, kisses, handshakes, back slaps, or with no touch at all, but how did one know whom to kiss and whom to hug and with whom to shake hands, and when?

"Day by day, things will be different," Grace told her whenever she felt discouraged. "Your future is bright. Other refugees come here and have to do things on their own. You have a good lawyer, you have a family who loves you. If you don't have faith, it's going to be hard." Grace and Sue Colussy both had found this to be true. Refugees who came without religious faith had a much harder time and, occasionally, a hard fall into alcoholism and homelessness. "You have to build up faith in your mind," Grace told Cynthia. "This family did not just come up from air. God was working. People picked up the phone, people made decisions. You have thousands of angels around you."

The Mizells refused to treat Cynthia as anything other than a Mizell. Jackson called her Cynthia Escargot or Cynthia Croissant, his adolescent way of saying, "Welcome." Before long, Sara was calling Cynthia her black twin. Robert bought her a computer and showed her how to go online. As her English progressed, he nagged her to keep reading in French. When she had court dates or appointments with Sue Colussy, Robert was usually the one who took her. He talked to her about everything, in English, whether she understood it or not. His animated monologues covered Buckhead, Eminem, Star Trek, the political significance of some ratty leather chair he found on the curb, and whatever other random bits of knowledge he felt she needed to know. The more confused Cynthia looked, the louder Robert talked. Sometimes Sara or Reid translated, but most of the time they let Robert and Cynthia find their way. Reid thought, "Every girl needs a father."

Cynthia began taping snapshots of the Mizells, even the grandparents, to the door and window frames in her room. If someone cut up a photo for a scrapbook, Cynthia kept the castoffs. If someone gave her a gift, she kept even the box. The Mizells rarely wanted the little Lego-like toys that came in cereal boxes, but Cynthia wanted them. She assembled the toys and lined them up for display in her room. She kept the "graduation" certificate the children's home had given her upon her departure, along with a sheet of notebook paper on which she'd penciled a prayer she heard the other children reciting: "Thank you, Lord, for the good things you did for us today. We need your help for our problems . . ."

It was spring before anyone heard her laugh. Only then did Reid think, "She's going to be okay."

No one would remember quite when this happened, or why, but Cynthia began calling Sara and Callie her sisters, and Jackson her brother, and introducing Reid and Robert as her mom and dad. Grace she called Auntie.

Only occasionally did anyone try to draw Cynthia out about her past. If Reid asked, "What kind of Burundian food did you eat?" Cynthia would say, "I prefer American food." Yet at Christmas, as the Mizells put up their North Carolina fir, Cynthia leaned into the fragrant branches and inhaled. "It smells like Burundi in the morning," she said.

Even Grace had never asked Cynthia about home. And Cynthia never asked Grace about Rwanda. They knew each other's souls without knowing each other's stories. The only ones who needed to know Cynthia's story were Sue Colussy and the government. Colussy hoped Cynthia's chances for asylum were better than most, given the tens of thousands dead in Burundi, but with the shock of 9/11 giving way to stricter laws and procedures under the newly created Department of Homeland Security, no one's security was guaranteed. For all her good fortune in finding Sue Colussy and the Mizells, Cynthia had walked into something of a snare by landing in Atlanta.

William Cassidy and Mackenzie Rast, the region's immigration judges, denied asylum 88 percent of the time, well above the national average of 62 percent. Cassidy was the tougher of the two. From the mid-nineties to 2000, only three judges in the country had denied asylum more often than Cassidy. Rast ranked twenty-first. A former assistant state attorney in Florida, he had been an immigration judge for eleven years. Between 1994 and 1999, he had granted asylum in only 55 out of 370 cases. Yet if you wanted a shot at asylum in Atlanta, you hoped for Rast.

Judges base a big part of their decision on instinct. Everyone knew the first rule of immigration law: Clients lie. Sue Colussy always told her clients straight away: You lie to me, I'm gone. And in the extremely rare event that a client did lie, Colussy kept her word and walked right out the door. She trusted her gut the way judges had to trust theirs when applicants came before them with only their word, which made for disparity among the courts and left little room for predicting which way a case would go. It all depended on the story.

Part 3

October 21, 1993

The president of Burundi went to bed with his cell phone on.

The palace occupied vast grounds surrounded by a high wall at the intersection of two broad avenues in Bujumbura. To the north lay the Hotel Meridien; to the west, a golf course. Army soldiers guarded the palace and lived in military camps a few miles away, across the Muha River. President Melchior Ndadaye, a forty-year-old ex-banker and the first Hutu president in history, had been in office since June. Barely a month after he assumed the presidency, army officers had attempted a coup that was quickly put down. Now, coup rumors were circulating again. The country was uneasy.

Ndadaye had been elected on a platform of land reform, and on the return of thousands of Hutus exiled after the 1972 genocide, and on allowing Hutus to join the Tutsi-dominated military. His landslide win, by 65 percent, was heralded as "one of the most remarkable transitions to democracy yet seen in Africa" and a promising step forward in the complicated, bloody history between Hutus and Tutsis.

The Hutu, farmers from the Niger-Congo region, settled modern-day Burundi and Rwanda in 200 A.D. The Tutsi, cattle-raising nomads, came later, from the upper Nile region in the mid-1500s, and began to rule peacefully, as overlords. From 1885 through the 1950s, the territory known as Ruanda-Urundi was colonized by Germany and later ruled by Belgium. In 1959, the region split into Burundi and Rwanda. In the early sixties, Burundi gained independence from Belgium, with Tutsis in power. Hutus and Tutsis had always lived together peacefully, and some intermarried. But independence triggered political power struggles, coups, and coup attempts that radiated mistrust, fear, hatemongering, and reactionary violence. During the 1972 genocide, hundreds of thousands of Hutu fled as refugees, fearful but furious. In the coming years, the so-called "Hutu commandments," published first in Rwanda, filtered south to Burundians. "Every Hutu should know that a Tutsi woman, wherever she is, works for the interests of her Tutsi ethnic group. As a result, we shall consider a traitor any Hutu who marries a Tutsi woman; befriends a Tutsi woman; employs a Tutsi woman," read commandment number one. Number eight was, "The Hutu should stop having mercy on the Tutsi." A Tutsi variation held that "Hutu kids are spoiled and insouciant: Just get hold of the kid who lost his way, then ask his father, elder brother, or mother to come and fetch him, and then kill them all."

Ndadaye's election had brought the nation months of unprecedented harmony and appeared to be the symbol of a new Burundi. Ndadaye was not only Hutu, he had also been a nineteen-year-old refugee during the genocide two decades earlier. As such, he had the heart of the people—the majority of the people, that is.

The coup rumors that had been circulating now appeared true. At one-thirty in the morning, the president's cell phone rang. The coup has started, a high-ranking official told him. "Il faut sortir," he said—you must leave. Ndadaye rose and quickly dressed.

Paratroopers from the Second Parachute Battalion had surrounded the palace. Gunfire and cannon blasts could be heard throughout the city. By now, the army had closed the borders, cut the phone lines. By seven in the morning, the president, his wife, and their children had been taken to an army base, where soldiers surrounded the car and forced the Ndadaye family out. "Tell me what you want, we can negotiate," the president told the soldiers in Kirundi. "But above all, do not spill blood. Think of your country. Think of your families."

As it became clear that the president was in trouble, Hutus across the country began destroying bridges and felling trees as roadblocks, remembering that in '72 the Tutsi came in caravans to haul away Hutus for slaughter. News of the president's detainment spread by radio and by provincial officials on motorcycles. Hutus were urged to take Tutsis hostage. By 10 A.M. the president had been executed, and then the orders were to kill.

Hutus began killing Tutsis. The Tutsi army began killing Hutus. Everybody seemed to be killing everybody, regardless of gender or age. Mothers watched their children be cut down and then were cut down, too. Women were raped. Homes were sacked. Tutsis were gathered in schoolhouses and hospitals and on riverbanks and executed. *The Hutu should stop having mercy on the Tutsi.* The people waged war with stones, spears, clubs, hammers, bayonets, bows and arrows. The soldiers used guns.

North of the capital, in the province of Bubanza, Cynthia Siyomvo sat watching nighttime television with her family. The country had one television station. It broadcast from four in the afternoon to eleven at night, and the Siyomvos watched together. They got the news in Kirundi, the news in French, and old music videos from the United States—Janet Jackson, Michael Jackson. They also got movies and, on Tuesday nights, an NBA game days or weeks old. Cynthia especially loved the basketball games. Her father, Paul, called her "Jordan," as in Michael. If girls played soccer, she would have joined in. Instead she tailed her brother Franck to his matches, where his friends teased, "Why you always got to bring your little sister?"

They lived better than most Burundians, in a small but nice brick house with three bedrooms and one bath, and a car. Paul Siyomvo worked as a liquor distributor; deliveries kept him on the road a couple of days a week. Like most Burundians, Marie grew their own food in their vast backyard. Their neighbors lived in similar homes within walking distance. Families knew each other. The children walked together to school.

Paul Siyomvo was Hutu. Marie was Tutsi. According to custom, their marriage made Cynthia and Franck Hutu. But the Siyomvos never talked about that. Older people talked about it, as in, "Oh, he is Hutu," but never once in her life had Cynthia asked another person, "Are you Hutu or Tutsi?" Marie had always told them, "That doesn't matter. If you are a good person, that is what matters." Marie had lived here for years among Hutus with no problem.

A knock on the door. Paul opened it. Outside stood a crowd of men: neighbors, friends—people they knew—including Cynthia's fourth-grade teacher. They held machetes. They called Paul out.

"We're on a mission," one said. "We're going to kill every Tutsi in the country. Your wife is Tutsi, your children are Tutsi. You must kill them."

"What is going on?" Paul said.

"Haven't you heard?" the leader said. "We're going to take over, kill all the cockroaches. We're actually late. All over the country, they have already started."

Paul said he needed time. He said he would take care of it. The men were angry and restless, but because they all knew each other, they agreed to give Paul time. "When we come back," the one said, "we want to see their bodies. We want to see them dead."

Inside, Paul told Marie and the children, "Right now they're just upset about what happened. In the morning it will be fine." But just in case, he said, hide.

Right away, Marie took Franck and Cynthia to the banana grove at the far, dark edge of the yard. There they waited all night. In the morning, they went back to the house and found Paul dead in the living room, the men's dark promise having been carried out for his failure to kill his family.

"Stop crying," Marie told Cynthia. They needed to move fast because the men would be back. Marie and the children gathered whatever clothing and food they could carry and went back to the banana grove to wait, to think about what to do. Soon the men returned.

Cynthia could see their shadows moving about the house, see them step out with their machetes, into the backyard. Then the house began to burn. It burned with Paul in it and with everything they owned. When morning came, Marie and the children ran.

.   .   .

Cynthia felt caught in a very bad dream. "Tomorrow is just going to be normal again," she kept thinking. She cried for her stuffed animals and for school and for the homemade french fries they used to eat at supper and for her favorite clothes. Marie slapped her right across the face.

"Stop crying," she said.

They made it to a refugee camp, thinking safety in numbers. Outside the camp, the killing continued. Schoolteachers killed their pupils. Pupils killed each other. Tutsis were locked inside an abandoned gas station and burned alive. The army randomly hunted down Hutus and shot them on sight. The Nyabarongo River flowed with bodies. Even most of the nation's cattle were killed. Ten, twenty, fifty thousand people lay dead in the early days, and more than 200,000 would be gone by the end. Some of the bodies would remain where they fell, going to bone, for many years to come. As one official put it, "Everybody has hands full of blood."

By the end of just the first week, 400,000 Burundians had fled to Rwanda and other neighboring countries. By the end of the month, 600,000. By Christmas Eve, one and a half million. "The situation is very complex," as Burundi's minister of communications, a Tutsi, explained it to the *New York Times.* "It is not a western. You don't have cowboys on one side and Indians on the other. It is not a moral problem, it is a political one. This will not be resolved in one week or two months."

In the camps, 180 people were dying each day, many of them children. They starved, or died of cholera, dysentery, malaria. In Cynthia's camp they had powdered milk and little else to eat. At first Cynthia refused it. She said, "No, I don't eat that." Soon, she was happy to eat anything at all. "If I could just get a handful of beans," she would think.

As a lifelong Catholic, she knew how to pray. She prayed for survival. But as she began to understand that her life would never be the same—that their home was gone, her father was gone, *bread* was gone—she prayed to die.

But she didn't die. For nearly a year, Marie, Franck, and Cynthia lived crowded into one small tent in a camp with little water and no place to wash and people pissing and shitting right on the earth.

Still, someone set up a school. First-graders attended with fifth-graders. No one took it very seriously because no one was sure they would survive to care about mathematics.

From time to time Marie cried for no reason. Franck grieved in dry silence. Cynthia thought, "This is my life now. I just need to get to tomorrow."

She learned to sleep through nighttime gunfire and grenades. "This will come to an end," she heard women in the camp say. "People cannot keep fighting forever." But the fighting continued. When soldiers attacked the camp, Marie took the children and fled to the forest, where they walked and walked and walked—for days, they walked. Sometimes they could see distant figures moving off among the trees, groups of people passing like ghost ships. Whenever Marie got a bad feeling, she and the children stopped to hide. They slept in the forest and scavenged for food. But mostly they just walked, in silence. There was nothing to discuss.

•   •   •

On the other side of the forest, they found a two-room cottage to rent behind a Hutu family's house. The arrangement violated the Hutu commandments about showing mercy to Tutsi women, but for all the killing, Hutus everywhere were hiding Tutsis at great risk to their own lives, and vice versa. For the next year, as the war continued, Marie worked for the landlords and in the fields. Cynthia studied with the landlords' tutored children.

One night, they heard arguing and screaming in the main house. Marie helped Franck and Cynthia scramble up into their crawl space of an attic but had no way or time to get up there herself. Hutu men broke down the door, found Marie hiding in a corner, and killed her on sight. Finding no others, they left.

For hours, Franck and Cynthia waited. Then they came down. The long night with their mother's body passed as they thought about what to do. At daybreak the landlady came and said the men had also killed her husband, for letting Tutsis live in his house. She gave Franck and Cynthia bus fare and told them to hurry away before the killers returned; she would take care of Marie.

The bus took them to Cibitoke, near the border of Zaire, where they rented a one-room cottage with a dirt floor and no kitchen or bath. Cynthia was twelve now, Franck sixteen. Cynthia enrolled in a school for orphans. The orphanage had no bed space but allowed Cynthia a uniform and a place in class. Franck took work and buried their savings in the floor. For three years they lived in the room—through another coup, more slaughters, through the genocide and its aftermath up north in Rwanda. Like the other families, they cooked outside and shared the communal bath. They concentrated simply on making it from one day to the next.

Behind their cottage stood the charred husk of an abandoned house. Weeds grew through the foundation. In duller moments Franck and Cynthia went to the house and played pretend, rebuilding it in their minds: Here is the living room, here is the kitchen; this could be your room, that could be mine.

One night, noise in the street. Men yelled, "Come here!" and "Who are you?" and "Where are you going?" Peeking out the door, they saw houses burning, women running, children standing stunned and screaming in the road. As Franck began gathering up their things he told Cynthia to run out the back, to the abandoned house; he would be close behind.

Cynthia slipped out the back and hid in an overgrown corner of the old house. A girl she knew ran past, holding her infant brother. Cynthia called the girl over and they huddled there together through the gunfire, trying to keep the baby quiet. All night they hid. Franck never came. At daybreak, Cynthia returned to the cottage and found him face down in the dirt.

The living began to tend to the dead. Some boys carried Franck down to the open field where they were burying people. They put him in the ground among the homemade crosses. Cynthia unearthed their money from the cottage floor, collected her school uniform, and got a bus to Bujumbura.

Her father's brother lived there as a successful businessman. Despite the intermittent killing, life in many ways went on. Schools convened. Buses ran. Bean fields were plowed. Businessmen conducted business. Cynthia had visited the uncle and his family in the capital in happier times. Yet she and Franck had come to believe the uncle was to blame for their mother's death because the uncle blamed Marie for Paul's death. Had Paul never married a Tutsi, he might still be alive.

"My brother is dead now, too," Cynthia said when the uncle came to the door. She thought, "How strange to look at this man and know he is the enemy."

"You can't stay here," the uncle said. "It's dangerous for me." He gave her money and told her to never come back.

Cynthia rented a room in a Tutsi neighborhood, found a job in a small market, and used her income for rent. Every day possible, she put on her uniform and took the bus to school. A year passed, maybe more. Peace talks progressed but the killing continued. No one ever really felt safe, especially people like Cynthia. Among Hutus, it was dangerous to be the child of a Tutsi;

among Tutsi, it was dangerous to be the child of a Hutu. She had no one and belonged nowhere.

One day, a man named Eddie showed up at Cynthia's home and said he knew all about her problems, said he could help her get out. "Soon they will find out that your dad was a Hutu and that you're here to spy," he said. "You will never find peace."

He offered to take her to Europe. Cynthia knew about Europe. People were happy there. Kids went to school. She had no real future in Burundi.

Together they traveled from Bujumbura to Paris, Cynthia as Eddie's "daughter." In Paris, he put her on a westbound plane alone.

.   .   .

Judge Rast granted Cynthia asylum on December 16, 2002, one year and three months after her arrival in the United States—one year and three months that she might have been in adult lockup, waiting. Sue Colussy was with her when she told her story. Grace testified on her behalf. Robert Mizell sat in the courtroom, just as he had sat in almost every other courtroom with Cynthia in the past fifteen months.

By then she had graduated from Atlanta International School and scored 1100 on her SAT. Without the proper papers, she couldn't enroll in college, or work, so as she waited for Rast to rule on her future, she had been volunteering at a center for refugee women.

With asylum, she applied for a green card, the hardest of all documents to procure, and there began more waiting. Once she got the work permit, she found a job—no, several. Working at Zaxby's. Conducting inventory at Abercrombie. Selling clothes to wealthy women at a boutique in Lenox Square, whose space and beauty mesmerized Cynthia; Lenox Square seemed like one big happy party.

She took driving lessons and got a license. She bought a cell phone that rang all the time. Her circle of friends now included not only Americans and Rwandans but also Somalis, Nigerians, Sudanese. Reid watched Cynthia move deftly between her American life with the Mizells and her African life with Grace's family in Lawrenceville.

One morning in early January 2004, Cynthia called Grace, crying.

"Cynthia, what happened?" Grace said.

Cynthia could barely talk.

"Please, tell me," Grace said.

"No, Auntie, I cannot say it."

"Tell me!"

"He died," Cynthia said.

"Who?"

And it was just beyond. Robert Mizell, such a good man. *For I was hungry, and you gave me food. I was thirsty, and you gave me something to drink. I was a stranger, and you welcomed me. I was naked, and you gave me clothing. I was sick, and you took care of me. I was in prison, and you visited me.* Yet on just another Saturday morning at the gym, a massive heart attack took him, at age fifty-two.

Two by two, the Mizells followed the casket into the Cathedral of Saint Philip: Reid with Callie, Jackson with Robert's sister, and Sara hand in hand with Cynthia.

"Why?" Cynthia asked. "I was happy that I had a second father, and now he is gone."

Grace told her, "But you still have a mother."

Two years after Robert's death, Cynthia opened her mail in Buckhead to find her green card. Grace could have heard her screaming all the way in Lawrenceville.

They drank champagne in the Mizell house that night. Cynthia wrote Sue Colussy a letter, telling her the news. She enrolled at Georgia Perimeter College and began earning the credits to get into a four-year college. In 2011, Cynthia will be eligible to apply to become a U.S. citizen. Citizenship will make everything complete. "Atlanta is my home now," she says.

Epilogue

The first person to save Cynthia's life was Paul Siyomvo, her father. The second person to save Cynthia was Marie Siyomvo, her mother. The third: Franck Siyomvo, her brother. The fourth person to save Cynthia was her uncle, through rejection and cash. The fifth: the mysterious Eddie, with a plane ticket and passport. The sixth? Irene Holth, of the INS, who made that critical phone call. The seventh was Sister Lucy—Sue Colussy. The eighth person to save Cynthia was Reid Mizell, by paying attention to what could have been just another e-mail. The ninth: Grace, by giving Cynthia another kind of home.

The tenth and perhaps most important person who saved Cynthia was Cynthia herself, by running when she needed to run, hiding when she had to hide, and by trusting when her instincts told her to trust.

After six years, she has known the Mizells almost as long as she knew her own family. She still lives in the room with photos taped to her wall and with framed pictures of an American boyfriend on her nightstand. She thinks in English now. But the bracelet Franck gave her still hugs her left wrist. She speaks as seldom of her past as she ever did. Sometimes when people ask about Burundi, Cynthia will say she does not remember. To those who know her this often means, *I don't want to talk about it.* The unabridged version is personal, and tightly contained, like the contents of Grace's gold locket.

In August, Cynthia enrolled at Georgia State University. A biology major with a year and a half to go, she plans to apply to medical school at Emory. She hopes to become a cardiac surgeon, a healer of broken hearts.

Rolling Stone

WINNER—COLUMNS AND COMMENTARY

Layering telling anecdotes beneath a veneer of gonzo brio, Matt Taibbi constructs some of the most insightful political profiles of the day.

Matt Taibbi

Obama's Moment

All love stories are beautiful at the beginning, and what we're witnessing now is the beginning of a new one: America and Barack Obama. The story begins with the world spinning off its axis, the country mired in dark times and the way of the fresh-faced savior seemingly blocked by a juggernaut agent of the Status Quo. Only in the end, in the moment that sportswriters die for and that comes once a generation in politics if we're lucky, the phenom rises to the occasion, gets the big hit in the big game and becomes a man before our very eyes. The old power recedes, and the new era is born.

That's grand language for a forum as vulgar and profane as presidential politics, but this is the moment that Barack Hussein Obama was born for, and it really is happening before our very eyes. Like Kennedy or Reagan or even Bill Clinton, Obama is a politician whose best chance for success has always been on the level of myth and hero worship; to win the Democratic nomination, he must successfully sell himself not just as a candidate but as an icon, a symbol of the best possible future for twenty-first-century multicultural America and an antidote to both the callous reactionary idiocy of the Bush administration and the shrewd but soulless corporatism of the Clinton machine.

With just weeks to go before Iowa, Obama is succeeding at that sales job, thanks in part to an unexpected avalanche of positive press and in even greater part to Hillary Clinton's recent performance as a creaky, suddenly vulnerable establishment villain. In just a few weeks, the first real votes in this insufferably long process will finally be cast, and when they are, the Powers That Be may find that they waited too long to get the real show started—that the long wait gave America just enough time to decide that it's ready to move on to something new.

For most of this campaign season, I doubted that Obama really was that new something. Now I'm not so sure he isn't. Whoever Barack Obama is, there's no doubting the genuineness of his phenomenon. And maybe, who knows, that's all that matters.

•   •   •

Covering presidential politics has devolved of late mainly into a matter of gauging levels of public disgust, along a narrow spectrum that runs from violent outrage to mere nausea; if you spend enough time out there in the Dubuques and Nashuas and Charlestons of the world, you learn pretty quickly that no matter what other problems America has, no crisis is more desperate in this country than the spiraling level of general disbelief of our political system.

After debacles in Iraq and New Orleans and mushrooming scandals that exposed much of Congress and the Cabinet as a low-rent crime family hired to collect protection money for the likes of Halliburton and Pfizer, people simply do not trust the politicians they vote for to be anything less than an embarrassment. You get the sense they approach the upcoming election with the enthusiasm of a two-time loser offered a selection of plea deals.

People hate the mechanized speeches, they hate the negative ads, and they especially hate venomous news creatures, myself included. It's now so bad that a poll last month found that 56 percent of all likely voters agreed with the phrase that the presidential race is "annoying and a waste of time"—a shocking number, given that it excludes the 40 to 50 percent of Americans who already don't vote in presidential races.

People don't want to feel this way, but the attitude everywhere is the same: What choice do these assholes give us? And it's that grim prejudice that has pervaded this process for a generation, forcing the public to choose from an endless succession of lesser evils and second-raters of the Kerry-Dole genus, stuffed suits who offered nothing like a solution to the main problem of feeling like shit about the American civic experiment.

Until now. Emphasizing that this is not necessarily a reflection of who or what Obama really is, he unmistakably and strikingly attracts crowds that, to a person, really seem to believe that his election will fundamentally change the way they feel about their country.

"I just want to see if there's going to be a difference with this cat," says Richard Walters, a forty-three-year-old New Yorker, who had come to hear Obama give a speech at Harlem's famed Apollo Theater. "Because if there's something different, we need it—now."

"At this point, I'd be glad if he recited the alphabet correctly," says Xiomara Hall, another New Yorker. Laughing, she and her friend add, "We got hope. Change is *goood!*"

"I just want to see if he can do something, anything, to change things," says Shirley Paulino, another visitor to the Apollo event. "See if he is what he says he is. We just—we need it, you know?"

Normally the sight of prospective voters muttering platitudes about "hope" and "change" would make any reporter erupt with derisive laughter, but at Obama events one hears outbursts of optimism so desperate and artless that I can't help but check my cynical instinct. Grown men and women look up at you with puppy-dog eyes and all but beg you not to shit on their dreams. It's odd to say, but it's actually moving.

An important component of this phenomenon is that the Obama crowds are surprisingly free of the usual anti-Republican venom. As much as anything, his rise is a reflection of the country's increasing boredom with partisan hatred.

"I'm so tired of the president just talking to one part of the country, or one group," says Malia Scotch-Marmo. "I was in my twenties with Reagan, but I felt he talked to me, even though we were all Democrats. It would be great to have a black president. It would be great for kids to see. It would be a nice mind shift."

It's a mood thing, not an issue thing, and it stems entirely from Obama's unique personal qualities: his expansive eloquence, his remarkable biography, his commanding physical presence. I saw this clearly on display at an event in Portsmouth, New Hampshire. It was a foreign-policy discussion arranged by his campaign that I thought was going to be a disaster. The candidate's handlers had announced a start time of 8:30 A.M., but when dozens of reporters and a hundred or so audience members arrived, we learned that the candidate wouldn't be showing up until eleven. Up to then, the room had to listen to a panel of academic corpses blather about the Middle East.

By 10 A.M., the press section was afire with sarcastic ripostes. "I slept in the car," said one hack. "I had to. I already checked out of my hotel in Manchester."

But once Obama showed up, the sarcasm evaporated. There was nothing remarkable about Obama's speech and subsequent Q&A session, except that he delivered every line with the force and confidence of someone who's already been president for years. Obama's shtick is to sell his future presidency as one that would recast America as the good guy of the world, one that would be guided by the principles of basic decency ("This isn't just about drawing contrasts. It's about doing what's right"), openness ("Not talking [to other countries] doesn't make us look tough. It makes us look arrogant"), and a vision that embraces the challenges of this century ("The task of the next president is to convince the American people that global interdependence is here to stay. Global trade is not going away. The Internet is not going away"). His presentation is deliberately vague on most counts, but the overall effect is augmented by his emphasis on easily remembered concrete positions—like his promise to withdraw all combat troops from Iraq within sixteen months.

But mostly, Obama is selling himself. When he talks about "showing a new face to the world," it's not exactly a mystery that he's talking about *his* face. In person, Obama is a dynamic, handsome, virile presence, a stark contrast to the bloated hairy shitbags we usually elect to positions of power in this country.

Moreover, he completely lacks that air of grasping, gutter-scraping ambition sickness that follows most presidential hopefuls around like a rain cloud—the vengeful impatience that hovers over Rudy Giuliani, or that creepy greediness for media attention that strikes one like an oar in the face in the presence of Mitt Romney. To use a sports cliché, Obama acts like he's been there before, and his handlers are aware enough of how well their candidate is wearing his climb to power that they've consciously chosen to contrast it with that of his rivals.

In particular, the Obama camp harps incessantly, without naming names, on the sense of entitlement that infects Hillary Clinton's campaign persona. Poor Hillary: While Obama glows like the chosen one, taking Kennedy-esque flight on the wings of destiny, next to him Hillary sometimes comes off like an angry drag queen, enraged that some other tramp has been allowed to "Danke Schoen" in her Las Vegas. Obama sees this and isn't above pointing at her Adam's apple. "I'm not running for president because I think this is somehow owed to me," Obama says. And people believe it. In Portsmouth, the same crowd that had to suffer through a two-and-a-half-hour wait sent Obama back on the road with a standing ovation. "There's just something about him," says one middle-aged gentleman. When I suggest that his comment was vague, he shrugs. "Yeah, but it's *good* vague."

●   ●   ●

Of course, underneath the veneer of fresh-faced optimism that Obama is pushing—note that the word "idealism" isn't appropriate here, because Obama isn't selling idealism so much as a kind of reinvigorated, feel-good pragmatism—there operates a massive, well-oiled political machine no less ruthless and ambitious than that of his establishment rival, Hillary Clinton. Obama has raised $80 million, and it would be a grievous mistake to describe his candidacy as a grassroots affair, particularly when he counts among his bundlers many of the lobbyists and political-finance pros who buttress the Clinton run.

Even a cursory glance at Obama's money men is enough to confirm that fact. The list includes Wall Street hotshots from Lehman Brothers, Oppenheimer and Co., and Citigroup, a smattering of Hollywood players and Native American casino interests, representatives of big pharmaceuticals and the insurance sector—in short, all the major food groups of reviled corporate influence-hunters.

Worse still, Obama's financial backing is reflected in some of his Senate votes and campaign positions, including most notably his support for expanding NAFTA to Peru, limiting the ability of injured workers and consumers to sue for damages, and pouring federal funds into E85 corn-based ethanol, an alternative fuel for which the market is dominated by the Illinois-based Archer Daniels Midland Company. More than once I heard Obama give stirring speeches, only to mar them with plugs for ethanol.

Obama's massive war chest allows him to compete not merely in the areas of personal charisma and "hope" but in the trench warfare of local pavement-pounding staff. He boasts thirty-seven offices in Iowa, maintaining a presence in towns with populations as low as 1,400.

In Iowa, New Hampshire, and South Carolina, three early-primary states, Obama has trotted out endorsements from an impressive cast of local pols—support that came under fire when it was learned that many of the politicians had received campaign contributions from Obama's cornball-titled political action committee, the "Hopefund." But here's the funny thing: When the Clinton campaign decided to take aim at Obama for "using his PAC in a manner that appears to be inconsistent with the prevailing election laws," the criticisms fell on deaf ears even among crusaders for campaign-finance reform. "Obama is being held to a higher standard," says Craig Holman of Public Citizen. "It's hard to criticize him as long as everyone else is doing it."

Indeed, it's Hillary Clinton—who, if not for Obama, would be the story of historic change in this race, the first woman ever to make a serious run at the Oval Office—who has been left to carry the million-pound cross of all the ugliest recent sins of the Democratic Party, dragging to Iowa her Iraq War vote, the Clinton record on NAFTA, and a list of corporate sponsors that could keep Bruce Reed and Al From hard all night long.

In what may turn out to be the final cruel irony in a career full of them, Hillary, at the climactic moment of her political life, now sees herself transformed into a symbol of the corrupt status quo. At multiple stops on the campaign trail, I've heard Obama voters say they rejected Hillary because she represents the "old-boys' network." The irony is doubly cruel because the same cozy coalition of moneyed insiders that foisted waffling yahoos like John Kerry on the party rank-and-file and urged Democrats toward cynical moves like support for the Iraq War, all in the name of "electability," now find their wagons circled around a candidate—Hillary—who may be the least electable of the Democratic contenders. In a stunning Zogby poll whose release coincided with Obama's recent charge to the top, a survey of prospective voters showed that Hillary would lose to all the top five Republicans in the election, while either Obama or John Edwards would defeat or tie every single one.

As for Edwards, he too lurks as a crucial character in a possible Hillary death drama, a passionate Cassius to Obama's coolly pragmatic Brutus. In town hall after town hall, in the remotest corners of states like Iowa and New Hampshire, Edwards casts Hillary as an elitist creature of political privilege bought off by lobbyists and indistinguishable from George Bush, charging audiences not to "trade corporate Republicans for corporate Democrats." Edwards delivers this argument with a healthy and convincing dose of class resentment—he is flawlessly playing the part of the small-town favorite son returned from the big city full of devastating tales of aristocratic treachery. He leaves behind crowds that are jazzed and angry and suddenly wanting no part of the Hillary-Evrémondes in charge of "their" party. But while Edwards is running the more revolutionary campaign, it's Obama (whose "differentness" is more visible on TV) who's getting traction as the candidate of "change."

All of which adds to the whiff of destiny that lately seems to surround Obama. At the outset of the campaign season, he was treated as a not-ready-for-prime-time sideshow, with media pundits all in one voice bitching about his "rookie mistakes" and "lack of aggressiveness." But now that he's got the numbers and the momentum, even the most hardened political cynic has to ask—why *not* this guy? Would it be such a terrible thing for America to show that it's big enough to elect a black president? Wouldn't that be something all by itself? The very fact that the public, mostly on its own, has lifted Obama past an arrogant establishment consensus adds to his appeal as a symbol of the idea that not everything in our politics is rigged, that not everything that they tell us is impossible really is.

So maybe it's OK to let the grandiose things that an Obama presidency could represent overwhelm the less-stirring reality— i.e., Obama as more or less a typical middle-of-the-road Democrat with a lot of money and a well-run campaign. Maybe it's OK because it's not always about the candidates; sometimes it's about us, what we want and what we want to believe. And if Barack Obama can carry that burden for us, why not let him? Seriously, why not? The happy ending doesn't *always* have to ring false.

5280: Denver's Mile-High Magazine

FINALIST—PUBLIC INTEREST

After a year-long investigation, 5280 writer Mike Kessler revealed the failure of the federal government to honor its promise to compensate cancer-stricken workers who assembled nuclear bombs at the Rocky Flats plant outside of Denver.

Mike Kessler

Out in the Cold

J udy Padilla was the last person you'd have pegged as a bomb builder. Five feet two inches tall with platinum blonde hair, she looked no more threatening than the pearl-white '75 Beetle that sat in the driveway of her Adams County home. Her idea of profanity was "shoot" and "booger." But Judy was stubborn, ambitious, and energetic, with the kind of piston-quick spirit that got her up every morning to ring-lead the family circus: She'd make breakfast and bag lunches for her three kids, feed the two lap dogs, and kiss her husband, Charlie, good-bye as he left for another morning shift on the factory floor at AT&T. Later, in the afternoon, Judy would leave for her own job. On her way out of the house, she'd reach for a small hook on the pantry door and grab a baseball-card-size instrument called a dosimeter.

It was 1984, Judy's second year on the job at the Rocky Flats Plant, the nuclear weapons facility just north of Golden on Highway 93. The communist threat was strong, or so we were told. Russia had troops in Afghanistan and the Berlin Wall stood tall. Production of nuclear weapons was in full swing, fueled by a defense budget that had swollen to nearly $300 billion.

A Coloradan since she was a teen, Judy was the daughter of an oilman who taught her to work hard and trust her government. She'd voted for Reagan once, and she'd do it again. Earning her keep at a nuclear weapons facility was a point of pride for Judy. Heaven forbid we'd ever need to use a nuclear weapon, but she was happy to be on the team that built it.

And she gladly took eleven dollars an hour at Rocky Flats over the seven dollars an hour that AT&T had paid her to stand at a table braiding wires. As a metallurgical operator at Rocky Flats—one of only four women to perform such a task—she loved being a "blue-collar rat" at the only United States Department of Energy site that manufactured plutonium pits. Heavy as a medicine ball and barely larger than a hockey puck, the pits were the triggers that made the bombs go BOOM!

At the east entrance of the plant, Judy flashed her badge to the guard, aimed the car over a gentle rise, and drove into a low basin that revealed Rocky Flats. The 6,500-acre facility was a small city unto itself. At least 20,000 people had worked there since it was built in 1951; at any given time there could have been 5,000 employees on-site. Main Street bustled with signs of productivity, even on weekends. There was a firehouse, a garage, a medical center, and seven cafeterias. Men and women scurried about on foot and bicycles and flatbed carts, weaving between clusters of administration trailers and warehouse-size buildings. The "Flats," as most workers called it, bore a striking resemblance to a thriving Hollywood back lot, except for the fact that so many buildings were decorated with the yellow and black "radioactive" symbol.

Buildings were grouped and numbered according to the work performed within them. Machining was in the 400 complex, for example. Paper pushers were in the 100 area. And radioactive material was typically "processed" in the 300 and 700 buildings; entering them required government "Q" clearance, the highest access granted to civilians. Judy worked in 707.

Through the metal detectors and into the locker room. Judy would change into her DOE-issued socks, underwear, white coveralls, and steel-toed boots. She'd report to her pre-shift meeting for what tended to be an unremarkable recitation of accidents that had occurred on the previous shift, production goals for the week, and new station assignments. But, on at least one morning that spring, as Judy recalls, superiors gave new orders: *Stop lolly-gagging in the glove boxes. Hanging in the glove boxes increases your chances of exposure to ionizing radiation. Many of your radiation counts are getting close to the allowable maximum.*

It was an odd set of instructions, to say the least. Reducing time in the glove boxes was nearly impossible. The massive metal-and-glass cubes—sometimes several hundred feet in length and fifteen feet tall—housed vital components for the manufacture of bomb triggers. The boxes, which looked like giant space-age fish aquariums, held equipment such as furnaces, melt coils, crucibles, conveyor belts, and that vital, silver-grey ingredient, plutonium 239. The only way to make a plutonium trigger was to approach a glove box, shove your hands and arms into portholes that housed the giant lead-lined rubber gloves, lean against the glass, and start working. Metallurgical operators spent at least five hours of every eight-hour shift in the glove boxes—it was their job—melting plutonium at 1,200 degrees Fahrenheit, pouring it into ingots, placing molds on the conveyor belt. *Shoot,* Judy thought, *no one lollygagged in the glove boxes.* The message was clear: Work faster, produce more, and don't let radiation exposure hinder productivity. Judy's supervisors then made what she remembers as a "strong suggestion"—a passive order that undermined one of the fundamental principles of safety. As Judy recently said to me, "I was told to put lead tape over my dosimeter."

A job at the Flats came with plenty of risks. Hot plutonium could spontaneously combust upon contact with water, and plutonium shavings could do the same when exposed to air. Small fires in the process areas were a matter of course. Gloves would often spring pinhole-size leaks where they attached to the ports, emanating radiation for minutes or hours before alarms would sound. Workers on one shift might have forgotten to decontaminate their gloves after pulling them out of the boxes. Sometimes a glove would come right off its port, instantly "crapping up" a room, and the people in it. They'd strip out of their work clothes, rush to the showers, and "scrub down" with chemical solutions and sharp brushes that rubbed their skin raw. You can't see, smell, hear, or taste radiation. A potentially hazardous mistake could go undetected for hours, even days. To monitor their radiation exposure, Rocky Flats workers relied on at least one of three instruments: machine-mounted "alpha mats," which measure alpha particles; handheld Geiger counters operated by radiological control technicians (RCTs); and personal dosimeters.

A dosimeter checked for gamma rays and neutrons; covering a dosimeter with lead tape could cause the device to give an artificially low reading. But even when used correctly dosimeters weren't fully reliable. For one thing, they had to be in the direct path of radiation. What's more, dosimeters were fickle, fragile devices; when workers would leave them in the sun or on top of the TV at home, other forms of radiation—less dangerous forms—could often throw off the instrument's readings.

Some workers willfully ignored safety regulations at the Flats. Overtime hogs would do anything not to "dose out" and be reassigned to another building. Workers with a certain esprit de corps would take their chances in the name of national pride. Others figured they were being looked after. Judy liked the extra cash, but she trusted that when things got too hazardous, her government would do everything to keep her out of harm's way, especially considering the nature of her work. "We were acutely aware of how important our jobs were for the country," Judy told me one recent afternoon. "We felt that the country would protect us in return."

Workers at the Flats referred to each other as "brothers and sisters." They didn't just build bombs—they built secrets. In the name of national security, what happened at the Flats stayed at the Flats. Even intimate groups of coworkers kept a muzzle on work chatter. "You could play cards with the same bunch of guys for years and barely even know what they did," Judy said while we sat at her kitchen table. "You'd say, 'I'm a welder,' or 'He's a machinist'—but that's about as far as it went." Information, she explained, was disclosed on a need-to-know basis.

So Judy kept her mouth shut and her hands in the glove box. Still, every time she pressed her breasts against the glass, she couldn't ignore what she held at arm's length—a manmade element that could decimate entire nations. She was working with the same material that caused the incineration of nearly 70,000 people in Nagasaki. "You lean against the glove box glass," she said, "and within minutes you can feel the heat."

•   •   •

Tom Haverty got the order from his foreman one fall afternoon in the early '90s. It could've been '91 or '93, but jobs like this were frequent, and today, after so many surgeries and medications, he has trouble fixing them in time. He and a few fellow electrical engineers were instructed to report to a storage room in building 371, one of the facility's hottest. As was the case since he started at the Flats in 1984, this was a need-to-know assignment: A criticality head, or crit-head—one of several types of radiation-detecting alarms—in the room needed to be moved.

Crit-head reinstallation was a common enough job in the early '90s, but the irony never escaped Tom. Just a few years earlier, in 1989, acting on an internal DOE memo that cited "serious contamination" and "patently illegal waste facilities," the FBI had raided the Rocky Flats site. The eighteen-day bust made headlines across the country. It was the first time that one federal agency had raided another federal agency. The FBI, along with the Environmental Protection Agency, uncovered a disturbingly high number of environmental and health-safety violations—everything from poor record keeping to dumping radioactive waste in on-site creeks to dilution of water samples so that plutonium levels would look less drastic. Jon Lipsky, one of the FBI's lead Flats investigators, recently told me there were "inconsistencies that were punishable under penalty of perjury. The DOE didn't let anyone know what went on out there."

The raid put Rocky Flats on the national map—as a disaster. The EPA declared it a Superfund site, the most severe ranking that an environmentally unsafe area can receive. There was a three-year investigation and a grand jury convened. Rockwell International Corp., the private contractor running Rocky Flats at the time, pleaded guilty to five felony charges and was fined $18.5 million. Conditions at the Flats were so abhorrent that the Feds shut down weapons production and halted waste disposal until the place could get its act together. As Tom recently said, "Rocky Flats was constipated, but no one was allowed to give it an enema."

In the wake of the raid, waste had piled up at such a rapid rate that crit-heads were increasingly likely to sound, signaling a potential "criticality"—a nuclear chain reaction that could cause an explosion and radiate a swath of the Front Range. Although the Flats never experienced a criticality, it was an incessant threat. In addition to the likely human devastation, a criticality would have required the expensive and dangerous decontamination of the building. In the early 1990s, Tom often found himself detailed to criticality head assignments. He would suit up in a pair of thick lead aprons—one for the front, one for the back—and set about moving the alarms away from areas with high levels of radiation. It was a stop-gap measure at best, like moving a smoke detector away from a pile of matches and gasoline.

Life at the Flats satisfied the two sides of Tom—engineering nerd and adrenaline junkie. He told me about his adventures one summer evening as we rode in his Jeep along a dark forest road near his Huerfano County mountain home. Talking in the certain but gravelly voice of a wizened uncle, Tom said that he'd joined the navy and quickly became a sonar man, fiddling with knobs and dials to his great delight. Tom the risk taker couldn't get near a small plane without wanting to fly it or jump out of it. Tom the nerd later worked as an electronics technician at NASA back in '69, when Apollo 11 touched down. It was a milestone in American history, and Tom, then twenty-nine and starting a family, was thrilled to be so close to the action. An electrical engineering gig at the Flats had everything Tom needed. "It was exciting, stimulating work that allowed me to serve my country," he told me. "I knew there were risks, but as an engineer this was as interesting and important as a job could get."

Tom worked lots of electrical engineering projects. For one, he recalls, he received a dire warning: *You have 90 seconds to complete the job.* A radiological control technician explained that the storage room that Tom was about to enter was so contaminated that any more than a minute or two inside was unsafe. White DOE barrels were stacked and scattered throughout the room. They held every radioactive item that a bomb factory could cook up—machine parts, laundry, glove-box parts, coveralls, remnants from small fires. Tom felt like he was looking at a gaping radioactive wound: "It was one of those times when I'd be in the process area, and I'd look around and think, 'My God. What have I gotten myself into?'"

Ninety seconds after entering the room, Tom was back out in the hallway, ditching his heavy lead aprons. A few weeks later, following Rocky Flats protocol, he dropped off his dosimeter at the lab for an official reading. He expected the worst. To his surprise, he received an impossible result: "no data available."

. . .

Judy Padilla didn't like what she saw. Too many of them were sick or dying or dead. Donald Gable died of a brain tumor after nine years working at the Flats—before he turned thirty-three. Robert Clompton, a process-area worker in his early forties, died of a brain stem tumor. Less than 1 percent of breast cancers occur in men, but Judy knew two process-area men who had malignant lumps.

In the late 1980s, Judy changed jobs, from metallurgical operator to a sheet-metal apprentice. The Flats facility newspaper profiled her as the plant's first "maid of steel." If a glove box needed to be repaired, she'd fix it. If a drill press needed a handle, she'd report to the machining area with her blowtorch. She was still around thorium, a radioactive element used in her welding equipment. And she spent significant chunks of time in the process areas within close range of plutonium. But, she reasoned, at least she wasn't standing in front of glove boxes with pinhole leaks or broken seals—at least she wasn't handling lava-like plutonium all day, feeling it radiate onto her torso.

Judy's sheet-metal job coincided with a major milestone in Rocky Flats history: the Cleanup. The Cold War was over, and in the wake of the negative publicity from the FBI raid, production at Rocky Flats remained at a standstill. Cleanup began in 1995, when a company named Kaiser-Hill signed the first of what became a two-part, $7 billion contract to demolish, decontaminate, and get rid of the site once and for all. .

Rocky Flats was being destroyed, not built, and the demand for sheet-metal workers dwindled, so Judy trained to become a radiological control tech, or RCT. The tests were daunting—a three-part series of obscure chemistry and physics and elemental equations that looked like hieroglyphics and sounded like a *Star Trek* script. She took night courses and studied RCT manuals for dozens of hours each week. "That's when I found out about the biological effects of what we were exposed to," she told me. "Unless you were an RCT or a scientist, you didn't know that stuff." Almost as soon as she learned the ugly details about radiation exposure, Judy had a routine mammogram that "came back a little funny." In June 1998, her doctor called her at work with the news: breast cancer.

After a mastectomy Judy felt asymmetrical, vulnerable, incomplete. Her insurance covered the bulk of her medical expenses, but Judy's condition blindsided the Padillas like the wrecking balls that were knocking down Rocky Flats. Blonde hair fell from Judy's head as quickly as her body caved in. During chemo, she lost more than twenty pounds and learned to vomit with her pistonlike efficiency. When she wasn't in class at Metro, Judy's nineteen-year-old daughter, Felicia, took care of her, as Judy's two sons were unable to be on the spot all the time. Judy's mother had the mornings. Charlie, who by now was driving an RTD bus for eleven dollars an hour, cut his schedule, causing a devastating wage loss. Judy had never been so dependent on others. When she wasn't throwing up, she was dry heaving. Two days a week of chemo for two weeks, then two weeks off, then repeat. Judy did her big round of chemo on Thursdays, a forty-five-minute IV drip that she could taste in her mouth the minute it entered her arm, "like when you're a kid and you suck on a penny." She endured bouts of blurry vision, lesions in her mouth, and trips to the bathroom when it "felt like I was passing glass," she said. "I don't know which is worse, the disease or the cure."

Eight months after her diagnosis, Judy was still weak and sick. But she'd only received 60 percent sick pay, and there was just one way for her to make the kind of money necessary to support the family. One day in March 1999, she woke up, made a sack lunch, and headed back to work at the Flats.

•　　　•　　　•

The cleanup looked messy to Tom Haverty, and to the more than a dozen Rocky Flats veterans and DOE experts I spoke with. Tom felt that the project was moving too fast. His disappointment was exacerbated by the bureaucracy at the Flats. Tom has a sharp, dark wit, but there was a saying around the plant that wiped the smile from his face: "For every person trying to do something at Rocky Flats, there's forty-seven others trying to prevent you from doing it, and fifty-one more yelling at you to do it faster." The status quo prevailed, and it crushed Tom's spirit. He tried to distract himself with hobbies and books. He made regular visits to the company shrink. In 2000, Tom decided he'd had enough.

The first five years away from the Flats, Tom road-tripped with his wife, Theresa, visited his children up and down the Front Range, and odd-jobbed around the little mountain getaway he'd finally managed to buy. One morning in November 2005, Tom checked into the emergency room at St. Joe's in Denver with an agonizing stomachache. He thought his appendix was about to burst. Tom woke up that afternoon to learn that thirteen cancerous inches of his colon had been removed. The oncologist, Dr. Thomas Hyde, was sorry to inform him that several small tumors had already begun forming throughout his digestive system. He put Tom on intravenous chemotherapy, but told him not to expect any miracles. In all probability, he said, Tom would be dead inside of six months. Tom and Theresa shopped for a life insurance policy, but his poor health precluded him from coverage.

He got through the chemo—nine months of puking and cloudy-headedness. But a round of tests in November 2006 revealed a tumor behind his bladder and several precancerous nodules on his liver and abdomen. Doctors opened Tom up, did their best to remove the rot from his guts, prescribed a slew of drugs, and told him not to make any big plans for the future. Capecitabine, the peach-colored chemotherapy pill that Tom will swallow by the handful for the rest of his life, is best known for the following side effects: nausea, itchiness, vomiting, fatigue, weight loss, dizziness, memory loss. And one other thing.

"Do you know what diarrhea is?" Tom recently asked me. I was walking next to him as he speed-waddled toward a hospital-lobby men's room.

"Yes," I replied. "Of course."

Tom turned his head, shot me a smile as wide as a mushroom cloud, and said, "No you don't."

·　　　·　　　·

The sick Rocky Flats veterans arrived by the dozens. They came on foot and in wheelchairs and on walkers, ambling through the conference center of the Westin hotel in Westminster this past May. They wore jeans and chinos and flannels and the occasional breathing apparatus. Some wore T-shirts that read, "Bury Rocky Flats, not the workers." Judy Padilla was there. Most were well into middle age and craggy-faced, with the calloused, meaty fingers of the blue-collar rats they once were. They had come to ask—to beg—the government to honor the law that it wrote for them.

The law is called the Energy Employees Occupational Illness Compensation Program Act, or EEOICPA (pronounced, e-oke-pah). Passed at the tail end of the Clinton Administration, EE-OICPA was championed by Colorado Republican Senator Wayne Allard and a long list of legislators from both sides of the aisle, especially those whose constituents had close ties to nuclear weapons production. From page one, EEOICPA sounds less like a legal document and more like a confession. The document begins:

> Since World War II, Federal nuclear activities have been explicitly recognized under Federal law as activities that are ultra-hazardous.

A few lines down:

> exposures to radioactive substances . . . even in small amounts,
> can cause medical harm. More than two dozen scientific findings have emerged that indicate that certain [nuclear weapons workers] are experiencing increased risks of dying from cancer.

The law's preamble acknowledges what people like Judy and Tom and the Rocky Flats veterans gathered at the Westin have believed for years. It read:

> Since the inception of the nuclear weapons program and for several decades afterwards, a large number of nuclear weapons workers at sites of the Department of Energy and at sites of vendors who supplied the Cold War effort were put at risk without their knowledge and consent for reasons that, documents reveal, were driven by fears of adverse publicity, liability, and employee demands for hazardous duty pay. . . . No other hazardous Federal activity has been permitted to be carried out under such sweeping powers of self-regulation.

EEOICPA's purpose is to recognize that nuclear weapons workers with any of twenty-two kinds of cancers (among them breast, colon, bladder, brain, and non-Hodgkin's lymphoma) are likely to have gotten their illnesses on the job, and that poor record keeping or gross health-safety negligence make it difficult to know exactly who was exposed, and to what extent. EEOICPA says that former weapons workers who are "at least as likely as not" to have gotten cancer from radiation are entitled to medical benefits and a lump-sum payment of $150,000. The law is an antidote to the legal action that workers might otherwise have to take, at their own expense, if they believe they are entitled to worker's comp. A hundred and fifty grand's not exactly pay dirt for people who've drained their bank accounts, taken out loans, or gone bankrupt fighting cancer. But, if nothing else, the measure was a gesture of appreciation. EEOICPA let workers believe that the government's heart was in the right place.

Seven years after the law passed, the crowd of Rocky Flats workers at the Westin saw a government that was heartless. As far as the Flats brothers and sisters were concerned, their piece of star-spangled legislation had been designed with loopholes and engineered to fail them. By now they had learned that EEOICPA was undermined by "dose reconstruction," a procedure that seemed more black magic than sound science.

Dose reconstruction is the responsibility of the National Institute for Occupational Safety and Health, or NIOSH. To reconstruct a radiation dose, NIOSH digs up whatever it can about a claimant—urinalysis, nasal swab results, medical files, DOE "incident" reports, dosimetry records, and personal histories. And therein lies the problem: Like Judy and Tom, *everyone* has a story. The more time I spent talking to former Rocky Flats employees, the more anecdotes I heard about faulty dosimeters and dubious orders. Two former government officials insisted that medical records "disappeared" during the 1989 FBI raid. A former administrative assistant says she was ordered to illegally shred workers' medical records in the 1990s. Some people I spoke to were still shackled by the culture of secrecy; when I'd press them for details, they'd clam up. One man simply quit talking to me the moment I opened my notebook. Despite overwhelming consistencies among workers' stories of questionable health safety, only a fraction of what they say can be corroborated. It's their word. None of them had the foresight to build a case history while they were producing bombs, cleaning up an environmental disaster, and tending to their lives. And the government's dose reconstruction program dismisses almost any anecdote that a worker cannot prove.

When a claimant's records are missing or incomplete, NIOSH will use "coworker data"—records from a colleague who performed a similar job at a similar point in time. NIOSH also refers to a "site profile"—a multipage report that the agency has created for some of the seventy-nine weapons facilities in the United States, that summarizes which parts of a site were most radioactive, and when. (Site profiles do not exist for all facilities.) In the end, the hard data get sent to the Department of Labor, plugged into a "matrix," and tallied to determine a figure known as "probability of causation," or POC. The POC is the claimant's final score; it informs Labor if the claimant was "at least as likely as not" to have gotten cancer due to work at a nuclear weapons facility. Claimants with a POC of 50 percent or higher are compensated. Claimants with a POC of 49.99 percent or lower are not.

Judy Padilla applied for compensation in August 2001—and waited nearly four years for a response. Her dose reconstruction score was 42.19; she was denied. She appealed the decision to the Department of Labor, explaining that she'd worked around ionizing radiation for the better part of fourteen years, and that six of those years were spent chest-to–glove box, handling plutonium. Seven of her remaining eight years, she reminded the DOL, were spent working with thorium-equipped welding gear and completing tasks in the process areas. Like her coworkers, she'd seen or been near more fires and spills and accidents—some reported, some not—than she could count. She was a healthy, exercising nonsmoker, and two genetic tests showed no history of breast cancer in her family. Judy's appeal was denied.

Tom Haverty applied in July 2006. DOL still hasn't issued a decision, but a NIOSH worker recently told him that his prospects weren't good. Speaking by phone, the representative, Brian, told Tom he couldn't give specifics, but he indicated that Tom's score was less than 50. He said that Tom's final answer from DOL could take another eight months. Tom matter-of-factly stated that he'd likely be dead by then. Brian delivered news to Tom with the detached aplomb of an airline gate agent telling a passenger that his flight's been canceled. It was clear that Brian had done this before.

Nearly 3,000 Rocky Flats workers have applied for compensation under this portion of EEOICPA; only 626, or 20 percent, have been paid. More than 69,000 weapons workers (or their families) across the country have submitted claims; at least one-third of them have been denied. The reason for their denials boils down to the dose reconstruction results—meaning they couldn't prove that they were "at least as likely as not" to have gotten cancer from radiation. They were given the burden of proof.

Larry Elliott oversees NIOSH's dose reconstruction program, and he defends his agency's work. "What most people don't understand is that dose reconstruction is an accepted scientific program to fill data gaps," he recently told me. "A high percentage of Rocky Flats workers have monitoring records, and NIOSH has those records." But, he went on, not all people were monitored. "We do not have individual monitoring records for every worker." He spoke of "unknown primaries" and "upper ranges." He assured me that dose reconstruction was set up to be as "claimant favorable" as possible.

Outside of NIOSH, it's tough to find anyone who supports the way the agency applies dose reconstruction. Richard Miller has worked as a senior policy analyst for the D.C. watchdog group Government Accountability Project and as a staff representative for DOE employees. Just last year, testifying before a House Judiciary Subcommittee, he said glove-box workers handling radiation at Rocky Flats (and other sites around the country) "were not adequately shielded for many years . . . [dosimeter] readings did not necessarily capture the neutron dose from leaky glove boxes, since the badges were not positioned near the parts of the glove box that leaked radiation." Tom Haverty's translation: "Radiation can blow up your skirt. It can radiate your skull. We wore dosimeters around our necks, not on our heads."

Even champions of the EEOICPA law acknowledge that the process of dose reconstruction is debatable. They point out that this particular brand of science was originally modeled to study large, unmonitored populations, like survivors of Hiroshima and Nagasaki, who were exposed to a single big blast, or atomic veterans who were involved in early weapons testing—not individuals who were exposed to low levels of radiation over long periods of time.

"When the bill was written, people on the Hill knew that any kind of science was imperfect—the law was even amended a few times to try to address that," Cindy Blackston, a former Judiciary staffer intimate with EEOICPA, recently told me. "But science is only as good as the perspective of the individual interpreting it. Some people within the system have interpreted the law so that claimants are placed on the defensive—which is exactly what the law was supposed to remedy. In many cases, the good intentions of EEOICPA have been abandoned."

In theory, claimants who are rejected have some recourse: They can form a group and petition to be added to the "special exposure cohort" (SEC). If an SEC petition gets the green light, the dose reconstruction process is effectively waived, and claims are more likely to be paid. In other words, legislators wrote a bill knowing that it was flawed, and built in a safety net that acknowledged those hiccups. The SEC isn't much different than the original law. If a group of cancer victims wants SEC status, NIOSH requires them to do what they failed to accomplish as individual claimants: Prove what cannot be proven.

In 2005, the Rocky Flats steelworkers' union, Local 8031, filed an SEC petition. NIOSH eventually adjusted the petition such that any eligible Rocky Flats veteran could apply. According to EEOICPA, approval can be granted by DOL only after the case has been reviewed by a twelve-person, presidentially appointed Advisory Board.

This board spends a good bit of its time traveling city to city for meetings about SEC petitions. And in May it wound up at the Westin in Westminster. The prospects looked grim for Rocky Flats vets: Since EEOICPA became effective in 2001, the board has been frugal about handing out Special Exposure Cohorts. For most of the day, board members talked at length about the vagaries of nuclear science and the legitimacy of dose reconstruction. They stopped a few times to listen as government officials phoned in to plead with them—to insist that the board vote in favor of the Rocky Flats petition. It was a full-court, bipartisan press. Governor Bill Ritter called in. So did Senators Ken Salazar and Wayne Allard, among others. The board members listened with chins in hands and furrowed brows. Everyone in the room perked up when Barack Obama called in and asked that the board give our Cold War veterans a "small measure of justice."

Public comments started late in the afternoon. The sign-up list was several pages long. Nearly everyone—even the leather-faced tough guys—couldn't finish speaking without crying. A security guard named Richard said he never even had a dosimeter. He believed he got cancer from background radiation emanating through a thin, unprotected wall that he sat against. Many of his records were missing, but his claim was denied anyway. Walter, a skinny man with thick glasses, had non-Hodgkin's lymphoma. He explained that, as his radiation counts got high in the early '90s, his records somehow went missing. He dealt with NIOSH for five years—then they denied him. There were more stories—of male breast cancer and dosimeters that read "no data available," of financial strain and bankruptcy and second mortgages taken out to cover medical costs and lost wages. Judy Padilla gave a long and impassioned speech. "As a former nuclear worker at Rocky Flats, I am a Cold War veteran," she said. "I feel that I sacrificed my health like the soldiers in Iraq are doing. And we got no acknowledgment—and no 'thank you'—from our government. We don't even get the courtesy of a flag on our coffins when we die." Fighting back tears of rage, she told the Advisory Board, "What some of us would give to be in your shoes. You have your health, and all that power! Our lives and peace of mind rest in your hands. We're like the men on death row waiting for a phone call from the governor."

When decision time came, board member Michael Gibson gave a short but poignant speech in favor of the petitioners. He cited the workers' stories of unrecorded exposure, their financial struggles, the fact that they were fighting with the government while fighting to stay alive. "I listened to all the presentations from NIOSH and heard all the stories from the workers," Gibson later told me. "I weighed both sides and came to the conclusion that these claimants were exposed to radiation in ways that could never be proven." Gibson, who worked for two decades as an electrician and union officer at the Mound facility in Miamisburg, Ohio, added, "Trying to reconstruct a dose from hard data is difficult enough. Reconstructing a dose with data that's absent of hard records is somewhat of an art. There were unexpected events that were not set up for monitoring. I know those sorts of things happened because I saw them first-hand when I worked for DOE. The people of Rocky Flats deserve to have this petition approved."

Another board member proposed partial approval for a sliver of Rocky Flats workers; his suggestion was as convoluted and confusing as EEOICPA and the science of dose reconstruction itself. Even the other board members looked dumbfounded. Yet inexplicably they voted for the cryptic measure, right then and there. The workers cocked their heads and mumbled. The room hummed with the sound of befuddlement and frustration, like a town hall meeting just before the fight scene in a Western. One might have expected the local drunk to stand up in back and start ranting. Confronted with the palpable tension in the room, the board deliberated for several minutes, collectively shrugging its shoulders and appearing to grow as confused and frustrated as the crowd. They decided that they should leave Denver, reconsider the petition, and return some other time for yet another round of deliberations.

A month later in the conference room of the Lakewood Sheraton, the Advisory Board decided that three small groups of workers who were at Rocky Flats before 1970 should be added to the Special Exposure Cohort. The Flats veterans saw it as an empty gesture, noting that by the time the board's decision is finalized, most of those workers would either be dead or close to dead. Anyone who worked at the Flats between 1970 and 2005 was out of luck: No Special Exposure Cohort. No compensation.

A few days later, I visited Tom Haverty at his mountain home. It was the first of many conversations we had over the summer. We ate dinner and took in the view of the Spanish Peaks. "I'm a Cold War veteran, like a veteran of any other war," Tom told me. "I didn't go to Iraq and take a bullet, but I went to Rocky Flats and took a neutron for my country." Tom and I talked late into the night—about the culture of secrecy at Rocky Flats, about the various private contractors that managed the site for more than fifty years. We talked about the "sweeping powers of self- regulation" noted in EEOICPA's preamble, and the half century of oftentimes unsavory management within the Department of Energy nuclear weapons complex—during production, during the FBI investigation, and during the cleanup. And we talked about how the government manages the EEOCIPA program with the same disregard for workers that DOE and its contractors practiced. From past to present, across multiple agencies, the flaws were as incessant as they were systemic. I asked Tom for his take. He paused for a moment, distilled his thoughts, and spoke. It was one of the few times I'd see him without a smile. "That's a simple question," he said. "Follow the money."

•   •   •

After a government subcontractor, Rockwell International Corp., rendered the Flats a Superfund site, a new government contractor, Kaiser-Hill, was hired to clean it up. In 1995, the Department of Energy estimated that the project would take more than sixty years and cost $37 billion dollars. Once the project was under way, Kaiser-Hill developed more ambitious goals: ten years, $7 billion. If the company could meet its target, it stood to make considerable cash incentives, paid by the DOE. The faster the job got done, the more Kaiser-Hill stood to earn.

On several occasions, the Department of Energy confronted Kaiser-Hill president Robert G. Card about "programmatic breakdown[s]" regarding health and environmental safety. A July 20, 1998, memo to Card from the DOE's Office of Enforcement and Investigation notes shoddy work that "led to potential violations of DOE [quality assurance] and radiological protection requirements." A follow-up memo to Card, in 2000, pointed out the "recurring nature of [safety] deficiencies" and "failures of the Kaiser-Hill Company . . . to correct quality assurance deficiencies." The list of previous safety concerns included insufficient storage of radioactive waste. Kaiser-Hill was fined $55,000.

Still the money flowed. One executive secretary told me she hand-delivered a bonus check for $257,000 to Card's office. If Kaiser-Hill could pull off the cleanup by 2006 as promised, institutionally it stood to make a "target payment" of $340 million. The contractor exceeded expectations. By 2001, Robert G. Card had done such a heck of a job that President Bush plucked him from Kaiser-Hill and appointed him undersecretary of the Department of Energy. While Card was a top man at DOE, the *New York Times* published a 2002 article called "Questions

Raised Over Energy Dept. Official's Industry Ties." The story noted that "Mr. Card supervises the Office of Environmental Management, which is in charge of cleaning up nuclear waste sites and manages the contracts of his old companies." In 2004, Card left the DOE. He's now working for CH2M Hill, the parent company of Kaiser-Hill.

Card did not respond to multiple e-mail and phone requests to be interviewed, but, a CH2M Hill spokesperson, John Corsi, said that Kaiser-Hill's management of the cleanup was executed with utmost concern for environmental and worker safety. He noted that Kaiser-Hill's work was widely recognized with awards from the American Council of Engineering Companies, the American Academy of Environmental Engineers, and the Project Management Institute. Corsi stated the amount of Card's $257,000 check is incorrect, adding, "It is not appropriate for us to discuss the details of compensation for any employee of the project." He also pointed out that many of the "spot recognition" bonuses received by Kaiser-Hill employees were the result of outstanding health safety practices. "On our watch it was much safer at Rocky Flats than it was at other times," he said.

Safety at the Flats has always been a relative term. But nothing is clearer than a bottom line. Pressure is still on the Department of Labor to nip and tuck its budget, including spending on EEOICPA. In late 2005, Shelby Hallmark, the deputy assistant secretary at DOL, sent a memo to the Office of Management and Budget with a five-point plan to reduce spending, or as he put it, "contain growth in the cost of benefits provided by [EEOICPA]." The memo was leaked, and Hallmark denied any intent to see his plan to fruition. But that didn't matter. The average annual budget for claims under this portion of EEOICPA hovers at a scant $100 million. Over the past six years, DOL has spent $869 million on radiation-induced cancer claims under EEOICPA—a pittance when compared with spending on other government programs, like defense ($432 billion) or homeland security ($32 billion).

What's more, the Department of Labor allows the National Institute of Occupational Safety and Health to pay private contractors to perform dose reconstruction. In other words, while the Department of Labor avoids paying millions on claims, people in the private sector are making millions from the government contracts—and from a program that denies payments to sick and dying claimants. The main contractor in charge of dose reconstruction is called Oak Ridge Associated Universities, or ORAU, a Tennessee–based 501(c)(3) that has received financial support and personnel from the Department of Energy for several decades. ORAU and DOE share such a cozy history that it's difficult to tell them apart. "ORAU was nurtured by the DOE," one well-placed source, who insisted on anonymity, recently told me. "No, ORAU *is* the DOE."

In 2002, not long after EEOICPA passed, NIOSH awarded Oak Ridge Associated Universities a $70 million contract to handle the bulk of its dose reconstruction work. ORAU, in turn, subcontracted some of its work to other firms. It could be a simple enough public-private arrangement, but it could be a conflict of interest. By law, DOE workers are forbidden to perform dose reconstruction, and technically no one at DOE does. But, as New Mexico Congressman Tom Udall pointed out last year to a judiciary subcommittee, an overwhelming number of dose reconstruction team members working for ORAU and its subcontractors built their careers working for the DOE, oftentimes at weapons facilities.

NIOSH requires dose reconstruction workers to fill out a conflict-of-interest form. But consider Roger Falk. Between 1996 and 1998, Falk was responsible for monitoring worker radiation at Rocky Flats, back when Kaiser-Hill was tearing the place down. Falk then went to work for ORAU, where he was partly responsible for creating the Rocky Flats site profile, the document that's considered the bible by dose reconstruction team members.

"When a site profile is put together by someone who worked at that very site, the accounts of workers are not given equal weight," Advisory Board member Michael Gibson told me. "It's a situation where these people from DOE have found a second life [at ORAU]. It's hard for them to criticize their own work, or the work of their colleagues. And those conflicts of interests are not exclusive to Rocky Flats." ORAU never took Falk off the Rocky Flats project, but it updated the site profile he created. However, critics have noted that the old document and the updated version are virtually identical. Little remains changed besides the signature on the cover sheets.

NIOSH's Larry Elliott says that former DOE workers are the most qualified to perform dose reconstruction. "The pool of dose reconstruction workers is shallow and narrow," he said. Indeed, health physics is a niche industry with roots in the weapons industry. But there are also health physicists without such direct ties to the weapons plants—such as those working for radiological-equipment vendors. As the well-placed source who insisted on anonymity put it, "It's not that ORAU has the best health physicists; they have the contracts. You could find someone to do a credible job of dose reconstruction who isn't mired in conflict of interest." What you're looking at here, the source said, is a "plug-and-chug gravy train."

By the end of 2006, ORAU's $70 million contract to perform dose reconstruction had ballooned to $280 million. That dollar amount, it's worth noting, would be enough money to pay 1,800 claimants.

·　　·　　·

Tom Haverty recently called me with some bad news. He'd sat down on the toilet and lost, by his own estimation, a pint and a half of blood. Doctors performed a colonoscopy and found another tumor. When I visited Tom at Good Samaritan in Lafayette, he was groggy from blood loss and four days on an IV. He told me he had three choices, each a slow version of certain death. First was complicated surgery that would require prostate and colon removal. As he put it, "They'd have to scoop out pretty much everything down there," leaving him to go through life with a colostomy bag. Choice number two was another round of intravenous chemotherapy. Option three: nothing at all. Tom told me, "I'm still deciding between extension of life and quality of life."

I stayed at Good Samaritan for an hour. Tom told me more stories about Rocky Flats with his usual understated wit. When the room grew quiet, we watched grizzly bears on TV with no volume. A chaplain stopped by, and Tom explained to her why I was in the room. The chaplain asked Tom if he thought his many cancers were the result of his sixteen years at a nuclear weapons facility. Tom just smiled. She then asked Tom if he'd like her services. Tom, a Catholic, said yes. The chaplain, a Lutheran, asked if her denomination was a problem. Without so much as a pause, Tom smiled at the chaplain and said, "God doesn't check your passport."

•   •   •

It's all gone now. Buildings 707, 771, 371, all of them. The barrels and the two-seater carts and the glove boxes and the trailers and the guard towers. All of it was deconstructed and demolished. Tens of thousands of cubic yards and containers full of radioactive waste—the secrets and ghosts of a bygone era. Some of it was buried out there. Some of it was shipped to New Mexico for deep-earth storage. Contamination levels in the ground are debated, inspected, and may still cause further damage in a few years, or a few decades. Today, in a twist that seems plausible only in an episode of *The Simpsons*, Rocky Flats is being turned into a wildlife refuge.

On a recent summer day, Judy Padilla's husband, Charlie, steered their old Ford Bronco onto a narrow shoulder on Indiana Avenue, where the east entrance to Rocky Flats used to be. The three of us hopped out of the vehicle and took in the view—Arvada and Broomfield to the east, the foothills to the west. A breeze blew tall grass over barbed wire decorated with old DOE signs. Judy pointed to the spot where the old checkpoint area stood, just before a small hill that concealed the little city of Rocky Flats. We took a walk along the shoulder of the road, past a small creek that once carried contaminated waste off the plant site. She pointed out the old Broomfield Reservoir, which had gotten so crapped up from the Flats that it could no longer be used as a drinking water source.

It was hard to imagine that this tiny woman once made the weapons that threatened to destroy the world. She looked like a little old lady in the making, someone who would chase off hooligans with an umbrella. Eight years after her cancer diagnosis, she finally felt healthy and strong. And nothing about Judy revealed how sick she once was, or so easily could be tomorrow. "I feel like a ticking time bomb," she said. "I could go off at any minute."

The New Yorker

FINALIST—COLUMNS AND
COMMENTARY

Most New Yorker *readers can recognize a Hendrik Hertzberg column on politics or policy in the very first sentence by its distinctive attributes: intellectual vigor, fresh insight, and smooth prose that always manage to pack a delightful punch.*

Hendrik Hertzberg

Brouhahaha

Q: What don't we know about your spouse?
A: She has the world's best laugh.
> —Interview with Bill Clinton, *Time.com, September 13, 2007*

In the great American tradition of Washington's teeth, Lincoln's Adam's apple, T.R.'s pince-nez, Nixon's five-o'-clock shadow, Ike's grin, Reagan's pompadour, and—more recently, less nostalgically—Gore's sigh, Dean's scream, and W.'s smirk, the small (but, thanks to the Internet, bigger than ever) universe of people who professionally or semiprofessionally obsess about presidential campaigns has been agog over Hillary Clinton's laugh.

This momentous subject began to elbow aside scarier topics like Iraq on September 23, when the junior senator from New York got herself interviewed on all five of the Sunday-morning political variety shows, a feat known as "the full Ginsburg," in honor of William Ginsburg, Monica Lewinsky's lawyer, who, on February 1, 1998, was the first to manage it. The Ginsburg may not be Clinton's favorite trophy, but she persevered. She met the press, she faced the nation, she rode down the fox. And, sure enough, whenever George or Wolf or Tim asked her something that struck her a certain way, she laughed.

The sound of Hillary's laughter, accompanied by urgent analyses thereof, has since been echoing from the tar pits of the Internet to the lofty peaks of the major mainstream media. It began with surprising amiability, on none other than *Fox News Sunday*, just after that program's contribution to the Ginsburg. Chatting with the interviewer, Chris Wallace, about the way Clinton had burst out laughing at the opening question (which was about why she has "a hyper-partisan view of politics"), Wallace's colleague Brit Hume remarked that her laugh "is always disarming, always engaging, and always attractive."

By midafternoon, the Republican National Committee had rushed out a corrective to Hume's lapse into graciousness: an electronic "research briefing" titled "Hillary: No Laughing Matter." It was studded with subheads like "When Asked Whether Her Plan Is a Step Toward Socialized Medicine, Hillary Giggles Uncontrollably" and festooned with video clips of the former First Lady engaged in giggle-related activities. From then on, the commentary alternated between judgments of the quality of the candidate's laughter and assessments of its hidden meaning.

Media Matters, the indefatigable Web site that chronicles conservative broadcasting, kept track. Sean Hannity played an audio clip seven times and described the candidate's laughter as "frightening." Bill O'Reilly trotted out a Fox News "body-language expert" to pronounce the laughter "evil." Dick Morris, the onetime Clinton adviser turned full-time Clinton trasher, described it as "loud, inappropriate, and mirthless." Further down the evolutionary scale, the right-wing blogs bloomed like a staph infection. "Shrillary's" laugh is "chilling." It's "fakey fake fake fake." It's a "hideous hyena mating call." It's "a signal to launch her flying monkeys."

The respectables joined in, too, in their mannerly way. In the *Times*, Frank Rich wrote, "Now Mrs. Clinton is erupting in a laugh with all the spontaneity of an alarm clock buzzer." His Op-Ed partner Maureen Dowd wrote that Clinton's "big belly laughs" were a way of making the transition "from nag to wag." Meanwhile, in the news section, a story explored the question "What's Behind the Laugh?" And *The Politico*, a new online political newspaper, identified the problem as "a laugh that sounded like it was programmed by computer."

How a given laugh sounds is, of course, a matter of personal taste. More than two dozen videos of Hillary laughing are available on YouTube, some of them edited so as to make her appear ridiculous or hysterical, and after repeated viewings one observer—this observer, actually—has concluded that she is in fact laughing. That is to say, she is responding in a more or less normal fashion to a comment or situation that she perceives as absurd or humorous. (As Jon Stewart, the well-known humor expert, noted in the course of his own riff on the Clinton laugh situation, being called hyper-partisan by Fox News is, to borrow his word, "funny.") Hillary's laugh is unusually uninhibited for a politician—especially, perhaps, for a female politician. It is indeed a belly laugh, if not a "big belly" laugh, and it compares favorably with the incumbent presidential laugh, a series of rapid "heh-hehs," at once threatening and insipid, accompanied by an exaggerated, arrhythmic bouncing of head and shoulders in opposite directions.

The just published *Journals: 1952–2000* of the late Arthur M. Schlesinger Jr., may shed some light on the question of whether Hillary Clinton is the sort of person who is capable of genuine laughter and, by extension, of the humanness that laughter is taken to signify. With reservations, Schlesinger liked the Clintons. But you don't have to take his word for it; you can take Jacqueline Kennedy Onassis's. Schlesinger's entry for February 4, 1993:

> Last night we dined at the [McGeorge] Bundys'. Jackie was also there. I asked her about Hillary Clinton. She could not have been more enthusiastic— so intelligent, so pretty, so cozy,

what a good sense of humor. This last item surprised me. I was ready to concede the first two adjectives and even the third, but I supposed her to be somewhat on the stern and humorless side.

In later entries, Schlesinger writes of Hillary's "charm and humor" and her "infectious joie de vivre." But it must be said that she doesn't always laugh, even when something's funny. In 1998, at the height of the Full Monica, Schlesinger, then eighty-one years old, is seated next to the first lady at a formal White House dinner celebrating the National Humanities Medals, one of which he has just been awarded. They're having a jolly, dishy time—she's "very easy to talk to"—when Arthur gets a little too expansive:

> I made the point that the liberals had stood by Clinton while the DLC [Democratic Leadership Council] people had deserted him and described the miserable [Senator Joseph I.] Lieberman as a "sanctimonious prick." Hillary said, "Well, he is certainly sanctimonious," but showed no eagerness to pursue this line of thought.

Speaking of which, or whom, if people want to find fault with Senator Clinton, there are juicier bones to pick than her funny bone. A week or so ago, for example, she was the only Democrat in the presidential race to support a Lieberman-sponsored resolution putting the Senate on record as urging the Bush administration to designate Iran's Islamic Revolutionary Guard Corps a foreign terrorist organization. Her fellow-candidate senators—Joseph Biden, Christopher Dodd, and Barack Obama—opposed it, not because they doubt that the Guard dabbles in terrorism but because they don't trust the administration not to treat the resolution as a green light for another war. A few days later,

Clinton did a course correction, signing on to a bill, sponsored by James Webb, of Virginia, that would bar funding for military action against Iran without explicit congressional authorization. Complain about her triangulation if you wish, but our unhappy country needs all the laughs it can get.

Vanity Fair

WINNER—PROFILE WRITING

Evan Wright's profile of a failed Hollywood agent turned documentary filmmaker chronicles his subject's harrowing but frequently amusing descent into drugs, madness, and violence and, improbably, his resurrection as a hero of the prowar right. "Pat Dollard's War on Hollywood" is a cautionary tale about what happens when Hollywood meets Baghdad.

Evan Wright

Pat Dollard's War on Hollywood

The day before Thanksgiving 2004, Pat Dollard, a Hollywood agent who represented Steven Soderbergh, sent an e-mail to just about everyone he knew containing one word: "Later." Friends worried it was a suicide note. Dollard, forty-two, had spent nearly twenty years in the film business. On a good day he seemed little different than any other successful operator, a sort of hipper version of *Entourage*'s Ari Gold. But often in his turbulent career, bad days outnumbered the good. Once a rising star at William Morris, he was fired in the mid-90s for chronic absenteeism brought on by drinking and drug abuse. He attended twelve-step meetings and bounced back, playing a critical role in getting Soderbergh's *Traffic* made. Propaganda Films tapped him to head its management division, and in 2002 he produced *Auto Focus*, the Paul Schrader–directed biopic about the murder of *Hogan's Heroes* star Bob Crane—a film in which Dollard has a cameo in drag. In 2004, Dollard cofounded Relativity, a firm which would assist the Marvel Entertainment Group in its half-billion-dollar production deal and went on to produce, after Dollard's exit, *Talladega Nights*. But Dollard was bingeing again. His fourth wife left him, and his third wife was suing for sole custody of their daughter. News that his daughter would be spending Thanksgiving at the home of Robert Evans—for whom his ex-wife worked as a development executive—sent Dollard into a morbid depression. Late one night he phoned a friend and suggested that everyone might be better off if he were dead. Then he sent his good-bye e-mail.

But Dollard was not planning a suicide, at least not a quick one. Dressed in what he would later describe as his "scumbag hipster agent's uniform"—Prada boots, jeans, and a black-leather jacket—he boarded a plane for New York, then Kuwait City. From there he hopped a military transport to Baghdad and embedded with U.S. Marines in order to make a "prowar documentary." Given the decades of substance abuse, the idea of the chain-smoking, middle-aged Hollywood agent accompanying marines into battle was sort of like Keith Richards competing in an Ironman Triathlon. But Dollard thrived. "My first time in a combat zone, I felt like I had walked into some bizarre fucking ultra-expensive movie set," he would later say. "I had this vivid clarity, like when I used to take LSD. I felt joy. I felt like I had a message from God, or whoever, that this is exactly what I should be doing with my life. I belong in war. I am a warrior."

To those at home it seemed that Dollard had entered dangerous mental territory. Around the New Year in 2005, he e-mailed a photo of himself to friends. In it he is clutching a machine gun, surrounded by marines. Dressed in combat gear, his hair in a mohawk and the word "die" shaved into his chest hair, Dollard looks like the mascot of camp *Lord of the Flies*.

The H'wood Warrior

Midsummer 2006. Dollard sits across from me at a hotel restaurant near the Los Angeles airport, tearing into a breakfast of waffles, bacon, and black coffee while talking about his ambition to become a "conservative icon, the Michael Moore of the right." He is well on his way, thanks in no small part to a terrible incident that occurred last February in Iraq. While filming U.S.

troops in Ramadi, a Humvee Dollard was riding in was struck by a bomb. Two marines were killed, but Dollard—in keeping with a streak of freakishly good luck—was thrown clear from the fiery wreckage and emerged unharmed but for a two-inch cut on his right leg. The bombing was, appropriately enough, first reported in *Variety*. Dollard was soon invited on Tony Snow's radio show on Fox and spent as much time railing against Hollywood liberalism as he did talking about Iraq. Snow, weeks away from becoming White House press secretary, loved it. He called Dollard a "true believer" and invited him back for two more appearances. Dollard was soon hailed by conservative columnists in *U.S. News & World Report* and the *Washington Times*. The *New York Post* dubbed him the "H'wood Warrior." No small part of his appeal to the right is the fact that Dollard was once a "doctrinaire liberal" who could even boast of close ties to Robert Kennedy Jr., but now speaks of his prowar stance in the most militant terms: "This is a propaganda war, and if I can fight with a camera the same as a marine with his rifle, I will."

Last May he launched a Web site (patdollard.com) and began airing a five-minute trailer of his as yet unfinished documentary, *Young Americans*. The response was overwhelming: 100,000 hits in the first week, hundreds of supportive e-mails, and unsolicited offers of money. "Dude, I'm becoming a national hero," Dollard tells me.

Compactly built, Dollard dresses in clothes—jeans, Wal-Mart work boots, and an olive-drab T-shirt—which look like they were slept in. His hair is close-cropped, but nevertheless manages to appear disheveled. He hasn't shaved in a few days. His teeth are cracked and stained, and, worst of all, from a health standpoint, his right eye is obscured by a milky blob: a cataract that developed in Iraq which he has never treated. Also in need of attention is a wretched cough, which sounds like a snow shovel scraping on the sidewalk. If he were a homeless man, you'd probably wash your hands after giving him your change.

Beneath the unkempt appearance, Dollard projects unnerving vitality. Even with the cataract, his green eyes are alert and engaging. Words tumble from his mouth at a rapid clip, his voice a parched growl acquired from a lifetime of cigarettes and liquor. One moment he is laughing about the time he picked up hookers on the set of *Dragon: The Bruce Lee Story*, a film his second wife worked on as an assistant to producer Raffaella De Laurentiis—a moment later he is pounding the table, railing against Cindy Sheehan's antiwar protests. "Cindy Sheehan is pathologically self-centered. It's a tragedy she lost her son. Anyway, we all lose family members. So, fuck Cindy Sheehan."

From hilarity to rage in less than two minutes. In laymen's terms, Dollard is "intense." Some might use words like "manic" or "bipolar"—a condition Dollard's mother believes he might suffer from—but Dollard bristles at any suggestion he is clinically off balance. "True," he says, chewing a strip of bacon, "I was told to get a CAT scan"—after being blown up in Iraq—"but I feel fucking fine."

And, true, Dollard was pretty much the same before he got blown up. He possesses a quality common among celebrities, children, and the insane. You are compelled to watch him because you never know what he will do or say next. His third wife, Alicia Allain, sums up her ex-husband, saying, "He may be the biggest asshole I've met, but he's got twisted charisma."

Not everyone succumbs to it. When Dollard first posted the story of escaping death in Iraq, his younger sister, deeply opposed to the war, speculated that her older brother was just "too evil to die." (Dollard dismisses her as a "nutcase—even nuttier than I am.")

When it comes to practicing the Hollywood art of salesmanship, Dollard was among the best. Steven Soderbergh says, "Pat has a quality that's essential to selling movies: making people see things that can't be seen yet. I mean, if Pat says he saw a U.F.O., he will convince me it was there, even if I didn't see it."

Upon returning from his second trip to Iraq, last March, Dollard moved from Los Angeles to an undisclosed location out of state to complete his film. (He is so obsessed with secrecy he recently had the OnStar system yanked from his S.U.V., fearing it might be used by "enemies" to locate him.) He is in L.A. today at the invitation of Andrew Breitbart—longtime contributor to the Drudge Report and self-described "right-leaning Hollywood basher," but, a free-thinker, who helped create the Huffington Post. Breitbart plans to introduce him to potential financial backers.

Dollard's film teaser is less like a documentary than agitprop. It opens on two young marines hunched over their machine guns at a roadblock. It's the winter of 2005. Both are shivering from the cold, warily eyeing the civilian cars which at any moment they may be called upon to shoot. The marines pass the time speculating about what kids their age might be doing back home. One of them turns to the camera, concluding, "They're over at home smoking blunts, fucking watching MTV, sitting on their fat ass. Well, fuck you."

A montage of violent clips slides past—an Arab fighter being shot to death by American soldiers; a marine rifleman dancing and clutching his groin, then firing a machine gun into an Iraqi town; the minaret of a mosque being blown to pieces. The violence is intercut with iconic images from American pop culture—the smiling face of *Jackass* prince Johnny Knoxville, college kids dancing at an MTV beach party, antiwar rallies, the faces of arch-liberals Jane Fonda and Michael Moore. The soundtrack is provided by Boston hard-core punk band Blood for Blood. Their song "Ain't Like You (Wasted Youth II)," with its chorus of "Fuck you, I ain't like you," becomes the refrain of the troops as they blow away insurgents and give the finger to antiwar activists and kids at home enjoying the fruits of America's mindless civilian culture.

There is evidence of a possible war crime in the trailer: a marine clutches the head of a dead Iraqi and raises it in front of the camera like a jack-o'-lantern. (This footage was given to Dollard by troops, and he claims not to know the provenance of the decapitated man, or why a marine was playing with his severed head.) In Dollard's presentation, the act of desecration, accompanied by the faces of grinning Marines, is treated as a macabre joke. By intercutting this with actual *Jackass* footage, the trailer seems to suggest that, for the young, wild, and patriotic American, war in Iraq is sort of like the ultimate *Jackass.*

When I mention to Dollard that his severed-head scene might turn more Americans against the war, or even against the troops, he laughs. "The true savagery in this war is being committed by the American left on the minds of the young men and women serving over there by repeatedly telling them that their cause is lost." He adds, "My goal is to desensitize young people to violence. I want kids to watch my film and understand that brutality is the fucking appropriate response to a brutal enemy."

Dollard's target audience is the same as any rock band's: kids—the more disaffected the better. He aims to alter the course of pop culture. "What we've celebrated since at least the 1950s is the antihero," Dollard says. "Today, even though our country has been attacked, nothing has changed. If you are a young man in America right now, the coolest fucking thing you can aspire to be is like a gangsta rapper, or a pseudo bad guy. The message of my movie is simple: If you're a young person in America, the coolest, fucking most badass and most noble thing you can be today is a combat marine. Period."

Breitbart believes Dollard is onto something important. "There needs to be a confrontation at the pop-culture level of the kids who are over there fighting versus the kids at home who are totally disconnected, immersed in this mindless Abercrombie & Fitch–MTV culture." Breitbart adds, "There needs to be a revolution, and Dollard is the man who can kick it off. I don't care if older conservatives are offended by Pat Dollard. I was not looking for someone pristine. He brings to our cause this whole spirit of, like, the Merry Pranksters Two."

Perhaps it's no surprise that Ann Coulter adores his work. Like Breitbart, she recognizes his ability to reach young people in ways that other conservatives don't. She says of his Web postings, "What's great about them is that they have the panache of a professional MTV video with a very un-MTV message." In an e-mail she sent to Dollard after an initial viewing of his trailer, she simply gushed, "wow! wow! that certainly is attention-grabbing! I like it—especially the 'fuck you' melange with michael moore and [former Democratic Party chairman] terry mccaulliffe. I like it!"

The reaction to Dollard from soldiers and their family members has been even more enthusiastic. One marine officer he encountered in Ramadi expressed his admiration in a terse note: "Thank God and Chesty Puller for people like you, Pat Dollard, who truly get us. Semper Fi."

As for those Americans who believe in the conspiracy of a liberal-controlled media, Dollard tells them that their worst fears are true, that the entertainment industry is run by a form of reverse McCarthyism. "If you're conservative in Hollywood today, you're not necessarily getting blacklisted, but you essentially are blacklisted. You are reviled and treated like shit." That a former Hollywood big shot would descend from the heights and admit to the people that he was once part of the liberal cabal electrifies them. The father of a marine Dollard met while filming in Ramadi wrote him, "[My son] told me that you were one of those very rare media types that didn't suck and had nuts equal to that of any Marine infantry rifleman. [Your film] will be mighty powerful ordnance deployed against the bed-wetting peaceniks on the left."

Most important from Dollard's standpoint, he is reaching his target audience—the MySpace crowd. Typical of the many e-mails he receives is this: "Hey Pat im a 17 year old high school student. I lived most of my life as a liberal and over the last year realized I was only a product of the leftist school system and the media. The clips I've seen of 'Young Americans' are an inspiration and it's time someone tells the truth. Thanks for putting your life on the line for the better of the country."

•   •   •

When you consider that just eighteen months earlier Dollard was a confessed whore-loving, alcoholic, coked-out Hollywood agent, his transformation into the great hope of conservative America is nothing short of astonishing. "It's fucking crazy, dude," he admits as he stands at the entrance of his hotel, smoking and watching planes take off from LAX. "I was afraid conservatives wouldn't have me, but they're fucking all over me."

He brings up George Clooney and Steve Gaghan, both of whom he knew through his work with Soderbergh. In Dollard's view, the two of them represent everything wrong and shallow about Hollywood liberalism. Dollard claims that he was having lunch with Gaghan—who wrote *Traffic*—a few years ago when Gaghan was struck by his inspiration to make *Syriana*. "He literally held up the bottle of olive oil on the table and said, 'Oh, my God! It's all about the oil.'"

(Though Gaghan remembers the lunch, his version of events differs from Dollard's. And by that point, Gaghan says, he was already a few years into his research for *Syriana*, which was based on Robert Baer's 2002 book, *See No Evil*.)

Nothing irks Dollard more than the praise Clooney received for making *Syriana* and *Good Night, and Good Luck*. "Clooney actually goes around letting people say he was 'brave' for making those movies. Everybody in Hollywood is obsessed with wanting to be perceived as tough. Is it brave making films that serve the agenda of every liberal in Hollywood, when real heroes are spilling their blood in Iraq?" Dollard sputters. "Clooney is a pompous jackass."

Another plane takes off from LAX. Lighting another post-breakfast cigarette, Dollard turns to me and laughs. "Dude, I spent twenty years being a pimp for the stars—now I'm becoming a political star."

The Young Turk

Billy Bob Thornton, a former client of Dollard's, once told a mutual friend, "Pat Dollard is the only person I know in Hollywood who's crazier than me." When Dollard was a teenager his goal in life was to become a "stoned artist." Inspired by his hero, Jim Morrison, Dollard dreamed of spreading a "metaphysical message throughout the world."

He grew up, the second eldest of five children, in a "Puerto Rican–Irish welfare family." When Dollard was three his mother, Eva, packed up the kids and fled from their alcoholic, Irish American father in New Jersey, moving to Paramount, California, a smog-bound blue-collar city on the southern fringes of the Los Angeles basin, where Eva took a job as a night-shift switchboard operator.

Dollard's father stalked the family to California. Living on skid row, the elder Dollard would show up at his ex-wife's house and terrorize the kids. As Dollard remembers it, his dad would inevitably end up leaping onto the cinder-block wall in the backyard to punch and threaten imaginary enemies. "My dad thought we were being attacked by pirates, and the police would come," he says. "But it wasn't my mom who called them. My dad would call the police to help him fight the pirates."

His mother again moved the family, but Dollard's father found them. Dollard was in first grade, a scholarship student at a Catholic elementary school, when his dad took a job parking cars nearby. During recess his father would approach the chain-link fence by the playground and call Pat's name.

According to Eva Dollard, she warned her son, "No matter what he asks, you don't answer any questions." Dollard remembers standing with friends on the playground when his dad, dressed in shabby clothes and an orange reflector vest, approached. "I told the other kids I didn't know him—he was a crazy drunk."

That was the last time Dollard saw his father. He died within a year, at age forty-five, of cirrhosis of the liver. "I was chewed up by guilt for treating him like that," Dollard says. "I stopped believing in God, and felt guiltier because my mom was this big Catholic. I seriously believed I must be some kind of psychopath."

In addition to her faith, Eva possessed a commitment to liberalism that was once almost a birthright of working-class Catholics. "My mother had this belief in, like, the nobility of being poor and the eternal fight for social justice," he says.

No one was more touched by Eva's faith than her eldest child, Ann, eight years older than Pat. Ann's involvement in activism would, strangely enough, put her on a fairy-tale ascent into the highest reaches of the American social strata. In 1976, a year after graduating from high school, Ann took a job as an extra in Hal Ashby's *Coming Home*, which was being filmed at a nearby hospital. During a break, Ann chatted up one of the film's stars, Jane Fonda. The conversation resulted in Ann's taking a job with Fonda's husband Tom Hayden's Campaign for Economic Democracy, then with César Chávez's United Farm Workers of America. Her work inevitably took her deeper into Hollywood's activist-entertainment circles. By the early 80s, Ann had found her professional niche as a junior agent at Leading Artists Agency. Her activism continued, particularly in the nuclear-freeze movement, which led to an intimate friendship with Robert Kennedy Jr., who says, "Ann was one of my closest friends.

She was extremely smart and extremely forceful and was absolutely committed to progressive issues, a vision of social justice for America."

In the Dollard family, no one was closer to Pat than Ann. Kennedy recalls, "Ann would bring Pat to whatever she was doing. Pat idolized her, and she adored him." Through his middle-school years, Dollard followed his older sister to marches and fund-raisers and spent weekends canvassing door-to-door for her.

But he was also beginning to follow in his father's footsteps. Dollard had become a blackout drinker by age fifteen. Nevertheless, with the help of his parish priest, he won a scholarship to a Jesuit prep school. The priests nicknamed him "Nemesis." He was the smart-ass who debated them about religion based on his extensive readings of South American writer Carlos Castaneda, and the kid who, when asked to do a book report on Colombia, brought in a live pot plant as a visual aid. Dollard claims he was nearly thrown out after being implicated in a plot to put LSD in the priests' drinking water. By his junior year, Dollard had discovered L.A.'s punk scene, which only accelerated his drinking. "I remember being in honors algebra, drunk out of my mind every fucking day."

.   .   .

Yet Dollard believed fate held something grand in store for him. Some nights he would take a girlfriend drunken-driving in the hills above Los Angeles, and when she would scream, "Slow down! You're going to kill us!" he would say, "Maybe you'll die. But not me. I can't die. I have a destiny." At seventeen, believing he was onto that destiny, he dropped out of high school to become a rock star. "I didn't play an instrument, and I couldn't sing," he says, "but I thought I could make it on ego and mouth."

He formed a band but admits, "I was too loaded to ever get up onstage." His most memorable performance would be at another band's show: the time he cracked his skull stage-diving at a Black Flag concert, then stayed in the mosh pit slamming for hours, despite later requiring twelve stitches. "I remember coming out covered in blood and everyone telling me how cool I looked," says Dollard. "That was as far as my career went in music." Married briefly and divorced at age twenty-one, Dollard became a telemarketer, spending the next few years in various boiler rooms, selling pens, printer ink, and charity vouchers for the Long Beach Police Department. "It was dismal," he says. "But I learned how to close."

When Dollard was twenty-two, Ann performed a career intervention, hiring him to answer her phone at Leading Artists. He lasted two years before she fired him. But destiny, which he still believed in, had other plans. He would get his break, but only through enduring the greatest tragedy of his life. Two days after Ann fired him, she was killed in a freak horse-riding accident. Dollard was offered her job and her client list, which included a then unknown Steven Soderbergh, about a year away from releasing his breakthrough, *Sex, Lies, and Videotape*.

Dollard was twenty-five when Soderbergh shot to fame, and quickly proved himself in his own right. In the early 90s he moved to William Morris, where he worked with Mike Simpson, today a senior vice president of the agency, whose best-known clients are Tim Burton, Quentin Tarantino, Wes Craven, and Trey Parker and Matt Stone. "Pat was outspoken, very articulate, and knew how to operate in the world," Simpson says. "He became an important soldier in our army."

His biggest contribution was to help establish the agency's independent-film division, which, Simpson says, "was extremely important to our success in the 90s." In addition to Soderbergh, Dollard represented Billy Bob Thornton and his writing partner Tom Epperson; Mike Werb, who wrote *The Mask* and *Face/Off*;

Don Mancini (writer of the *Child's Play* series); director Alan Rudolph; writer Fina Torres; and actor Malcolm-Jamal Warner.

．　　　．　　　．

To Dollard, the sudden success felt as if "someone handed me a basket of power." One of his favorite movies as a teenager had been Stanley Kubrick's *Barry Lyndon*, based on the Thackeray novel about a fatherless Irish rogue who fakes his way into the aristocracy. For Dollard, becoming an agent fulfilled this fantasy. "It was like being a fucking duke or count in Europe back in the day," he says.

Dollard did what many other twentysomethings in his shoes would have done: he became a swine of the first order. He wore Armani suits, drove whatever car was "tasty" at the time—from a Miata to a Porsche to a Range Rover—and "plowed through more pussy than I thought was imaginable."

Outwardly, Dollard was the consummate Hollywood player. A former client says, "Pat seemed like the archetypical agent. He was hyper-slick in that hyper-glib, dismissive, hipper-than-thou, bullshit-Hollywood way. He was your basic Young Turk prick."

Simpson saw something different in him. "The main thing I always liked about Pat from day one is that I felt like he had a soul. There was something else going on besides just who his clients were, what the deal was, that kind of agent veneer."

Dollard was earning a reputation for intense but passing infatuations, such as the time in the early 90s when he converted to Judaism and took the name Schlomo Bin Avrihim. ("The rabbis who held my beth din," says Dollard, referring to the council that determines a candidate's suitability for conversion, "told me afterwards that they wished all converts could reach my spiritual level.") The conversion didn't last. Dollard's second wife, for whom he'd become a Jew, divorced him not long after his romp with hookers on the set of *Dragon: The Bruce Lee Story*.

While visiting his wife on the *Dragon* set, Dollard found the time to chat up one of the hairdressers, Alicia Allain, who would become his third wife, in 1994. Alicia, nineteen, had come to Los Angeles from Louisiana with ambitions of becoming a producer, though was still relegated to the hair-and-makeup department.

The Dollard Alicia met "always wore these very tasteful Italian suits and was so gifted I believed he was going to end up running a studio." Alicia was open-minded in a way that should have made theirs the ideal Hollywood marriage. When I ask her if she was aware that her future husband was having sex with hookers at the same time he was wooing her on the set of *Dragon*, she corrects me. "No, Pat didn't have sex with those girls," she says. "They just gave him some blow jobs."

But as tolerant as Alicia was, Dollard's increasing drug use plunged her into despair. While he controlled it at the office, after hours he typically functioned in a chemically induced haze. She says, "Those guys at William Morris loved Pat. They saw him as this happy-go-lucky dude. They didn't see Pat locking himself in his bedroom at our apartment, him high as a kite, and me and his mother finally having the police and firemen get him because we're afraid he's killing himself in there. I saw he hated himself for what he was doing. After these runs Pat would just be balled up on the floor crying."

Dollard estimates that he wound up in emergency rooms half a dozen times for overdoses.

By 1995, at age thirty, Dollard was barely functioning. Mike Simpson tried to intervene. He says, "I talked to him, kind of like up against the wall, and said, 'What are you doing, man? You're gonna kill yourself.'"

According to Simpson, Dollard simply laughed and said, "You're right."

That year, he was fired from William Morris. Pat and Alicia moved back to her hometown, near Baton Rouge, Louisiana, where initially she supported them working at a hair salon. "We lived on clipping coupons for pizzas," Dollard recalls. He began attending A.A. meetings and took a job at a Baton Rouge commercial-production house, and in 1996, Alicia gave birth to their daughter. He and Alicia produced two independent films, *Notes from Underground* and *Lush*, a portrait of a man suffering from alcoholic blackouts who is accused of murder. Neither film put Dollard back on the map. Nor was Soderbergh, who remained a client, doing especially well. After he failed to connect with audiences with films like *The Underneath* and *Schizopolis*, Soderbergh's relations with major studios had chilled. "For a while there," says Dollard, "the most successful film I was involved with was a Louisiana State Lottery commercial I worked on."

.   .   .

Everything changed in 1998 when Soderbergh's *Out of Sight* was released to critical acclaim. Dollard's career came roaring back to life. In short order he set up lucrative deals for Soderbergh to make *The Limey*, *Full Frontal*, and *Erin Brockovich*. But *Traffic* was Dollard's biggest coup. Dollard is credited by Soderbergh and others with getting the film made after it fell apart during preproduction. When *Traffic* won four Academy Awards, including Soderbergh's first as a director, Dollard was a made man in Hollywood.

Propaganda Films hired Dollard to be president of its management division. Then at its peak as a commercial- and feature-production company, Propaganda's stable included some of the hottest directors in town, including David Fincher, Michael Bay, and Spike Jonze. Dollard moved into a home in Bel Air. He and Alicia had separated in 1999, but continued to work together as a producing team.

With *Traffic* having moved the national debate on the war on drugs to the forefront, Dollard spoke candidly to the press about his own struggles with addiction, telling one reporter that his practices as an agent were now "consistent with A.A. principles."

Despite preaching about sobriety, Dollard began using again. Initially, he attempted to hide it. "I would take drug vacations," he explains. "I'd check into a hotel on Sunset and just binge for a few days." Soon his addictions spilled into his work life. According to Dollard, in 2001, after starting at Propaganda, he initiated monthly drug-and-hooker parties, which he dubbed "the Hotel Club."

Dollard claims that the Hotel Club became part of his executive plan at Propaganda. "I'm not saying we expensed any of this," Dollard says. "Once a month, a variety of executives at the company would have non-wedding-connected bachelor parties with drugs and hookers we'd book at all the different trendy hotels—the Avalon, Four Seasons, Argyle. We would invite potential clients and get them loaded and get them laid. I was participating in the fucking Roman orgy."

Propaganda soon went belly-up—industry-watchers blame a post-9/11 recession in commercial production, not Dollard—but he landed on his feet, taking a senior position at Catch-23, the management firm that represented Renée Zellweger, among others. In 2004 he and manager Ryan Kavanaugh cofounded Relativity Management, with $150 million in financing and ambitious plans to produce films as well as manage talent. "My career had never been better," Dollard says. "My personal life was this ongoing disaster."

In 2000 he had married for the fourth time. He and his wife moved into a Hollywood Hills mansion previously inhabited by Kirstie Alley. It was owned by Alley's former boyfriend, *Melrose Place* actor James Wilder, who lived next door. After Dollard reverted to old habits and began locking himself in the master bedroom to binge in privacy, his new wife enlisted Wilder's help breaking in—by climbing across a walkway that connected the two homes—in order to check on her husband. She says, "Poor James went from Kirstie Alley to Pat and me."

At a dinner party at Stockard Channing's house, Dollard's third wife, Alicia, heard alarming stories about her ex-husband. She says, "Pat was seen running naked down the street waving a sword." (Dollard disputes key details of the account, saying, "I was wearing my boxers and I never left my balcony.")

What's not in dispute is that police were called to Dollard's house in the spring of 2004, handcuffed him, and took him to the psych unit at Cedars-Sinai for observation. Around this time he began his political conversion. Somewhere between the Roman orgy and the mental ward he became a staunch supporter of George W. Bush's.

To show his support for the war in Iraq, he acquired vanity plates for his Hummer that spelled, US WINS. He told friends, "President Bush is the Che Guevara of our time. He's already liberated two countries from tyranny. Those kids walking around in T-shirts with Che on them in a red beret, someday they'll be wearing shirts with Bush's face on them in a cowboy hat."

Paul Schrader, who became close to him during the making of *Auto Focus*, says, "Pat is a passionista, just like Jimmy Toback or John Milius. These are guys who have never allowed logic or, actually, their own thought process to interfere with the progress of an interesting argument. The danger with Pat comes when he moves into that territory where everything gets blurred, and he becomes the object of his own imagination."

Soon, Dollard was telling people that it was his intention to "personally fight al-Qaeda." As he told me, "If I could, I'd kill jihadis with my bare hands. That's really the goal."

Kidnapped

My first encounter with Dollard takes place in the spring of 2004. We are introduced by a mutual friend who believes Dollard might be interested in representing the film rights of a book I wrote about marines in Iraq. "He's a little crazy," my friend warns, "but he's Steven Soderbergh's agent. This guy makes movies."

We meet in the offices of Relativity, on the fourth floor of a reassuringly stolid concrete-and-glass building on Beverly Drive. The reception area is a jumble of cardboard boxes and partially assembled desk components, with phone lines snaking through the mess. It looks like the company is just moving in, rapidly expanding, or folding. (As it would turn out, it was doing all three at once.) It's populated by attractive, young, female assistants who seem to be doing nothing when Dollard—still in his Prada-boots-jeans-and-silk-T-shirt phase—strides in, shakes my hand, and tells me he'll be right back. He has to go to the bathroom. I can wait in his office down the hall.

Dollard returns twenty minutes later. We sit on black leather chairs around a chrome-and-glass coffee table. He smokes, ashing in a paper cup, and rambles about killing jihadis and his dream of making a prowar film.

Despite his ease in discussing his travails with drugs, he lowers his voice when discussing his incipient Republicanism. "Dude," he says, "when I have meetings with George Clooney, I'm afraid to drive my Hummer on the lot. I'm afraid if I come out as a Republican it will jeopardize my business relations. How fucked is that, dude? I live in fear of George Clooney."

At the end of our meeting Dollard offers to become my manager. "Seriously, dude, I could get something set up for you like *that*," he says, clapping his hands to indicate how fast he is going to make a deal.

But Dollard never becomes my manager. In the coming weeks, he breaks several appointments. One day he phones. Rapid, shallow breaths come across the line. "Dude, I am so, so, so fucking sorry for not calling you." No explanation is required, but Dollard offers one anyway. "I was fucking kidnapped."

Dollard claims that members of an A.A. meeting abducted him after promising his wife to get him sober. Instead, they held him prisoner at a hotel in Palm Springs while plying him with call girls and coke. Meanwhile, they used his credit cards to charter a yacht and a plane for business deals they were conducting. The story is incredible, but Dollard's fourth wife later confirms its essential truth, adding, "I'm sure those A.A. people started with good intentions, but Pat twisted their intervention around until they thought the right thing to do was buying coke and hiring prostitutes for him."

On Election Day 2004, I receive an urgent phone call from Dollard. I must come to his office immediately. When I show up, two agents from Relativity are on the couch. Dollard paces, making introductions at a rapid clip.

His eyes are glassy. He speaks with those shallow breaths I'd heard when he phoned after the "kidnapping." I get the feeling he may be seriously messed up. The two agents slink from the room.

Dollard reveals why he asked me over. *New York Times* reporter Sharon Waxman, a friend of mine, has completed a book on directors of the 90s, *Rebels on the Back Lot*, for which she interviewed him. He wants to know if he is quoted in it. I tell him I believe he is.

Dollard summons an assistant. "I want you to take a letter for me," he tells her. "Send it to all my clients. Tell them I might be quoted in Sharon Waxman's book. I don't recall what I told her. I was on drugs and I retract my quotes."

"Hollywood Yuppie Faggot"

Three weeks later Dollard leaves for Iraq. He persuaded a former client—a director who had previously won accolades at Sundance for a small, gritty film—to accompany him. The director says that when he first glimpsed Dollard on their way to the airport "he looked like he was detoxing. He didn't have any proper gear. I knew this would be a disaster."

As it turned out, disaster befell Dollard's partner. Shortly after their arrival, he was severely injured in a Humvee accident and had to be medevac'd home. Dollard decided to push ahead on his own. The military embedded him with marines at a forward operating base about twenty-five miles south of Baghdad in an area troops dubbed "the Triangle of Death." About 200 marines occupied the camp, a dusty crater surrounded by concrete blast barriers and razor wire, which insurgents showered with mortars every other day or so.

Dollard wandered the camp befriending anyone who would talk to him. Sergeant Brandon Welsh, then twenty-two, recalls their first encounter. "He came up and said, 'I'm Pat Dollard from Hollywood.' He talked fast, was all uppity and shit. We thought he was a cokehead."

The troops nicknamed him "Hollywood Yuppie Faggot." Welsh's section leader, Sergeant John Callan, says, "Pat came up with these stories about partying with movie stars and rock stars and models, and the marines just ate it up."

Dollard pulled the ultimate trump card. Using his sat phone, he called Lucy Walsh, daughter of former Eagles guitarist Joe Walsh. Lucy, a client of Dollard's, had toured as a keyboardist for Ashlee Simpson. Dollard managed to catch her when she was visiting with Simpson. Callan says, "Pat put this kid from West Virginia on the line with Ashlee Simpson. I was told she was like, 'Well, thanks for going out there and getting your dumb ass blown up. I gotta go.'"

•   •   •

As far as the troops were concerned, Dollard was now in. Says Callan, "For the younger guys he became, like, their leader. Nobody from the command ever told us he was attached to us. He just kind of went out for a ride with us one time, then said, 'I'm gonna get my stuff,' and he moved in."

From a First Amendment standpoint, it's to be applauded that commanders never sought to supervise the activities of their embedded reporter from Hollywood. But to Callan, Dollard was a constant headache. "I'm the guy that has to talk to these guys' mothers if one of them gets killed. With Pat around, it was hard to get people to do their jobs."

Dollard claims he was sober when he arrived in Iraq, but he soon fell off the wagon. As one marine describes it, "One afternoon, on patrol, we bought beer from a hajji." Later, back at the base, he says, "we all got buzzed, and Pat was like, 'Let's get mohawks.'"

After Dollard shaved the word "die" in his chest hair, the night was immortalized in the photo he e-mailed back to friends in Hollywood. By then, Dollard was wearing marine fatigues. Another reporter at the camp recalls, "I was there when the commander, a lieutenant colonel, saw this clown running around in cammies with a mohawk. The colonel called over the platoon sergeant of the unit he was with and asked, 'Is that your fucking reporter?'"

Welsh and the others were ordered to shave off their mohawks. Shortly after the incident, the platoon Welsh and Callan belonged to was ordered to Al-Musayyib, a town of an estimated 10,000 on the Euphrates where a few days earlier insurgents had destroyed one of two main bridges with a truck bomb. Their platoon was sent in to hold the remaining bridge. Dollard accompanied them—fewer than two dozen troops in three light armored vehicles—as they rolled into the center of Al-Musayyib. At sunset, a muezzin sang calls to prayer from loudspeakers on a nearby mosque, and the marines were ordered on foot patrols through the narrow streets surrounding their position. Dollard joined them.

Unfortunately, the patrol Dollard accompanied encountered an Iraqi selling whiskey. Dollard purchased several bottles and drank himself into a blackout. Callan says, "He was wandering around singing and spewing stupid shit. It was the middle of the night, and he was turning on the light to his camera to film us, putting a spotlight on us in the middle of our security patrols."

Sergeant Brandon Wong, another marine in the unit, who was then twenty-two, says, "When Pat first showed up in Iraq he was all, like, he's an alcoholic and can't drink.

"We saw what he meant that night. He was fucking trashed. Pat ran up to a mosque and ripped the fucking sign off it"—a cloth banner with hand-painted Arabic on it. Later that night, Wong says, "a patrol of Humvees was driving by and I look and there's Pat just standing in the middle of the fucking road trying to wave them through, like he's directing traffic."

The marines returned from their patrol before dawn and were allotted a couple of hours to sleep. Dollard continued babbling and singing—a sort of shanty that went, as Callan recalls, " 'Three bottles of whiskey and a couple of hajji sodas and just got shitty.' "

The antics pushed Wong to the breaking point. "I could not fucking sleep because of his ass," he says. "I flipped out on him." Wong, who later became friends with Dollard, regrets what happened next. "I pulled my gun on him. I put it to his head and told him he'd better shut the fuck up or I would pull the trigger." Wong adds, "It's fucked up to say now, but I really didn't care if he lived or died."

Other marines talked Wong out of shooting Dollard. Callan wasn't told about Wong's threat on Dollard's life until the next day. He recalls, "When I heard about it, I said, 'You should have just shot him.' "

The following morning Dollard returned to the main base with another unit, while Callan's platoon remained in Al-Musayyib. At about noon, a mob gathered in front of the mosque whose banner Dollard had stolen as the imam delivered an angry denunciation of the American occupiers. Soon, the marines came under fire from gunmen around the mosque. "Our whole platoon opened up on that side of the city," says a Marine. "We could never prove Pat is the one who caused it, but that's what we thought started it."

No Marines were injured in the engagement. Among some, affection for Dollard actually grew. "It wouldn't make sense to anyone who wasn't there," says Welsh, "but Pat brought this civilian craziness to our lives. He made being in Iraq fun."

·   ·   ·

Among troops, Dollard's next stunt gave him almost mythic status as a wild man. For several weeks an urban legend circulated on the base that a derelict former palace beyond their perimeter was a whorehouse. Marines talked of seeing attractive young women, dressed in provocative clothes and makeup, coming and going from it. But given the abductions and beheadings meted out to unaccompanied Westerners, no one dared leave their fortified perimeter to investigate—until Dollard informed them that he was going out alone to search the alleged whorehouse.

According to Wong, he and other young marines decided to help. "We gave him a pistol and a grenade and showed him how to work the shit. We told him, 'If you start shooting, we'll come running after you,' but, you know, we weren't allowed to leave the patrol base."

As marines watched from the base, Dollard walked alone into the city. He says all he found in the shattered palace was a family living in the rubble. Walking to the rear of the building he found a hole blasted through the back wall, which offered a view into the city, where something caught his eye. "It was like this blue sign. I don't remember if there was a crescent on it or not," Dollard says, "but something about it said 'pharmacy' to me."

He set off into the city toward the blue sign. His instincts proved correct. The shop with the sign was a pharmacy, where

Dollard lived out a drug addict's dream. Armed, dressed in American military attire, he entered the shop to take anything he wanted. "The man at the counter just looked at me," Dollard says. "I showed my weapons and pointed at the stuff on the shelves. The man started speaking in Arabic, but I heard the word 'analgesics.' I knew that was the shit I wanted."

Dollard left with several bottles of liquid Valium and other substances he wasn't quite sure of. "I never pointed my gun at the guy," he explains. "But it was robbery at gunpoint by implication."

Dollard at one point claimed that his dealer in L.A. sent him an unsolicited care package of coke through military mail. Later, he retracts this story and denies robbing a pharmacy of Valium. But several marines I interview confirm that Dollard shared liquid Valium and other substances with men in the unit, and say he told them they were legally acquired in Iraq. Two marines claim to have done rails of coke provided by Dollard on top of their armored vehicle after their tour of duty on the way back to Kuwait. "The shit we got into with Pat was crazy," says one.

Dollard himself contradicts one of his retractions later while showing me raw footage he shot. "You can tell we're all on Valium," he says, "because everyone is heavy-tongued when we talk."

·   ·   ·

Hours of tape Dollard has shown me but not yet made public reveal an embedded reporter running out of control. In one sequence, filmed at a checkpoint where marines are stopping civilian cars, Dollard himself cuts in front of the marines to accost the driver. He leans in the window and shouts, "You got any bombs, dickface? Any booms? Any women?"

Dollard backs away, laughing, then shouts to nearby Marines. "Will you fucking kill something while I am here?"

Dollard argues that his reckless behavior was calculated to get the marines to loosen up in front of his camera. Leaving aside whatever damage he did to the combat effectiveness of the unit by distributing drugs, as well as the harm he did to American-Iraqi relations by vandalizing a mosque and robbing a drugstore while dressed as a U.S. soldier, his footage from Iraq stands as a peculiar and often compelling record of war.

Most documentaries emerging from Iraq, no matter how scrupulously their makers strive to be neutral, have the feel of an adult presence, an intermediary at the controls. In Dollard's work, there is no filter. It's not the work of a grown-up. There's no authority interpreting how the young troops ought to feel about their experiences. It's the kind of film a nineteen- or twenty-year-old marine would make to show his buddies. It captures the raw experience of a combat zone about as well as anything I have seen—short of actually going to a combat zone. No small part of the loyalty Dollard engenders among young marines stems from what they see as the honesty of his work. "No one else out there I know of," says Wong, "has gone as far as Pat to show people what our lives are like."

There are some marines Dollard never won over. "His presence endangered lives," says Callan. "I have no doubt that he's insane."

Escape and Evasion

Dollard returned to L.A. in March 2005 to find that his business and personal affairs had imploded. Relativity was in the process of ousting him. An ex–business partner in an unrelated venture was seeking a $700,000 judgment against him. His fourth wife, Megan, had filed for divorce. Even worse, the three most influential women in his life—Megan, Alicia, and his mother—had sided together, like a freak alignment of stars, in a legal action to deny him custody of his daughter. His Porsche and Range Rover were repossessed. Megan sold their furniture to pay bills. Dollard still had his Hummer, but a thief stole his US WINS vanity plates.

Dollard dealt with everything by going on a massive binge, living alone in the empty Hollywood Hills home. The four-story house was built into the side of a cliff, with panoramic views, an open steel-cage elevator running through its center, and walls adorned with his collections (not yet sold off) of African art, swords, and battle helmets. Soon he was living like a bum. The electricity was turned off. He slept on a mattress on the floor of a bathroom.

In mid-April, when an agent colleague showed up at his house to check on him, she found the front door open. The place was filled with trash. It smelled. As she entered the kitchen, Dollard stumbled in, so filthy she initially thought he was a homeless man. Dollard lunged and threatened, "I'm going to fucking kill you."

She fled and called the L.A.P.D., who showed up in force. "They had shotguns out," she says. "I was terrified they were going to kill him."

Dollard left peacefully, but given his proximity to neighbors like Bill Condon, Russell Crowe's agent Bill Freeman, and James Wilder, his arrest was a bizarre industry event. "Everyone came out to see what was going on, and there was Pat being taken away in handcuffs," says Dollard's colleague. "It was one of the most traumatic experiences of my life."

No criminal charges were filed. Police deposited him at the Los Angeles County/U.S.C. Medical Center for psychiatric evaluation. Dollard describes the place as a "ghetto psych ward full of true nut jobs and power-mad nurses." They tied him down and shot him full of Ativan. He was held for three days and released.

Dollard returned to his home and picked up where he'd left off. Two of the marines he'd befriended in Iraq, Welsh and Wong, flew out to L.A. to visit. Dollard was still wearing his hospital bracelet, doing lines, and downing jug vodka when his visitors showed up.

As the marines left, Dollard promised them he'd taper down. Shortly thereafter, someone—Dollard still doesn't know who—again called the cops. This time Dollard, on foot, led police on a pursuit through the hills. Even his landlord, James Wilder, became involved, grabbing a stick and thrashing the bushes in an attempt to corner Dollard. But Dollard evaded capture. He crawled into a hole and hid out Saddam-style through the night. "In my ability to run and find cover, my experience in Iraq really paid off," Dollard would later tell me. "It's what the Marines call 'E and E,' escape and evasion."

By May, Dollard was ready to call it quits. He voluntarily entered Impact House, a live-in, highly regimented rehab in Pasadena.

Always the Truth

In early June 2005, I see Dollard after his departure from Impact House. Friends have helped him move into an apartment on Sunset Boulevard, where he is staging a comeback. Outside his window the dome of the ArcLight Cinemas appears to be melting in a liquid sunset. Inside, the air-conditioning blasts. It's on because Dollard actually abhors cigarettes: the smell, the taste, the ruinous effects on the lungs—everything about cigarettes, except, of course, smoking them. He paces beneath the ceiling vents, chain-smoking and discussing his newfound sobriety. "I had this realization about my drug use," he tells me. "Until my last binge, I held on to the idea that I could just drop out for a day or two and do drugs. I would have this James Bond fantasy where I'm in, like, the Mondrian [hotel], drinking martinis and shit with beautiful women, then having, like, great coked-out sex." He laughs. "But I always seem to end up, like, homeless within a matter of hours."

Dollard has acquired his new, post-agent look: crew cut, Marine Corps fatigues, the haggard, unshaven face. The cataract is just starting to appear over his right eye. He looks wrecked, but Dollard insists he has never felt better, saying, "I wasted twenty years of my life on the narcotic of being a Hollywood agent. Iraq gave me a shot at redemption, but I didn't realize it, dude, until it was almost too late."

Dollard is full of new morality. "Ultimately, you realize that the purpose of life isn't just to take from it whatever you can get," he says, bending over the stove to light another cigarette on the gas flame. "You can't spend your life as a sexual libertine and end up being at peace." He walks up to me and points to my chest. "We were not just born to be sexual pirates."

I ask if he is involved in outpatient therapy or going to A.A. meetings. "I've just been through a war," he says. "How can I sit around listening to a bunch of grown men whine about their fucked-up childhoods? I'm part of something bigger than myself—the war, the conservative cause. I can't get loaded anymore."

Dollard shares a profound discovery he's recently made. "I'm a warrior, dude. I am of the class of people whose role has been genetically determined to be protectors. My role is to fight the battle against Islamic-fundamentalist fascism."

There are people in Dollard's life who believe he's gone completely out of his mind. His mother believes that at a minimum he may be bipolar. His third wife, Alicia, offers a blunter assessment: "I think he brain-damaged himself in one of those last drug runs."

Exhibit A in her argument that he has gone mad is his recent announcement that he is terminating his relationship with Soderbergh. "Pat owned 10 percent of Steven Soderbergh, and he goes and fires him," Alicia says. "How crazy is that?"

Dollard tells me, "I'm a director now. A director can't represent a director."

His future lies in 243 hour-long videocassettes piled on the floor in the corner. There is no furniture, just wall-to-wall white carpet and a sleeping bag. Dollard can't afford a computer yet on which to edit his tapes. What keeps him motivated is a tattered Iraqi flag tacked to the wall, signed by marines and inscribed, "Always the truth." I later ask Captain Brian Iglesias, who signed the flag, about the inscription. He answers, " 'Always the truth,' because the truth is what Pat Dollard champions."

Most people in Dollard's life have written him off. Yet for an industry where relationships are reputed to be calculated solely on the basis of self-interest, loyalists remain, from Soderbergh—who helped pay for Dollard's stay at rehab—to William Morris's Mike Simpson. (After my visit, Simpson will give Dollard an editing system.) Prior to moving into his apartment Dollard couch-surfed at the Bel Air home of Erik Hyman, an entertainment lawyer and the partner of photographer Herb Ritts until his death, in 2002. Explaining his surprising bond with Dollard, Hyman says, "Our friendship transcends whatever nuttiness he's involved in at the moment. After Herb died, Pat showed up for me. He wouldn't let me be alone. He is an extremely caring friend."

Dollard argues that those most critical of his career abandonment are either his ex-wives and mother, who depend on him financially, or those whose "empty lives making crap films" he now rejects. "People expect me to regret going to Iraq, because I lost everything," he says. "What's really going on here is I left the whorehouse. The people who stayed behind are the ones saying I'm a psychopath. Why? Because I rejected being a self-centered, moneygrubbing pig, which is what you are supposed to be in this town if you want to be considered sane."

Dollard's mother believes that her son is a near genius "at taking any information and transferring it into self-serving data." A case in point is his argument that his recent trips to area mental wards prove his mental health is solid. "Psychiatrists checked me out. If I were truly pathological, they never would have released me," he says, accidentally banging his cigarette against the side of his face. Sparks fly from his smoldering whiskers. "I have often asked myself the question 'Am I a psychopath?' But it just doesn't add up. I am one of the sanest people I know."

Dollard sucks mightily on his mangled cigarette. The aroma of burnt hair lingers. "The only exception is if you fill me with drugs and alcohol I do become insane. I concede that point."

I ask him whether there is any difference in his thought process when he's sober or on drugs. Dollard laughs. "None. When I'm on drugs, the same garbage comes out of my mouth, only it's amplified."

The Pitch

Late August 2005. Pat Dollard is bombing down Sunset Boulevard at the wheel of his new, gray Hummer, on his way to a meeting at William Morris. He handles the massive vehicle with about as much caution as the average eleven-year-old at the wheel of a carnival bumper car. "I love the Hummer," he says, weaving through the lanes. "It's like driving your fucking living room from your Barcalounger."

Sober for nearly 120 days now, Dollard's comeback is well under way. He has created a ninety-minute rough cut of his documentary, now titled *Young Americans*. Both Soderbergh and Simpson viewed it in his apartment and, as they say in Hollywood, "went crazy." Soderbergh has offered to help arrange distribution. Simpson has scheduled a screening at William Morris this morning at eleven, with the idea that the agency that once fired Dollard will take him on as a client.

A couple of weeks ago, Dollard received an unexpected cash windfall. Hence, the new Hummer, including a new set of US WINS plates. His military fatigues—what he now refers to as his

"Travis Bickle uniform"—are neatly pressed. His hair is slicked flat on his head, and he is clean-shaven.

Three days a week he's been training in *krav maga*, Israeli martial arts. "I have to get my body up to the level my mind is at," he says. "When I was in Iraq, I learned all this will-to-power shit. I could kill now."

The exception to his new, squared-away life is his failure to obtain treatment for the cataract clotting his right eye—a result of Dollard's fear of doctors and hospitals. Driving partially blind has become a sort of experiment. Cutting recklessly through traffic, Dollard laughs. "I'm just a puppet in the hands of God, dude," he says, repeating a saying he picked up at an A.A. meeting.

Nowhere is God's grace more evident than in Dollard's resurrection in Hollywood. People who long ago wrote him off have begun to pop out of the woodwork. In the past few days, even one of the most powerful men in town, ICM's chairman, Jeff Berg, has been asking him for a chance to see *Young Americans.*

"Berg's a sensitive matter," Dollard says, sounding oddly calculating—more like an agent than I am accustomed to hearing. "I can't blow him off, but I have an obligation to show it to Mike Simpson first."

"How do you know Berg?" I ask.

"Business," Dollard says. "We crawled through the slime together." (Dollard later explains that Berg once provided him with helpful advice on a deal.)

Outside William Morris, Dollard is seized by a fit of self-objectivity. He admits to qualms about involving an old, loyal friend like Simpson in his current scheme. "People who get involved with me tend to end up feeling that they've been put through the wringer at some point," he says. "Oh, well. What the fuck."

Inside the lobby, receptionists do double takes as he approaches their desk and announces himself. God only knows what they make of him. He's too old to be a recent vet, but his digital camouflage trousers, with their futuristic abstract pattern, have only recently become standard issue. Perhaps they think he's a homeless man from the future.

An assistant escorts us to a screening room on the fourth floor. Mike Simpson, over six feet tall, lanky and fair-haired, approaches in the hall, grinning. In his early fifties and dressed in his regulation William Morris blue suit, Simpson looks more like a small-town banker than an industry player. Originally from Texas, Simpson's voice retains a rural twang. Patting Dollard's shoulder, Simpson seems slightly in awe of him, like the straitlaced kid in high school who secretly yearns to be accepted by the delinquents.

To help evaluate the potential of Dollard's film, Simpson has invited fellow agent John Ferriter to the screening. Simpson believes the agency ought to sell *Young Americans* as a hybrid documentary/reality-TV series, for which Dollard's rough cut would be a pilot.

When I ask Simpson if he's at all worried about representing Dollard, whose drug lunacies are a known quantity, he replies, "What we look at is the success of films like *Fahrenheit 9/11* and the ability to go into that territory with Pat's very different point of view. As far as his personal issues, this is the entertainment business. It's not banking."

John Ferriter enters the room, dressed in a baggy black suit like the hit men from *Pulp Fiction*—a look that has never gone out of style among some agents. In his early thirties, Ferriter has earned a reputation as one of Hollywood's top reality-TV agents. As they make introductions, Ferriter drops his business card (Senior Vice President Worldwide Head of Non-Scripted Television) on the table, then flips it like a blackjack dealer. Dollard appears momentarily unsure of himself. He tries shaking Ferriter's hand, but fails to connect on the first pass.

"How are you?" Ferriter asks.

"Fine, good," Dollard says, sitting down.

"You just got back from Iraq?"

"A few months ago."

"Are you O.K.?" Ferriter leans closer to Dollard.

"Fucking fine." Dollard fidgets.

"I mean, how are you *doing*?" Ferriter radiates deep concern.

"Dude, I didn't fucking come here for fucking psychotherapy," Dollard says.

(Dollard later tells me, "It's important to show your agent he's just the fucking cleaning lady. Ferriter obviously has good agent training. He didn't even act insulted when I insulted him.")

Simpson, watching from the back, laughs quietly.

Dollard feeds his DVD into the player by the TV at the head of the conference table. Ferriter sits about four feet from the TV screen, shaking his foot, tugging at his cuffs, running his hand through his longish black hair. When the Blood for Blood song begins to blast, Ferriter seems to relax, bopping his head to the rhythm. At about the twenty-minute mark, he stands and hits the stop button.

"Great, great," Ferriter says. "I totally get it."

"Is that all you want to see?" Dollard asks.

"This is going to be like *The Aristocrats*," Ferriter says. "Every college kid in America is going to want to see this. It's like Tom Green, *Jackass* in a war zone. And it's real."

Ferriter asks Dollard the most important question. "Can we get Steven [Soderbergh] to come in the room with us?"

"Yeah," Dollard says.

Ferriter and Simpson discuss possible buyers, then a price. "What do you think?" Ferriter asks. "Eight to ten million?"

"Sounds about right to me," Simpson says.

Ferriter tells Dollard to shorten the rough cut at future screenings. "This is like a drug. You've got to give them just a little bit, so they want more."

A few minutes later, as we emerge into the brightness of the street, Dollard seems amazed Ferriter went for it. "He didn't even watch it. The guy was twitching the whole time." Dollard is incredulous. "He bought it on a vibe and the fact I can bring Steven Soderbergh into the room with me."

Dollard turns to the William Morris sign on the building. "This is the place that fired me. Now I'm the fucking getting-my-ass-licked client. How cool is that?"

In the Room with Soderbergh

Later that afternoon, Dollard has an appointment with Soderbergh on the Paramount lot to deliver a copy of *Young Americans*. Soderbergh is then flying to Italy, where he plans to hand-deliver the film to entrepreneur and HDNet founder Mark Cuban at the Venice Film Festival.

Bouncing through traffic on his way to the meeting, Dollard is on a high, dreaming of the millions he stands to make, which has made him forgetful of the lecture on sexual continence he delivered weeks earlier. "Once I get some production money, this is my M.O.," Dollard says. "Hire a hot, twenty-one-year-old assistant, get her to do all my shit—paying bills, laundry—then I start banging her. Serious, dude. I had one in the 90s I literally trained to lick my ass. She was so good I even took her to Italy once. Two weeks. But all we did was stay in the hotel room so she could lick my ass."

Soderbergh's office is off Gower, where he is in preproduction for *The Good German*. Soderbergh enters the reception area wearing jeans and heavy black shoes that look as if they have paint spattered on them. He greets Dollard with a quiet hello. Like Simpson, Soderbergh is genuinely enthusiastic about Dollard's project. He believes *Young Americans* transcends Dollard's political message and is simply "riveting." He tells me, "I knew Pat was going to come back with something pure. I believe in Pat's sense of what's compelling."

Soderbergh works from a drab office fairly typical of those on studio back lots. He and Dollard sit opposite each other on threadbare lounge chairs. Soderbergh has often spoken of his need for anonymity in order to function as an artist—"So I can eavesdrop, sit in an airport behind somebody and listen to their conversation, spy on people and hear stuff in undiluted form." The drive for self-effacement seems to guide his social interaction as well.

Soderbergh's presence in the room is like this: he arranges his body on the chair, then somehow astrally projects himself into a corner of the ceiling to watch himself interacting with his guests. To a guest, being seated across from Soderbergh is like sitting in front of a two-way mirror. You know someone is there, but you can't quite make him out, just shadows and indecipherable movements. A throat clears. A chair scrapes. Dollard fidgets nervously, as if he's straining to rein in his normal impulses to do and say the wrong things. He appears paralyzed.

Soderbergh breaks the ice: "Did you bring the DVD?" His voice is as lively as a prerecorded message.

It turns out Dollard had a change of heart. He doesn't want Mark Cuban to have it. He wants Cuban to see it, but he doesn't trust him to possess it. "It's like laying my dick out," Dollard tells Soderbergh. "This guy could be in a hotel and might lose it."

Soderbergh reveals the faintest annoyance: "Pat, we should move fast on this."

"I'll fly to New York or something, and show it to him there," Dollard says.

Soderbergh shakes his head.

"We'll work something out." Dollard grins, as if oddly satisfied to have put a spanner in the works. I am seated between Dollard and Soderbergh, what would be the therapist's position if they were a couple in need of help, which they in fact are. I ask Soderbergh if he was surprised when he found out Dollard had gone to Iraq.

"No," Soderbergh says, "I've known him a long time. When you get a call from Pat you never know what to expect. It could be 'I just got married,' 'I'm making a new film,' 'I'm in Mexico getting an operation.' Pat is sort of an adrenaline junkie."

Dollard leans around me to bicker with Soderbergh. "I have no history of being the adrenaline junkie, an adventurer, blood-fucking-thirsty, or anything like that," he says.

"I'm saying you were looking for a change in your life," Soderbergh says.

"I didn't change intentionally by going to Iraq," Dollard argues. "It wasn't so much this noble thing where I was trying to change myself."

Soderbergh measures his words carefully. "I think you had created a circumstance last fall in which, if there was ever a time when going to Iraq would seem like an appealing thing, that was the time."

"It's really easy to say that," Dollard says, "but I was not going to go to Iraq and risk my life just to not deal with some hassles. It's almost insulting to, like, fucking say that."

Soderbergh sticks to his point. "Do you think if you'd been totally happy and things were great, would you still have gone to Iraq?"

"There was no fucking way I was running away." Dollard gives a feeble wave of his hand, running out of steam. "That's my argument and whatever."

Soderbergh turns to me, now animated. "When you look at Pat's narrative, which I think for Pat is probably really exciting, for a lot of the supporting people it can be crazy."

It's an odd reversal that he, the star director, would cast himself in the supporting role with his agent. I ask Soderbergh about his friendship with Dollard, and he says, "The formative years of our relationship were strange because we were really young"— Soderbergh twenty-three and Dollard twenty-two when they first met. "We had nothing in common with people in Hollywood," Soderbergh says, "no interest in the high-school aspects of the social life in Hollywood."

Dollard says, "We'd just sit around fucking talking about chicks."

"Yeah, we would," Soderbergh says, laughing. "We'd swap stories about fucking chicks." Soderbergh corrects himself. "I don't mean *fucking* chicks. I mean . . ."

"Steven, we would talk about *fucking* chicks," Dollard insists.

Soderbergh leans closer to me. "I was just so close to Pat's family. And of course because of the horrible event that happened, it stepped up the relationship with Pat several levels. It made us much closer."

Dollard twists in his chair. The subject of his sister's death makes him uncomfortable. He says, "Let's talk about whatever, dude."

Soderbergh ignores Dollard. He says, "There are certain people who have an integrity, whether you can articulate it or not." He pauses. "I guess I fall back to the word 'soul' for lack of a better term. It's just a feeling. You meet them and you have an instantaneous reaction to them. It's certainly the reaction I had when I met Ann."

Ann

It was Pat Dollard's great fortune and misfortune to have Ann as his sister. She was so good, when people talk about her, you wonder if canonization would do her justice. Robert Kennedy Jr. says, "She was beautiful and she was charming and you couldn't meet her without loving her." Larry Jackson, the president of Northern Arts Entertainment and former executive V.P. of acquisitions and coproductions at Miramax, says, "There was something magical about Ann. She had such a rosy expectation of what the world could become."

No small part of Ann's expectations were poured into her little brother, Pat. Their mother, Eva, says, "Ann was probably more of a mother figure to Pat than I was." Both Ann and Eva believed Pat would be the first in the family to attend college. After he dashed those hopes by dropping out of high school, Ann continued to try to guide him until finally hiring him as her assistant at Leading Artists.

Initially, Dollard cleaned up his act. Other agents nicknamed him "Beaver Cleaver." Ann began grooming him to become an agent, but Dollard began screwing off on the job. On the last workday before the Fourth of July weekend in 1988, Ann fired him. Dollard claims he had already decided he didn't want to be an agent and was relieved.

Two days later, Ann went horseback riding with friends and fell while crossing a field. Though it was a relatively minor fall, Ann wasn't wearing a helmet and her brain stem was crushed. She lingered for two days in the hospital before being removed from life support. Scott Kramer, a producer and close friend, arrived at the hospital about the same time as Dollard. "Pat literally couldn't bear to see her," Kramer recalls. "He began hitting his head on the wall to the point where we had to grab him and hold him down and take him out of the hospital."

Dollard says, "I was blown apart by the horror. I'll never forget trying to see Ann's face and looking down at these two massive purple lumps of flesh sticking out like eggs where her eyes were supposed to be. For years after, if I saw a hospital I would start crying."

Her death was no less mourned in Hollywood. Ann's memorial service, held at the Wilshire Ebell Theatre, became an industry event, drawing more than 700 people. Julia Phillips described the gathering in her 1991 book, *You'll Never Eat Lunch in This Town Again*, as "all of young Hollywood looking stricken." Stephen Stills sang, and eulogies were delivered by filmmaker Lionel Chetwynd and Robert Kennedy Jr., who later held a private ceremony with Eva at his home in Mount Kisco, New York, where they spread her ashes.

Among Ann's clients, Steven Soderbergh was one of the closest to her. When they met, Soderbergh was twenty-two and had just finished directing his Grammy-nominated documentary about the band Yes, but a couple years later he was drifting, uncertain of his next move. Their meeting wasn't so much a typical agent-client encounter but the start of an intense creative collaboration. Ann encouraged Soderbergh to continue work on his own scripts. Scott Kramer says, "Ann believed in Steven in such a way that it filled him." Production on *Sex, Lies, and Videotape* was about to begin when she died.

Soderbergh was devastated. "The idea of replacing Ann was something I couldn't contemplate," he says. He and a few of Ann's other clients decided to ask Pat to fill her shoes, which, Soderbergh explains, "felt like a way to process and transcend the awful thing that had happened." He approached Dollard and told him, "I want you to be my agent. If you won't be my agent, I just won't have an agent, because I can't."

"My family was ripped apart by Ann's death," says Dollard. "I felt like I had to take her job, to hold it together." At the time of her death, Ann hadn't yet come into her own as an agent. Had she lived another year, it would have been a different story.

In addition to Soderbergh, clients on her list such as screenwriters Michael Blake (*Dances with Wolves*) and Scott Frank (*Out of Sight, The Interpreter*) became major successes shortly after her death.

Inheriting most of Ann's list, Dollard had assumed his sister's life (much as the protagonist of his favorite film, *Barry Lyndon*, had risen by assuming the life of a deceased nobleman), and though he loved the trappings of success and power that came with it, he says it filled him with self-loathing. "I had this idea that I was going to be a subversive inside the system and do great things," he says. "But when they said, 'O.K., you're Steven Soderbergh's agent'—and suddenly Steven becomes the biggest filmmaker in the world in terms of the hype—all my greed and power lust and alcoholism kicked in." He adds, "It's like I went to hell when I became an agent, and I've been trying to fight my way out ever since."

The Dark Arts

A day after his meeting at William Morris, Dollard sits across from me at Kabuki, a restaurant near his apartment, eating a celebratory meal of ribs and flan, while unloading on his former profession. All the clichés are true, he tells me: Agents are "assholes, these morons who have an entirely superior attitude. They believe that they are better than everybody else because they think they've pulled off this scam, where they're doing the coolest thing in the world."

Though Dollard is loud and obnoxious in most matters, when it comes to discussing the dark Hollywood arts he practiced as an agent, he looks over his shoulders, as if expecting a squad of agent hit men to show up in their black suits, armed with bland smiles and Uzis. Leaning forward, he claims that, as much as he embraced every possible excess during his rise to the top, the life appalled him. "There was just so much fucking money and whores and power that people actually got bored with it," he says. "An agent I worked with—I guess he was bored out of his fucking mind—he trained his fucking Chihuahua to lick his balls and would have people come into his office to watch."

He continues: "There was another guy I worked with"— Dollard names a prominent manager—"who was such a pathological liar they did a whole intervention, like a twelve-step thing on him to get him to stop lying, hired fucking psychiatrists and brought, like, his mother and wife in to confront him in his office."

What troubles Dollard the most about his past as an agent were the business practices. "A lot of what we did was just your basic nasty, lying, backstabbing stuff that's part of the normal business world," he says. "But some of what we did, it's like *The Firm*, like over-billing." He explains that during the heyday of the speculative- script market, in the 90s, a form of over-billing commonly perpetrated against clients was cutting side deals with producers for secret commissions. He says, "You're talking about, like, white-collar crime here—virtually—about some of this stuff."

He adds, "I was taught when I was a kid that you're supposed to grow up and contribute to society and be a good person. No kid thinks, When I grow up, I want to fuck other people." He laughs. "I always used to tell myself it's all going to be worth it because eventually I'm going to make good films."

The Delivery Dude

A few days later Dollard phones with good news. One of the marines from *Young Americans* is visiting him. Sergeant Brandon Welsh greets me at the door of Dollard's apartment. Dressed in jeans and a knit surf shirt, Welsh is compactly built and fair-haired with a gravity to him which seems at odds with his boyish smile.

Dollard saunters in, looking unusually relaxed. His apartment has been transformed. There's an Oriental rug, velvet couches, African art on the walls, and a six-foot-tall statue of Buddha by the entry—all purchased out of hock with his recent cash windfall. Dollard drops onto a velvet chaise.

For Welsh the war is a deeply personal matter. Friends of his died in Iraq. Welsh nearly died. And he believes the fatal patrols undertaken by his unit helped stabilize the area and will in the long run improve the lives of Iraqis. Still, terrible things, which trouble him today, did happen. He tells me of one instance when his unit came under fire and, in the confusion that followed, marines may have ended up killing innocent civilians. Welsh shakes his head. "It was so fucked up."

"Welsh, you're a killer, and that's a good thing," Dollard says, walking up behind him and gesturing toward him like he is an exhibit in a science project. "Earlier today Welsh was having anxiety about killing and I had to tell him, 'Look, dude, appropriate killing is one of the most sacred and noble and greatest things to go on in the world. The world cannot survive without killing. Good killing is required to hold society together and to protect it. This involves nobility and sacrifice. It's about subsuming the self to the whole.' Welsh volunteered to kill on behalf of our society. That is a good, noble thing."

I point out that Welsh's anxiety was about killing innocent people.

"Chaotic and terrible and tragic things are just part and parcel of the natural laws of war," Dollard says, pacing. "War is its own state of being. It's like another planet, Planet War. And the people who live on Planet Peace read about the terrible things that happen on Planet War—friendly fire, innocents killed—and are shocked. They naturally say we need to punish these boys"—Dollard points to Welsh—"because they're not playing by the rules of civilization. The point is these are two worlds, each with their own set of natural laws. And they just don't get it. Everything that's happening in Iraq is completely in line with the rules of war state."

Welsh runs his hands through his hair, worn out by Dollard's frenetic arguing. "I'm fucking hungry," Welsh says. "You said we were going to get takeout."

"We can't call on my phone," Dollard says. "You've got to make the fucking call on your fucking phone."

Dollard explains the problem: His favorite delivery place is a nearby Brazilian restaurant, but a couple of nights ago he had a run-in with the delivery dude. Dollard ordered a meal, and the delivery dude showed up more than an hour late. Dollard demanded the delivery dude give him his chocolate cake for free, but he refused. Dollard sent him packing. He fears the restaurant won't deliver to his address. The plan is for Welsh to have the food delivered to the security guard in the lobby.

But Welsh runs into an unforeseen glitch. The woman taking our order doesn't understand English very well. He tells her we are at the building on the corner of Sunset and Vine, but she doesn't understand. Welsh holds the phone up. We hear the heavily accented voice of the woman on the other end. "Vane?" she asks. "Where is Vane Street?"

Dollard grabs the phone and shouts, "Vine, you dumb bitch!" He throws the phone across the room. Welsh collapses, laughing. Dollard broods. "There are all these people in this town I've been waiting to get back at. It's going to start now."

Dollard suggests the three of us go to the restaurant, hide out in the parking lot until closing time, and fuck up the delivery dude. "This whole war started with him," Dollard says. "Fucking delivery dude was two hours late and wouldn't comp me with a $4 slice of chocolate cake on a $50 order."

Welsh punches his fist into the palm of his hand. "I'm down." (Welsh later says he wasn't serious.)

Dollard rushes to the front door, then hesitates. "The thing is, this restaurant has gotten me through so many binges."

They decide not to fuck up the delivery guy, and instead we go to the 101 Coffee Shop. Welsh leaves the next day.

American Jihadi

In mid-September, Dollard screens *Young Americans* for Bob Greenblatt, the president of entertainment for Showtime. Afterward, Dollard leaves a message for me: "Hey. Dude. They fucking loved it, man. I was fucking shocked. They watched the whole thing. First thing out of Greenblatt's mouth: 'These marines are movie stars!'"

The next day I visit. He greets me at the door drinking root beer and ice cream from an enormous bowl. "You want a root-beer float?" he asks, nodding toward a quart of Häagen-Dazs vanilla melting on the counter. Dollard admits last night was a little rough. After the fantastic news from Showtime, he learned of a setback in his custody battle for his daughter. Dollard is particularly incensed that his ex-wife Alicia has been taking their daughter to Robert Evans's house. Dollard fumes, "Alicia tells me that Bob bought a fucking bicycle for her." (Evans recalls Alicia bringing her daughter to his home a few times, but laughs at the suggestion he bought her a bicycle.)

He stayed up all night writing letters to a therapist and a lawyer involved in his custody battle. Dollard insists I read some of these communications. He says, "You will uncover the fact that I am not a paranoid schizophrenic about all of these people. But I am right. They are all psychopaths."

I have scarcely digested this letter when Dollard leads me into the editing room to reveal his next inspiration. The editing system is set up against the back wall of the bedroom. Along the opposite wall is a child's bed, with an ornate iron frame and a ruffled cover, which was his daughter's in his old home and is set up for a visit from her that never happens. I sit on the bed as Dollard plays jihadi videos: YouTube-quality clips made by insurgents to showcase attacks on Americans, beheadings, and other violent doings. Designed to recruit young men into the insurgency, many are set to jihadi hip-hop. Watching them, Dollard becomes outraged (even as I am struck by how similar they are to his own film). "This is the Islamo-fascist death machine at work," he says. "This is the breath of Darth Vader."

Dollard has long conceived of his film as a work of guerrilla cinema, a sort of American version of a jihad video to galvanize the domestic audience. But recently the videos have inspired him further. Dollard wants to launch an anti-jihadi action cell in the West. He explains, "This will be an educational, activism, and political organization dedicated to waging final war on modern jihadism. There will be a manifesto, guides for maintaining political pressure in favor of the overthrow of the Syrian and Iranian governments. Aggressive militarism in support of these goals will generally be encouraged, dependent on current conditions within the target nations and regimes."

He tells me that he has already registered the domain name, jihadikiller.com, then shows me a note to his business manager, Evan Bell, telling him to incorporate a business named Jihadi Killer, Inc.

(Dollard forwards me the e-mail from Bell responding to his request: "Pat you sure you want this name? . . . I do think it is a mistake.")

I leave at about ten as a delivery guy shows up from a corner store with cigarettes and more root beer and vanilla ice cream. "You sure you don't want a root-beer float?" Dollard asks, grabbing his bowl from the sink.

The Buddy System

A few days later, Dollard calls, sounding rattled, to tell me that the night before "the Devil was back." Driving alone in Hollywood, he was seized by a powerful urge to get loaded. Though he resisted, he says that since then he's "just felt literally sick."

Dollard assures me he's taken steps to maintain his sobriety. He's having a young man he met in rehab move in with him. "I'm doing it just like the marines," he says. "I'm going on the buddy system."

Dollard describes his new roommate as a "metrosexual gangbanger." Josiah Hernandez is twenty-two and slight of stature, about five two, but with eyes so large his face looks like that of an anime character. His dark hair is fragrantly pomaded. He dresses like any kid in a low-rent Hollywood club—black Skechers, a dark striped shirt, and pressed jeans worn so low his plaid boxers fluff out like feathers. When I meet him at Dollard's place, Josiah shakes my hand, grinning. His smile is so big it makes his eyes squint.

Before he and Dollard met at Impact House, in May, Josiah had recently finished serving three and a half years in prison for armed robbery. "Josiah has a long history of occasionally going crazy and stabbing people," Dollard explains, eyeing the young man with a look of paternal pride.

Josiah had been folding Dollard's laundry on the coffee table when he let me in. In addition to serving as Dollard's sobriety helpmate, he works around the house as a sort of manservant (while also working as a busboy at Hamburger Hamlet). Josiah fetches me a drink, then resumes sorting Dollard's socks. He tells me about his past.

"I used to be a stickup kid, eh?" He finishes his sentences with an "eh?" like Canadians do, but in L.A. it's part of the *cholo* slang. "Fifteen years old, eh? Fucking tweaked out on meth, eh? My homey and me would just rob people on the street."

Josiah was an industrious petty criminal, but also an unlucky one. He was in and out of various youth facilities until the age of eighteen, when the state of California sent him to prison. After his release, seven months earlier, he began smoking meth again, fell in with his old homeys, and was arrested and charged with possession of stolen checks. He is out now on bail, pending trial. If convicted, he could face another four years in prison.

Josiah claims he is a changed man since going to rehab and meeting Dollard. "I fucking take responsibility for my actions," he says. "They want to throw me back in prison, so be it, eh? But if I stay out, I've got a new life now. I'm fucking clean, eh? I work for Pat fucking Dollard. I'm a movie assistant."

Dollard gazes affectionately at Josiah. "For the first time in probably six, eight years, Josiah's clean and sober. He's working for me and flourishing at Hamburger Hamlet. He's leading a really good, squared-away life. I trust Josiah completely."

There's no more compelling evidence of his trust than the large sums of cash piled on the coffee table where Josiah is sorting laundry. Owing to Dollard's pronounced fear of banks, he prefers to keep his money in liquid form. One-hundred-dollar bills are bundled in $10,000 bricks, which Josiah delicately brushes aside as he stacks the socks.

Josiah says when he met Dollard—whom the staff nicknamed "Saddam Manson" due to his crazed appearance and wild talk of Iraq—he "had no idea Pat was a rich Hollywood agent."

Dollard checked himself out of Impact ahead of Josiah. The day Josiah left, Dollard picked him up and drove him to his father's house. "I told Josiah's father I was adopting him," Dollard says. "He turned Josiah over to me." Though Dollard's claim has no legal standing whatsoever, Josiah enthusiastically nods.

Dollard himself had no money or place to go. He and Josiah spent a weekend sleeping at Dollard's mother's house, then split up. But the two have kept tabs on each other ever since. In the wake of Dollard's recent scare over using drugs, both feel it's prudent to live together.

For Josiah, the move comes at a convenient time. As he explains it, owing to his incredible good looks, charm, and sexual prowess, he has been experiencing female trouble. Until a couple of days ago he had been living with a girlfriend. But, according to Josiah, she had recently grown unreasonable. "Dumb bitch didn't want me seeing other bitches," Josiah says. Their contretemps grew to a head. The other morning Josiah awakened to find himself being held prisoner. "Bitch took all my clothes, told me I couldn't leave," Josiah says. "I don't hit bitches. But I said, 'You don't give me my clothes, I'm gonna kick the shit out of you, bitch.'"

"Tell him about the bitch you fucked up in seventh grade," Dollard says, egging him on.

"It only happened one time," Josiah says. "In elementary school there was this bitch, she was so big she used to fuck up the dudes."

Although he was the smallest boy in his grade, Josiah stood up to the giant bully girl, telling her he wasn't afraid. "Bam!" Josiah says. "Bitch hit me in the face. Tore off my shark-tooth necklace."

Josiah reenacts the fight, throwing kicks and punches to demonstrate how he felled her. "I got that big bitch down and whaled on her, eh?" Josiah straddles an imaginary human on the floor and pummels. "Boom, boom, boom," he says. "Bitch was all lumped up and drooling."

．　　　．　　　．

Warmed up by the fight tale, Josiah dances across the room, recounting his years of being the littlest guy in youth camps, county jail, and then prison, but who was always ready to throw *chingasos* with the big *vatos*. He drops onto a couch, seemingly exhausted. "I been fighting my whole life."

Josiah points to Dollard. "But thanks to this dick, for the first time I got a reason to stay clean." Josiah's mouth wobbles. He chokes back tears, thumping his chest to regain composure. "This motherfucker's been there for me."

Dollard turns to me. "We're friends against all probability. When we met at Impact, we were a gangbanger and a Hollywood agent. It was funny because Josiah came from this hard prison culture and yet he became my vassal. Everyone thought he was my bitch."

"I wasn't his bitch, eh?" Josiah clarifies.

"Josiah," Dollard explains, "in the sense that I was your friend and protector, you were my bitch."

"I wasn't your fucking bitch." Josiah's face darkens.

"Josiah, you are my lieutenant. I am the general." Dollard gestures to the apartment. "Someday, you will inherit everything."

On Fire with Sobriety

September 19, 2005. I accompany Dollard to a screening of his film for a small company seeking content for Spike TV. Dollard meets the head of the firm's film division—a tall, wiry, cerebral-seeming man whom Dollard nicknames "Spock"—in a spacious Beverly Hills suite. A few minutes into the screening, things start to go badly when Spock leaps from his couch to turn down the obscenity-laden soundtrack. "They can hear this outside," he says.

Dollard immediately jumps from his seat and twists the volume up. To my astonishment, the two go back and forth like this until Spock finally has enough. He hits the pause button and stands blocking the equipment from any more interference from Dollard. "This is great," Spock says through a tight grin, "but I'm having trouble getting my head around it."

"This is cinéma vérité," Dollard says, standing up, beginning to rant. I time Dollard on my watch. He talks for twelve straight minutes. The cords on his neck pop out. Spit flies. By the end of the tirade he paces, talking about whores in Iraq, robbing pharmacies, liberals, Valium. He finally sputters to a stop.

Spock breaks the silence. "I don't even know how we could market this."

"I don't want you to market it." Dollard yells, "I don't want an audience talked into watching this by marketing tricks. Fuck that."

Spock shakes Dollard's hand. "The thing is, I totally respect you as an artist."

Careening down Wilshire Boulevard minutes later, Dollard grouses, "He turned my shit off. You do not tell the artist to turn his shit off early." Then his face brightens with inspiration. "Let's take $10,000, go to Las Vegas, get a bunch of hookers and blow, and have fun for a few days."

"What makes you think you'd be able to stop?" I ask.

"What we'll do is hire a couple of big niggers to shut us down at the end of five days and put us in suitcases and bring us home."

Dollard catches me writing down the word "nigger" in my notes.

"I can say that word," he says. "I'm half Puerto Rican, and if I'm Puerto Rican, then I'm a nigger. End of story."

He also insists for the record that he has no desire to actually get high, that he is merely joking. "The fact is Josiah and I are on fire with sobriety."

Megan

It seems the gods do favor Pat Dollard. Mike Simpson informs him that the HBO executives who saw the film in L.A. have recommended it to the head of the documentary division in New York, Sheila Nevins, arguably the single most influential person in America in the realm of documentary. The plan is for Dollard to fly to New York for a screening.

After sharing this news with me, Dollard says, "I called Megan"—his fourth wife, who left him a year ago. "I told her I'm going to be getting eight million bucks. I told her I'd pay her $10,000 if she'd come over here and suck my dick."

"Calling me up and saying disgusting things like that to me is Pat's idea of a joke," Megan tells me when we meet a few days later. She is twenty-five, tall and blonde, and speaks in a silky Louisiana accent. We sit outdoors at a restaurant near Dollard's apartment. He has invited her over to watch his film. She has agreed to go only because she needs to pick up papers related to their divorce.

When I sit down, Megan is reading a cheap romance novel. "One of my vices," says Megan, who has been known to often carry one in her purse. But her worst vice, she allows, is still caring about her soon-to-be ex-husband.

From the moment Megan met Dollard it was as if his almost supernaturally good luck was working on her, only in reverse. She was twenty-one, about to graduate from college in Baton Rouge, when early one evening she burned down her apartment trying to heat potpourri on the stove—something she'd read about in a magazine article. After the firemen left, Megan walked to the bar where she worked part-time as a waitress to commiserate with some coworkers, who plied her with free drinks. Soon she was plastered. Then her girlfriend pointed out that there was a celebrity in the bar, Billy Bob Thornton, who was in town filming.

Megan's friend dared her to say hello. At that moment Billy Bob happened to be sharing a cigarette with his former agent, Pat Dollard, who was in town visiting his ex-wife, Alicia. Megan approached Billy Bob and said, "I'm Megan. Want to drink some martinis with me?"

Billy Bob declined the invitation. He was due to pick up Angelina Jolie at the airport and excused himself. Megan was alone with Dollard. She admits that by this point "I was too drunk to know anything." (Dollard claims, "Megan was so drunk she thought I was Billy Bob.") All Megan knows is that when she woke up the next day she was smitten. A couple months later, they flew to Las Vegas, where Soderbergh had just wrapped the location shooting for *Ocean's Eleven* at the Bellagio, where Dollard was comped a suite. According to Megan, "Our second night there Pat was like, 'Hey, you want to marry me?' and I was like, 'Yeah,' and we got married at the Little White Wedding Chapel."

A few days later she moved into Dollard's Bel Air home. "My first week in L.A.," Megan says, "I met Brad Pitt and George

Clooney. Pat introduced us on the *Ocean's Eleven* set, and Brad gave me this knowing look and said, 'I've heard a lot about you.' And I was like, Holy shit, Brad Pitt has heard about me? Then I went to Cannes with Pat, and I hung out with Julia Roberts. I would call my friends back home every night and I'd be like, 'Guess who I just met tonight.'"

Megan tamps out her cigarette. "It was very surreal, for sure." She adds, "I grew up with very little, and Pat offered me this total fantasy of staying at home, not working, and raising children."

The fantasy quickly bumped into the realities of his addictions. Initially, Megan was prepared to help. She encouraged him to attend A.A. meetings and opened their home to informal gatherings of recovering addicts. It didn't work. Once, she says, she saw "a vagrant walking around" outside the house who turned out to be "Pat's drug dealer leaving coke underneath the rocks."

The relationship went terminal soon after Dollard began "sponsoring"—serving as a twelve-step adviser to—a young, recovering female crack addict he'd met at an A.A. meeting. "Pat told me it would help him stay sober if he was helping another addict," Megan explains. Dollard got his "sponsee" a job and moved her into their house. Megan moved out and later discovered e-mails Dollard had written his "sponsee" in which he suggested that both their lives would be better off if she killed Megan. (Dollard says, "Anyone who knows me knows I was only joking.") As the controversy played out, Dollard made his first trip to Iraq.

Megan now works as a waitress at a swanky Sunset hotel. As a result of her three years of marriage to Dollard, she is left with tens of thousands of dollars in debts. "Pat told me when we first got married that it would help build my credit if we put everything in my name," Megan says as we enter his building. "As awful as this sounds," she confesses, "sometimes I wish he was dead."

Dollard greets us at the door. He is neatly shaved. The living room is pristine. Josiah kneels in front of a TV Dollard purchased for him and is playing *Hitman 2*, a game he likes because "it teaches you how to become a professional killer."

"Is this your new little slave?" Megan says, nodding toward Josiah. She says to me, "Pat always manages to get a little slave. Like I was."

Dollard laughs indulgently and corrals her into the editing room for her viewing of *Young Americans*. Megan sits on the bed and watches the first few minutes with a stony expression. Then she starts to sob.

"Jesus, they're so young," she says of the Marines on-screen. "They're like the boys I went to school with."

"I told you this was good," Dollard says.

"Have you talked to your mother?" Megan asks. "You need to call her."

"How's that fucking bitch?" Dollard says.

"You don't talk about your mother that way."

"Watch me—I just did. I just did."

"Your mother is the most wonderful woman that I've ever met," Megan says. "I want to punch you in the face right now."

She sits up and inadvertently knocks over an ashtray concealed under the blanket on the bed. She leaps up, brushing ashes from her jeans. "This brings back memories," she says, growing angry. "This is definitely why I left you."

"You left because you're a quitter," Dollard says.

"I left because you are an alcoholic and you won't get help," Megan says.

"You didn't stick around like Bill Wilson's wife," Dollard says, referring to the wife of the founder of A.A. "If Bill Wilson's wife hadn't stuck by his side when he was drinking there would be no A.A."

"My husband was hiring hookers on my credit card—to buy coke [for him]," Megan says to me.

She walks to the door. Dollard hurries after her and hands her the papers he promised her. She kisses him on the cheek and leaves.

Dollard stares at the door. "This really hurts," he says. "Am I over her? Maybe not. But the question with having a woman is, to what extent do I want to continue to engage with civilization?"

"Jesus Christ, Pat," Josiah says, still playing *Hitman 2*. "You said she was hot, eh? But she's really fucking hot."

The Jesus Room

Dollard's screening with Sheila Nevins, in New York, is scheduled for mid-October. During the two weeks before his scheduled departure, his behavior becomes increasingly bizarre. He phones early one morning and says, "I need your help."

I ask him what's going on.

"I'm taking steps," he says, "but they ain't *the* 12 steps." He won't explain any further, because he feels it's unsafe to talk on the phone. A couple hours later he shows up at my apartment. There is a massive safe in the back of his Hummer. All his money is in there, he tells me. He plans to hide it. To that end, he needs to leave his cell phone at my house so no one will track him while he's on his mission. Several days later he phones from a new telephone number and leaves a message: "Driving on Washington Boulevard I clutch the receipt for my new .45-caliber Glock and the feeling that I will be very disappointed if I die before I kill jihadis with this gun."

It turns out that in the state of California people who have been taken into custody and held for psychiatric evaluation and determined to be a danger to self and others, as Dollard has, are ineligible to purchase firearms for the next five years. Later, when the gun shop gives Dollard his money back, he calls: "Yo, call me as soon as you get this, please. I need to know if you have a clean record in California, and if you could purchase guns. I will pay you."

I decline the offer.

Dollard is eager for me to accompany him to New York and witness what he expects will be his triumphant screening for HBO. The day we are to fly out, a girl named Sunshine (I've changed her name) phones and introduces herself as one of Pat Dollard's assistants. She is calling to arrange the final details of our flight. An hour later Dollard phones to say his new assistant will be flying to New York with us. "Oh, yeah," he adds. "Sunshine will be smoking meth."

The two never show up for the flight.

Josiah phones the next morning from New York. He has taken it upon himself to rescue Dollard's appointment with Nevins by hand-delivering the screener DVD. He took the red-eye to New York—his first time on an airplane and his first trip outside of California. When he checked into the Times Square Quality Inn moments before phoning me, something happened that totally tripped him out. The hotel put him in room 316. "Can you fucking believe it?" Josiah shouts. "I'm in 316, the Jesus room. That's who I am. My middle name is Jesus."

I tell Josiah I don't get the relationship between the number 316 and Jesus.

"God so loved the world that he gave his only begotten son," Josiah says, quoting the Scriptures. "John 3:16."

"Have you guys been smoking meth?" I ask.

"Yeah, I ain't going to lie," Josiah answers. "Pat's fucked up. He's fucking psychotic, fucking psycho, fucking, a fucking weirdo. We all are, you know?"

Dollard phones minutes after Josiah hangs up. Unlike Josiah, Dollard sounds supremely relaxed, groggy, maybe a little drunk. He informs me that he was unable to fly to New York because he has fallen in love with Sunshine. "She has a golden heart," he tells me.

There is a complication. Sunshine is Josiah's girlfriend, one who, at times, meant a great deal to him. "This is rough for Josiah," Dollard says. "She came here to see him and . . ." He whispers. "What happened between us had to happen. She's the one."

I ask him why he skipped his meeting in New York, and he cuts me off. "Dude, I can't talk right now. I'm having my dick sucked."

No Redemption

Auto Focus, the film that Dollard produced and Paul Schrader directed, is about *Hogan's Heroes* star Bob Crane's self-destruction through his addiction to sex as well as the murky homoeroticism of his relationship with a hanger-on who films Crane's exploits with women and ultimately beats him to death with a camera tripod. The film did not do well at the box office, but Schrader remains pleased with his collaboration with Dollard. "He wasn't scared about doing stuff that may offend people," Schrader tells me. "I knew that if we did something warped he would get it." Despite its lackluster reception, Schrader believes the film stands as a pure story, unencumbered by hack studio convention, which he attributes in part to Dollard's influence. "Pat was attracted to the idea that we just weren't going to redeem or glorify our main character. That this was the story of the life of an extremist, what happens if you release the reins on a normal powerful passion and let the horse run. Will you achieve some kind of balance, or will it break you apart?"

Unlike the fictionalization of Bob Crane's life in *Auto Focus*, Dollard since I have known him has been obsessed with redemption. This was the whole point of going to Iraq. While I'm not totally surprised that he has apparently gone out on a bender, I hadn't expected he would so casually skip the all-important meeting with Nevins. As a practical matter it also seems potentially dangerous to be having sex with the girlfriend of a violent felon.

Josiah phones after delivering the film to Nevins's apartment. "There I was, eh, in this rich bitch's apartment," Josiah says. "These broads were fucking all into me, saying how handsome I am. They thought me and Pat were gay. I was all 'Wait, I know I'm fucking fine, eh? But that doesn't mean I have to be gay and shit.'" Josiah states for the record, "Gay is not my position."

I ask Josiah what's going on with Dollard and his girlfriend. "He's fucking fucking her," he says. Josiah admits this was initially hard for him to take. He and Sunshine have known each other for several years. "Then I got busted and went to prison and she wrote me, giving me hope, 'cause she was the only broad there for me," Josiah says.

But when Sunshine, who hadn't seen Josiah in months, showed up at Dollard's apartment several days ago, she turned the tables. She refused to have sex with him and, as Josiah saw it, was trying to make him jealous by flirting with Dollard. "It hurt, eh, 'cause I fucking love that girl."

About this time, Josiah says, he and Dollard, then Sunshine, began smoking meth. Soon, Dollard advised Josiah on the best way to handle the situation with Sunshine. Josiah says, "Pat told me she was trying to play a game on me." Dollard gave Josiah a pep talk to remind him who he is: "I'm the pimp. I'm the one that plays the games. She thinks she's playing me? I'll use her to my fucking advantage. So I pimped her out." Josiah laughs. "Last night he gave me $5,000. She got fucked, and I got paid."

When I later speak with Dollard, he laughs off the notion that he talked Josiah into pimping his girlfriend to him. "The fact is," Dollard says, "Josiah can't stop watching her fuck me." Dollard informs me that Josiah filmed him as he had sex with his girlfriend.

I point out to Dollard that he has now entered the realm of *Auto Focus.* He says, "The difference is in *Auto Focus* the girls Bob Crane was fucking were just girls, but Josiah's filming me fucking the love of his life." Dollard laughs. "People get killed over this."

Three Days

Mike Simpson phones me in the midst of this to ask how my story on Dollard is going. I don't want to divulge anything that will screw up Dollard's prospects at William Morris. Moreover, there's something so strangely decent about Mike Simpson, so at odds with Dollard's portrayals of agents as whoremongering, borderline white-collar criminals, I'm at a loss to say anything. I tell him Pat is certainly an interesting subject. "We're hearing such good things about his project at Showtime and now HBO," Simpson says, sounding pleased. "Pat is really coming into his own as a filmmaker."

On an unseasonably hot October afternoon Dollard invites me to his apartment to show me something. Josiah greets me outside the door. He asks if I've come alone. Dollard is afraid I might have brought his mother. Ever since the first time his family had the police take him to the psych ward, he's grown wary. (As he once told me, "They figured out they could pick up the phone, and, boom, I'm in a mental hospital. It fucking sucks, dude.") I assure Josiah I've come alone.

The apartment is a rat's nest. One couch is overturned. Cigarette butts are burned into the carpet. Tear-gas grenades—part of an arms cache Dollard hoped to acquire to launch his anti-jihadi network—are scattered on the floor. The bathroom looks like someone skinned a deer in it: everything is covered in tufts of hair and blood from Dollard's effort to cut off the beard that grew during the past couple of weeks.

Dollard enters in shorts and sandals, drinking vodka and cranberry juice from a plastic cup. "I'm tapering down," he says. "This is medicine."

Gesturing to the wrecked apartment, Dollard attempts a joke. "I go on a drug binge for ten days, and when I come out of it I find out my agents have done less work than I have."

Dollard boasts he has just completed a new film which he plans to send to Sheila Nevins. "This is the woman who is the grande dame of interesting, weird documentaries. Part of what I am trying to sell them is that I am a madman—this, quote, insane genius."

"It's called *Three Days*," says Josiah, kneeling at the coffee table and playing with a large hunting knife.

Dollard says, "I want to send *Three Days* to Sheila as an explanation as to why I missed my meeting with her." He adds that *Three Days* may be one of the greatest films ever made, whose meaning is, well . . . I just have to watch it.

I sit on the tiny bed in the editing room. Josiah is next to me, his hunting knife now sheathed. Dollard hunches by the monitor and starts the film. The face of a girl with long black hair fills the screen. Sunshine. Though she is of legal age, she speaks in a child's voice, plaintive and quavering, as Dollard, still offscreen, barks at her, "What's your job on the team?"

She giggles. "To sexually satisfy you and clean the house."

Dollard enters the frame, totally nude, a decrepit satyr. A montage ensues of him performing various sex acts with her, intercut with close-ups of the girl smoking a glass pipe. There is unintended comedy: while Dollard is having sex with her on the couch, it catches fire, and the two fail to notice until flames engulf their feet. There is intended comedy: Dollard performs anal sex with her while simultaneously talking on the phone with an agent at William Morris.

In the film, Josiah, who serves as cameraman, does not have sex with Sunshine. He later explained that he enjoyed watching it and pleasuring himself. His most significant on-screen presence is to lean close to Sunshine and offer encouragements: "What's his name? Say Pat. You're fucking a rich man with accomplishments, not a fucking loser."

In the room with me, Dollard and Josiah howl and tap knuckles. I stand up.

Dollard shoots me an annoyed glance. "You have to pay attention," he says. "You're going to miss that this is not really a porn film."

The film fades to black. Jim Morrison comes across the loudspeakers singing "The End." Dollard narrates in the background about immortality, death, and the horrors he witnessed in Iraq. It cuts to Dollard readying to make his money shot on Sunshine.

In *Auto Focus*, when Bob Crane and his sidekick watch their homemade porn together, they masturbate. Thankfully, Dollard takes a different route. He turns to Josiah, speaking excitedly. "You love this girl, Josiah. But you know what? You wandered off into a room by yourself to fucking jerk off to a tape of her fucking somebody else. That's who we are. That's who people are! They're scumbags!"

"This is so fucked up," Josiah shouts, "but I like it."

"Exactly, dude!" Dollard claps his hands, like a teacher whose pupil is about to achieve satori. "That's what I told you! That's the whole point to everything around here, with this whole thing, all of it, beyond! It's what everything in my life is about. It's about finding all those truths and those fucking experiences that other people just don't get."

Josiah seems paralyzed, staring at the screen, his huge eyes unblinking. "This is so fucked up," he repeats.

"That's what we do here," Dollard says, pounding the editing table. "We take everything to its furthest limits. We go out. We go get in cars. We fucking kill people. We kill terrorists."

I'm guessing that Dollard has veered into the realm of his jihadi-killer fantasies, or that he is in some sort of meth psychosis. The final moments of the film play. Dollard stares at the decrepit-satyr version of himself on-screen executing the money shot. When it's over, he turns to me. "So what do you think?"

All I can think of is Ben Stiller's line in *Meet the Parents* after Robert De Niro asks Stiller for his reaction to the awful poem he reads about his deceased mother. "Wow," I say. "Your film contains a lot of information." I urge Dollard not to send it to HBO.

"Our taste may be too cutting-edge, too extreme." Despite these reservations, Dollard stands. "We need to film Sunshine more." He tells Josiah to phone her and ask her to come back over. It turns out Sunshine has a responsible day job. Josiah reaches her, but she refuses to come over. Dollard takes the phone and pleads, "We'll make right on the mistake from when you were here the last time. I promise."

He hangs up and drops onto the partially burned couch in the living room. "Josiah," he says, "we need to reconcile ourselves to the fact that she may not be coming back."

The Geographic Cure

Dollard does not get a deal for *Young Americans*. Nor does he send Nevins a copy of *Three Days*. He drops out of sight for nearly a month. About a week before Thanksgiving he resurfaces in a phone message: "Where you been, dude? I'm having the D.T.'s—it's awesome. Give me a call. Bye."

We speak. "I feel like suicide, or going into a hospital," he tells me. Dollard says he nearly died recently while smoking meth. "I couldn't move. It was like my body had turned to ice." He mourns wrecking the prospects of his film, then adds, "I failed Josiah in all of this." A few days ago Josiah totaled the Humvee, and Dollard kicked him out. (Dollard subsequently found an attorney and helped pay nearly $5,000 to defend Josiah in his outstanding case, but in March 2006, he was convicted of receiving stolen property and sent back to prison with a four-year sentence.) "Do you think you could help get me to a hospital or something?" Dollard asks.

I call Impact House, and they agree to take Dollard back. I don't reach him again until after midnight. I am about to deliver the good news when Dollard cuts me off. "I need a favor," Dollard says. He informs me that he e-mailed a Marine Corps public-affairs officer who offered him an embed spot if he could get to Kuwait in the next seventy-two hours. The only problem is Dollard's credit card is maxed out and he can't buy tickets. He wants to know if he can use my credit card to buy the tickets. "What am I going to do in a rehab?" Dollard asks. "I'm going to feel like shit no matter where I am. I'd rather be lying in a hole in Iraq than in a bed somewhere in L.A."

Brian Michael Jenkins, a counterterrorism analyst with Rand, has argued, like other experts in his field, that a primary lure of jihad in radical Islam is the notion that war offers "purification." I am beginning to think that it's much the same for Dollard in his indomitable drive to purge himself of his afflictions.

I give him my credit-card number. In recovery-speak, people might say I'm "enabling" the "untreated alcoholic" by helping him run away from his troubles with a "geographic cure." I know this because I have had my own struggles with drugs and alcohol. It's probably why I like Dollard, feel a kinship with him in his madness. Unlike him, I haven't had bad experiences with people in twelve-step meetings. But from what I have seen you just can't force it on someone. The way I look at it, if the untreated alcoholic wants to take his geographic cure by going to Iraq, that's his business.

The night before Thanksgiving a taxi delivers him to my apartment. Dollard wants to say good-bye. He gets out of the cab lugging his camera equipment, a few changes of underwear, and a jacket, all packed in several shopping bags. I give him an old suitcase. Stuffing his possessions into it, Dollard laughs, watching how badly his hands shake. He is totally blind in his right eye from his cataract, and the contact lens in his left eye—which he hasn't removed for more than six months—is infected. He nearly tumbles down the steps when he walks out my door. The apartment below mine belongs to a devout Mormon woman, who every year puts up a large fir tree in her window facing the courtyard. The tree is up, but not yet decorated. My neighbor opens her door as Dollard clatters past. "Hey, it's fucking Christmas," he tells her. "Put some shit on your tree."

I yell after him, "It's Thanksgiving, Pat, not Christmas."

"Fuck it, dude. Whatever."

The Third Act

The Marine Corps sends Dollard to Ramadi. After the relatively calm national elections on December 15, 2005, a new wave of insurgent attacks erupts in Ramadi, making it one of the most dangerous cities in Iraq for U.S. troops. The media largely ignore the city. Dollard becomes one of the few Western journalists to continuously cover the battle for the city throughout the winter and early spring of 2006.

Dollard is the first reporter on the scene on January 5, 2006, when insurgents bomb a recruitment center for Iraqi police. An estimated forty men are killed and eighty wounded. Lieutenant Aaron Autry, a marine platoon commander who arrived with

Dollard at the blast site, says, "We were the first ones at the scene, where a formation of Iraqis had been blown apart. Body parts were everywhere. Pat was really struggling with what we were seeing. We both were, but Pat was doing his job filming. On that day, he became part of our platoon like any other marine."

This time in Iraq, Dollard does not engage in the antics that had so entertained and enraged troops on his first tour. In the course of nearly five months, Dollard films marines on well over 200 combat patrols. Says Lieutenant Autry, "Nobody covered the war like he did."

While in Iraq, Dollard sends me an e-mail, revisiting his Hollywood past:

> I was like a junky who never kicked because someone kept throwing me a bag of heroin every Friday Who loves you, baby? If you're an agent, you really don't want to know the answer. . . . You ever watch terrified 55 year-old men begging for praise every week in a staff meeting . . . ? It's not pretty. Any Hollywood agent or executive whwo criticizes my career doesn't understand how much of a geek they sound like. "He wasn't really one of us." No shit, Maynard, I didn't want to be a geek like you. Go back to your cappuccino, auto-fellatio, and faux tough-guy posturing. It took me forever to escape, and that's arguably pathetic, but I have the whole third act of my life left, and there's an old Hollywood maxim: The first two acts of a movie can suck, but if the third act rocks, everyone leaves the theater saying, "Damn, that was a great movie."

All of Dollard's efforts seem geared toward that third act. When he survives the February 18 bombing that killed two marines, Dollard continues to join patrols, surviving yet another vehicle bombing on March 9. At the ceremony troops hold in

Iraq for their brother marines killed there, Dollard is given a place of respect.

Homecoming

In late March, Dollard flies home with the marines. An ex-girlfriend of Dollard's drives to the base at Twenty-Nine Palms, California, to join military families at the welcoming ceremony. Dollard had phoned her asking if she would take him back to L.A., promising that he had cleaned up his act. "The parents of the boy Pat was with when he died met him and were hugging him and it was so powerful," she says. "Then we went out to a restaurant and Pat started drinking and told me he wasn't coming back to L.A., and he disappeared."

In April he calls me from an undisclosed location. Dollard says he is not doing well, and insists he must tell me about the February 18 bombing which killed Second Lieutenant Almar L. Fitzgerald, twenty-three, and Corporal Matthew D. Conley, twenty-one. Dollard says he was in the lead Humvee of a patrol going through Ramadi when a bomb hit the Humvee behind his. The patrol stopped. Nobody could see what was going on, because it was the middle of the night and the city, with no electricity, was pitch-black. Adding to the confusion, the Marines' radios stopped working. Lieutenant Fitzgerald, the officer seated next to Dollard, ordered Conley, the radioman, to exit the vehicle and see what was going on with the Humvee behind them that had just been hit. As Conley stepped out, insurgents detonated a second bomb buried in the asphalt, underneath their Humvee. Conley was blown to pieces. Dollard's armored door flew open, and he was thrown from the Humvee. A four-inch piece of shrapnel had penetrated his calf muscle, and he was covered in diesel fuel, but he was otherwise O.K. As insurgents began to rake the area with machine-gun fire, he crawled back to the crumpled, smoking Humvee and climbed inside for cover.

I ask him what happened to Fitzgerald. "He was next to me," Dollard says, "pushed forward in a prone position, dying." Over the phone Dollard emits a series of sharp noises. He's sobbing. He hangs up, then phones back about half an hour later. "This is why I've got to stop doing drugs and finish this project," he says, sounding desperate. "It's their film."

He turns to two former marines to help him complete his project. Sergeant Brandon Welsh, honorably discharged in early 2006, and another young vet offer Dollard a place to stay at a town house they rent in a Sunbelt metropolis. (Dollard requests that the city not be named.) By early May, Welsh helps Dollard create the Web site that draws the attention of Andrew Breitbart and his invitation to return to Los Angeles for a series of meetings with operatives on the right.

The Evil Genius

Our breakfast at the LAX hotel is the first time I have seen Dollard since his return from Iraq. A couple days later I accompany him to an invitation-only pool party on the roof of the downtown Standard hotel. Breitbart has introduced Dollard to Morgan Warstler, a thirtysomething entrepreneur who dabbles as a conservative operative. Warstler has promised to be Dollard's "evil genius."

We meet Warstler, an impish redhead (with an uncanny resemblance to Danny Bonaduce), by the pool. Dressed in jeans and a green baseball cap, he invites Dollard to sit on some plastic cube chairs by the dance floor. While sipping a rum-and-Coke, Warstler lists his credentials. "I was a national-champion debater," he says. "I made the president of the Yale debate team cry. I called him a dildo in front of 500 people."

"Mad props to you," Dollard says, drinking a black coffee.

"I deal in ideas," Warstler continues. "People are hosts to ideas, like viruses. When two people meet, ideas jump out of their heads, looking for new hosts. What I'm after is for my idea to jump out of my head and crush the ideas in someone else's head."

Warstler lays out a series of schemes for Dollard to spread his conservative, prowar views, using viral-marketing techniques. "There is a whole vast, untapped market of Americans who don't know shit about geopolitical bullshit, but who want this war to succeed," Warstler says. "Those people need arguments. So if they're in a bar somewhere arguing with somebody they can just hold up their cell phone, play the latest installment from you, and be like, 'End of argument.'"

Dollard warms to the plan. "I'm like this gonzo character, but I fucking support the whole conservative agenda."

Warstler takes a long, reflective pull from his drink. He tells Dollard that he personally digs "the whole Hunter S. Thompson direction you've been going in." He says, "I loved the guy. I once spent a night drinking with him, but once he killed himself, that brand died."

Blowing Smoke

A few days later, Breitbart arranges Dollard's introduction to Ann Coulter. They meet after she tapes an appearance on *The Tonight Show*, rendezvousing at the Acapulco, across from the NBC studios in Burbank. When I enter, Coulter is standing on the patio surrounded by about thirty fans, leading them in a chorus of "God Bless America." Coulter wears a black dress stretched tightly over her thin, angular, almost starved-looking frame.

Dollard hovers by the entrance, dressed in a MORRISON HOTEL T-shirt, waiting for their dinner, which will take place at a nearby steak house. When Coulter finally walks out, Breitbart hustles Dollard over for the introduction.

Dollard attempts to ditch his cigarette. "No, no," Coulter tells him. "Blow smoke in my face." She leans her oblong, Brazil-nut-shaped face toward Dollard's lips, and he exhales through his yellow, cracked teeth. Coulter, who later explains she recently quit smoking and is still jonesing for tobacco, shuts her eyes and coos, "Thank you."

A few days after their dinner Coulter e-mails me her impression of Dollard: "The main thing I'd say about Dollard is that when you first meet him, he looks like a bad-ass degenerate and then the moment he starts talking, you realize he's highly intelligent, interesting and funny.... I would trust anything he says implicitly."

Through Breitbart's tireless networking, Dollard travels to New York in July to meet with a magazine editor, who offers him a job as a war correspondent. In an e-mail to Dollard, the editor reveals the mixture of awe and obsequiousness Dollard increasingly receives from the swelling ranks of new acolytes:

> So ... I shit my pants just thinking about all the shit you've been through Your shit is so raw and real.... The knives must be out for you.... Hollywood eats its young so my God they must be sending some liberal fucking hit squad out after you.... I want to know everything about your project and I want to promote it in a good way with your voice and diary.... I'm sure you think [the magazine] is frivolous shit that is part of the problem but we are read by the soldiers We are the dick that is to be sucked by the vapid, MTV bullshit, I know all that but imagine if your shit ran on MTV.... You can trust me, I'm one of the good guys ...

While in New York, Dollard also appears on *Hannity & Colmes*. Introduced by Colmes as a former talent agent who left

"Tinseltown behind to see what the Iraqis themselves think of the liberal antiwar movement," Dollard plays a clip of an Iraqi translator who calls Michael Moore a "little bitch" and crushes a DVD purported to be *Fahrenheit 9/11* (but appears to be *I, Robot*). Dollard rambles about "an incredibly strong [anti-Republican] bias in Hollywood that denies people work." Hannity adds, "The truth isn't being told, is it? The left is undermining [the soldiers'] effort and stabbing them in the back."

After viewing her ex-husband on the show, Megan Dollard tells me, "It's really scary that a person who is completely crazy can go on TV and have that influence." Having seen him come unglued so many times in front of me, I hadn't anticipated how effective he would be on TV. Isn't somebody going to notice he's insane, I had wondered while watching him trade sound bites with Hannity? But of course he would fit in. In the pro-wrestling world of opinion TV, Dollard is a natural.

In conversations I've had with Breitbart, he, like other conservatives, harps on the "nihilism of the left." Breitbart brings up anti–Vietnam War protesters, like yippies, who attacked the Establishment "by spitting on people. They debased people and institutions and values with anger and disrespect."

Despite his outrage, Breitbart advocates a right-wing version of the Merry Pranksters led by people like Coulter and Dollard. Perhaps America has experienced a circular movement in its social history. The freaks are now on the right. Dollard takes this even further. With his drug-fueled excursions into combat zones, his lust for booze and hookers and porn, and, above all, his madness for life, he is an authentic anti-Establishment figure and is certainly in the running to be the first true gonzo journalist to emerge from this war. And yet he supports the Republican Party platform, George Bush, and the Pledge of Allegiance.

Four days after Dollard's *Hannity & Colmes* appearance, I receive a call from a security guard at the W Times Square hotel, where Dollard is staying. The guard tells me the N.Y.P.D. is on their way to possibly arrest Dollard. Throughout the call, I hear a drunk slurring in the background. It's Dollard. The guard tells me that earlier that morning a woman from room service had brought him cigarettes and found the room trashed, covered in what she thought was blood. (Dollard would later claim it was coffee.) Dollard allegedly told the woman from room service, "I killed someone." Welsh, who accompanied Dollard to New York, tells me that after his appearance on *Hannity & Colmes* a magazine editor "trying to kiss Pat's ass and believing all his Hunter S. Thompson bullshit" gave him "a bunch of coke, and Pat got all retarded as usual." Welsh left him a few days ago.

When the cops show up at the W, instead of arresting him, they have an ambulance take him to St. Vincent's hospital for observation. He is released hours later and flies back home.

Welsh informs me that he and an ex-marine buddy plan to tie Dollard up and use a Taser gun if he acts out. Dollard sobers up for a few weeks. But in early September, Welsh moves out after an incident in which Dollard shoots a hole through the ceiling of his bedroom while playing with a .45. "The motherfucker's out of his mind," Welsh tells me. "I'm just fucking tired of being a twenty-three-year-old babysitting a forty-two-year-old."

Two weeks after Welsh's departure, Dollard contacts me. He has finished cutting his second version of *Young Americans* (without any pornographic scenes). According to Dollard, since the new version of his film includes footage of the two bombings he survived and graphic footage of marines in close-quarters firefights, "William Morris thinks it's going to be fucking big. Fucking liberals are going to buy this. That's the thing about all the dark-side stuff I've done, which I didn't truly understand until now: it's appealing to everybody. I guess that's why in the bottom of their hearts most people fucking love war."

Epilogue

Dollard and I meet for dinner at a Santa Monica steak house a couple of nights before Christmas. He claims that on September 11 he underwent an experience—part spiritual, part patriotic—in which he was struck sober and has been clean ever since. He certainly looks better than I expected. A few weeks earlier he had cataract surgery, and for the first time in more than a year his gaze is clear. Over Caesar salads and steaks, Dollard tells me it's important that people in the public realize he doesn't "advocate drugs or the drug lifestyle. I don't think taking drugs is cool. I suffer from the disease of alcoholism like millions of other people." Unable to stomach the "whiny assclowns" at A.A. meetings, Dollard remains in solo combat with his personal demons.

In the battle against Islamo-fascism he is gaining new allies. He says that Frank J. Gaffney Jr., an assistant secretary of defense during the Reagan administration and charter member of the Project for the New American Century, has begun discussions with him about helping to distribute *Young Americans.* (Gaffney's Center for Security Policy has produced TV ads and promoted documentaries aimed at stiffening the American public's resolve to carry on the war in Iraq.) Dollard is also in direct negotiations with Fox News V.P. Ken LaCorte to provide clips to the network. "I'm becoming a member of the Fox family," he tells me.

·   ·   ·

In mid-January, Andrew Breitbart hosts a conservative coming-out party for Dollard to celebrate his upcoming Fox deal. (According to Dollard, Fox News head Roger Ailes was "stoked" about bringing him into the Fox fold after viewing his Web site.) About thirty people gather at Breitbart's hillside home in Brentwood to view Dollard's clips. When I enter, Ann Coulter stands by a bowl of guacamole, eating tortilla chips and venting about the lack of spine shown by her own partisans. "I meet so many conservative men afraid to say they still support the war," she says. "Conservatives are pussies. That should be the title of my next book." The large man behind her in a double-breasted, white linen suit is Richard Miniter, author of *Losing Bin Laden* (plot spoiler: it's Clinton's fault). Miniter, chewing an unlit cigar, huddles in conversation with a bald guy in a baseball cap, discussing battle plans to promote more "prowar content" in the movies. The guy in the baseball cap is part of a small contingent of movie-industry people on hand, a writer and a couple of producers, who represent the new face of butch Hollywood. While maintaining the same careers they had before 9/11, at parties like this they now talk forcefully of the need to confront the Islamo-fascist threat. I find Dollard—who flew in from his undisclosed location—in the living room wrestling with loudspeakers and computer cables in preparation for his screening. When he sees me, Dollard throws his arm around my shoulder and asks, "Dude, how's your fucking mother?"

Having recently learned of an illness in my family, Dollard has bombarded me with phone calls and e-mails inquiring about my well-being, providing me with leads on experimental medical clinics offering nontraditional cures. Dollard, when he is not off in a war, on an antiliberal rant, or locked away on a binge, becomes an obsessively and at times intrusively caring friend. Tonight, he scolds me for not being at the hospital with my mother, and offers "anything, anything I can do to help. Just ask, dude." After I decline, Dollard switches gears, asking if I have read his latest e-mail. In it he writes that liberal enclaves in Manhattan and Los Angeles "basically need to be exterminated in order for the planet to move ahead into peace." In Dollard's view, the liberal media based on both coasts are "literally allied with the Islamic Fascist Imperialists out of a short-sighted grab for domestic political power. You are seeing the age of treason in America."

The screening—a series of interviews Pat conducted with marines complaining about the liberal bias of the media—concludes with polite applause.

．　　　．　　　．

Back in the kitchen, Ann Coulter resumes her assault on the guacamole and chips. A male guest approaches, slips Coulter his number, and delivers what must be the ultimate pickup line at a conservative party. "I'm having dinner tomorrow night with Richard Perle. Would you like to join us?"

I find Dollard on the balcony conferring with a producer. The producer tells him he could help him walk into a major studio and get a deal. Dollard listens attentively. The producer says, "My problem is the title. *Young Americans*—I don't like it."

One thing you can't criticize is Dollard's title. He believes it is not only one of the best things he's ever come up with but that it's been plagiarized at the highest levels. He believes that last summer President Bush himself checked out his Web site, saw the trailer, and began slipping the phrase "young Americans" into speeches as a not-so-subtle nod to his film. Dollard turns from the producer and pulls the last cigarette from a pack of Marlboro Lights. "Fuck, I'm out."

The producer slinks back into the living room. Dollard lights his last cigarette and looks up at the twinkling lights on the hills. I point out that he is now essentially back at a Hollywood party.

"It's like I never left," he says.

I remind him of his latest e-mail, arguing that Los Angeles needs to be wiped off the face of the planet.

"After I get my deal." Dollard shrugs. "Fuck that. I just want to get back to Ramadi this spring. I'm supposed to die there."

He turns to me. "Dude, drive down to a gas station and buy me some cigarettes."

The Atlantic

FINALIST—ESSAYS

The rise of personalized technology was supposed to give us time and freedom. Instead, argues Walter Kirn, it has imprisoned us. With self-deprecating wit, Kirn takes us along on a bruising ride through multitasking hell, and explains why "parallel processing" threatens both the brain and the GNP.

Walter Kirn

The Autumn of the Multitaskers

I think your suggestion is, Can we do two things at once?
Well, we're of the view that we can walk and chew gum at
the same time.
> —Richard Armitage, *deputy secretary of state, on the wars in
> Afghanistan and Iraq, June 2, 2004 (Armitage announced
> his resignation on November 16, 2004.)*

To do two things at once is to do neither.
> —Publilius Syrus, *Roman slave, first century* B.C.

I n the midwestern town where I grew up (a town so small that the phone line on our block was a "party line" well into the 1960s, meaning that we shared it with our neighbors and couldn't use it while one of them was using it, unless we wanted to quietly listen in—with their permission, naturally, and only if we were feeling awfully lonesome—while they chatted with someone else), there were two skinny brothers in their thirties who built a car that could drive into the river and become a fishing boat.

My pals and I thought the car-boat was a wonder. A thing that did one thing but also did another thing—especially the *opposite* thing, but at least an *unrelated* thing—was our idea of a great invention and a bold stride toward the future. Where we got this idea, I'll never know, but it caused us to envision a world to come teeming with crossbred, hyphenated machines. Refrigerator–TV sets. Dishwasher–air conditioners. Table saw–popcorn poppers. Camera-radios.

With that last dumb idea, we were getting close to something, as I've noted every time I've dropped or fumbled my cell phone and snapped a picture of a wall or the middle button of my shirt. Impressive. Ingenious. Yet juvenile. Arbitrary. And why a substandard camera, anyway? Why not an excellent electric razor?

Because (I told myself at the cell-phone store in the winter of 2003, as I handled a feature-laden upgrade that my new contract entitled me to purchase at a deep discount that also included a rebate) there may come a moment on a plane or in a subway station or at a mall when I and the other able-bodied males will be forced to subdue a terrorist, and my color snapshot of his trussed-up body will make the front page of *USA Today* and appear at the left shoulder of all the superstars of cable news.

While I waited for my date with citizen-journalist destiny, I took a lot of self-portraits in my Toyota and forwarded them to a girlfriend in Colorado, who reciprocated from her Jeep. Neither one of us almost died. For months. But then, one night on a snowy two-lane highway, while I was crossing Wyoming to see my girl's real face, my phone made its chirpy you-have-a-picture noise, and I glanced down in its direction while also, apparently, swerving off the pavement and sailing over a steep embankment toward a barbed-wire fence.

It was interesting to me—in retrospect, after having done some reading about the frenzied activity of the multitasking brain—how late in the process my prefrontal cortex, where our cognitive switchboards hide, changed its focus from the silly phone (*Where did it go? Did it slip between the seats? I wonder if this new photo is a nude shot or if it's another one from the topless series that seemed like such a breakthrough a month ago but now*

I'm getting sick of) to the important matter of a steel fence post sliding spear-like across my hood . . .

(*But her arms are too short to shoot a nude self-portrait with a camera phone. She'd have to do it in a mirror . . .*)

The laminated windshield glass must have been high quality; the point of the post bounced off it, leaving only a star-shaped surface crack. But I was still barreling toward sagebrush, and who knew what rocks and boulders lay in wait . . .

Then the phone trilled out its normal ringtone.

Five minutes later, I'd driven out of the field and gunned it back up the embankment onto the highway and was proceeding south, heart slowing some, satellite radio tuned to a soft-rock channel called the Heart, which was playing lots of soothing Céline Dion.

"I just had an accident trying to see your picture."

"Will you get here in time to take me out to dinner?"

"I almost died."

"Well, you *sound* fine."

"Fine's not a *sound*."

I never forgave her for that detachment. I never forgave myself for buying a camera phone.

●   ●   ●

The abiding, distinctive feature of all crashes, whether in stock prices, housing values, or hit-TV-show ratings, is that they startle but don't surprise. When the euphoria subsides, when the volatile graph lines of excitability flatten and then curve down, people realize, collectively and instantly (and not infrequently with some relief), that they've been expecting this correction. The signs were everywhere, the warnings clear, the researchers in rough agreement, and the stories down at the bar and in the office (our own stories included) revealed the same anxieties.

Which explains why the busts and reversals we deem inevitable are also the least preventable, and why they startle us, if briefly, when they come—because they were inevitable for so long that they should have come already. That they haven't, we reason, can mean only one of two things. Thanks to technology or some other magic, we've entered a new age when the laws of cause and effect (as propounded by Isaac Newton and Adam Smith) have yielded to the principle of dream-and-make-it-happen (as manifested by Steve Jobs and Oprah). Either that, or the thing that went up and up and up and hasn't come down, though it should have long ago, is being held aloft by our decision to forget it's up there and to carry on as though it weren't.

But on to the next inevitable contraction that everybody knows is coming, believes should have come a couple of years ago, and suspects can be postponed only if we pay no attention to the matter and stay very, very busy. I mean the end of the decade we may call the Roaring Zeros—these years of overleveraged, overextended, technology-driven, and finally unsustainable investment of our limited human energies in the dream of infinite connectivity. The overdoses, freak-outs, and collapses that converged in the late '60s to wipe out the gains of the wide-eyed optimists who set out to "Be Here Now" but ended up making posters that read "Speed Kills" are finally coming for the wired utopians who strove to "Be Everywhere at Once" but lost a measure of innocence, or should have, when their manic credo convinced us we could fight two wars at the same time.

The Multitasking Crash.

The Attention-Deficit Recession.

·　　　·　　　·

We all remember the promises. The slogans. They were all about freedom, liberation. Supposedly we were in handcuffs and wanted out of them. The key that dangled in front of us was a micro-chip.

"Where do you want to go today?" asked Microsoft in a mid-1990s ad campaign. The suggestion was that there were endless destinations—some geographic, some social, some intellectual—that you could reach in milliseconds by loading the right devices with the right software. It was further insinuated that where you went was purely up to you, not your spouse, your boss, your kids, or your government. Autonomy through automation.

This was the embryonic fallacy that grew up into the monster of multitasking.

Human freedom, as classically defined (to think and act and choose with minimal interference by outside powers), was not a product that firms like Microsoft could offer, but they recast it as something they *could* provide. A product for which they could raise the demand by refining its features, upping its speed, restyling its appearance, and linking it up with all the other products that promised freedom, too, but had replaced it with three inferior substitutes that they could market in its name:

Efficiency, convenience, and mobility.

For proof that these bundled minor virtues don't amount to freedom but are, instead, a formula for a period of mounting frenzy climaxing with a lapse into fatigue, consider that "Where do you want to go today?" was really manipulative advice, not an open question. "Go somewhere now," it strongly recommended, then go somewhere else tomorrow, but always go, go, go—and with our help. But did any rebel reply, "Nowhere. I like it fine right here"? Did anyone boldly ask, "What business is it of yours?" Was anyone brave enough to say, "Frankly, I want to go back to bed"?

Maybe a few of us. Not enough of us. Everyone else was going places, it seemed, and either we started going places, too—especially to those places that weren't *places* (another word they'd redefined) but were just pictures or documents or videos or boxes on screens where strangers conversed by typing—or else we'd be nowhere (a location once known as "here") doing nothing (an activity formerly labeled "living"). What a waste this would be. What a waste of our new freedom.

Our freedom to stay busy at all hours, at the task—and then the many tasks, and ultimately the multitask—of trying to be free.

> While the president continued talking on the phone
> (Ms. Lewinsky understood that the caller was a Member of
> Congress or a Senator), she performed oral sex on him.
> —The Starr Report, 1998

It isn't working, it never has worked, and though we're still pushing and driving to make it work and puzzled as to why we haven't stopped yet, which makes us think we may go on forever, the stoppage or slowdown is coming nonetheless, and when it does, we'll be startled for a moment, and then we'll acknowledge that, way down deep inside ourselves (a place that we almost forgot even existed), we always knew it *couldn't* work.

The scientists know this too, and they think they know why. Through a variety of experiments, many using functional magnetic resonance imaging to measure brain activity, they've torn the mask off multitasking and revealed its true face, which is blank and pale and drawn.

Multitasking messes with the brain in several ways. At the most basic level, the mental balancing acts that it requires—the constant switching and pivoting—energize regions of the brain that specialize in visual processing and physical coordination and simultaneously appear to shortchange some of the higher areas related to memory and learning. We concentrate on the act of concentration at the expense of whatever it is that we're supposed to be concentrating *on*.

What does this mean in practice? Consider a recent experiment at UCLA, where researchers asked a group of twenty-somethings to sort index cards in two trials, once in silence and once while simultaneously listening for specific tones in a series of randomly presented sounds. The subjects' brains coped with the additional task by shifting responsibility from the hippocampus—which stores and recalls information—to the striatum, which takes care of rote, repetitive activities. Thanks to this switch, the subjects managed to sort the cards just as well with the musical distraction—but they had a much harder time remembering what, exactly, they'd been sorting once the experiment was over.

Even worse, certain studies find that multitasking boosts the level of stress-related hormones such as cortisol and adrenaline and wears down our systems through biochemical friction, prematurely aging us. In the short term, the confusion, fatigue, and chaos merely hamper our ability to focus and analyze, but in the long term, they may cause it to atrophy.

The next generation, presumably, is the hardest-hit. They're the ones way out there on the cutting edge of the multitasking revolution, texting and instant messaging each other while they download music to their iPod and update their Facebook page and complete a homework assignment and keep an eye on the episode of *The Hills* flickering on a nearby television. (A recent study from the Kaiser Family Foundation found that 53 percent of students in grades seven through twelve report consuming some other form of media while watching television; 58 percent multitask while reading; 62 percent while using the computer; and 63 percent while listening to music. "I get bored if it's not all going at once," said a seventeen-year-old quoted in the study.) They're the ones whose still-maturing brains are being shaped to process information rather than understand or even remember it.

This is the great irony of multitasking—that its overall goal, getting more done in less time, turns out to be chimerical. In reality, multitasking slows our thinking. It forces us to chop competing tasks into pieces, set them in different piles, then hunt for the pile we're interested in, pick up its pieces, review the rules for putting the pieces back together, and then attempt to do so, often quite awkwardly. (Fact, and one more reason the bubble will pop: A brain attempting to perform two tasks simultaneously will, because of all the back-and-forth stress, exhibit a substantial lag in information processing.)

Productive? Efficient? More like running up and down a beach repairing a row of sand castles as the tide comes rolling in and the rain comes pouring down. *Multitasking*, a definition: "The attempt by human beings to operate like computers, often done with the assistance of computers." It begins by giving us more tasks to do, making each task harder to do, and dimming the mental powers required to do them. It finishes by making us forget exactly how on earth we did them (assuming we didn't give up, or "multiquit"), which makes them harder to do again.

·   ·   ·

Much of the problem is the metaphor. Or perhaps it's our need for metaphors in general, particularly when the subject is our minds and the comparison seems based on science. In the days of rudimentary chemistry, the mind was thought to be a beaker of swirling volatile essences. Then came classical physical mechanics, and the mind was regarded as a clocklike thing, with springs and wheels. Then it was steam-driven, maybe. A combustion chamber. Then came electricity and Freud, and it was a dynamo of polarized energies—the id charged one way, the superego the other.

Now, in the heyday of the microchip, the brain is a computer. A CPU.

Except that it's not a CPU. It's whatever that thing is that's driven to misconstrue itself—over and over, century after century—as a prototype, rendered in all-too-vulnerable tissue, of our latest marvel of technology. And before the age of modern technology, *theology*. Further back than that, it's hard to voyage, since there was a period, common sense suggests, when we didn't even know we *had* brains. Or minds. Or spirits. Humans just sort of *did* stuff. And what they did was not influenced by metaphors about what they *ought* to be *capable* of doing but very well might not be equipped for (assuming you wanted to do it in the first place), like editing a playlist to e-mail to the lover whose husband you're interviewing on the phone about the movie he made that you're discussing in the blog entry you're posting tomorrow morning and are one-quarter watching certain parts of as you eat salad and carry on the call.

Would it be possible someday—through drugs, maybe, or esoteric Buddhism, or some profound, postapocalyptic languor—to stop coming up with ideas of what we are and then laboring to live up to them?

The great spooky splendor of the brain, of course, is that no matter what we think it fundamentally resembles—even a small ethereal colosseum where angels smite demons and demons play dead, then suddenly spit fire into the angels' faces—it does a good job, a *great* job, of seeming to resemble it.

For a while.

I do like to read a book while having sex. And talk on the phone. You can get so much done.

—Jennifer Connelly, movie star, 2005

After the near-fatal consequences of my 2003 decision to buy a phone with a feature I didn't need, life went on, and rather rapidly, since multitasking eats up time in the name of saving time, rushing you through your two-year contract cycle and returning you to the company store with a suspicion that you didn't accomplish all you hoped to after your last optimistic, euphoric visit.

"Which of the ones that offer rebates don't have cameras in them?"

"The decent models all do. The best ones now have video capabilities. You can shoot little movies."

I wanted to ask, *Of what? Oncoming barbed wire?* The salesman was a believer, though—a zealot.

"Oh, yeah," he said, "as well as GPS-based, turn-by-turn navigation systems. Which are cool if you drive a lot."

"You have to look down at the screen, though."

"They're paid subscription services, you need to know, but we're giving away the first month free, and even after that, the rates are reasonable."

I shook my head. I was turning down whiz-bang features for the first time, and so had some of my friends, one of whom had sprung for a new BlackBerry that he'd holed up in his office to learn to use. He'd emerged a week later looking demoralized, muttering about getting old, although he'd just turned thirty-four.

"Those little ones there—the ones that aren't so slim, that you give away free."

"That too is an option. Mostly they're aimed at kids, though. Adolescents."

I wanted one anyway. I'd caught air in my Land Cruiser off a sheer embankment, lost my girlfriend, chucked my dream of snapping a hog-tied terrorist, and once, because of another girl—a jealous type who never trusted that I was where I said I was—I'd been forced to send on a shot of L.A. palm trees to prove that I was not in Oregon meeting up with yet another girl whom I'd drunk coffee with after a poetry reading and who must have been bombed a few weeks later when she sent me a text message at 3 A.M. while I was sleeping beside the jealous girl. My bedmate heard the ring, crept out of bed, and read the message, then woke me up and demanded that I explain why it seemed to suggest we'd shared more than double espressos—an effect curiously enhanced by the note's thumb-typed dyslexic style: *Thuoght I saw thoes parkly eyes this aft, that sensaul deivlish mouth, and it took me rihgt in again, like vapmires do.*

"I'll take the fat little free one," I told the salesman.

"The thing's inert. It does nothing. It's a pet rock."

I informed him that I was old enough to have actually owned a pet rock once and that I missed it.

·   ·   ·

Here's the worst of the chilling little thoughts that have come to me during microtasking seize-ups: For every driver who's ever died while talking on a cell phone (researchers at the Harvard Center for Risk Analysis estimate that some 2,600 deaths and 330,000 injuries may be caused by drivers on cell phones each year), there was someone on the other end who, chances are, was too distracted to notice. Too busy cooking, NordicTracking, fluffing up his online dating profile, or—most hauntingly of all, I'd think, for a listener destined to discover that the acoustic chaos he'd interpreted as the other phone going out of range, or perhaps as a network-wide disturbance triggered by a solar flare, was actually a death, a human death, a death he had some role in— sitting on the toilet.

Trading securities.

Or would watching streaming pornography be worse?

Not that both of these activities can't be performed on the same computer screen. And often are—you can bet on it. In bathrooms. Even *airport* bathrooms, on occasion. In some of which, via radio, the latest business headlines can be monitored, permitting (in theory and therefore in *fact*, because, as the First Law of Multitasking dictates, any two or eight or sixteen processes that *can* overlap *must* overlap) the squatting day trader viewing the dirty Webcast (while on the phone with someone, don't forget) to learn that the company he just bought stock in has entered merger talks with *his own employer* and surged almost 20 percent in under three minutes!

"Guess how much richer I've gotten while we've been yakking?" he says into his cell, breaking his own rule about pretending that when he's on the phone, he's on the phone. Exclusively. Fully. With his entire being.

No reply.

Must be driving through a tunnel.

.   .   .

I've been fired, I've been insulted in front of coworkers, but the time I flew thousands of miles to meet a boss who spent our first and only hour together politely nodding at my proposals while thumbing out messages on a new device, whose existence neither of us acknowledged and whose screen he kept tilted so I couldn't see it, still feels, five years later, like the low point of my career.

> This is the perfect "one plus one equals three" opportunity.
> — Robert Pittman, *president and COO of America Online,*
> *on the merger between AOL and Time Warner,* 2000

There may be a financial cost to multitasking as well. The sum is extremely large and hard to vouch for, the esoteric algorithm that yielded it a puzzle to all but its creator, possibly, but it's one of those figures that's fun to quote in bars.

Six hundred and fifty billion dollars. That's what we might call our National Attention Deficit, according to Jonathan B. Spira, who's the chief analyst at a business-research firm called

Basex and has estimated the per annum cost to the economy of multitasking-induced disruptions. (He obtained the figure by surveying office workers across the country, who reported that some 28 percent of their time was wasted dealing with multitasking-related transitions and interruptions.)

That $650 billion reflects just one year's loss. This means that the total debt is vastly higher, since personal digital assistants (the devices that, in my opinion, turned multitasking from a habit into a pathology, which the advent of Bluetooth then rendered fatal and the spread of wireless broadband made communicable) are several annums old. This puts our shortfall somewhere in the trillions—even before we add in the many billions that vanished when Time Warner and AOL joined their respective corporate missions—so ably accomplished when the firms were separate—into one colossal mission impossible.

And don't forget to add Enron to the tab, a company that seemed to master so many enterprises, trading everything from energy to weather futures, that the Wall Street analysts' brains froze up trying to "recontext" (another science term) what looked at first like a capitalist dynamo as the street-corner con that it turned out to be. Reports suggest that the illusion depended nearly as much on cunning set design as it did on phony accounting. The towering stack of Broadway stages that Enron called its headquarters—with its profusion of workstations, trading boards, copiers, speakerphones, fax machines, and shredders—made visiting banker-broker types go snow-blind. When the fraud was exposed, the press accused the moneymen of overestimating Enron. In truth, they'd underestimated Enron, whose hectic multitasking front concealed the managers' Zenlike focus on one proficiency, and only one.

Hypnotism.

Which is easy to practice on an audience whose brains are already half dormant from the stress of scheduling flights on fractionally owned jets and changing the tilt and speed of treadmills according to the shifting readouts of miniature biofeedback monitors strapped around their upper arms.

What has the madness of multitasking cost us? The better question might be: What hasn't it?

And the IOUs keep coming, signed at the bottom with millions of our names. We issued this currency. We're the Federal Reserve of the attention economy, the central bank of overcommitment, keeping the system liquid with adrenaline. The problem is that we, the bankers, are also the borrowers. That's multitasking for you. It moves in circles. Circles that we run around ourselves, as we try to pay off the debts we owe ourselves with funny money engraved with our own faces.

•   •   •

Here's one item from my ledger:

Cost of pitying Kevin Federline while organizing business trip online and attaching computer peripheral: $279.

Federline—I know. A mayfly on the multimedia river who, now that he has mated, deserves to break back up into pixels. That he hasn't means pixels are far too cheap and plentiful, particularly on the AOL welcome page, where for several months last year Federline's image was regularly positioned beside the icon I click to get my e-mail. With practice, I learned to sweep past him the way the queen sweeps past her guards, but one afternoon his picture triggered a brainslide that buried half my day.

What the avalanche overwhelmed was a mental function that David E. Meyer, a psychology professor at the University of Michigan, calls "adaptive executive control." Thanks to Federline, I lost my ability, as Meyer would say, to "schedule task processes appropriately" and to "obey instructions about their relative priorities."

Meyer, it's worth noting, is a relative optimist among the researchers studying multitasking, since he's convinced that some people can learn, with enough practice, to perform two tasks simultaneously as successfully as if they were doing them sequentially. But "enough practice" turns out to mean at least 2,000 tries, and I had just the one chance at the cheap fare to San Francisco that I'd turned on my laptop to reserve, only to be distracted by the picture of Federline winking at me from one browser window over.

The photo, a link explained, was taken while Federline was taping a TV show and happened to peer down at his phone, only to learn that what's-her-hair, his wife, the psycho, bad-mother rehab-escapee (I had last caught up on her misadventures weeks or months before, while waiting out an eBay auction for an auxiliary hard drive "still in box"), had sent him a text message asking for a divorce. Federline's face looked as raw as a freshly unbandaged plastic-surgery patient's, but the aspect of the photo that grabbed me (as the promotional fare hovered in the ether, still unbooked and up for grabs) was the idea I suddenly entertained about its origins. The picture of Federline in cell-phone shock had been snapped on the sly by another phone, I sensed, and possibly by a hanger-on whom Federline regarded as a "bro." It also seemed plausible that after the taping, Federline bought dinner for this Judas—who, in my reconstruction of events, had already beamed the spy shot to a tabloid and been wired big money in return. If so, he was probably richer than Federline, who depended for funds on the wife who'd just dumped him.

This thought sequence caused me to remember the hard drive—still sitting unopened in a closet—that I'd bought in that Internet auction way back when, while catching up on the Hollywood gossip news. Here's the mental flowchart: Federline dumped > story about his prenuptial with Britney Spears > story was read during eBay auction > time to get some use out of my purchase.

Removing the hard drive from its shell of molded Styrofoam sloppily wrapped in masking tape stirred serious doubts about the seller's claim that the gadget was unused. This put me in a quandary. Should I send the hard drive back? Blackball its seller on a message board? Best to test it first. I riffled through drawers to find the proper cable, plugged the device into a USB port, and only then became aware of the fluorescent Post-it note stuck in the corner of my laptop screen. "Grab discount SF fare," the note read. Where had it gone? Where had *I* gone, rather? How could a piece of paper in a color specially formulated to signal the brain *Important! Don't Ignore!* be upstaged by a picture of a sad minor celebrity? If the Post-it note had been a road sign warning of a hairpin mountain curve and Federline's photo a radio interview, I and my car would be rolling down a cliff now.

Back to the San Francisco ticket, then. I brought up the main Expedia/Orbitz/Travelocity page and typed in the code for the San Francisco airport, which I couldn't believe I got wrong. To fix it, I was forced to use one of those drop-down alphabetized lists that the highlight line always moves too fast through, meaning I click my mouse several entries too late. Seattle this time. I scrolled back up.

All tickets sold out.

The scientists call this ruinous mental lurching "dual task interference," or just plain bottlenecking. I call it the reason Keven Federline cost me a cheap flight to San Francisco. (It also explains, perhaps, why sexual threesomes are often disappointing.)

I just wish the military understood the concept. They might understand then why "walking and chewing gum" in Afghanistan and Iraq is no way to catch bin Laden.

My hunch is that when we look back on it someday, at our juggling of electronic lives and the array of subtly different personas that each one encourages (we're terse when texting, freewheeling on the phone, and in some middle state while e-mailing), the spectacle will appear as quaint and stylized as those scenes in old movies of stiff-backed lady operators, hair in bobby pins, rapidly swapping phone jacks from hole to hole as they connect Chicago to Miami, reporter to city desk, businessman to mistress. Such scenes were, for a time, cinematic shorthand for the frenzy of modern life, but then communications technology changed, and those operators lost their jobs.

To us.

We've got to be patient and committed [in Iraq], but we've got to multitask. . . . We've got to talk about Iran—Iran is more dangerous than Iraq—and we have got to get the job done in Afghanistan and in Pakistan.

—Rudolph Giuliani, Republican presidential candidate, July 2007

The night the bubble finally popped for me began when I pushed a button on my hospital bed to summon the gray-haired night nurse. To convey my appreciation when she arrived and to help establish a relationship that I hoped would lead her to agree with me that my morphine drip was far too slow, I did as the gurus of management urge executives to do when they engage in important negotiations. I "reallocated" my "presence" and "enriched" my "medium." I removed my headphones, closed my book, aimed the remote and clicked off the TV, and looked the old woman in the eye.

"What?" she said.

Her question came too quickly. Because of the way the human brain works—always lagging slightly, always falling a bit behind itself when it has to drop many things, one thing at a time, and refocus on a new thing—my attention had not yet caught up with my expression. Also, perhaps because of the way that morphine works, I was unnaturally aware of the mechanisms inside my mind. I could actually feel the neurological switching, the mental grinding of fine, tiny gears that makes multitasking such an inefficient, slow, error-prone, tiring way to get things done.

"Still hurts," I finally said. "Wondering if you'd shorten up the intervals." I left out the *I*'s, text message–style, because that's how people in agony communicate. Teenagers, too, but aren't they also in agony, with the shy self-consciousness of partials who don't show all their cards, out of fear that they haven't yet drawn many worth playing?

The nurse made a face that the gurus would call "equivocal"— meaning that it can support conflicting interpretations, even in a real-time, face-to-face, "presence-rich" exchange—and then glanced down at the iPod on my blanket.

"Music lover?"

"Book on tape," I said.

"You can do those both at once?" She eyed the real book lying on my lap.

"Same one," I said. "I like to double up."

"Why?"

I had no answer. I had a comeback—*Because I can, because it's possible*—but a comeback is just a way to keep things rolling when perhaps they ought to stop. When the nurse looked away and punched in new instructions on the keypad attached to my IV stand, I heard her thinking, *No wonder this guy has kidney stones. No wonder he's so hungry for narcotics.* She turned around in time to see my hands moving from the book they'd just reopened to the tangled wires of the earphones.

"I'm grateful that you came so quickly and showed such understanding," I said, not textishly, relaxing my syntax to suit the expectations of the elderly.

"Maybe more dope will be just the thing," the nurse said, shedding equivocation with every word, as a dreamy warmth spread through my limbs and she soft-stepped out and shut the door. When I woke in the wee hours, my book, in both its forms, had slid off the bed onto the floor, the TV remote was lost among the blankets, and the blinking "sleep" indicator of the laptop computer I've failed to mention (delivered to my bedside by a friend who'd shared my delusion that even twenty-five-bed Montana hospitals must offer wireless Internet these days) was exhaling onto the walls a lovely blue light that tempted me never to boot it up again.

That night, last May, as I drowsed and passed my stones, the mania left me, and it hasn't returned.

·   ·   ·

What happened to the skinny brothers' car-boat was that it sank the third time they took it fishing. It cracked down the length of its hull, took on water, then nose-dived into the sandy bottom, leaving its revved-up rear propeller sticking up two feet out of the river, furiously churning air until its creators returned in a canoe and whacked it silent with a crowbar.

The catastrophe, visible from half the town, was the talk of the party line that night, with most of the grown-ups joining in one pooled call that was still humming when I was sent to bed.

·   ·   ·

"Where do you want to go today?" Microsoft asked us.

Now that I no longer confuse freedom with speed, convenience, and mobility, my answer would be: "Away. Just away. Someplace where I can think."

The New Yorker

FINALIST—PUBLIC
INTEREST

George Packer's exhaustively reported article is on one level the story of Iraqi interpreters who risk their lives to help the United States—and how the United States very often abandons them. On another level, it illustrates the plight of millions of Iraqi refugees.

George Packer

Betrayed

On a cold, wet night in January, I met two young Iraqi men in the lobby of the Palestine Hotel, in central Baghdad. A few Arabic television studios had rooms on the upper floors of the building, but the hotel was otherwise vacant. In the lobby, a bucket collected drips of rainwater; at the gift shop, which was closed, a shelf displayed film, batteries, and sheathed daggers covered in dust. A sign from another era read, "We have great pleasure in announcing the opening of the Internet café 24 hour a day. At the business center on the first floor. The management." The management consisted of a desk clerk and a few men in black leather jackets slouched in armchairs and holding two-way radios.

The two Iraqis, Othman and Laith, had asked to meet me at the Palestine because it was the only place left in Baghdad where they were willing to be seen with an American. They lived in violent neighborhoods that were surrounded by militia checkpoints. Entering and leaving the Green Zone, the fortified heart of the American presence, had become too risky. But even the Palestine made them nervous. In October 2005, a suicide bomber driving a cement mixer had triggered an explosion that nearly brought down the hotel's eighteen-story tower. An American tank unit that was guarding the hotel eventually pulled out, leaving security in the hands of Iraqi civilians. It would now be relatively easy for insurgents to get inside. The one comforting thought for Othman and Laith was that, four years into the war, the Palestine was no longer worth attacking.

The Iraqis and I went up to a room on the eighth floor. Othman smoked by the window while Laith sat on one of the twin beds. (The names of most of the Iraqis in this story have been changed for their protection.) Othman was a heavyset doctor, twenty-nine years old, with a gentle voice and an unflappable ironic manner. Laith, an engineer with rimless eyeglasses, was younger and taller, and given to bursts of enthusiasm and displeasure. Othman was Sunni, Laith was Shiite.

It had taken Othman three days to get to the hotel from his house, in western Baghdad. On the way, he was trapped for two nights at his sister's house, which was in an ethnically mixed neighborhood: gun battles had broken out between Sunni and Shiite militiamen. Othman watched the home of his sister's neighbor, a Sunni, burn to the ground. Shiite militiamen scrawled the words "Leave or else" on the doors of Sunni houses. Othman was able to leave the house only because his sister's husband—a Shiite, who was known to the local Shia militias—escorted him out. Othman took a taxi to the house of Laith's grandfather; from there, he and Laith went to the Palestine, where they enjoyed their first hot water in several weeks.

They had a strong friendship, based on a shared desire. Before the war, they had both longed for the arrival of the Americans, expecting them to change their lives. They had told each other that they would try to work with the foreigners. Othman and Laith were both secular, and despised the extremist militias on each side of Iraq's civil war, but the ethnic conflict had led them increasingly to quarrel, to the point that one of them—usually Laith—would refuse to speak to the other.

Laith began to describe these strains. "It started when the Americans came with Shia leaders and wanted to give the Shia leadership—"

"And kick out the Sunnis," Othman interrupted. "You admit this? You were not admitting it before."

"The Americans don't want to kick out the Sunnis," Laith said. "They want to give Shia the power because most Iraqis are Shia."

"And you believe the Sunnis did not want to participate, right?" Othman said. "The Americans didn't give them the chance to participate." He turned to me: "You know I'm not just saying this because I'm a Sunni—"

Laith rolled his eyes. "What*ever.*"

"But I think the Shia made the Sunnis feel that they're against them."

"This is not the point, who started it," Laith said heatedly. "Everybody is getting killed, the Shia and the Sunnis." He paused. "But if we think who started it, I think the Sunnis started it!"

"I think the Shia," Othman repeated, with calm knowingness. He said to me, "When I feel that I'm pushing too much and he starts to become so angry, I pull the brake."

Laith had a job with an American organization, affiliated with the National Endowment for Democracy, that encouraged private enterprise in developing countries. Othman had worked with a German group called Architects for People in Need, and then as a translator for foreign journalists. These were coveted jobs, but over time they had become so dangerous that Othman and Laith could talk candidly about their lives with no one except each other.

"I trust him," Othman said of his friend. "We've shared our experiences with foreigners—the good and the bad. We don't have a secret life when we are together. But when we go out we have to lie."

Othman's cell phone rang: a friend was calling from Jordan. "I had a vision that you'll be killed by the end of the month," he told Othman. "Get out now, please. You can stay here with me.

We'll live on pasta." Othman said something reassuring and hung up, but his phone kept ringing, the friend calling back; his vision had made him hysterical.

A string of bad events had given Othman the sense that time was running out for him in Iraq. In November, members of the Mahdi Army—the Shia militia commanded by the radical cleric Moqtada al-Sadr—rounded up Othman's older brother and several other Sunnis who worked in a shop in a mixed neighborhood. The Sunnis were taken to a local Shia mosque and shot. Othman's brother was only grazed in the head, but a Shiite soldier noticed that he was still alive and shot him in the eye. Somehow, he survived this, too. Othman found his brother and took him to a hospital for surgery. The hospital—like the entire Iraqi health system—was under the Mahdi Army's control, and Othman decided that his brother would be safer at their parents' house. The brother was now blind, deranged, and vengeful, making life unbearable for Othman's family. A few days later, Othman's elderly maternal aunts, who were Shia and lived in a majority-Sunni area, were told by Sunni insurgents that they had three days to leave. Othman's father, a retired Sunni officer, went to their neighborhood and convinced the insurgents that his wife's sisters were, in fact, Sunnis. And then, one day in January, Othman's two teenage brothers, Muhammad and Salim, on whom he doted, failed to come home from school. Othman called the cell phone of Muhammad, who was fifteen. "Is this Muhammad?" he said.

A stranger's voice answered: "No, I'm not Muhammad."

"Where is Muhammad?"

"Muhammad is right here," the stranger said. "I'm looking at him now. We have both of them."

"Are you joking?"

"No, I'm not. Are you Sunni or Shia?"

Thinking of what had happened to his older brother, Othman lied: "We're Shia." The stranger told him to prove it. The boys had left their identity cards at home, for their own safety.

Othman's mother took the phone, sobbing and begging the kidnapper not to hurt her boys. "We're going to behead them," the kidnapper told her. "Choose where you want us to throw the bodies. Or do you prefer us to cut them to pieces for you? We enjoy cutting young boys to pieces." The man hung up.

After several more phone conversations, Othman realized his mistake: the kidnappers were Sunnis, with Al Qaeda. Shiites are not Muslims, the kidnappers told him—they deserve to be killed. Then they stopped answering the phone. Othman called a friend who belonged to a Sunni political party with ties to insurgents; over the course of the afternoon, the friend got the kidnappers back on the phone and convinced them that the boys were Sunnis. They were released with apologies, along with their money and their phones.

It was the worst day of Othman's life. He said he would never forget the sound of the stranger's voice.

Othman began a campaign of burning. He went into the yard or up on the roof of his parents' house with a jerrican of kerosene and set fire to papers, identity badges, books in English, photographs—anything that might incriminate him as an Iraqi who worked with foreigners. If Othman had to flee Iraq, he wanted to leave nothing behind that might harm him or his family. He couldn't bring himself to destroy a few items, though: his diaries, his weekly notes from the hospital where he had once worked. "I have this bad habit of keeping everything like memories," he said.

Most of the people Othman and Laith knew had left Iraq. House by house, Baghdad was being abandoned. Othman was considering his options: move his parents from their house (in an insurgent stronghold) to his sister's house (in the midst of civil war); move his parents and brothers to Syria (where there was no work) and live with his friend in Jordan (going crazy with boredom while watching his savings dwindle); go to London and ask for asylum (and probably be sent back); stay in Baghdad for six more months until he could begin a scholarship that he'd won, to study journalism in America (or get killed waiting). Beneath his calm good humor, Othman was paralyzed—he didn't want to leave Baghdad and his family, but staying had become impossible. Every day, he changed his mind.

From the hotel window, Othman could see the palace domes of the Green Zone directly across the Tigris River. "It's sad," he told me. "With all the hopes that we had, and all the dreams, I was totally against the word 'invasion.' Wherever I go, I was defending the Americans and strongly saying, 'America was here to make a change.' Now I have my doubts."

Laith was more blunt: "Sometimes, I feel like we're standing in line for a ticket, waiting to die."

·   ·   ·

By the time Othman and Laith finished talking, it was almost ten o'clock. We went downstairs and found the hotel restaurant empty, with no light or heat. A waiter in a white shirt and black vest emerged out of the darkness to take our orders. We shivered for an hour until the food came.

There was an old woman at the cash register, with long, dyed-blond hair, a shapeless gown, and a macramé beret that kept falling off her head. I recognized her: she had been the cashier in 2003, when I first came to the Palestine. Her name was Taja, and she had worked at the hotel for twenty-five years. She had the smile of a mad hag.

I asked if there had been any other customers tonight. "My dear, no one," Taja said, in English. The sight of me seemed to jar loose a bundle of memories. Her brother had gone to New Orleans in 1948 and forgotten all about her. There was music here in the old days, she said, and she sang a few lines from the Spaniels' "Goodnight, Sweetheart, Goodnight":

> Goodnight, sweetheart,
> Well it's time to go.
> I hate to leave you, but I really must say,
> Goodnight, sweetheart, goodnight.

When the Americans first came, Taja said, the hotel was full of customers, including marines. She took the exam to work as a translator three times, but kept failing, because the questions were so hard: "The spider is an insect or an animal?" "Water is a beverage or a food?" Who could answer such questions?

Taja smiled at us. "Now all finished," she said.

My Time Will Come

Millions of Iraqis, spanning the country's religious and ethnic spectrum, welcomed the overthrow of Saddam Hussein. But the mostly young men and women who embraced America's project so enthusiastically that they were prepared to risk their lives for it may constitute Iraq's smallest minority. I came across them in every city: the young man in Mosul who loved Metallica and signed up to be a translator at a U.S. Army base; the DVD salesman in Najaf whose plans to study medicine were crushed by Baath Party favoritism, and who offered his services to the first American Humvee that entered his city. They had learned English from American movies and music, and from listening secretly to the BBC. Before the war, their only chance at a normal life was to flee the country—a nearly impossible feat. Their future in Saddam's Iraq was, as the Metallica fan in Mosul put it, "a one-way road leading to nothing." I thought of them as oddballs, like misunderstood high-school students whose isolation ends when they go off to college. In a similar way, the four years of the war created intense friendships, but they were forged through collective disappointment. The arc from hope to betrayal that traverses the Iraq war is nowhere more vivid than in the lives of these Iraqis. America's failure to understand, trust, and protect its closest friends in Iraq is a small drama that contains the larger history of defeat.

An interpreter named Firas—he insisted on using his real name—grew up in a middle-class Shia family in a prosperous Baghdad neighborhood. He is a big man in his mid-thirties with a shaved head, and his fierce, heavily ringed eyes provide a glimpse into the reserves of energy that lie beneath his phlegmatic surface. As a young man, Firas was shut out of a government job by his family's religious affiliation and by his lack of connections. He wasted his twenties in a series of petty occupations: selling cigarettes wholesale; dealing in spare parts; peddling books on Mutanabi Street, in old Baghdad. Books, more than anything, shaped Firas's passionately melancholy character. As a young man, he kept a credo on his wall in English and Arabic: "Be honest without the thought of Heaven or Hell." He was particularly impressed by *The Outsider*, a 1956 philosophical work by the British existentialist Colin Wilson. "He wrote about the 'non-belonger,'" Firas explained. Firas felt like an exile in his own land, but, he recalled, "There was always this sound in the back of my head: the time will come, the change will come, *my* time will come. And when 2003 came, I couldn't believe how right I was."

Overnight, everything was new. Americans, whom he had seen only in movies, rolled through the streets. Men who had been silent all their lives cursed Saddam in front of their neighbors. The fall of the regime revealed traits that Iraqis had kept hidden: the greed that drove some to loot, the courage that made others stay on the job. Firas felt a lifelong depression lift.

"The first thing I learned about myself was that I can make things happen," he said. "When you feel that you are an outcast, you don't really put an effort in anything. But after the war I would run here and there, I would *kill* myself, I would focus on one thing and not stop until I do it."

Thousands of Iraqis converged on the Palestine Hotel and, later, the Green Zone, in search of work with the Americans. In the chaos of the early days, a demonstrable ability to speak English— sometimes in a chance encounter with a street patrol—was enough to get you hired by an enterprising marine captain. Firas began working in military intelligence. Almost all the Iraqis who were hired became interpreters, and American soldiers called them "terps," often giving them nicknames for convenience and, later, security (Firas became Phil). But what the Iraqis had to offer went well beyond linguistic ability: each of them was, potentially, a cultural adviser, an intelligence officer, a policy analyst. Firas told the soldiers not to point with their feet, not to ask to be introduced to someone's sister. Interpreters assumed that their perspective would be valuable to foreigners who knew little or nothing of Iraq.

Whenever I asked Iraqis what kind of government they had wanted to replace Saddam's regime, I got the same answer: they had never given it any thought. They just assumed that the Americans would bring the right people, and the country would blossom with freedom, prosperity, consumer goods, travel opportunities. In this, they mirrored the wishful thinking of American officials and neoconservative intellectuals who failed to plan for trouble. Almost no Iraqi claimed to have anticipated videos of beheadings, or Moqtada al-Sadr, or the terrifying question "Are you Sunni or Shia?" Least of all did they imagine that America would make so many mistakes, and persist in those mistakes to the point that even fair-minded Iraqis wondered about ulterior motives. In retrospect, the blind faith that many Iraqis displayed in themselves and in America seems naïve. But, now that Iraq's demise is increasingly regarded as foreordained, it's worth recalling the optimism among Iraqis four years ago.

.   .   .

Ali, an interpreter in Baghdad, spent his childhood in Pennsylvania and Oklahoma, where his father was completing his graduate studies. In 1987, when Ali was eleven and his father was shortly to get his green card, the family returned to Baghdad for a brief visit. But it was during the war with Iran, and the authorities refused to let them leave again. Ali had to learn Arabic from scratch. He grew up in Ghazaliya, a Baathist stronghold in western Baghdad where Shia families like his were rare. Iraq felt like a prison, and Ali considered his American childhood a paradise lost.

In 2003, soon after the arrival of the Americans, soldiers in his neighborhood persuaded him to work as an interpreter with the Eighty-second Airborne Division. He wore a U.S. Army uniform and a bandanna, and during interrogations he used broken Arabic in order to make prisoners think he was American. Although the work was not yet dangerous, an instinct led him to mask his identity and keep his job to himself around the neighborhood. Ali found that, although many soldiers were friendly, they often ignored information and advice from their Iraqi employees. Interpreters would give them names of insurgents, and nothing would happen. When Ali suggested that soldiers buy up locals' rocket-propelled grenade launchers so that they would not fall into the hands of insurgents, he was disregarded. When interpreters drove onto the base, their cars were searched, and at the end of their shift they would sometimes find their car doors unlocked or a mirror broken—the cars had been searched again. "People came with true faces to the Americans, with complete loyalty," Ali said. "But, from the beginning, they didn't trust us."

Ali initially worked the night shift at a base in his neighborhood and walked home by himself after midnight. In June, 2003, the Americans mounted a huge floodlight at the front gate of the base, and when Ali left for home the light projected his shadow hundreds of feet down the street. "It's dangerous," he told the soldiers at the gate. "Can't you turn it off when we go out?"

"Don't be scared," the soldiers told him. "There's a sniper protecting you all the way."

A couple of weeks later, one of Ali's Iraqi friends was hanging out with the snipers in the tower, and he thanked them. "For what?" the snipers asked. For looking out for us, Ali's friend said. The snipers didn't know what he was talking about, and when he told them they started laughing.

"We got freaked out," Ali said. The message was clear: You Iraqis are on your own.

A Person in Between

The Arabic for "collaborator" is *aameel*—literally, "agent." Early in the occupation, the Baathists in Ali's neighborhood, who at first had been cowed by the Americans' arrival, began a shrewd whispering campaign. They told their neighbors that the Iraqi interpreters who went along on raids were feeding the Americans false information, urging the abuse of Iraqis, stealing houses, and raping women. In the market, a Baathist would point at an Iraqi riding in the back of a Humvee and say, "He's a traitor, a thug." Such rumors were repeated often enough that people began to believe them, especially as the promised benefits of the American occupation failed to materialize. Before long, Ali told me, the Baathists "made the reputation of the interpreter very, very low— worse than the Americans'."

There was no American campaign to counter the word on the street; there wasn't even a sense that these subversive rumors posed a serious threat. "Americans are living in another world,"

Ali said. "There's an Iraqi saying: 'He's sleeping and his feet are baking in the sun.'" The U.S. typically provided interpreters with inferior or no body armor, allowing the Baathists to make a persuasive case that Americans treated all Iraqis badly, even those who worked for them.

"The Iraqis aren't trusting you, and the Americans don't trust you from the beginning," Ali said. "You became a person in between."

•   •   •

Firas met the personal interpreter of L. Paul Bremer III, the head of the Coalition Provisional Authority—which governed Iraq for fourteen months after the invasion—in the fall of 2003. Soon, Firas had secured a privileged view of official America, translating documents at the Republican Palace, in the Green Zone.

He liked most of the American officials who came and went at the palace. Even when he saw colossal mistakes at high levels— for example, Bremer's decision to abolish the Iraqi Army—Firas admired his new colleagues, and believed that they were helping to create institutions that would lead to a better future. And yet Firas kept being confronted by fresh ironies: he had less authority than any of the Americans, although he knew more about Iraq; and the less that Americans knew about Iraq the less they wanted to hear from him, especially if they occupied high positions.

One day, Firas accompanied one of Bremer's top political advisers to a meeting with an important Shiite cleric. The cleric's mosque, the Baratha, is an ancient Shiite bastion, and Firas, whose family came from the holy city of Najaf, knew a great deal about the mosque and the cleric. On the way, the adviser asked, "Is this a mosque or a shrine or what?" Firas said, "It's the Baratha mosque," and he started to explain its significance, but the adviser cut him short: "O.K., got it." They went into the meeting with the cleric, who was from a hard-line party backed by Tehran but who spoke as if he represented the views of all Iraqis. He didn't represent the views of many people Firas knew, and, given the chance, Firas could have told the adviser that the mosque and its imam had a history of promoting Shia nationalism. "There were a million comments in my head," Firas recalled. "Why the hell was he paying so much attention to this imam?"

Bremer and his advisers—Scott Carpenter, Meghan O'Sullivan, and Roman Martinez—were creating an interim constitution and negotiating the transfer of power to Iraqis, but they did not speak Arabic and had no background in the Middle East. The Iraqis they spent time with were, for the most part, returned exiles with sectarian agendas. The Americans had little sense of what ordinary Iraqis were experiencing, and they seemed oblivious of a readily available source of knowledge: the Iraqi employees who had lived in Baghdad for years, and who went home to its neighborhoods every night. "These people would consider themselves too high to listen to a translator," Firas said. "Maybe they were interested more in telling D.C. what they want to hear instead of telling them what the Iraqis are saying."

Later, when the Coalition Provisional Authority was replaced by the U.S. Embassy, and political appointees gave way to career diplomats, Firas found himself working for a different kind of American. The embassy's political counselor, Robert Ford, his deputy, Henry Ensher, and a younger official in the political section, Jeffrey Beals, spoke Arabic, had worked extensively in the region, and spent most of their time in Baghdad talking to a range of Iraqis, including extremists. They gave Firas and other "foreign-service nationals" more authority, encouraging them to help write reports on Iraqi politics that were sometimes forwarded to Washington. Beals would be interviewed in Arabic on Al Jazeera and then endure a thorough critique by an Iraqi colleague—Ahmed, a tall, handsome Kurdish Shiite who lived just outside Sadr City, and who was obsessed with Iraqi politics. When Firas, Ali, and Ahmed visited New York during a training trip, Beals's brother was their escort.

Beals quit the foreign service after almost two years in Iraq and is now studying history at Columbia University. He said that, with Americans in Baghdad coming and going every six or twelve months, "the lowest rung on your ladder ends up being the real institutional memory and repository of expertise—which is always a tension, because it's totally at odds with their status." The inversion of the power relationship between American officials and Iraqi employees became more dramatic as the dangers increased and American civilians lost almost all mobility around Baghdad. Beals said, "There aren't many people with pro-American eyes and the means to get their message across who can go into Sadr City and tell you what's happening day to day."

Badges

On the morning of January 18, 2004, a suicide truck bomber detonated a massive payload amid a line of vehicles waiting to enter the Green Zone by the entry point known as the Assassins' Gate. Most Iraqis working in the Green Zone knew someone who died in the explosion, which incinerated twenty-five people. Ali was hit by the blowback but was otherwise uninjured; two months later, he narrowly escaped an assassination attempt while driving to work. Throughout 2004, the murder of interpreters and other Iraqi employees became increasingly commonplace. Seven of Ali's friends who worked with the U.S. military were killed, which prompted him to leave the army and take a job at the embassy.

In Mosul, insurgents circulated a DVD showing the decapitations of two military interpreters. American soldiers stationed there expressed sympathy to their Iraqi employees, but, one interpreter told me, there was "no *real* reaction": no offer of protection, in the form of a weapons permit or a place to live on base. He said, "The soldiers I worked with were friends and they felt sorry for us—they were good people—but they couldn't help. The people above them didn't care. Or maybe the people above *them* didn't care." This story repeated itself across the country: Iraqi employees of the U.S. military began to be kidnapped and killed in large numbers, and there was essentially no American response. Titan Corporation, of Chantilly, Virginia, which until December held the Pentagon contract for employing interpreters in Iraq, was notorious among Iraqis for mistreating its foreign staff. I spoke with an interpreter who was injured in a roadside explosion; Titan refused to compensate him for the time he spent recovering from second-degree burns on his hands and feet. An Iraqi woman working at an American base was recognized by someone she had known in college, who began calling her with death threats. She told me that when she went to the Titan representative for help he responded, "You have two choices: move or quit." She told him that if she quit and stayed home, her life would be in danger. "That's not my business," the representative said. (A Titan spokesperson said, "The safety and welfare of all employees, including, of course, contract workers, is the highest priority.")

A State Department official in Iraq sent a cable to Washington criticizing the Americans' "lackadaisical" attitude about helping Iraqi employees relocate. In an e-mail to me, he said, "Most of them have lived secret lives for so long that they are truly a unique 'homeless' population in Iraq's war zone—dependent on us for security and not convinced we will take care of them when we leave." It's as if the Americans never imagined that the intimidation and murder of interpreters by other Iraqis would undermine the larger American effort, by destroying the confidence of Iraqis who wanted to give it support. The problem was treated as managerial, not moral or political.

.　　　.　　　.

One day in January 2005, Riyadh Hamid, a Sunni father of six from the embassy's political section, was shot to death as he left his house for work. When Firas heard the news at the embassy, he was deeply shaken: he, Ali, or Ahmed could be next. But he never thought of quitting. "At that time, I believed more in my cause, so if I die for it, let it be," he said.

Americans and Iraqis at the Embassy collected $20,000 in private donations for Hamid's widow. At first, the U.S. government refused to pay workmen's compensation, because Hamid had been traveling between home and work and was not technically on the job when he was killed. (Eventually, compensation was approved.) A few days after the murder, Robert Ford, the political counselor, arranged a conversation between Ambassador John Negroponte and the Iraqis from the political section, whom the ambassador had never met. The Iraqis were escorted into a room in a secure wing of the embassy's second floor.

Negroponte had barely expressed his condolences when Firas, Ahmed, and their colleagues pressed him with a single request. They wanted identification that would allow them to enter the Green Zone through the priority lane that Americans with government clearance used, instead of having to wait every morning for an hour or two in a very long line with every other Iraqi who had business in the Green Zone. This line was an easy target for suicide bombers and insurgent lookouts (known in Iraq as *alaasa*—"chewers"). Iraqis at the Embassy had been making this request for some time, without success. "Our problem is badges," the Iraqis told the ambassador.

Negroponte sent for the embassy's regional security officer, John Frese. "Here's the man who is responsible for badges," Negroponte said, and left.

According to the Iraqis, they asked Frese for green badges, which were a notch below the official blue American badges.

These allowed the holder to enter through the priority lane and then be searched inside the gate.

"I can't give you that," Frese said.

"Why?"

"Because it says 'Weapon permit: yes.'"

"Change the 'yes' to 'no' for us."

Frese's tone was peremptory: "I can't do that."

Ahmed made another suggestion: allow the Iraqis to use their embassy passes to get into the priority lane. Frese again refused. Ahmed turned to one of his colleagues and said, in Arabic, "We're blowing into a punctured bag."

"My top priority is embassy security, and I won't jeopardize it, no matter what," Frese told them, and the Iraqis understood that this security did not extend to them—if anything, they were part of the threat.

After the meeting, a junior American diplomat who had sat through it was on the verge of tears. "This is what always calmed me down," Firas said. "I saw Americans who understand me, trust me, believe me, love me. This is what always kept my rage under control and kept my hope alive."

When I recently asked a senior government official in Washington about the badges, he insisted, "They are concerns that have been raised, addressed, and satisfactorily resolved. We acted extremely expeditiously." In fact, the matter was left unresolved for almost two years, until late 2006, when verbal instructions were given to soldiers at the gates of the Green Zone to let Iraqis with embassy passes into the priority lane—and even then individual soldiers, among whom there was rapid turnover, often refused to do so.

Americans and Iraqis recalled the meeting as the moment when the embassy's local employees began to be disenchanted. If Negroponte had taken an interest, he could have pushed Frese to change the badges. But a diplomat doesn't rise to Negroponte's stature by busying himself with small-bore details, and without his directive the rest of the bureaucracy wouldn't budge.

In Baghdad, the regional security officer had unusual power: to investigate staff members, to revoke clearances, to block diplomats' trips outside the Green Zone. The word "security" was ubiquitous—a "magical word," one Iraqi said, that could justify anything. "Saying no to the regional security officer is a dangerous thing," according to a second former embassy official, who occasionally did say no in order to be able to carry out his job. "You're taking a lot of responsibility on yourself." Although Iraqi employees had been vetted with background checks and took regular lie-detector tests, a permanent shadow of suspicion lay over them because they lived outside the Green Zone. Firas once attended a briefing at which the regional security officer told newly arrived Americans that no Iraqi could be trusted.

The reminders were constant. Iraqi staff members were not allowed into the gym or the food court near the embassy. Banned from the military PX, they had to ask an American supervisor to buy them a pair of sunglasses or underwear. These petty humiliations were compounded by security officers who easily crossed the line between vigilance and bullying.

One day in late 2004, Laith, who had never given up hope of working for the American embassy, did well on an interview in the Green Zone and was called to undergo a polygraph. After he was hooked up to the machine, the questions began: Have you ever lied to your family? Do you know any insurgents? At some point, he thought too hard about his answer; when the test was over, the technician called in a security officer and shouted at Laith: "Do you think you can fuck with the United States? Who sent you here?" Laith was hustled out to the gate, where the technician promised to tell his employers at the National Endowment for Democracy to fire him.

"That was the first time I hated the Americans," Laith said.

Corridors of Power

In January 2005, Kirk Johnson, a twenty-four-year-old from Illinois, arrived in Baghdad as an information officer with the United States Agency for International Development. He came from a patriotic family that believed in public service; his father was a lawyer whose chance at an open seat in Congress, in 1986, was blocked when the state Republican Party chose a former wrestling coach named Dennis Hastert to run instead. Johnson, an Arabic speaker, was studying Islamist thought as a Fulbright scholar in Cairo when the war began; when he arrived in Baghdad, he became one of U.S.A.I.D.'s few Arabic-speaking Americans in Iraq.

Johnson, who is rangy, earnest, and baby-faced, thought that he was going to help America rebuild Iraq, in a mission that was his generation's calling. Instead, he found a "narcotic" atmosphere in the Green Zone. Surprisingly few Americans ever ventured outside its gates. A short drive from the embassy, at the Blue Star Café—famous for its chicken fillet and fries—contractors could be seen, in golf shirts, khakis, and baseball caps, enjoying a leisurely lunch, their Department of Defense badges draped around their necks. At such moments, it was hard not to have uncharitable thoughts about the war—that Americans today aren't equipped for something of this magnitude. Iraq is that rare war in which people put on weight. An Iraqi woman at the embassy who had seen many Americans come and go—and revered a few of them—declared that 70 percent of them were "useless, crippled," avoiding debt back home or escaping a bad marriage. I met an American official who, during one year, left the Green Zone less than half a dozen times; unlike many of his colleagues, he understood this to be a problem.

The deeper the Americans dug themselves into the bunker, the harder they tried to create a sense of normalcy, resulting in

what Johnson called "a bizarre arena of paperwork and booze."
There were karaoke nights and volleyball leagues, the Baghdad
Regatta, and "Country Night—One Howdy-Doody Good Time."
Halliburton, the defense contractor, hosted a Middle Eastern
Night. The cubicles in U.S.A.I.D.'s new Baghdad office building,
Johnson discovered, were exactly the same as the cubicles at its
headquarters in Washington. The more chaotic Iraq became,
the more the Americans resorted to bureaucratic gestures of
control. The fact that it took five signatures to get Adobe Acro-
bat installed on a computer was strangely comforting.

Johnson learned that Iraqis were third-class citizens in the
Green Zone, after Americans and other foreigners. For a time,
Americans were ordered to wear body armor while outdoors;
when Johnson found out that Iraqi staff members hadn't been
provided with any, he couldn't bear to wear his own around
them. Superiors eventually ordered him to do so. "If you're still
properly calibrated, it can be a shameful sort of existence there,"
Johnson said. "It takes a certain amount of self-delusion not to
be brought down by it."

In October 2004, two bombs killed four Americans and two
Iraqis at a café and a shopping center inside the Green Zone,
fueling the suspicion that there were enemies within. The Iraqi
employees became perceived as part of an undifferentiated menace. They also induced a deeper, more elusive form of paranoia.
As Johnson put it, "Not that we thought they'd do us bodily
harm, but they represented the reality beyond those blast walls.
You keep your distance from these Iraqis, because if you get
close you start to discover it's absolute bullshit—the lives of
people in Baghdad aren't safer, in spite of our trend lines or
ginned-up reports by contractors that tell you everything is going great."

After eight months in the Green Zone, Johnson felt that the
impulse which had originally made him volunteer to work in

Iraq was dying. He got a transfer to Falluja, to work on the front lines of the insurgency.

•　　　　•　　　　•

The Iraqis who saw both sides of the Green Zone gates had to be as alert as prey in a jungle of predators. Ahmed, the Kurdish Shiite, had the job of reporting on Shia issues, and his feel for the mood in Sadr City was crucial to the political section. When a low-flying American helicopter tore a Shia religious flag off a radio tower, Ahmed immediately picked up on rumors, started by the Mahdi Army, that Americans were targeting Shia worshippers. His job required him to seek contact with members of Shiite militias, who sometimes reacted to him with suspicion. He once went to a council meeting near Sadr City that had been called to arrange a truce between the Americans and the Mahdi Army so that garbage could be cleared from the streets. A council member confronted Ahmed, demanding to know who he was. Ahmed responded, "I'm from a Korean organization. They sent me to find out what solution you guys come up with. Then we're ready to fund the cleanup." At another meeting, he identified himself as a correspondent from an Iraqi television network. No one outside his immediate family knew where he worked.

Ahmed took two taxis to the Green Zone, then walked the last few hundred yards, or drove a different route every day. He carried a decoy phone and hid his embassy phone in his car. He had always loved the idea of wearing a jacket and tie in an official job, but he had to keep them in his office at the embassy—it was impossible to drive to work dressed like that. Ahmed and the other Iraqis entered code names for friends and colleagues into their phones, in case they were kidnapped. Whenever they got a call in public from an American contact, they answered in Arabic and immediately hung up. They communicated mostly by text message. They never spoke English in front of their children. One Iraqi employee slept in his car in the Green Zone parking lot for several nights because it was too dangerous to go home.

Baghdad, which has six million residents, at least provided the cover of anonymity. In a small Shia city in the south, no one knew that a twenty-six-year-old Shiite named Hussein was working for the Americans. "I lie and lie and lie," he said. He acted as a go-between, carrying information between the U.S. outpost, the local government, the Shia clergy, and the radical Sadrists. The Americans would send him to a meeting of clerics with a question, such as whether Iranian influence was fomenting violence. Instead of giving a direct answer, the clerics would demand to know why thousands of American soldiers were unable to protect Shia travelers on a ten-kilometer stretch of road. Hussein would take this back to the Americans and receive a "yes-slash-no kind of answer: We will take it up, we'll get back to them soon—the soon becomes never." In this way, he was privy to both sides of the deepening mutual disenchantment. The fact that he had no contact with Sunnis did not make Hussein feel any safer: by 2004, Shia militias were also targeting Iraqis who worked with Americans.

As a youth, Hussein was an overweight misfit obsessed with Second World War documentaries, and now he felt grateful to the Americans for freeing him from Saddam's tyranny. He also took a certain pride and pleasure in carrying off his risky job. "I'm James Bond, without the nice lady or the famous gadgets," he said. He worked out of a series of rented rooms, seldom going out in public, relying on his cell phone and his laptop, keeping a small "runaway bag" with him in case he needed to leave quickly (a neighbor once informed him that some strangers had asked who lived there, and Hussein moved out the same day). Every few days, he brought his laundry to his parents' house. He stopped seeing friends, and his life winnowed down to his work. "You have to live two separate lives, one visible and the other one invisible," Hussein told me when we spoke in Erbil. (He insisted on meeting in Kurdistan, because there was nowhere else in Iraq that he felt safe being seen with me.) "You have to always be aware of the car behind you. When you want to park, you make sure that the car passes you. You're always afraid of a person staring at you in an abnormal way."

He received three threats. The first was graffiti written across his door, the second a note left outside his house. Both said, "Leave your job or we'll kill you." The third came in December, after American soldiers killed a local militia leader who had been one of Hussein's most important contacts. A friend approached Hussein and conveyed an anonymous warning: "You better not have anything to do with this event. If you do, you'll have to take the consequences." Since Hussein was known to have interpreted for American soldiers at the start of the war, he said, his name had long been on the Mahdi Army's blacklist. It was not just frightening but also embarrassing to be a suspect in the militia leader's death; it undermined Hussein in the eyes of his carefully cultivated contacts. "The stamp that comes to you will never go—you will stay a spy," he said.

He informed his American supervisor, as he had after the previous two threats. And the reply was the same: lie low, take a leave with pay. Hussein had warm feelings for his supervisor, but he wanted a transfer to another country in the Middle East or a scholarship offer to the U.S.—some tangible sign that his safety mattered to them. None was forthcoming. Once, in April 2004, when the Mahdi Army had overrun Coalition posts all over southern Iraq, he had asked to be evacuated along with the Americans and was refused; his pride wouldn't let him ask again. Soon after Hussein received his third threat, his supervisor left Iraq.

"You are now belonging to no side," Hussein said.

·   ·   ·

In June 2006, with kidnappings and sectarian killings out of control in Baghdad, the number of Iraqis working in the embassy's public-affairs section dropped from nine to four; most of those who quit fled the country. The Americans began to replace them with Jordanians. The switch was deeply unpopular with the remaining Iraqis, who understood that it involved the fundamental issue of trust: Jordanians could be housed in the Green Zone without fear (Iraqis could secure temporary housing for only a limited time); Jordanians were issued badges that allowed them into the embassy without being searched; they weren't subject to threat and blackmail, because they lived inside the Green Zone. In every way, Jordanians were easier to deal with. But they also knew nothing about Iraq. One former embassy official, who considered the new policy absurd, lamented that a Jordanian couldn't possibly understand that the term "February 8th mustache," say, referred to the 1963 Baathist coup.

In the past year, the U.S. government has lost a quarter of its 206 Iraqi employees, and many have been replaced by Jordanians. Not long ago, the U.S. began training citizens of the Republic of Georgia to fill the jobs of Iraqis in Baghdad. "I don't know why it's better to have these people flown into Iraq and secure them in the Green Zone," a State Department official said. "Why wouldn't we bring Iraqis into the Green Zone and give *them* housing and secure *them*?" He added, "We're depriving people of jobs and we're getting them whacked. It's not a pretty picture."

On June 6, amid the exodus of Iraqis from the public-affairs section, an embassy official sent a six-page cable to Washington whose subject line read "Public Affairs Staff Show Strains of Social Discord." The cable described the nightmarish lives of the section's Iraqi employees and the sectarian tensions rising among them. It was an astonishingly candid report, perhaps aimed at forcing the State Department to confront the growing disaster. The cable was leaked to the *Washington Post* and briefly became a political liability. One sentence has stuck in my mind:

"A few staff members approached us to ask what provisions we would make for them if we evacuate."

I went to Baghdad in January partly because I wanted to find an answer to this question. Were there contingency plans for Iraqis, and, if so, whom did they include, and would the Iraqis have to wait for a final American departure? Would any Iraqis be evacuated to the U.S.? No one at the embassy was willing to speak on the record about Iraqi staff, except an official spokesman, Lou Fintor, who read me a statement: "Like all residents of Baghdad, our local employees must attempt to maintain their daily routines despite the disruptions caused by terrorists, extremists, and criminals. The new Iraqi government is taking steps to improve the security situation and essential services in Baghdad. The Iraq security forces, in coordination with coalition forces, are now engaged in a wide-range effort to stabilize the security situation in Baghdad. . . . President Bush strongly reaffirmed our commitment to work with the government of Iraq to answer the needs of all Iraqis."

I was granted an interview with two officials, who refused to be named. One of them consulted talking points that catalogued what the embassy had done for Iraqi employees: a Thanksgiving dinner, a recent 35 percent salary increase. Housing in the Green Zone could be made available for a week at a time in critical cases, I was told, though most Iraqis didn't want to be apart from their families. When I asked about contingency plans for evacuation, the second official refused to discuss it on security grounds, but he said, "If we reach that point and have people in danger, the ambassador would go to the secretary of state and ask that they be evacuated, and I think they would do it." The department was reviewing the possibility of issuing special immigrant visas.

To receive this briefing, I had passed through three security doors into the embassy's classified section, where there were no Iraqis and no natural light; it seemed as if every molecule of

Baghdad air had been sealed off behind the last security door. The embassy officials struck me as decent, overworked people, yet I left the interview with a feeling of shame. The problem lay not with the individuals but with the institution and, beyond that, with the politics of the American project in Iraq, which from the beginning has been conducted under the illusion that controlling the message mattered more than the reality. A former official at the embassy told me, "When we say that the corridors of power are insulated, is it that the officials aren't receiving the information, or is it because the construct under which they're operating doesn't even allow them to absorb it?" To admit that Iraqis who work with Americans need to be evacuated would blow a hole in the administration's version of the war.

Several days after the interview at the embassy, I had a more frank conversation with an official there. "I don't know if it's fair to say, 'You work at an embassy of a foreign country, so that country has to evacuate you,'" he said. "Do the Australians have a plan? Do the Romanians? The Turks? The British?" He added, "If I worked at the Hungarian Embassy in Washington, would the Hungarians evacuate me from the United States?"

When I mentioned these remarks to Othman, he asked, "Would the Americans behead an American working at the Hungarian Embassy in Washington?"

The Hearts of Your Allies

In the summer of 2006, Iraqis were fleeing the country at the rate of 40,000 per month. The educated middle class of Baghdad was decamping to Jordan and Syria, taking with them the skills and the more secular ideas necessary for rebuilding a destroyed society, leaving the city to the religious militias—eastern Baghdad was controlled by the poor and increasingly radical Shia, the western districts dominated by Sunni insurgents. House by house, the capital was being ethnically cleansed.

By that time, Firas, Ali, and Ahmed had been working with the Americans for several years. Their commitment and loyalty were beyond doubt. Just going to work in the morning required an extraordinary ability to disregard danger. Panic, Firas realized, could trap you: when the threat came, you felt you were a dead man no matter where you turned, and your mind froze and you sat at home waiting for them to come for you. In order to function, Firas simply blocked out the fear. "My friends at work became the only friends I have," he said. "My entertainment is at work, my pleasure is at work, everything is at work." Firas and his friends never imagined that the decision to leave Iraq would be forced on them not by the violence beyond the Green Zone but from within the embassy itself.

After the bombing of the gold-domed Shia mosque in Samarra that February, Sadr City had become the base for the Mahdi Army's roving death squads. Ahmed's neighborhood fell under their complete control, and his drive to work took him through numerous unfriendly—and thorough—militia checkpoints. Strangers began to ask about him. A falafel vender in Sadr City whose stall was often surrounded by Mahdi Army *alaasa* warned Ahmed that his name had come up. On two occasions, people he scarcely knew approached him and expressed concern about his well-being. One evening, an American official named Oliver Moss, with whom Ahmed was close, walked him out of the embassy to the parking lot and said, "Ahmed, I know you work for us, but if something happens to you we won't be able to do anything for you." Ahmed asked for a cot in a Green Zone trailer and was given the yes/no answer—equal parts personal sympathy and bureaucratic delay—which sometimes felt worse than a flat refusal. The chaos in Baghdad had created a landgrab for Green Zone accommodations, and the Iraqi government was distributing coveted apartments to friends of the political parties while evicting Iraqis who worked with the Americans. The interpreters were distrusted and despised even by officials of the new government that the Americans had helped bring to power.

In April, a Shiite member of the parliament asked Ahmed to look into the status of a Mahdi Army member who had been detained by the Americans. Iraqis at the embassy sometimes used their office to do small favors for their compatriots; such gestures reminded them that they were serving Iraq as well as America. But Ahmed sent his inquiry through the wrong channel. His supervisor was on leave in the U.S., and so he sent an e-mail to a reserve colonel in the political section. The colonel refused to provide him with any information, and a couple of weeks later, in May, Ahmed was summoned to talk to an agent from the regional security office.

To the Iraqis, a summons of this type was frightening. Ahmed and his friends had seen several colleagues report to the regional security office and never appear at their desks again, with no explanation; one had been turned over to the Iraqi police and was jailed for several weeks. "Don't go. They're going to arrest you," Ali told Ahmed. "Just quit. It's not worth it." Ahmed did not listen.

The agent, Barry Hale, who carried a Glock pistol, questioned Ahmed for an hour about his contacts with Sadrists. The notion that Ahmed's job required him to have contact with the Mahdi Army seemed foreign to Hale, as did the need to have well-informed Iraqis in the political section of the embassy. According to an American official close to the case, Hale had a general distrust of Iraqis and wanted to replace them with Jordanians. Another official spoke of a "paranoia partly founded on ignorance. If Ahmed wanted to hurt an American, he could have done it very easily in the three years he worked with us."

Robert Ford, the political counselor, spoke to top officials at the embassy to insure that Ahmed—whom several Americans described as the best Iraqi employee they had worked with—

would be "counseled" but not fired. Everyone assumed that the case was closed. But over the summer, after Ford's service in Baghdad ended, Hale started to pursue Ahmed again. "It was a witch hunt," one of the officials said. "They wanted to fire him and they were just looking for a reason. They decided he was a threat." The irony of his situation was not lost on Ahmed: he was suspected of giving information to a militia that would kill him instantly if they knew where he worked.

In late July, Hale summoned Ahmed again. On Hale's desk, Ahmed saw a thick file marked "Secret," next to a pair of steel handcuffs.

"Did you ever get a phone call from the Mahdi Army?" Hale asked.

"I'll be lucky if I get a phone call from them," Ahmed replied. "My supervisor will be very happy."

The interrogation came down to one point: Hale insisted that Ahmed had misled him by saying that the reserve colonel had "never answered" Ahmed's inquiry, when in fact the colonel had sent back an e-mail asking who had given Ahmed the detainee's name. Ahmed hadn't considered this an answer to his question about the detainee's status, and therefore hadn't mentioned it to Hale. This was his undoing.

When Ahmed returned to his desk, Firas and Ali embraced him and congratulated him on escaping detention. Meanwhile, lower-ranking embassy officials began frantically calling and e-mailing colleagues in Washington, some of whom tried to intervene on Ahmed's behalf. But by then it was too late. The new ambassador, Zalmay Khalilzad, and his deputy were out of the country, and the official in charge of the embassy was Ford's replacement, Margaret Scobey, a new arrival in Baghdad, who had no idea of Ahmed's value. Firas said of her, "She was really not into the Iraqis in the office." Some Americans and Iraqis described her as a notetaker for the ambassador who sent oddly upbeat reports back to Washington. Two days after the second interrogation, Scobey signed off on Ahmed's termination, and ordered a junior officer named Rebecca Fong to go down to Ahmed's office and, in front of his tearful American and Iraqi colleagues, fire him.

Ahmed later told an American official, "I think the U.S. is still in a war. I don't think you're going to win this war if you don't win the hearts of your allies." The State Department refused to discuss the case for reasons of privacy and security.

Ahmed's firing demoralized Americans and Iraqis alike. Fong transferred out of the political section. For Firas, it meant that, no matter how long he worked with the Americans and how many risks he took, he, too, would ultimately be discarded. He began to tell himself, "My turn is coming, my turn is coming"—a perverse echo of his mantra before the fall of Saddam. The Iraqis now felt that, as Ali said, "Heaven doesn't want us and Hell doesn't want us. Where will we go?" If the Americans were turning against them, they had no friends at all.

Three days after Ahmed's departure, Scobey appeared in the Iraqis' office to say that she was sorry but there was nothing she could have done for Ahmed. Firas listened in disgust before bursting out, "All the sacrifices, all the work, all the devotion mean nothing to you. We are still terrorists in your eyes." When, a month later, Khalilzad met with a large group of Iraqi employees to hear their concerns, Firas attended reluctantly. After the Iraqis raised the possibility of immigrant visas to the U.S., Khalilzad said, "We want the good Iraqi people to stay in the country." An Iraqi replied, "If we're still alive." Firas, speaking last, told the ambassador, "We are tense all the time, we don't know what we are doing, right or wrong. Some Iraqis are more afraid in the embassy than in the Red Zone"—that is, Baghdad. There was a ripple of laughter among the Iraqis, and Khalilzad couldn't suppress a smile.

At this point, Firas knew that he would leave Iraq. Through the efforts of Rebecca Fong and Oliver Moss—who pulled strings with counterparts in European embassies in Baghdad—Ahmed, Firas, and Ali obtained visas to Europe. By November, they were gone.

Johnson's List

On the morning of October 13, an Iraqi official with U.S.A.I.D. named Yaghdan left his house in western Baghdad, in search of fuel for his generator. He saw a scrap of paper lying by the garage door. It was a torn sheet of copybook paper—the kind that his agency distributed to schools around Iraq, with date and subject lines printed in English and Arabic. The paper bore a message, in Arabic: "We will cut off heads and throw them in the garbage." Nearby, against the garden fence, lay the severed upper half of a small dog.

Yaghdan (who wanted his real name used) was a mild, conscientious thirty-year-old from a family of struggling businessmen. Since taking a job with the Americans, in 2003, he had been so cautious that, at first, he couldn't imagine how his cover had been blown. Then he remembered: Two weeks earlier, as he was showing his badge at the bridge offering entry into the Green Zone, Yaghdan had noticed a man from his neighborhood standing in the same line, watching him. The neighbor worked as a special guard with a Shia militia and must have been the *alaas* who betrayed him.

Yaghdan's request for a transfer to a post outside the country was never answered. Instead, U.S.A.I.D. offered him a month's leave with pay or residence for six months in the agency compound in the Green Zone, which would have meant a long separation from his young wife. Yaghdan said, "I thought, I should not be selfish and put myself as a priority. It wasn't a happy decision." Within a week of the threat, Yaghdan and his wife flew to Dubai, in the United Arab Emirates.

Yaghdan sent his résumé to several companies in Dubai, highlighting his years of service with an American contractor and U.S.A.I.D. He got a call from a legal office that needed an administrative assistant. "Did you work in the U.S.?" the interviewer asked him. Yaghdan said that his work had been in Iraq. "Oh, in Iraq . . ." He could feel the interviewer pulling back. A man at another office said, "Oh, you worked against Saddam? You betrayed Saddam? The American people are stealing Iraq." Yaghdan, who is not given to bitterness, finally lost his cool: "No, the Arab people are stealing Iraq!" He didn't get the job. He was amazed—even in cosmopolitan Dubai, people loved Saddam, especially after his botched execution, in late December. Yaghdan's résumé was an encumbrance. Iraqis were considered bad Arabs, and Iraqis who worked with the Americans were traitors. The slogans and illusions of Arab nationalism, which had seemed to collapse with the regime of Saddam, were being given a second life by the American failure in Iraq. What hurt Yaghdan most was the looks that said, "You trusted the Americans—and see what happened to you."

Yaghdan then contacted many American companies, thinking that they, at least, would look favorably on his service. He wasn't granted a single interview. The only work he could find was as a gofer in the office of a Dubai cleaning company.

Yaghdan's Emirates visa expired in mid-January, and he had to leave the country and renew the visa in Amman. I met him there. The Jordanians had been turning away young Iraqis at the border and the airport for several months, but they issued Yaghdan and his wife three-day visas, after which they had to pay a daily fine, on top of hotel bills. After a week's delay, the visas came through, but, upon returning to Dubai, Yaghdan learned that the Emirates would no longer extend the visas of Iraqis. A job offer as an administrative assistant came from a university in Qatar, but the Qataris wouldn't grant him a visa without a security clearance from the Iraqi Ministry of the Interior, which was in the hands of the Shia party whose militia had sent him the death threat. He couldn't even become a refugee, which would have given him some protection against deportation, because the United Nations High Commissioner for Refugees had closed its Emirates office years ago. Yaghdan had heard that the only way to get a U.S. visa was through a job offer—nearly impossible to obtain—or by marrying an American, so he didn't bother to try. He had reached the end of his legal options and would have to return to Iraq by April 1. "It's like taking the decision to commit suicide," he said.

· · ·

While Yaghdan was in Dubai, news of his dilemma made its way through the U.S.A.I.D. grapevine to Kirk Johnson, the young Arabic speaker who had asked to be transferred to Falluja. By then, Johnson's life had been turned upside down as well.

In Falluja, Johnson had supervised Iraqis who were clearing out blocked irrigation canals along the Euphrates River. His job was dangerous and seldom rewarding, but it gave him the sense of purpose that he had sought in Iraq. Determined to experience as much as possible, he went out several times a week in a marine convoy to meet tribal sheikhs and local officials. As he rode through Falluja's lethal streets, Johnson eyed every bag of trash and parked car for hidden bombs, and practiced swatting away imaginary grenades. After a local sniper shot several marines, Johnson's anxiety rose even higher.

In December 2005, after twelve exhausting months in Iraq, during which he lost forty pounds, Johnson went on leave and met his parents for a Christmas vacation in the Dominican Republic. In the middle of the night, Johnson rose unconscious from his hotel bed and climbed onto a ledge outside the second-floor window. A night watchman noticed him staring at an unfinished concrete apartment complex across the road. The night before, the sight of the building had triggered his fear of the sniper, and he had instinctively dropped to the floor of his room. Standing on the ledge, he shouted something and then fell fifteen feet.

Johnson tore open his jaw and forehead and broke his nose, teeth, and wrists. He required numerous surgeries on his shattered face, and stayed in the hospital for several weeks. But it was much longer before he could accept that he would not rejoin the marines and Iraqis he had left in Falluja. There were rumors in Iraq that he had been drunk and was trying to avoid returning. Back home in Illinois, healing in his childhood bed, he dreamed every night that he was in Iraq, unable to save people, or else in mortal peril himself.

In January 2006, Paul Bremer came through Chicago to promote his book, *My Year in Iraq.* Johnson sat in one of the front rows, ready to challenge Bremer's upbeat version of the reconstruction, but during the question period Bremer avoided the young man with the bandaged face who was frantically waving his arms, which were still in casts.

Johnson moved to Boston, but he kept thinking about his failure to return to Iraq. One day, he heard the news about Yaghdan, whom he had known in Baghdad, and that night he barely slept. It suddenly occurred to him that this was an injustice he could address. He could send money; he could alert journalists and politicians. He wrote a detailed account of Yaghdan's situation and sent it to his congressman, Dennis Hastert. But Hastert's office, which was reeling from the Mark Foley scandal and the midterm elections, told Johnson that it could not help Yaghdan. Johnson wrote an op-ed article calling for asylum for Yaghdan and others like him, and on December 15 it ran in the *Los Angeles Times.* A U.S.A.I.D. official in Baghdad sent it around to colleagues. Then Johnson began to hear from Iraqis.

First, it was people he knew—former colleagues in desperate circumstances like Yaghdan's. Iraqis forwarded his article to other Iraqis, and he started to compile a list of names; by January he was getting e-mails from strangers with subject lines like

"Can you help me Please?" and "I want to be on the list." An Iraqi woman who had worked for the Coalition Provisional Authority attached a letter of recommendation written in 2003 by Bernard Kerik, then Iraq's acting minister of the interior. It proclaimed, "Your courage to support the Coalition forces has sent home an irrefutable message: that terror will not rule, that liberty will triumph, and that the seeds of freedom will be planted into the hearts of the great citizens of Iraq." The woman was now a refugee in Amman.

A former U.S.A.I.D. procurement agent named Ibrahim wrote that he was stranded in Egypt after having paid traffickers $12,000 to smuggle him from Baghdad to Dubai to Mumbai to Alexandria, with the goal of reaching Europe. When the Egyptian police figured out the scheme, Ibrahim took shelter in a friend's flat in a Cairo slum. The Egyptians, wary of a popular backlash against rising Shia influence in the Middle East, were denying Iraqis legal status there. Ibrahim didn't know where to go next: in addition to his immigration troubles, he had an untreated brain tumor.

By the first week of February, Johnson's list had grown to more than a hundred names. Working tirelessly, he had found a way to channel his desire to do something for Iraq. He assembled the information on a spreadsheet, and on February 5 he took it with him on a bus to Washington—along with Yaghdan's threat letter and a picture of the severed dog.

•　　　•　　　•

Toward the end of January, I traveled to Damascus. Iraqis were tolerated by Syria, which opened its doors in the name of Arab brotherhood. Yet Syria offered them no prospect of earning a living: few Iraqis could get work permits.

About a million Iraqis were now in Syria. Every morning that I visited, there were long lines outside the United Nations High

Commissioner for Refugees office in central Damascus. Forty-five thousand Iraqis had officially registered as refugees, and more were signing up every day, amid reports that the Syrian regime was about to tighten its visa policy and had begun turning people back at the border.

One chilly night, I went to Sayyida Zainab, a neighborhood centered around the shrine of the sister of Hussein, grandson of the Prophet and the central martyr of Shiism. This had become an Iraqi Shia district, and on the main street were butcher shops and kebab stands that reminded me of commercial streets in Baghdad. There were pictures of Shia martyrs, and also of Moqtada al-Sadr, outside the real-estate offices, some of which, I was told, were fronts for brothels. (Large numbers of Iraqi women make their living in Syria as prostitutes.) Shortly before midnight, buses from Baghdad began to pull into a parking lot where boys were still up, playing soccer. One bus had a shattered windshield from gunfire at the start of its journey. A minibus driver told me that the trip took fourteen hours, including a long wait at the border, and that the road through Iraq was menaced by insurgents, criminal gangs, and American patrols. And yet some Iraqis who had run out of money in Damascus hired the driver to take them back to Baghdad the same night. "No one is left there," he said. "Only those who are too poor to leave, and those with a bad omen on their heads, who will be killed in one of three ways—kidnapping, car bomb, or militias."

In another Damascus neighborhood, I met a family of four that had just arrived from Baghdad after receiving a warning from insurgents to abandon their house. They had settled in a three-room apartment and were huddled around a kerosene heater. They were middle-class people who had left almost everything behind—the mother had sold her gold and jewelry to pay for plane tickets to Damascus—and the son and daughter hadn't been able to finish school. The daughter, Zamzam, was seventeen, and in the past few months she had been seeing corpses in the streets on her way to school, some of them eaten by dogs because no one dared to take them away. On days when there was fighting in her neighborhood, Zamzam said, walking to school felt like a death wish. Her laptop computer had a picture of an American flag as its screen saver, but it also had recordings of insurgent ballads in praise of a famous Baghdad sniper. She was an energetic, ambitious girl, but her dark eyes had the haunted look of a much older woman.

I spent a couple of hours walking with the family around the souk and the grand Umayyad Mosque in the old city center. The parents strolled arm in arm—enjoying, they said, a ritual that had been impossible in Baghdad for the past two years. I left them outside a theater where a comedy featuring an all-Iraqi cast was playing to packed houses of refugees. The play was called *Homesick.*

•　　•　　•

In the past few months, Western and Arab governments announced that they would no longer honor Iraqi passports issued after the 2003 invasion, since the passport had been so shoddily produced that it was subject to widespread forgery. This was the first passport many Iraqis had ever owned, and it was now worthless. Iraqis with Saddam-era passports were also out of luck, because the Iraqi government had canceled them. A new series of passports was being printed, but the Ministry of the Interior had ordered only around 20,000 copies, an Iraqi official told me, far too few to meet the need—which meant that obtaining a valid passport, like buying gas or heating oil, would become subject to black-market influences. In Baghdad, Othman told me that a new passport would cost him $600, paid to a fixer with connections at the passport offices. The Ministry of the Interior refused to allow Iraqi embassies to print the new series, so refugees outside Iraq who needed valid passports

would have to return to the country they had fled or pay someone a thousand dollars to do it for them.

Between October 2005 and September 2006, the United States
admitted 202 Iraqis as refugees, most of them from the years
under Saddam. Last year, the Bush administration increased the
allotment to 500. By the end of 2006, there were almost 2 million Iraqis living as refugees outside their country—most of
them in Syria and Jordan. American policy held that these Iraqis
were not refugees, that they would go back to their country as
soon as it was stabilized. The U.S. embassies in Damascus and
Amman continued to turn down almost all visa applications
from Iraqis. So the fastest-growing refugee crisis in the world
remained hidden, receiving little attention other than in a few
reports from organizations like Human Rights Watch and Refugees International.

Then, in early January, U.N.H.C.R. sent out an appeal for $60
million for the support and eventual resettlement of Iraqi refugees. On January 16, the Senate Judiciary Committee's subcommittee on refugees, chaired by Senator Edward M. Kennedy, of
Massachusetts, held hearings on Iraqi refugees, with a special
focus on Iraqis who had worked for the U.S. government. Pressure in Congress and the media began to build, and the administration scrambled to respond. When an Iraqi employee of the
embassy was killed on January 11, and one from U.S.A.I.D. on
February 14, statements of condolence were sent out by Ambas-
sadorKhalilzadandthechiefadministratorofU.S.A.I.D.—gestures
that few could remember happening before.

In early February, the State Department announced the formation of a task force to deal with the problem of Iraqi refugees.
A colleague of Kirk Johnson's at U.S.A.I.D., who had been skeptical that Johnson's efforts would achieve anything, wrote to
him, "Interesting what a snowball rolled down a hill can cause.
This is your baby. Good going." On February 14, at a press conference at the State Department, members of the task force

declared a new policy: the United States would fund $18 million of the U.N.H.C.R. appeal, and it would "plan to process expeditiously some seven thousand Iraqi refugee referrals," which meant that two or three thousand Iraqis might be admitted to the U.S. by the end of the fiscal year. Finally, the administration would seek legislation to create a special immigrant visa for Iraqis who had worked for the U.S. Embassy.

During the briefing, Ellen Sauerbrey, the assistant secretary of state for population, refugees, and migration, insisted, "There was really nothing that was indicating there was any significant issue in terms of outflow until—I would say the first real indication began to reach us three or four months ago." Speaking of Iraqi employees, she added, "The numbers of those that have actually been seeking either movement out of the country or requesting assistance have been—our own embassy has said it is a very small number." Sauerbrey put it at less than fifty.

The excuses were unconvincing, but the stirrings of action were encouraging. When Johnson, wearing the only suit he owned, took his list to Washington and dropped it off at the State Department and the U.N.H.C.R. office, the response was welcoming. But he pressed officials for details on the fates of specific individuals: Would Yaghdan be able to register as a refugee in Dubai, where there was no U.N.H.C.R. office, before he was forced to go back to Iraq? How could Ibrahim, trapped in Egypt without legal travel documents, qualify for a visa before his brain tumor killed him? Would Iraqis who had paid ransom to kidnappers be barred entry under the "material support" clause of the Patriot Act? (One embassy employee already had been.) How would Iraqis who had no Kirk Johnson to help them—the military interpreters, the embassy staff, the contractors, the drivers—be able to sign up as refugees or candidates for special immigrant visas? Would the U.S. government seek them out? Would they have to flee the country and find a U.N.H.C.R. office first?

Thanks in part to Johnson's list, Washington was paying attention. Privately, though, a former U.S.A.I.D. colleague told Johnson that his actions would send the message "that it's game over" in Iraq, and America would end up with a million and a half asylum seekers. Johnson feared that the ingrained habit of giving yes/no answers might lower the pressure without solving the problem. His list kept growing after he had delivered it to the U.S. government, and the desperation of those already on it grew as well. By mid-March, Iraqis on the list still had no mechanism for applying to immigrate. According to the State Department, a humanitarian visa for Ibrahim would take up to six months. And Yaghdan's situation was just as dire now as it was when Johnson had written his op-ed. "No matter what is said by the administration, if Yaghdan isn't being helped, then the government is not responding," Johnson told me.

For him, it was a simple matter. "This is the brink right now, where our partners over there are running for their lives," he said. "I defy anyone to give me the counter-argument for why we shouldn't let these people in." He quoted something that President Gerald Ford once said about his decision to admit 130,000 Vietnamese after the fall of Saigon: "To do less would have added moral shame to humiliation."

Evacuation

In 2005, Al Jazeera aired a typically heavy-handed piece about the American evacuation from Saigon, in April 1975, rebroadcasting the famous footage of children and old people being pushed back by marines from the embassy gates, and kicked or punched as they tried to climb onto helicopters. The message for Iraqis working with Americans was clear, and when some of those who worked at U.S.A.I.D. saw the program they were horrified. The next day at work, a small group of them met to talk about it. "Al Jazeera has their own propaganda. Don't believe it," said Ibrahim, the Iraqi who is now hiding out in Cairo.

Hussein, the go-between in southern Iraq, had also begun to think about Vietnam. He had heard that America had left the Vietnamese behind, but he couldn't believe that the same thing would happen in Iraq. "We might be given a good chance to leave with them," he said. "I think about that, because history is telling me that they always have a moral obligation." To Hussein, the obligation was mutual, because he still felt indebted to the Americans for his freedom. I asked him what he would do if he found himself abandoned. Hussein thought about it, then said, "If I reach this point, and I am still alive when I see moral obligation taking the incorrect course, I will say, 'I paid my debt. I am free.'"

At the end of the Vietnam War, Frank Snepp was the C.I.A.'s chief analyst at the American Embassy in Saigon. His 1977 book about the last days of the Vietnam War, *Decent Interval*, describes how the willful ignorance and political illusions of top U.S. officials prevented any serious planning for an evacuation of America's Vietnamese allies. Thousands were left to the mercy of the Communists. The book contains a photograph of the author, thirty-one at the time, standing on the bridge of the U.S.S. *Denver* in the South China Sea, three days after being evacuated from Saigon by helicopter. He is leaning against the rail, his tan, handsome face drawn taut as he stares slightly downward. Recently, I asked Snepp what he had been thinking when the picture was taken.

"I was overwhelmed with guilt," he said. "I kept hearing the voices on the C.I.A. radios of our agents in the field, our Vietnamese friends we wouldn't be able to rescue. And I had to understand how I had been made a party to this. I had been brought up in the Old South, in a chivalric tradition that comes out of the Civil War—you do not abandon your own. And that's exactly what I had done. It hasn't left me to this day."

No conquering enemy army is days away from taking Baghdad; the city is slowly breaking up into smaller, isolated enclaves, and America's Iraqi allies are being executed one by one. It's hard to imagine the American presence in Iraq ending with a dramatic helo lift from a Green Zone landing pad. But, in some ways, the unlikelihood of a spectacularly conclusive finale makes the situation of the Iraqis more perilous than that of the South Vietnamese. It's easier for the U.S. government to leave them to their fate while telling itself that "the good Iraqis" are needed to build the new Iraq.

American institutions in Vietnam were just as unresponsive as they are in Iraq, but, on an individual level, Americans did far more to evacuate their Vietnamese counterparts. In Saigon they had girlfriends, wives, friends, whereas Americans and Iraqis have established only work relationships, which end when the Americans rotate out after six months or a year. In the wide-open atmosphere of Saigon, many officials, including Snepp, broke rules or risked their lives to save people close to them. Americans in Baghdad don't have such discipline problems. A former embassy official pointed out that cell phones and e-mail connect officials in Iraq to their bosses there or in Washington around the clock. "When you can always connect, you can always pass the buck," he said. For all their technology, the Americans in Baghdad know far less about the Iraqis than those in Saigon knew about the Vietnamese. "Intelligence is the first key to empathy," Snepp said.

I asked Snepp what he would say to Americans in Iraq today. "If they want to keep their conscience clean, they better start making lists of people they must help," he said. "They should also not be cautious in questioning their superiors, and that's a very hard thing to do in a rigid environment."

Richard Armitage, who was deputy secretary of state under Colin Powell during the first years of the Iraq war, served as a naval officer in Vietnam. In the last days of that war, he returned as a civilian, on a mission to destroy military assets before they fell into North Vietnamese hands. He arrived too late, and instead turned his energy to the evacuation of South Vietnamese sailors and their families. Armitage led a convoy of barely seaworthy boats, carrying 20,000 people, 1,000 miles across the South China Sea to Manila—the first stop on their journey to the United States.

When I met Armitage recently, at his office in Arlington, Virginia, he was not confident that Iraqis would be similarly resettled. "I guarantee you no one's thinking about it now, because it's so fatalistic and you'd be considered sort of a traitor to the president's policy," he said. "I don't see us taking them in this time, because, notwithstanding what we may owe people, you're not going to bring in large numbers of Arabs to the United States, given the fact that for the last six years the president has scared the pants off the American public with fears of Islamic terrorism."

Even at this stage of the war, Armitage said, officials at the White House retain an "agnosticism about the size of the problem." He added, "The president believes so firmly that he is president for just this mission—and there's something religious about it—that it will succeed, and that kind of permeates. I just take him at his word these days. I think it's very improbable that he'll be successful."

· · ·

I was in Baghdad when the administration announced its new security plan—including an effort to stabilize Baghdad with a "surge" of 20,000 additional troops. I spent a day with Lieutenant Colonel Steven Miska, who commands a small American base surrounded by a large Iraqi one in the old-line Shia district of Kadhimiya. Everywhere we went, Iraqi civilians asked him when the surge would begin. Two dozen men hanging out at a sidewalk tea shop seemed to have the new strategy confused with the Iraq Study Group Report; I took the mix-up to mean that they were desperate for any possible solution. A Shia potentate named Sheikh Muhammad Baqr gave me his version of the new plan over lunch at his house: the Americans were trying to separate the 10 percent of the population that belonged to extremist militias—whether Shia or Sunni—from what he called the "silent majority." If families evicted from mixed areas could be convinced to return to their homes, and if unemployed young men could be put to work, the plan had a chance of restoring confidence in the Americans. The sheikh warned, "In six months you will have to see this plan work, or else the Iraqi people will tell the Americans to find another venue." The sheikh had even less faith in the government of Prime Minister Nuri al-Maliki, which he called a collection of "sectarian movements" brought to power by American folly. "We don't need democracy," he said. "We need General Pinochet in Chile or General Franco in Spain. After they clear the country, we'll have elections."

Lieutenant Colonel Miska, for his part, described the security plan as an attempt to get Americans off the big bases and into Iraqi neighborhoods, where they would occupy small combat outposts on the fault lines of sectarian conflicts and, for the first time, make the protection of civilians a central goal. The new plan represented a repudiation of the strategy that the administration had pursued for the past two years—the handover of responsibility to Iraqi security forces as Americans pulled out of the cities. President Bush had chosen a new commander in Iraq, General David Petraeus, who recently oversaw the writing of the Army and Marine Corps's new counterinsurgency manual. Petraeus has surrounded himself with a brain trust of counterinsurgency experts: Colonel H. R. McMaster, who two years ago executed a nearly identical strategy in the northern city of Tal Afar; Colonel Peter Mansoor; and David Kilcullen, an Australian strategist working at the State Department. Bush named

Timothy Carney, a retired ambassador, to be his reconstruction czar in Iraq; Carney had left the Coalition Provisional Authority in disgust after seeing Bremer make mistake after mistake. After four years of displaying resolve while the war was being lost, the president has turned things over to a group of soldiers and civilians who have been steadfast critics of his strategy. It is almost certainly too late.

In Baghdad, among Iraqi civilians and American soldiers, it's impossible not to want to give the new strategy a try. The alternative, as Iraqis constantly point out, is a much greater catastrophe. "I'm still hoping Bush's new plan can do something," Othman told me. In the weeks after the surge was announced, there were anecdotal reports of Shia and Sunni families returning to their homes. But even if this tentative progress continues, three major obstacles remain. The first is the breakdown of U.S. ground forces, in manpower and equipment; it isn't clear that the strategy can be sustained for more than six months—nowhere near enough time to repair the physical and social destruction of Baghdad.

The second obstacle was described to me by an international official who has spent the past three years in Iraq. "The success of the American strategy is based on a premise that is fundamentally flawed," he said. "The premise is that the U.S. and Iraqi governments are working toward the same goal. It's simply not the case." Shia politicians, the official said, want "to hold on to their majority as long as they can." Their interest isn't democracy but power. Meanwhile, Sunni politicians want "to say no to everything," the official said; the insurgency is politically intractable.

Finally, there is the collapse of political support at home. Most Americans have lost faith in the leadership and conduct of the war, and they want to be rid of it. More important than all the maneuverings in Congress, at the White House, and among the presidential candidates is the fact that nobody wants to deal with Iraq anymore. The columnist Charles Krauthammer, the most ardent of neoconservative hawks, has found someone to blame for the war's failure: the Iraqis. He recently wrote, "We midwifed their freedom. They chose civil war." John Edwards, the Democratic presidential candidate, is also tired of Iraqis. "We've done our part, and now it's time for them to step up to the plate," he recently told this magazine. "When they're doing it to each other, and America's not there and not fomenting the situation, I think the odds are better of the place stabilizing." America is pulling away from Iraq in the fitful, irritable manner of someone trying to wake up from an unpleasant sleep. On my last day in Baghdad, I had lunch with an embassy official, and as we were leaving the restaurant he suddenly said, "Do you think this is all going to seem like a dream? Is it just going to be a fever dream that we'll wake up from and say, 'We got into this crazy war, but now it's over and we never have to think about Iraq again'?" If so, part of our legacy will be thousands of Iraqis who, because they joined the American effort, can no longer live in their own country.

.   .   .

Othman and Laith are still in Baghdad. Earlier this month, Othman spent more than $2,000 on passports for his mother, his two younger brothers, and himself. He is hoping to move the family to Syria. Laith wants to find a job in Kurdistan.

Firas, Ali, and Ahmed are now in Sweden. All three of them would have preferred to go to America. Ali had spent his childhood in the United States; Ahmed was fascinated with American politics; Firas never felt more at home than he had on their training trip, listening to jazz in Greenwich Village. Like all Iraqis who worked with Americans, they spoke in American accents, using American idioms. Ahmed delighted in using phrases like "from the horse's mouth" and "hung out to dry."

I asked Firas why he hadn't tried to get a visa to the United States. "And what would I do with it?" he said.

"Ask for asylum."

"Do you think they would give me an asylum in the U.S.? Never."

"Why?"

"For the U.S. to give an asylum for an Iraqi, it means they have failed in Iraq."

This wasn't entirely true. Recently, Iraqis who made it to America have begun filing petitions for asylum, and, because they undoubtedly face a reasonable fear of harm back home, a few of them have been accepted. A much larger number of Iraqis are still waiting to learn their fates: U.S.A.I.D. employees who jumped ship on training trips to Washington; Fulbright scholars who have been informed by the State Department that they have to go back to Iraq after their two- or three-year scholarships end, even if a job or another degree program is available to them in America. The U.S. government, for which Firas worked for three and a half years, had given him ample reason to believe that he could never become an American. Still, if he had somehow made it here, there is a chance that he could have stayed.

Instead, he is trying to become a Swede. I met him one recent winter morning in Malmö, a city of eighteenth-century storefronts and modern industrial decay at the southern tip of Sweden, just across the Öresund Strait from Copenhagen. He was waiting to hear the result of his asylum petition while living with Ahmed in a refugee apartment block that was rapidly filling up with Iraqis. Since the war began, nearly 20,000 Iraqis had arrived in the country. Firas was granted asylum in February.

Sweden amazed Firas: the silence of passengers on trains; the intolerance for smoking; the motorists that wait for you to cross the street, as if they were trying to embarrass you with courtesy. When I joked that he would be bored living here, he laughed grimly and said, "Good. I want to be like other people—normal.

How long before I can be afraid or shocked? There is nothing that makes me afraid or shocked anymore."

We walked from the train station to the Turning Torso, a new apartment tower, designed by Santiago Calatrava, that twists ninety degrees on its axis as it rises fifty-four stories into the slate-gray sky, and drank Swedish pilsners at the Torso Bar and Lounge. When the Americans came to Iraq, four years ago, Firas felt that he could finally begin his life. Now, at thirty-five, he was starting over yet again.

I asked him if he felt betrayed by America.

"I have this nature—I don't expect a lot from people," Firas said. "Not betrayed, no, not disappointed. I can never blame the Americans alone. It's the Iraqis who destroyed their country, with the help of the Americans, under the American eye." I was about to say that he deserved better, but Firas was lost in thought. "To this moment," he said, "I dream about America."

The Atlantic

WINNER—REVIEWS AND
CRITICISM

Caitlin Flanagan is an insightful observer of modern culture, an engaging writer who brings a unique, intensely personal perspective to a wide range of contemporary issues. Her work is an example of criticism at its best—thoughtful and bracingly honest, filled with humor and empathy, and free of clichés or political correctness.

Caitlin Flanagan

Babes in the Woods

I spent the summer I was nineteen at my parents' house on the north shore of Long Island, which was pleasant enough but hardly the last word in teenage excitement. When a friend called and invited me to spend a weekend with her family in Delaware, I was packed by bedtime. At first light, I was sitting at the Stony Brook train station with a round-trip ticket and a tin of cookies for my friend's mother. Life had taken a delightful turn, and the only fly in the ointment was that a young man was trying, desperately, to catch my eye.

He walked past me once, turned around and walked by again, and finally made a wide circle around the bench, sat down next to me, and said, "Hi, Caitlin!" That caught my attention. "Hi," I said politely and tried to place him. He was scruffy and a few years older than me—was he a handyman my mother had hired? There was something mocking about him, but he asked about my parents very respectfully, calling my father "Mr. Flanagan." He wanted to know if I still lived on Gnarled Hollow Road. I did. He said that he'd called me the week before, but that no one had answered. And then he did something that changed my feeling of annoyance to one of alarm: He rattled off my parents' phone number.

My mother had taught me quite a few things about men: I should be wary of those I did not know, polite to those I did, and tough as nails with those who were disrespectful or in any way threatening. But none of these rules seemed to apply in this situation.

That young man didn't do me any harm, but neither was he a good-natured kidder. The train arrived, and he lingered behind me as I boarded it. Then he pulled himself up to the bottom step and called my name. When he had my attention, he said—quietly, but with just enough menace that I have remembered him to this day—"You ought to be more careful about what you write on that tag." I stared dumbly at the cardboard luggage tag I had filled in so carefully. He jumped back down to the platform, the train pulled away, and that was the last I saw of him.

He'd tricked me by using two things against me: some personal information and my youth. My ability to recognize social cues, to distinguish an approach that was well-intentioned from one that was threatening, was not what it would be in five years' time. I wasn't an unworldly person or an especially naive one; I was just young. My mother hadn't left me at the train station for five minutes before someone caught sight of me—a pretty girl, dressed for an excursion. That's the way of things, I suppose: Set your children loose, as you someday must, and there will be all kinds of people waiting for them.

*   *   *

The history of civilization is the history of sending children out into the world. The child of a seventeenth-century weaver would have been raised and educated at home, prey to the diseases and domestic accidents of his time, but protected from strangers who meant him harm. As the spheres of home and work began to separate, cleaving parents from their sons and daughters, children faced dangers of an altogether different kind. The world is not, nor has it ever been, full of people who prey upon children. But it has always had more than enough of them, and it always will. Think of the Children's Crusade: Several thousand children marched out of Cologne to liberate the Holy Land but barely made it to Brindisi; they ended up dead or sold into sex slavery, an army of innocents easily picked off within a few weeks' march from home.

With the Internet, children are marching out into the world every second of every day. They're sitting in their bedrooms—wearing their retainers, topped up with multivitamins, radiating the good care and safekeeping that is their lot in life in America at the beginning of the new century—and they're posting photographs of themselves, typing private sentiments, unthinkingly laying down a trail of bread crumbs leading straight to their dance recitals and Six Flags trips and Justin Timberlake concerts, places where anyone with an interest in retainer-wearing thirteen-year-olds is free to follow them. All that remains to be seen is whether anyone *will* follow them, and herein lies a terrifying uncertainty, which neither skeptics nor doomsayers can deny: The Internet has opened a portal into what used to be the inviolable space of the home, through which anything, harmful or harmless, can pass. It won't be closing anytime soon—or ever—and all that parents can do is hope for the best and prepare for the worst.

Those preparing for the worst will find their darkest fears realized in *To Catch a Predator.* The show is a spin-off of the news program *Dateline NBC,* and every episode features the same satisfying format: The network has partnered with an organization called Perverted Justice, which is dedicated to luring and then busting the creepy men who use the Internet to seduce youngsters. The team creates a decoy: an online presence claiming to be a teenager who eagerly participates in increasingly pornographic online chat with an adult male. The "teen" arranges an assignation—the parents are supposedly out of town for the weekend—and the scumbag wanders into a setup par excellence: NBC has the house rigged with cameras and microphones, local law enforcement is watching the whole thing from a van parked at the curb, and cops are hiding in the bushes ready to bring the guy down if he bolts.

What makes the show so fantastic is not only the deeply satisfying element of watching justice instantly meted out. It's also that before the perp gets cuffed and loaded into the paddy wagon he's grilled by the show's host/anchor, a journalist named Chris Hansen, who in every episode gets to deliver, straight-faced, lines that sound like they come from a Will Ferrell movie, as when he confronts a pedophile (hell-bent on bestiality and dessert) with the evidence against him: "You're naked. There's a fourteen-year-old girl. You're chasing a cat around. You've got Cool Whip." The show's been on the air long enough that when Hansen suddenly walks into the room and confronts the predator, it's a bit like the moment when Allen Funt would suddenly show up in the middle of a screwy day at the dry cleaners. ("I knew it!" the perps sometimes say when Hansen appears.)

To Catch a Predator puts an innocent in contact with a trickster and then allows the inevitable to take place. But after you watch a few episodes, it dawns on you that the naifs in this equation are actually the idiot perverts who take the bait and end up in the slammer. Calling this sad-sack collection of wankers and flashers "predators" accords them a level of evil genius they haven't earned; most of them look like they couldn't track down the towel department in a Wal-Mart. I won't lie: Sweet little Mary may swear like a sailor when she logs on to MySpace; but unless she's the kind of gal who responds to a stranger's request to "cum in you" with a cheery "I don't want to get preggers!" she should be safe. And a significant number of the decoys who successfully lure predators are male, a fact that one senses is a grave disappointment to the producers and probably reveals less about Internet crimes than about one of the sad, old truths about sexual initiation for gay teenage boys.

Hansen has written a book about the program, which he created. The book is also called *To Catch a Predator*, and its subtitle—*Protecting Your Kids From Online Enemies Already in Your Home*—is true to the spirit of the show, which involves both informing viewers and scaring the bejesus out of them. When I was a kid, the most frightening moment in horror movies occurred when the terrified girl learned that the creepy telephone caller was making his calls from "inside the house." It never made any sense—nobody had two phone lines back then. But the idea itself was horrifying enough to warrant a bit of poetic license. The sensation of being home—safe, behind locked doors—must have some strong hold on the human psyche, because we're particularly outraged and horrified by crimes that occur to people in their own houses. As hideous as the Polly Klaas kidnapping-and-murder case was, it had an added resonance because the twelve-year-old had been in her own room—*home*—before she was taken into the night and killed. Hansen's subtitle, lurid though it may be, speaks to the fear that makes parents so queasy: Flooding through that Internet connection are any number of people whose interest in their children could be predatory.

The National Center for Missing and Exploited Children maintains that one out of five kids who use the Internet has been propositioned for sex. It's hard to know just how accurately such events can be quantified, and when I first read the statistic, I found it hard to believe that, if indeed so many children were being propositioned, more parents weren't uniting in outrage, rather than wiring up their kids at a blistering pace. My friends with teenagers were very open with them and were well-informed about the dangers of the Internet; I couldn't imagine one out of five of those kids being propositioned by a stranger and not telling their parents.

But Hansen provides a second bit of information that made me wonder if that statistic wasn't in fact on the low side. As part of the first episode of his show, Hansen convened a panel of tweens and teens, among them children of some of his colleagues at NBC, and asked how many of them had been "approached online by someone in a sexual way that made you feel uncomfortable." Almost all the kids raised their hands. Then he asked how many had told their parents. Not a hand went up. And when he asked why they hadn't told their parents, all the kids in the room said they didn't tell because they didn't want their parents to take away their Internet connections.

Suddenly, it all made sense to me: Teenagers don't tell their parents that someone nasty got through to them for the same reason I didn't tell my parents that kids were dropping acid at a party—because they wouldn't let me go to those parties anymore. That's the horrible, inescapable fact of coming of age: The moment you choose the world over your parents, you've chosen to make your own decisions about what's safe and what's not, with only your own wits to protect you.

·　　·　　·

Just how dangerous is the unsupervised use of the Internet by adolescents? Nobody knows. I suspect that in a decade or so we'll all have a very different set of beliefs about how and when and for what purposes teenagers should be allowed to go online. When something new comes along, it takes a while for parents to sort out what's safe and what isn't, and even longer for their conclusions to become commonly held assumptions about good parenting. In the future it may be unheard-of for a teenage girl from a loving family to disappear into her room every night for two hours of unsupervised e-chatting and instant messaging and MySpacing. Then again, it may be even more common than it is today. All we know for sure is that our children are living in the midst of a technological revolution, and that they're drawn to it like moths to a flame.

Most parents of teenage girls with Internet connections will tell you that their daughters' physical safety isn't in jeopardy—they've taken all kinds of precautions they think ensure this—but that the online experience is doing nothing for the girls' peace of mind. Not many people are as ill-served by having their natterings subjected to instantaneous, global transmission as adolescent girls. In the first place, these girls' feelings can be hurt by even a well-intentioned comment or question, and having a caustic remark that would have been bad enough if kept between two people suddenly unleashed to the whole clique, team, or school can be a wretched experience. Furthermore, because this new technology can make the old girl standbys of gossip and social exclusion and taunting more efficient—and therefore more cruel—many girls arrive at school each morning having experienced the equivalent of a public hazing in the privacy of their own rooms. While Johnny's upstairs happily sneaking hard-core pornography past his Internet filter, poor Judy is next door weeping into her pillow because everyone in the eighth grade now knows that she still uses pads, not tampons. (Meanwhile, in a galaxy far, far away, Mom and Dad are trying to figure out how to watch *Dancing With the Stars* now that the remote's on the fritz again.)

If you have an adolescent and you're clueless about the "social networking" sites they love, it's probably a good idea to pick up a copy of a first-rate new guidebook, *Generation MySpace*, by Candice M. Kelsey, a teacher at a private high school in Los Angeles. She's the kind of super-pretty, nonjudgmental young adult kids adore, and seems to have a sensible grasp of both the fears of parents and the desires of teenagers. She's also particularly perceptive about why MySpace can cause a teenage girl so much pain. As she began to understand the site's increasing hold on her students, she writes, fewer and fewer days would go by that didn't end with a distraught student sitting on the floor of my office in search of advice about how to respond to various MySpace-related dilemmas.

Kelsey describes an experiment she conducts each year in which kids are asked not to log on for an entire week. Many of them can't hack it, but the ones who do often find themselves happier and calmer.

Some of the most harmless aspects of MySpace would have crushed me at fourteen. Members get to list their "Top 8" friends, a list they can change at whim. It's an ingenious number, because it's just large enough to make exclusion really hurt—*eight* people, and there wasn't any room at all for me?

One of the great paradoxes of our age is that at the exact moment when a huge number of teachers, parents, and school administrators have dedicated themselves to the emotional well-being and self-confidence of adolescent girls, a technology has come along that's virtually guaranteed to undermine that confidence. A girl can go to school and happily discover that it's possible for her to become a scientist when she grows up, but that may be cold comfort when she comes home to discover that five people just dropped her from their Top 8.

The primary engine of MySpace's stupendous growth isn't the Internet or the additional opportunities for cattiness it provides, but the fathomless narcissism of the young. There's no more ardent devotee of a MySpace profile than its creator, lovingly adjusting the lighting on the perfect self-portrait, changing the song that serenades it, the graphics that surround it. The page can speak broadly to others, but others are almost beside the point; every profile is a sonnet to the self. Today's girls spend hours looking at their MySpace profiles, fiddling and tinkering with them—much as I once sat in front of my vanity mirror, holding my hair up and letting it fall, smiling one way and then the other. For girls, the powerful need to be alone in their bedrooms—dreaming, writing in diaries, looking at themselves in the mirror—is married to a kind of exhibitionism. Why was I trying out my hair so many different ways, if not to calculate its potential effect on others? The Internet makes it possible to combine these two opposed desires: to be alone trying something out and to be exposed in public for everyone to see. A decade from now, a large group of parents may be telling anyone who will listen that this is a very dangerous combination indeed.

•   •   •

Last year, all of a sudden, the phrase "Club Penguin" entered my house via my eight-year-old twin sons, and they were so completely immersed in recounting to me its endless complexities that there was no way to slow them down and elicit a concise definition. I did grasp that it was on the Internet and that it was "safe"—they kept repeating this to me, as though somehow they'd absorbed (accurately) that it was an essential part of the incantation that gets a mother to allow you to do something online. So one day, with me sitting beside them and feeling as though I were summoning Beelzebub, they logged on and played for a while—their first Internet gaming experience.

What fun they had! Club Penguin is a cute, happy virtual world in which you create an adorable little penguin in whose guise you can travel to all sorts of fun spots and play video games (making pizzas against the clock, playing ice hockey, going inner-tubing), for which you win coins. With the coins you can buy clothes and furniture and cool stuff for your virtual igloo. The boys loved it. Everyone loved it. Club Penguin was the most happening event of the second grade; to be denied it was to be denied not just a pleasure but an essential mode of schoolyard discussion and inclusion, a way of being a second grader.

But I never let them play again, because something about it scared me: The penguins could chat with each other. True, the chatting is monitored by paid professionals and a citizens' army of tattlers, children who've been members for more than thirty days and who've been commissioned as "Secret Agents" to loiter in the public spaces and report on inappropriate chat, including the exchange of telephone numbers and e-mail addresses. But these protocols only highlight the paradox at Club Penguin's core: It's certainly the safest way for unsupervised children to talk to potentially malevolent strangers—but why would you want them to do that in the first place?

Shortly after that first visit, once my interfering children had been packed off to school, I made myself a nice cup of coffee and logged on. I chose a pink penguin, and because no versions of my real name were available, I picked one of my mother's nicknames for me. But—O, hated Internet, and its font of unwanted knowledge—even that turned out to be taken, so I had to be "Tootsabella2."

For a long while nobody wanted anything to do with me (I cannot adequately describe how much this felt like a real-life snubbing), so I just waddled around, wallflower at the orgy. It was immediately apparent that girls and boys have very different attitudes about what to do in Club Penguin. The girls want to hang out, chat, and send little hearts to people, and the boys want to play video games. It's this dynamic that makes social-networking sites so much more dangerous for girls than for boys: It's in girls' nature to form relationships, to trade intimacies, to console and confide. It's also in the nature of the Internet to allow emotions to escalate in the blink of an eye; indeed, many of the traits that concern parents of adolescent girls—meanness, aggressive flirting with boys, budding Internet addictions—are clearly being born out there on the icebergs and snowcaps of Club Penguin. It has lowered the point of entry to social-networking sites from middle school to elementary school, opening up young children to a type of interaction that even tweens and teenagers often find overwhelming and hurtful. Did I see anything dangerous happen? I did not. But I saw any number of flame wars, and—more unsettling—even more cases of penguins deep in happy conversation who suddenly vanished from the scene, perhaps off to a private chat in an out-of-the-way igloo, safe from the prying eyes of the Secret Agents.

The next time I logged on, I was at last befriended—or should I say, courted—by a wonderful blue penguin whom I'll call "Denks." He treated me the way a girl wants to be treated: He took me to great places, he paid for everything, and he showed me how to do things. We went sledding, we played Mancala, and Denks turned out to be excellent at Connect Four, so we played a lot of that, too.

I realized, during our second or third game, that I was having my very first online relationship. And as I sat there, dropping my blue pieces into the grid (something I'd done countless times in the real world with my own children), I wondered who was playing the game with me. The thought that Denks might actually be a pervy adult wasn't nearly as unsettling as the thought that he might really be a little boy somewhere, home from school for the day, entertaining himself by logging on to a safe Web site and making friends with someone he thought was a little girl named Tootsabella.

•   •   •

MySpace has more than 100 million members and an unknown number of unregistered lurkers. Last spring, I became one of the latter. The site seemed hopelessly confusing at first, so to get started, I went to the search box and typed in the name of the high school closest to my house. It's the best girls' school in Los Angeles, with a walled and beautiful campus. As soon as I entered the name, the profiles of several girls popped up, and I clicked on the first one, a girl I'll call "Jenna." (Protecting her identity seems at once important and ridiculous: I am taking pains to make private information that she has taken pains to make public.)

I could tell in a minute that this was no fake profile. I taught at a Los Angeles private school for many years, and the associations and places to which she made reference were all of a piece—at once too prosaic and too specific to be fabricated. She was a nice girl, you could tell that right away: Her profile picture showed her in a bikini at the beach, but it wasn't posed or self-consciously provocative. There were pictures from all kinds of parties and from trips to Disneyland and the Santa Monica Pier, and she had a steady boyfriend who posted to her page all the time, as well as a group of friends and family members who clearly thought the world of her. As I read her messages (especially the charming ones between her and her boyfriend, who had moved from "best friend" to "lover" status over the course of many sweet and well-documented months), I felt guilty, as though I were looking at things I shouldn't have been, as though I were lingering at a doorway, overhearing something private. And yet all of them were posted in a place that was designed not just to allow me in but to welcome me.

In that moment, the reality of my new life on the far side of a generation gap hit me fully. My fundamental understanding of privacy—the notion that one shouldn't listen in on the personal conversations of others—marked me as old. I'm not old because I like to peek into people's private lives; I'm old because I feel guilty about it. And I couldn't shake the feeling that—merely by trolling slowly and patiently through her pictures and conversations and lists of favorite things—I had become predatory. Dwelling secretly in the private life of a beautiful young girl seemed inherently sinister, and I had to remind myself, over and over, that I was doing nothing wrong.

Because I'm the mom of two preteens growing up in a social milieu not so different from Jenna's, her MySpace page was a

comfort to me. Her friends were nice, their pursuits and plea-
sures were wholesome enough (much more wholesome than
what my friends and I were up to a quarter century ago), and her
boyfriend was pure gold—a stalwart encourager of her studies,
a champion of her parents and family whose own MySpace
photo was a picture of the two of them. And because I'm someone who loves to read about the day-to-day nature of people's
lives, the page was very interesting to me. But if I were the kind
of person who regards beautiful teenage girls—especially clois-
tered ones from good families—as objects of irresistible erotic
desire, I would not have been comforted or merely "interested";
I would have been excited, perhaps unbearably so.

The current resurgence of girls' schools like Jenna's is based
on the idea that to become strong and powerful, girls need an
environment in which they are protected from the various energies and appetites of adolescent boys. Free of the sexually charged
atmosphere that will always pervade coed high schools, they
can emerge and evolve in ways they never could in the presence
of ogling, domineering boys. What contemporary parents of
daughters—among them some of the most liberal-minded—have
come to believe is not so different from what nineteenth-century
parents believed: The sexual unfolding of a young girl is such a
fraught process emotionally as well as physically that she needs
to be carefully sheltered from the myriad forces that would seek
to exploit or coarsen her as she reconciles the girl that she was
with her biological destiny. That Jenna's parents would pour
such a river of cash into her school tuition to grant her that safe
and gentle place, and that—at the cost of not one cent—she
would have created a MySpace page so dangerously revealing (in
every sense of the word) is a terrific irony.

In the middle of Jenna's profile was a calendar relentlessly
ticking down the days, hours, minutes, and seconds until graduation, which was a little more than a week away. I glanced up
from the computer screen, through the scrim of leafy branches

and out in the general direction of the school, startled by the realization that Jenna—this person I had never heard of twenty minutes before and about whose intimate life I now knew quite a bit—was a flesh-and-blood human being who was at that moment sitting in a building a few blocks away. I minimized the MySpace page on my screen and typed the name of Jenna's school into my search engine; the school's home page had a calendar button, and I clicked on it. I waited for the site to ask me for a password, but it didn't. Up came a complete record of Jenna's whereabouts for the following week: the exam schedule, the school awards ceremony, the graduation exercises, the faculty-appreciation luncheon.

Just about every kid in the country knows not to post his or her last name or address or phone number on the Internet. The paltry set of facts that I so innocently wrote on my luggage tag so long ago are the only bits of information that kids guard jealously today. What they don't realize is that when the vast matrix of information easily available on the Internet is cross-referenced to the bountiful data they supply on MySpace, it can lead right to them. You tell me where your daughter goes to school and what sport she plays, and I'll tell you what day and time she'll be playing a game in a public park. Look around that park while you're watching the game—it's not inconceivable that one of the men there has come to catch a glimpse of a particular girl on the team.

I'm a well-intentioned, busybody mom who's forever sharing snacks and finding Kleenexes for kids I don't know. Like most former high-school teachers, I can't help thinking that whenever there are teenagers in a crowd, they must be on a field trip that I'm chaperoning. Something in my mien and voice must make them think so too—I've scolded some pretty tough-looking teenage boys for swearing around my children, and I've never received anything other than an embarrassed apology. There couldn't be any stranger in the world less inclined to cause harm to Jenna than I was—and thank God for that, because when I saw on the school's Web site that her graduation rehearsal was the following week, I flipped open my calendar and jotted down the day and time.

The day of the rehearsal was glorious, the way days in early June often are in this part of Los Angeles. I wore a pink linen skirt, a white sleeveless top, and a pair of low-heeled leather sandals, and I was so caught up in congratulating myself for approximating so exactly the look of a middle-aged, private-school mom that I had to remind myself that that's exactly what I am.

At the school, things were hopping: Younger girls were being dismissed, a party-supply truck was delivering hundreds of white folding chairs for the ceremony, a uniformed guard was waving car-pool drivers onto the horseshoe drive in front of the school. I walked down the sidewalk and passed the front gate—something I've done literally hundreds of times (I used to live just down the street), but this time my heart was racing. I gave the guard a big, familiar smile, and she nodded and smiled back—she had the look of someone trying to place a familiar face. I kept walking down the block.

I wasn't sure what I was trying to prove to myself, but it certainly wasn't that someone like me could slip onto the campus—the school that several of my friends' children attend and that is my own polling place. I got to the end of the block and turned the corner; I knew the rehearsal was to be held in the field behind the main building, and I was hoping that maybe I could get at least a glimpse of the seniors. And that's when I heard them: Girls, a lot of them, were laughing and talking, and a teacher—her voice much louder, coming through speakers—was trying to impose some order. A piano played the first notes of something that sounded like a processional march, and it was soon joined by the sweet music of a hundred girls singing: They were preparing for graduation by practicing their alma mater. They started, they stopped, they squealed with laughter. The teacher spoke into the microphone, more sternly this time, and they began again.

But that, you will be relieved to know, was as close as I got: The campus was surrounded by a wall as thick and imposing as any ever built around a school dedicated to the teaching and sheltering of girls. So I stood there feeling foolish, slid my camera back in my purse, and slunk away. The place to meet Jenna (without breaking the law) was not on the walled campus of a private school.

•   •   •

There would be other opportunities. Every so often, for the rest of the summer, I'd log on to Jenna's profile. I just missed the gang's trip to a hot-dog stand in Hollywood, and I would have gone to the fast-food place on Wilshire where they went for burgers one afternoon, but Jenna said she wasn't going, so I skipped it, too. Whenever a group of girls came bouncing down my neighborhood shopping street, I scanned their faces, and once I thought I saw her through the big plate-glass window of Jamba Juice, but I wasn't sure. Her boyfriend went away on vacation for a couple of weeks, and she missed him terribly. But then he came back, and before you knew it, they were both ready to go off to college.

I sort of drifted away after that, although I keep an eye on Jenna now and then. Her university has a helpful online student directory, so I know her campus address and phone number; it was also surprisingly easy to learn the times and locations of two of her courses. According to Mapquest, I could be waiting outside her French class in a little over two hours. But what do you think I am—some kind of creep?

GQ

FINALIST—FEATURE
WRITING

In a powerfully understated narrative, Jeanne Marie Laskas offers a window into the lives of coal miners in southeastern Ohio, transporting readers deep into a claustrophobic subterranean world. The men—who go by such nicknames as Smitty, Pap, Hook, Duke, and Ragu—slowly reveal themselves to be tough but nuanced characters, veritable diamonds in the dust, portrayed by Laskas with humor, grace, and compassion.

Jeanne Marie Laskas

Underworld

He handed me a salt-and-vinegar potato chip. We were more than 500 feet underground, sitting on a blanket of powdered limestone, up in section two and a half south. I asked him if there was anything he enjoyed about coal mining.

He thought a moment.

"I'm gonna say no," he said.

"Oh, come on," I said.

"You gotta stop shining your frickin' light in my eye," he said. "What did I tell you about that?"

He told me that the one thing that was going to piss off Billy, Smitty, Pap, Ragu, and the rest of the guys in the crew was if I pointed my light directly in their eyes. It's a common early mistake. The normal human urge is to look a person in the eye, and when your only visibility is from a hard hat shining a pinpoint of light through the darkness, naturally you're going to aim that sucker right at the eyeball.

"Sorry," I said.

"Go for the shoulder," he said. "Or the chin."

I asked him how he got the nickname Foot.

"The first day I went into the coal mine, a guy looked down and said, 'Damn, how big are your feet?' I said, 'Fifteen.' He said, 'You're a big-footed son of a bitch.' And that was it. One guy had a huge head, so of course we called him Pumpkin. One guy had a big red birthmark on his face, so of course his name was Spot. They don't cut you any slack. They'll get right on you. A coal miner will get right on you."

I shined my light on his boots and he wagged them, like puppets.

It was tough getting used to identifying people, in the darkness, just as feet, shoulders, chin, teeth. As for Foot, he was a truck of a man, forty-nine years old, a wide load in both girth and spirit. He had a messy mop of gray hair and a rugged, intelligent face that often wore one expression: "You gotta be kidding me." He was proud of a lot of what he'd done with his life—his three kids, his stint as a county commissioner, his coal-mining expertise—but his heart, he said, belonged to his fifty-two head of beef cattle: Pork Chop, Frick and Frack, and, aw, Bonehead, with the amazing white eyelashes.

He'd been in and out of coal mines since graduating high school and had just been promoted to assistant safety director of the Hopedale Mining coal company in Cadiz, Ohio, a small operation in the eastern part of the state, just beyond the panhandle of West Virginia. Aboveground, the area looks a lot more New England—rolling farmland dotted with tall oaks, white church steeples, geranium pots hanging on front porches—than it does the tar-paper-shack Appalachia people tend to associate with coal mining. Underground, I wasn't permitted to go anywhere without Foot, even though I did. He got sick of me, and I got sick of him, and so he got even *more* sick of me in what became, over a four-month period, an easy friendship.

"It's kind of peaceful down here," I said to him.

"Yeah," he said.

We were not at the face, not "up on section," where the bellow and whir and *hucka-chucka-hucka-chucka* of the toothy, goofy, phallic continuous miner machine was extracting coal and dumping it, load after load, onto buggies that zoomed like lunatic roaches through the darkness. We were over in B entry, or A entry, or perhaps room 3; I had no idea. I rarely knew where I was in that endless catacomb of tunnels, on and on and on, about fifteen square miles in all, where the quiet, when you found it, felt like an embrace. You could sit there. You could shut your light off, sit there in the perfectly dark silence. Nothing. Just—nothing.

Until: *Pop!*

Hisssss.

A crackle like a fireplace.

Hisssss.

When you're inside the earth, this is what it sounds like. The earth isn't some stupid rock, isn't inert, isn't just a solid mass for people to stand on. The earth is always moving, constantly stretching and squawking and repositioning itself like anyone else trying to get comfortable.

"Down here," I said to Foot, "it's like you're away from all your problems. Do you think that's part of the allure for you guys, that you escape your problems down here?"

He looked at me, laughed. "This *is* our problem," he said.

．　　　　．　　　　．

I live on top of a massive vein of medium-sulfur bituminous coal—the very famous Pittsburgh Number 8 Seam that extends from eastern Ohio to western Maryland, where coal has played a vital role in the economy and culture for over a century. The fact that it still does takes a lot of people by surprise. *We still have coal mines?* I got that question a lot when I told people that I was hanging out in a coal mine.

In this way, I was slightly ahead of the learning curve: I knew coal mines *existed*. And not just in pockets of some America that never caught up, not as funky remnants of a bygone era, but as current places of work, day after day, guys with lunch buckets heading in and heading out, taking home sixty, seventy, eighty thousand dollars a year. To live where I live, in western Pennsylvania, is to occasionally get stuck behind a coal truck, to be vaguely cognizant of boxcars full of coal snaking in between the hills, to see a guy covered in coal dust up at the Toot-*N*-Scoot paying for an iced tea.

Coal, if it disappeared from the nation's consciousness, never went away. This is America, and this is *our* fossil fuel, a $27.6 billion industry that employs nearly 80,000 miners in twenty-six states. We are sitting on 25 percent of the world's supply—the "Saudi Arabia of Coal!"—and lately we've been grabbing it in record amounts, gorging on the black rock the Bush administration calls "freedom fuel."

The question I had going in was almost ridiculous in nature: If coal is really this big, and all these people really exist, how is it that I know nothing about them?

It took me months to even gain access to a coal mine—this is not an industry that welcomes publicity, perhaps because the publicity it gets is always so horrific. Coal mines make the news only when they explode, collapse, kill. It's exciting! Tragedy! Fodder for a cable-news frenzy. *Look at these poor, stupid rednecks who work these awful jobs. Trapped! Suffocating! Buried alive!*

Repeatedly, the guys at the Hopedale Mining company asked that I not portray them as poor, stupid rednecks. This characterization, they said, would only display my own ignorance. They were shy at first, eager to impress, and with little other apparent motivation, welcomed me in. I followed one crew, "the E rotation"—Billy, Smitty, Scotty, Pap, Rick, Chris, Kevin, Hook, Duke, Ragu, Sparky, Charlie—who worked in the Cadiz portal, one of two the company owned. I followed them underground, home, to church, to the strip club where they drink and gossip and taunt and jab and worry about one another. I listened while they worried about Smitty, the loner of the group, who had just ordered himself a mail-order woman. Smitty had been talking to her on the Internet for more than a year; he was shipping her over from Russia and she was supposed to arrive, beautifully, on the first day of buck season. I listened while they mercilessly mocked Scotty, a disarmingly cheerful guy who often talked to himself, especially in the bathhouse, where the guys gathered after each shift to wash off the filth before reentering life aboveground. Scotty would be scrubbing away, smiling, telling himself all about this and all about that and sometimes he'd come out with a laugh that would about bust your ear off. "What the hell is wrong with you, Scotty?" said Foot, who was showering next to Scotty when he recently did this.

"I'm going to be in jail tomorrow for murder," Scotty said to Foot.

"For what?"

"I'm gonna kill this son of a bitch I'm fighting, I'm gonna *kill* him!"

"Yeah, well, don't get too far ahead of yourself there, buddy," Foot said. Fight Night XV at Wheeling Island Racetrack & Gaming Center would feature its first-ever junior-middleweight championship, pitting Scott "the Rock" Tullius against Todd Manning, and a lot of the guys from the mine were going.

These were men who lived underground together for ten-hour shifts, five days at a stretch, often spending more time with each other than they did with their families, so they knew everything about each other. They knew all about Billy's brand-new house and the barn siding he used to panel his basement, all about Chris's kid getting his second bone-marrow transplant, all about Pap's wife getting her damn knee replaced—and they knew there was no sense in asking Pap what the hell he was doing, a sixty-two-year-old man still mining coal. Pap should have retired long ago. Or he should have had a job outside. A lot of guys put in years underground with the hope of moving aboveground; Pap could have had almost any job he wanted outside.

But he chose to stay under, working what was widely regarded as the worst job of all: roof bolting. He was the guy drilling six-foot rods up into the top of the mine as the coal got dug out and the earth complained, hissing its hissy methane fits and collapsing more or less on a regular basis.

Of course I asked him why. Every which way I could think of, I asked Pap why he chose to stay under, but he, like so many of the miners I met, had a way of talking in circles. I asked Pap's wife, Nancy, the woman he called "the old bag I live with," why Pap still worked underground. She had no idea what I was talking about. "I don't know nothing about nothing that goes on in that mine," she said. (She did not mind being called an old bag and referred to Pap as "my Frankie" or, sometimes, "Lucifer.") She, like so many of the people I visited, always gave me a care package to take home, a few chunks of Edam cheese and a pear. Pap gave me two bottles of homemade blackberry wine to take home to my husband. I never once mentioned that I *had* a husband, but everyone kept sending home presents for him. Family was the assumption. Family-to-family interaction was the natural order of communication.

I spent months trying to position myself and my world around these people—people who seem stuck in a bygone era that isn't bygone at all. If anyone is gone, it's us, the consumer. We forgot, or we lost touch, or we grew up with our lives already sanitized. We live over *here* and they live over *there*, and we have almost no access to a way of life that we are so unwittingly dependent on. What disturbed me was nothing I found so much as the nature of the experiment itself: How is it that our own neighbors are the stuff of *anthropology*? If that says anything about us, it's probably not flattering.

Why do we even have coal mines? said some blond-haired TV news lady last year, when those twelve miners famously trapped in West Virginia's Sago mine were first pronounced alive and then, whoops, dead. All of a sudden, the nation's attention was on coal miners, zoo animals—specimens of humanity—while the coal miners looked back.

Why do we even have coal mines? The miners I talked to remembered listening and laughing, having great fun with that one. "Whenever you plug your vibrator in and it doesn't work, okay, that's why we have coal mines!" one of them shouted at the TV. Okay, that might not have been the best example, seeing as your sex-toy industry is more or less dependent on batteries, which have nothing to do with coal. But the point is: power. Coal is power. "Yeah, turn the lights on, lady. That's why you need coal mines. Where do you think electricity comes from?"

Every time we flip on a light switch, we burn a lump of coal, each of us consuming about twenty pounds of those lumps a day. Fully half of our electricity comes from coal—and that's nothing compared with China, which leads the world both in the production and the consumption of coal, accounting for a whopping 70 percent of that country's total energy consumption. Coal is the fastest-growing energy source on the planet (much to the planet's reported gasping dismay).

And so, the coal miner. He shows up in country-music songs and poetry, a working-class hero. He works a job that has killed more than 100,000 since we started, over a century ago, sending people underground. It's enough to make you shake your head, sigh a grateful sigh, and go on and bond with the guys over at ABC News waxing philosophical: *"If there is such a thing as a mystique associated with a hard, dirty, and dangerous life, that mystique is attached to the miners who are such a part of the nation's consciousness and soul."*

That's where we start. That's where I started. I wanted the mystique. I wanted to discover that the guys who make their living underground do it because of some attachment to the earth, or to history, or to their own ancestry, or to further some fundamental masculine need for brotherhood, or—yes!—on behalf of the nation's consciousness and soul.

You talk like that in a coal mine, you'll get your lunch bucket nailed shut. Seriously. That's a beauty.

.   .   .

If you want a job at the Hopedale Mining company, the first thing they do is bring you down for a tour to see if you can mentally handle it. You pretty much know instantly if you can take the confinement, the lack of light, the very real worry about the roof caving in or the air supply shutting off or something blowing up. And if you don't know instantly, there's a team of guys watching you to see if you twitch, shake, turn pale. Some guys say, "Yeah, never mind" and ask to leave. One guy recently passed out.

When Billy Cermak Jr. first went under six years ago, he was trying to convince himself he was doing the right thing—*I can do this, I can do this, I can do this*—because coal mining was exactly the thing he swore he'd never do; he'd never allow the Cermaks to become *fourth*-generation coal miners. First his great-grandfather, recruited from what is now the Czech Republic by the coal companies; then his grandfather, who started working in the mines at twelve and died of black lung; then Billy's dad, working most of his life in the strip mines. *That won't be me*, Billy grew up thinking. He would be a man of *his* generation, get himself a job somewhere at least air-conditioned. He'd become sick of the family farm, of a life so dependent on brawn. He went to college to study nursing, tried to pretend he didn't hate it, kept thinking *It's gotta get better, it's gotta get better*, but it never did. He graduated, but ended up leaving the air-conditioned world for jobs in construction, on pipelines, and on the railroads. Muscles. Might. Sweat. It just felt better. Soon he had a wife. He imagined sons on four-wheelers, boys raking hay. The farm. Leaving it only proved how much he loved it. And there he was, days at a time, off on that railroad. He just wanted to figure out a way to stay on the farm. And coal mining was right there in his backyard.

So, in walks Billy Cermak to the Cadiz portal on Old Hopedale Road. *I can do this, I can do this, I can do this.* The building itself is blue corrugated steel with a big American flag hanging from a pole out front, struggling rhododendrons along the walkway, and a giant happy face painted on a fuel tank in the parking lot. The whir of the massive fan sucking bad air out of the mine is loud, obnoxious, and constant.

Billy gets suited up: coveralls, steel-reinforced boots, hard hat, light, and on his belt a battery pack, methane detector, and W65 self-rescuer—a breathing mask intended to filter out carbon monoxide for about an hour. If there's an explosion or fire, you wrap that around your face until you can get yourself to an SCSR apparatus, many of which are stationed throughout the mine, and which provide a full hour of actual oxygen. He's given a metal tag with his name on it and told where to hang it on the peg board. In case of a collapse, they want to know who to go looking for. He gets on the elevator, plunges 500 feet down, fifty stories just—down. The elevator opens up and everything is white. That's the first weird thing. *White?*

Everyone, I was told, gets jolted by the white. You try to make sense of it. "They just paint this opening part white to cheer everyone up?" I said to Foot the first time I saw it. He didn't even dignify that guess with a response. "It's, like, a joke?" I said. "Irony? A little humor to start your day before you move into black?" I figured we'd hit the black part of a coal mine as soon as we moved further in. Foot looked at me in that way he came to look at me, a stillness, a flatness to his gaze, an expression that said, "You just keep turning into more of an idiot." He said, "I think you'll find there are no aesthetic choices, nor is there irony, in a coal mine."

The white is on account of "rock dust," powdered limestone, a fire retardant that you throw on every exposed inch of coal, which, were it not rock-dusted, is spontaneous combustion waiting to happen. One small explosion could trigger a series of explosions, on and on, *fwoom, fwoom, fwoom*, through the mine, but not if you've got it rock-dusted. Explosion is nothing to flirt with. I was not permitted to even use a tape recorder when we were at the face of the mine, where the coal was exposed and the methane was bleeding, nor could our photographer use a flash. The smallest spark could cause a blast.

So, 500 feet down. White. That's just hello. You are not, technically, even at work yet. Once you step off the elevator, you climb onto a mantrip, a small train car. You don't sit so much as lie on that thing, a crawling convertible, you lean way back on it so as to avoid scraping your head on the ceiling as you whiz on in through a cool, damp tunnel, mud, slush, *clunk, clunk, rattle, hiss*. You travel a mile in, two miles in, sometimes as far as six or seven miles in and away from the elevator shaft where you first dropped down. It depends on where they're digging coal. The guys, of course, are used to this, an everyday commute. Some of them break into their lunch buckets, Scotty sharing M&Ms, Hook downing a Mountain Dew. They keep their lights off, conserving battery power, but the mantrip has a headlight, so you can watch the underworld whiz by, all of it crusty white, eerily frosty. Everything is crooked, bent, leaning; there are posts jammed in here and there to keep the top up, rusted reinforcement bolts jutting out, power cables hanging—the net effect is an endless crawl of abandonment and prayer. *Just keep the damn thing from caving in.* There is nothing aesthetic about a coal mine. There is no design, no geometry, no melody. A coal mine greets you with only one sentiment, then hammers it: *This is not a place for people, this is not a place for people, this is not a place for people.*

So, 500 feet down, a couple of miles in. You are under somebody's house, or a grocery store, or, in this case, the Wendy's up there off Route 22. The guys joke about yelling up for a burger, maybe some chili. You roll off the mantrip and stand up. The ceiling is five feet high, and so you can't, actually, stand up. You look around and everyone is walking around like the freaks in *Being John Malkovich.*

"Okay, they should make it higher," I said to Foot the first time I experienced this. I wanted to call a congressman or something. This was ridiculous. There are *people* in here! Everyone's doing a duck walk, hands clasped behind their backs to give the body balance as they lean over and waddle. You work your whole ten-hour shift like that, duck-walking through the darkness, nothing but a pinpoint of light shining from your hat to tell you which rat tunnel is which. A rat. You feel like a rat.

I could not get used to the height. Every time I went down, I asked, "Is this lower than last time? Are we in a lower spot?"

"Same spot," Foot said, explaining that there was nothing to be done about the height. "A coal seam is a coal seam."

A coal seam is a coal seam, and this one was five feet high, and so that was how high the mine was. The height got decided a long time ago, like 300 million years ago, way before dinosaurs, when the coal seam was a ribbon of dead plants, slime. It sat there, buried sludge, covered up over millions of years. It turned to peat, lignite, then subbituminous, bituminous, or anthracite coal, depending on how many millions of years it had a chance to sit there and store energy and depending on the geologic forces surrounding it. A coal seam is an act of nature. If you want the coal, you just mine the coal. You don't mine above it or below it. Take any higher and you're mining rock, mixing rock in with the coal, a messy product that will have to get "washed." Take any lower and you're doing the same, plus probably hitting water and making yourself a mud hole and Billy will have to go get the fucking sump pumps. You just take the coal. And shut up, because Foot could tell you about plenty of mines where the seam is thirty-six inches, thirty-two inches. Pap could tell you about working on his stomach, his *stomach*, down in Saginaw "scratch your back" mine.

There is good news. Every once in a while you find the good news, or hear about the good news: A glory hole! Come on over. A glory hole is a place where the "top" has opened up, forming a dome. Heaven. You can stand. Thank the Lord! Guys hang out in glory holes, Scotty stretching, Sparky rolling his neck around. Standing in a glory hole, you can feel your spine thank you even as you work on denying the fact that a glory hole is, technically, a cave-in, a place where the top fell down, maybe yesterday or maybe the day before.

The "top" is certainly the main topic of conversation in a coal mine. Bad top. Hey, that top over there is bad. Aw, this is some bad top here. Look out. Okay, that's coming down. Move. The top is falling. "Go on over to C entry at ten-plus-thirty and you'll see where the fucking top collapsed."

It's not always this bad. The top conditions in two and a half south, where the E rotation was mining, were especially crappy. Every coal miner I talked to had, in his history, at least one story of a cave-in. "Yeah, he got covered up," is a way coal miners refer to fathers and brothers and sons who got buried alive.

Air is probably the second most common topic of conversation in a coal mine. With every fresh cut of coal, the earth leaks explosive methane. You need to get that out of there. Guys up at the face are constantly getting off their machines to control and direct the airflow: tacking up tarps, taking them down, checking their methane detectors in an effort to keep fresh air sweeping across the face of the mine.

A coal miner is busy. A coal miner doesn't have time to sit around and ponder all of this: methane, bad top, no light, no standing, no bathroom, no water fountain, no phone, no radio, no windows, 500 feet down, a couple of miles in. If I found that I could, in fact, mentally handle being inside a coal mine, it was only because I knew I was leaving. No matter how many times I went under, I would always be a tourist. I could ooh and I could ahh and I could leave. But Smitty and Kevin and Ragu couldn't, and Pap wouldn't. The Cadiz mine operates twenty-four hours a day, seven days a week.

The "face crew" works up at the face of the mine, operating the cacophony of machinery. At the head of the line you have Rick, the miner operator chewing off the coal with the *hucka-chucka-hucka-chucka* continuous miner machine and its rolling drums of teeth. Behind him, two roof bolters, Pap and Charlie, with their mighty orange hydraulic jack machine that holds the top up with one arm, then slams four- or six-foot rods into that top, reinforcing it. Behind them, three buggy runners zooming—Scotty, Ragu, Smitty—each capturing the coal and hauling it to conveyor belts. Behind them, the scoop man, Kevin, who pulls up in his scoop machine to capture the loose coal. Then Rick moves in with the miner again, making another cut, and the cycle repeats.

All of these men and all of these machines keep in constant motion, chewing, hauling, bolting, scooping, in what becomes a kind of dance. It's a factory that keeps going forward, sixty feet per shift, deeper into the mine and farther from the power center, the base of the operation. Every two weeks or so, you have to pack up the power center, move the whole factory forward.

Now, Billy Cermak, when he went down the first time, six years ago, to see if he could mentally handle it, he was elated. It wasn't so bad! It was . . . white! Kind of pleasant that way, really. Not all doom and gloom. And other than the height issue, it was just learning equipment—farm boys make the best miners because farm boys know equipment—it wasn't bad at all. *I can handle it!* He started work the next week, a rising star from the moment he got there. He was put right up at the face, a roof bolter, and soon enough he shot up to crew chief. A boss. Smitty, Scotty, Pap, Rick, Chris, Kevin, Hook, Duke, Ragu, Sparky, Charlie—eleven workers under Billy's direction. The E rotation.

Billy was a gentleman. He wore cologne. If there's an upwardly mobile coal miner, it's Billy. He tries. He *believes*. He even shows up at the company picnics. Even his house, brand-new, with a big, bright porch and cats running around, says "winner." An eighteen-foot Playtime motorboat in the drive-way, a shiny Dodge, and a Suburban. His house sits across from his dad's place, over from his brother's. The original family farm, intact. Billy has two boys now, and can't you just picture little Brody and Gage riding four-wheelers real soon? They have three miniature horses. Next year, an in-ground pool. For Billy, this whole thing is like the most unbelievable dream come true, even though he swore he'd never be a fourth-generation coal miner.

"The only thing I think about is the danger part of it," his wife, Tynae, said one day when we were all sitting in the living room, watching Brody tumble.

"It's not that bad," Billy said to her. "I mean, the danger isn't even a thought for me anymore."

"I know," she said, even though you could tell she didn't.

"Anything that happens is just a freak accident."

"I know."

"That's the only stuff that happens is *freak accidents.*"

"*I know.*"

Then she turned her attention to a Smurfs cartoon Brody had settled on, and nobody said anything.

A few days later, when I was in the mine, up on section, Billy said, "Look, I don't talk about the bad stuff in front of my wife, okay?"

Billy was there the day Albert got crushed. Billy was only two months into his happily-ever-after, just two months into learning that he could mentally handle it. An explosion. The power out. And the section foreman called, "We're gonna need some help!" It was over at the bottom of the slope, where supply cars travel from outside down into the mine, carrying tons of equipment. The cars had let loose, fell through the air at maybe sixty miles an hour—one car, two cars, three loaded cars did a free fall on top of Albert, killing him instantly. Chip was the one who found him. Billy and Boomer helped dig. They found half of Albert. About half. Then they looked around for the rest. They wrapped what they found in blankets and drug it on out.

·   ·   ·

Up at the Joy Spot, where the strippers were said to strip anytime, even nine o'clock in the morning if you wanted them to, a bunch of the E-rotation guys were putting back a truly outstanding quantity of Coors Light while inviting me to consider the positive side of a coal miner's life. We sat engulfed by the blare of Metallica on the jukebox, beneath a sign advertising the day's feature shot: JAGGER BOMBS, $4.50. On the positive side of coal mining, they said, there was the weather. Seriously, year-round, a steady average of fifty-five degrees underground. No rain. They sang the praises of working for Hopedale Mining, believing themselves to be the envy of area coal miners because of the five-and-three schedule (five days on, three days off; some mines are as high as six and one) and because it's a nonunion mine, meaning a lot less crap to deal with. The guys thought their pay, an average of $21.15 an hour for face rate, was excellent.

Sparky: "The paycheck is the reason we're there."

Hook: "You get your check and first thing is, I'll go straight down to Dillonvale. We got seven bars in one mile. Ain't nothing but opportunity right there."

Kevin: "Usually, I'll just buy twelve beers, and I'll go ride around and look at deer. I take my wife, my kid, hell, we usually see about seventy, eighty deer a night. It's all dirt roads; I ain't never passed a cop yet."

Rick: "Jackass, how many DUIs have you had?"

Kevin: "Two. But it wasn't looking for deer; it was for doing stupid shit, like doing burnouts in front of the bar and fucking going to the city drunk at three in the morning. Stupid shit. I don't do that now. I stick to dirt roads."

Sparky: "We're applauding."

Duke: "What does this have to do with mining coal? Tell her the good parts of mining coal."

Hook: "Okay, here's what it is: Everybody is there for the same reason. You mine coal, you get money, you go home."

Duke: "That's what it is. It's simple. Coal is your goal."

They ordered another round. They talked coal. They talked about how Rick, who runs the miner machine, was in charge. He wasn't the boss, but he was in charge and everyone knew it. Whoever runs the miner machine runs the show.

Duke: "He's got one priority, and that's penetrating. That's your job if you're on that miner. You're penetrating. And if you've got three shitbag buggy runners behind you loading off you and you gotta wait for them, you're not penetrating. And if you got shitbag bolters supposed to bolt these cuts behind you, then it's even worse. Then if you got a scoop man that cries all the time, it's real bad."

Sparky: "It's the dependency you have on each other. That's what it is."

Hook: "That's it."

They talked coal, ordered another round. They wondered why they just talk coal all the time.

Kevin: "If you're down there, you're trying to make everything all right for the next guy. Like, Pap brings me a sandwich every day, a bull coon sandwich. It's Amish salami or Amish ham. A lot of the guys bring extra food, in case you get trapped. I always eat everything I bring, but Pap has something left. A bull coon sandwich. But come after lunchtime, Pap knows I'm ready to kill him. I tell him, *You old fucking bastard*. You know. Everybody gets along in the beginning of the day. But anything after lunch, you're ready to fucking kill."

Hook: "If anybody wants to kill you, Kev, it's because you just busted something again."

Kevin: "That ain't true."

Sparky: "It's true."

Kevin: "Will you tell me, Rick, do I not do my job to the best of my ability?"

Rick: "No, you're a good scoop man. You scoop good."

Kevin: "Am I not the best scoop man you have ever had?"

Rick: "I told you, you scoop good."

Kevin: "See? I don't care what you mechanics think. If a machine is meant to fucking break and it's gonna break, well, guess what? You're looking at the fucking guy that's gonna break it. That's the way I've been my whole life."

Duke: "My priority is, I produce. When I worked the miner, that's what I cared about. I produce. I don't care what the fuck else is going on or where anybody is, I produce."

Kevin: "But see, I do. I care. I do care. I care because that man cares. And that man cares. That man wants it rock-dusted, you bet your fucking ass if I got the opportunity and I can scoop it and rock-dust it, then I will scoop it and rock-dust it."

Hook: "It's the same as any family, bottom line."

Duke: "Bottom line. Because these fuckholes, every one that goes down there each and every day, depends on the next fuckhole. Bottom line."

Rick: "Bottom line is, he loves him and he loves him and he loves him and he loves him just like I love him."

Kevin: "You might hate them, but you love them."

Sparky: "Bottom line."

Hook: "That's it right there."

Kevin: "I'll tell you what I do a fucking good job at. I keep the fucking deadbeat fucking mechanics off their asses."

Rick: "A little rough there, Kevin, a little rough."

Kevin was not, in my estimation, any rougher than any of the others, but the deeper we got into drunkspeak, man love and man hate and bottom lines and fuckholes, Kevin was the one singled out. Rick slipped him a note. I WILL NOT SAY THE F-WORD, it read. He told Kevin to put it in his pocket.

Kevin: "I have a four-year-old kid I don't say it in front of."

Rick: "All right. Well, you got a lady here."

Kevin: "I'm sorry."

Rick: "All right."

Kevin: "Now you think I'm a shitbag."

Rick: "No, I don't."

Kevin: "I know, Rick. I ain't good now, huh? You gave me a compliment and now you're taking it back."

Rick: "I'm not taking it back."

Kevin wanted to go home. Sparky said he'd drive him to his place, where he could just go ahead and pass out. Kevin refused. It was nearly midnight, and the guys had to be back at the mine by six.

Kevin: "I got a wife and a kid to get home to. I got two DUIs, and I'm a shitbag."

Sparky: "Seriously, you'll stay at my place. I'll even pack your lunch for tomorrow."

Kevin: "I got to go home with my family. That's why I'm going home, because I'm a shitbag."

With that, he took off. No one said much. No one even felt like bothering with the strippers.

Rick: "I thought we were gonna tell her the good parts about coal mining."

Hook: "We more or less covered most of it, wouldn't you say?"

·　　　·　　　·

Everyone I talked to in the coal mine had a reason for being there that had nothing to do with coal, even if the reason was beer. Coal was currency, just as it is for the coal consumer, only in the case of the coal miner it is literally so. Coal is a good provider, but coal isn't free. Coal is dirty and dangerous—for the coal miner getting it out of the ground and for the planet burning it. Same deal. No kidding, no fooling, nothing subtle, nothing virtual. Coal doesn't play with you. The thing you can say about coal is, coal is honest.

"They say if you truly find a job you love, then you'll never work a day in your life," Foot told me, and he wasn't talking about coal mining. Fifty-two head of beef cattle, a brand new Massey Ferguson 390 tractor, a Krone 125 baler, and a 995 Case with a loader on it—that's why he mined coal, to afford his farms, two of them, 280 acres in all. He was hoping to buy a third, because he had three kids and it only seemed right to leave each kid a farm. "There ain't nothing I like more than to smell that fresh-cut hay, throw that hay, rake that hay," he said. Sometimes neighbors offer to help him; they'll say, *You work down in that mine all night and then you're out on that damn farm.* "And I just tell them, 'If I was sitting here on the bank with a fishing pole in my hand, fishing, would you come to take it out of my hand?' *Well, no.* And I say, 'Well, this is my fishing.' You know. This is my fishing."

I heard that kind of story over and over again. Only a few of the coal miners I met *didn't* own at least a hundred acres of Ohio farmland, chunks passed through the generations, added to, divided among brothers and sisters. Farming doesn't pay the bills, so you go into the coal mines. The deep, rich, plentiful mines of the Appalachia region are what have helped keep so many family farms east of the Mississippi intact for over a century.

If there was a threat to this natural order, it began thirty years ago, when coal suffered its first serious reputation problem. The Federal Clean Air Act of 1970 and its amendments in 1977 and 1990 placed stringent controls on the sulfur-dioxide emissions from burned coal. Acid rain was the thing. Power plants were forced to turn to more expensive but cleaner-burning natural gas, while the industry flirted with nuclear technology.

Coal? Suddenly, you could hardly give away the stuff they mined in the East, the medium sulfur bituminous coal of the Pittsburgh Number 8 Seam, and the similar-grade stuff of the 6A seam where I hung out with the E-rotation guys in Cadiz. That coal burned dirty. Power companies turned to the far less efficient but cleaner coal out West, where very-large-scale strip mines became coal's new cash crop. Mines throughout Pennsylvania, Ohio, Kentucky, and West Virginia closed as the industry in Appalachia went into a free fall.

Cadiz felt the punch. It was 1980 and Cadiz, home to what was once the largest shovel in America—the Silver Spade, twelve stories high, capable of scooping 315,000 pounds of earth in a single bite—struggled with its very identity. Even the coal festival held every summer, the Coal Queen pageant, the coal-shoveling contest, the heavy-mining-equipment parade—even that became a sour joke. They stopped calling it the Coal Festival. They changed the name to Heritage Days.

Guys scrambled for work, left town. Foot moved to Connecticut to manage two Wendy's fast-food restaurants—him in one, his wife, Jackie, in the other. It was ridiculous. It was like putting a buffalo in some kind of hat boutique or something. The suburbs were nice but oppressive. "You go to work, come home, and what do you do?" he said to me. No square bales to haul, no manure spreader to repair, no wandering steer to chase home under the light of the moon. "*How many movies can you go to?*" He lasted a year. Him and Jackie came back from Connecticut with their tails between their legs, moved in with her mom, who, at that time, owned the farm. The farm. That was all that mattered.

So when the eastern mines started reopening in the late 1990s, it seemed like God Himself was answering prayers. The mines reopened because the power plants had figured out how to burn that gloriously efficient dirty coal and wash the emissions, meeting EPA standards. They're still reopening today, at a fierce rate, thanks to "clean-coal technology," a controversial term if you talk to environmentalists who aren't buying the sudden image change. Scientists are figuring out how to convert coal into liquid fuel to power cars and jets. The country is in a decidedly passionate mood to let go of its dependency on foreign oil. This is America, and this is *our* fossil fuel. Freedom fuel! Coal.

.   .   .

For Scotty, the mine was a way of funding his boxing career, such as it was.

It wasn't so much that Scott "the Rock" Tullius lost that fight to Todd Manning at Fight Night XV, it was that he was so widely expected to win, and not just in his own murderous heart, but even by the way the promoters were promoting it. On the radio. Talk shows. Scotty saying into the microphone yeah, heck yeah, he was back, he took a year's hiatus but he was back. He took the hiatus on account of his hand getting crushed in the mine, smashed on the bolter. But it healed up. And he got back into fighting shape, eating nothing but raw eggs and chicken and water for weeks, no pop, no iced tea, nothing—and there you are, working in a coal mine. Hardly ideal conditions for an athlete. But he was back, and he had always wanted to fight Manning, and he was seriously worried about killing the poor bastard.

So it wasn't just that he lost. Worst of all—way worse than his mouth guard getting knocked clear out of his mouth in the second round, worse than even his eardrum getting busted in the third—worst of all was that the ref called the fight in the fifth. Called it. Now, Scotty had fought over a hundred fights and never had a fight called. Scott the Rock had started competing at sixteen, had amassed a 92-17 record, and there he was, thirty-one years old, down on one knee in the fifth when the ref called it. The place went nuts. *He got back up! He wasn't down!* He had fans in the audience throwing their T-shirts into the ring, everyone screaming, and then there was Scotty's mother up there chewing out the ref for calling that fight he should not have called. *He got back up! He wasn't down!* And then out comes the championship belt, that belt was worth over $600, that belt is what you fight all your life for, and there was Todd Manning wearing it. It was bad. It was so ugly. Just . . . ugly.

The guys from the mine who were there saw Scotty getting whupped, and you can be sure he heard about it two days later when he showed up for work, all bruised and with a busted eardrum, and having to go back down 500 feet under and run that buggy. The guys were like, *Oh, Scotty thought there were four guys punching him in that ring, oh, Scotty got his ass kicked.* It was bad. It was ugly. It might have been the low point of his life, all around.

He decided it was over. He was going to retire from the ring. Hang up his gloves.

"Yeah, I'm done," he told me. "I'm never gonna be a world champion. That's what I always wanted to be, and I'm never gonna get there. I'm not. You know. I'm just . . . not."

He didn't look sad. Or he was the happiest sad man I'd ever met. It's possible that Scotty had lived a previous life as a golden retriever, a tail-wagging pal who keeps coming back around no matter how mean you are to him.

"Boxing has given me a lot," he said. We were at his house in a remote area of Wheeling, up a hill, where there's nothing but woods out back, and so you can go on out and target practice on pumpkins whenever you feel like it. His wife, Eddie, had a Playboy T-shirt stretched tight over her pregnant belly. She was about due. She was a boxer, too. They had met at a fight.

"Boxing gave me a family," he said. "And I was close. Real close to going somewhere and getting the world title. But what are you gonna do? You're not good enough to make a living at it, so you gotta work."

He smiled, laughed into the air. "Jeez!"

He said he was, anyway, amassing a fortune. He laid out the numbers. The house needed work but was about paid off. Him and Eddie drove old cars. Between his job and hers at the plastics factory, they brought home $100,000 a year, most of which went straight to the bank. The plan was to work, save, and as soon as they had enough cash on hand, quit. Retire. "We want to live our life. That's what our plans are."

I asked him what his life would look like once he started living it. He couldn't think of anything besides boxing, which was sort of where he had started out in the first place and what got him into this situation, so he didn't know.

The main thing was he didn't want to be sixty years old working in a coal mine. He didn't want to be an old man like Pap, down there bolting every day. Nobody wanted to be Pap. Everyone spoke of Pap with respect, even kindness, but also with a certain amount of horror. The ghost of a future that was to be avoided.

"One day I was boltin', me and Pap, the roof was real bad," he said. "And all of a sudden, it started sprinkling all around us, and it just come in behind us. About buried us alive. We was goin', '*Ptuh, ptuh.*' We thought we was dead. I mean, we should have been dead. But we weren't."

He laughed. "*Ptuh, ptuh!* Aw, that was *bad!*"

I asked him if he thought that putting himself in such dangerous conditions upped the odds that he would die young, that he might, that is, never make it to retirement.

"You can't think like that," he said. "It's the chance you take. You don't think like that. I mean, sometimes you think about it, you know, you go, *Man!* Huh. Sometimes you do. But you get used to it. You get brave. You really do. I'm serious. You get brave."

He asked me if I wanted a drink of water or something like that. I said no, I was good. He asked me if I wanted to watch something on the big-screen TV, said maybe later we could watch tapes of some of his fights.

"Now, a buddy of mine, Robby Dutton, he's dead," he said. "We were pretty good friends. And we was on the same crew. And the miner, there was something wrong with it, a hose was leaking, and they were turning it and a bit got caught and come down and mangled his leg. We had to drag him outta there on a stretcher, all bleedin' *bad.* Aw, he was . . . we thought he was gonna die. Huh. But he didn't die."

"I thought you said he's dead," I said.

"Yeah. He come back like a year and a half later to the mine and he was having a hard time. Then, Memorial Day weekend. On his Harley. He was riding down the interstate and a woman was screamin' at her kid and pulled out, started screamin' at her kid, *POW!* Smothered him all over his Harley.

"Huh. *Pow!* Can you believe that?"

·   ·   ·

With the obvious exception of combat soldiers, I'd never been around people who knew so many dead people.

Pap's son was dead. Got smashed by a coal truck in 1993. Pap told me this with no break in his voice or release of his gaze. "It was quick," he said. "Oh, he never knew what hit him."

Death was a shame, a crying shame. Other than that, as a subject it wasn't near as interesting as Smitty's mail-order woman who did not, by the way, arrive on schedule. There was a lot of chatter about this.

"*She didn't show up?*"

"She was sick. She couldn't board the plane."

"The way I heard it, there was a flu epidemic and they wouldn't let any planes out."

"Out of Russia?"

"That's the way I heard it—or maybe just the town she was in."

"It's her turn to come over, and everybody's got the flu and they can't come over? I think I would check into that. That would have been on the news somewhere."

"He said she was coming later."

"He already paid for her plane ticket?"

"That's the way I heard it."

"Aw, Smitty."

Pap was good friends with Smitty, thought of him as a kind soul. I rode with Pap in his pickup, through his hay fields. He was the only coal miner I met who had actual positive words to say about coal mining. Then again, Pap was a man of very, very many words, so this might have been a matter of odds. He was compact, rosy cheeked, and his teeth were worn from left to right onward down a hill. "I come home from work," he said. "And I don't complain, 'Oh, John made me mad,' or 'Bob made me mad.' Like I tell my mom: The gloopies were there. My mom, she knows. She always called them gloopies. Crazy coal miners. So I tell her, 'The gloopies were there,' and that's it."

As we drove around, it wasn't the gorgeous views he pointed out, the patchwork of hills rolling into the horizon, but instead various piles of rocks. Sometimes, he said, all you want to do is go out and pile up rocks. It's relaxing. It makes you feel good to know the hay fields are clear, to know your baler won't get banged up. He told me his wife used to help him on the farm, but ever since she got that job up at Sam's Club she's too busy. Now *that*, he said, was a stupid job. "All them people do is eat," he said, blaming retail sales for Nancy's weight gain. Now, instead of just "the old bag I live with," he had started calling her Moo.

I asked him why he still worked in the mine, doing one of the hardest jobs.

"Oh, I don't know," he said. He talked about being "Little Frankie" in high school, only five feet tall, making the varsity football team. He said he was always very athletic. He was always a good worker. That started even earlier, in grade school, Father Coleman pulling him out, almost every day, just him and Dickie Angelo got pulled out every day after Mass to go on down and clean up the old cemetery. Tombstones were falling in, and it was all unlevel. So him and Dickie would wheelbarrow dirt in, smooth it out. Someone had to do it, and those boys were strong, good workers. Good workers. He worked instead of going to school, a choice decided for him by his church.

"I've always been a good worker," he said. "Me and Dickie were goats."

You work. If you're healthy, you work. You don't quit work until something bad happens, which is your sign to move on. Pap's own belligerent father sanctioned this pattern. "He got covered up two days after I got hired," he told me. "I took my physical on a Wednesday, I started on a Thursday, and Friday morning he got covered up. The boss working with him never made it. Crushed him. He was standing there, a guy knocked a post out, and the whole place tumbled. Killed the boss dead. Oh, they had to get jacks to get the stuff off my dad. Broke both his pelvises. He had pins in his pelvises, but it was the best thing that ever happened to my dad. He quit drinking after that, which was always his worst problem."

We drove past a doghouse with BUTTERCUP written on it. Buttercup, a yellow lab, was a pup out of his son's dog's litter. "Ol' Buttercup," he said, tooting his horn.

"You want to go on up and meet my mom now?" he asked. She was eighty-seven, hadn't been sleeping well, but lately she had started eating a little bit. She lived in the original house, at the top of the hill, where Pap's grandparents had lived and died. There was pride in this: dying on the farm.

He rolled down his window, said it felt like spring was coming.

When we got to his mom's house, there were about twenty cats snaking on and around the porch. Inside was a small kitchen with a thin curtain leading to the living room where his mom was, in a hospital bed in front of a TV. She was tiny, swallowed up by that bed. On the opposite wall tick-tocked a clock that had family members' pictures instead of numbers. She lit up when she saw him enter. He called her Bubba and spoke to her in Polish. When they switched to English, they talked about cabbage— the whole backyard used to be cabbage, and that's what the kids did: cut it, trampled it, put it in big barrels, and then it would foam up. They'd take the foam off every day, and when it quit foaming, you got your sauerkraut. "In the wintertime, that's what we ate about 70 percent of the time," he said. "Sauerkraut's what we ate. Isn't that right, Bubba?"

She closed her eyes, fell sound asleep.

"Okay, Bubba," he said. "Okay."

She was dying in that room. Of course she was. And there was nothing shameful, or odd, or worrisome about it.

I stood in the room with Pap and his mom, wondering what to say, where to look, and how it would be to live a life so coolly close to death.

.   .   .

One of the things that happened was, way after I was finished researching coal mines, I kept going down into the coal mine. Explain that. I couldn't seem to quit. A couple of more hours down, a couple of more, a full ten-hour shift. Friends would leave me voice mail: "You're not down in that coal mine again, are you?" My husband, despite being the recipient of many gifts, would call and say, "Okay, come on home now." My children missed me, and my mother was sick of this particular prayer added to her daily prayer ritual.

I had no explanation as to why I kept going back, other than that I was fooling myself into believing that I needed to go one more time. "It gets in your blood after a while, I think," Scotty said to me once. "You know what I mean? After a while, it kinda sticks with you a little bit."

Foot said, "Isn't it about time you got back to your life? I can't take babysitting you anymore."

"Yeah, okay," I said, pointing my light at his chin. I told him I wanted to leave, but I didn't want to leave. I started to go all *Wizard of Oz* on him. "I think I'm going to miss you most of all, Scarecrow," I said.

"Oh, Christ almighty."

I asked him if he wouldn't feel just a little bit nostalgic for the Cadiz portal, which first opened in the 1970s and would be closing soon, nearly all of the coal gone. By summer the E-rotation guys would all be over in the company's other mine, in Hopedale. "You don't think it's kind of sad to say good-bye to this place?"

"Uh," he said. "No."

We were sitting at the power center, up on section, the place where they park all the generators and batteries running the equipment and the place where the microwave is and the couch. It was about eight P.M., and some of the guys were taking dinner breaks, Rick with a Philly steak and cheese, cupcakes, Slim Jims. Chris had steak and a baked potato. Billy had homemade beef jerky. Foot was having chicken Alfredo, a Pepsi, and a Rice Krispy treat. The guys were, of course, covered in coal dust, their hands mostly black, but Billy said it wasn't like eating in *dirt* dirt. "It's *clean* dirt," he said. "It's just coal."

Hook, chewing Copenhagen, wanted to know if anyone thought Rod Stewart was gay.

No one did.

"Mick Jagger, he could go either way."

"He messed around with that what's-her-face all his life. Aw, come on. Help me out here. What's her name? That blond? I'm narrowing it down here, ain't I?"

"Bianca!"

"No, that might have been their kid."

"Bianco, isn't that that black girl dancing around?"

"No, that's Beyoncé."

"We're not really doing too good here, are we?"

"Hey, I got the latest scoop on Smitty's woman. He said she got to be asking too many questions, so he told her to go fuck herself."

"What about the flu epidemic?"

"She wanted more money for a flu vaccine."

"Oh, man."

"He sent her $1,800 for the flight over. She does that to two or three guys a month, holy hell, she's making a good living."

"He's window shopping again. He told me he's shopping again."

"Sooner or later, you gotta trust somebody."

They talked about killing coyotes. You make a cry like a wounded animal and you can call them in, shoot 'em dead.

They talked about Freddie Mercury wearing assless chaps.

They talked about why Smitty uses a spoon to eat grapes.

They talked about it being Billy's turn to relieve Pap on the bolter so Pap has a chance to eat.

Billy stood, ready for duty. "Okay, give me something to think about," he said, before heading off. He was a man who needed to keep his mind occupied while running equipment, to keep himself from going mad.

They thought about what to offer up to Billy's mind.

"Okay, I got one," Hook said. "If everyone is going to wang chung tonight, and everyone is going to have fun tonight, what is everyone doing?"

No one felt they could top that one.

Scotty came over, sat next to me. He told me his wife had had a baby boy. He told me how happy he was, holding his son. "It was just like looking at a little *me*," he said. He named him King.

At about midnight, Foot drove me out in our own private mantrip, him slouched down as he steered, me leaning on my side trying to find the one spot of my hip best able to cushion the bumpy ride. We went rattling through the darkness, and I guess he could see me shivering. The drive out was always cold because you were moving into the wind, into all the fresh air whooshing through the mine. Foot grabbed somebody's jacket lying behind him, offered it to me. I cuddled under that sooty thing and thanked him. "Yeah, okay," he said. "I don't know why you never listened to me and brought a damn jacket in." He said he was glad our time was up so he could get back to his normal life, just dealing with the state inspectors he had to drag through the mine four and five days a week. I flipped my light on for one last look at the coal seam all frosted white, moving the light around with my head, drawing with that light on the walls.

Oftentimes, but only on the drive out of the mine, Foot got to philosophizing. This time he mused on how it was a man became a good man. Not that he was calling himself a good man, but he felt more and more that he'd been leaning in the direction.

"You're away from your kids," he said. "You work all kinds of crazy hours. Now, what happens when you work those kinda hours?"

I wasn't sure where he was going, so I didn't answer.

"What happens is you come home and your kids say they love you. Now, they're not saying that because they *know* you. They're saying that because of what their mom instilled in them kids. She's instilled in them kids that this is a good man."

"I guess so," I said.

"Because my kids didn't know me. You know what I mean? I wasn't there. So why do my kids think so much of their dad? It's because of what their mom has instilled in them. Now, my portion of that is that everything she says about me, I have to make it more or less be true. That's my portion of the equation.

"Do you see? Do you know what I mean? If I'm a good man, it's because of the people I got around me expecting *good* out of me."

"Yeah, okay," I said, considering the theory.

"Down here, this kind of shit kicks in," he said.

New Letters

WINNER—ESSAYS

Thomas Kennedy's account of his prostate-cancer scare is wince-inducing, shockingly honest, and wickedly funny. Laugh all the way through, then ponder the subtext of medical testing gone awry.

Thomas E. Kennedy

I Am Joe's Prostate

The year is 1994. You are fifty years old. It is three domiciles and one wife ago. In the bathroom of your somewhat classy north Copenhagen bungalow, you stand over the porcelain and pee. You have not yet learned the word *micturate*. You are so innocent. Finished, you wash your hands and open the door, startled to find your wife of twenty-years marriage listening there.

She says, "You piss like an old man." She is a physician. She says, "You need to have that checked. I'll make an appointment for you."

Three weeks later, you ride your classic, green, three-speed Raleigh twenty-five minutes north to G—— Hospital. Through the maze of hallways without a thread or a clue as to what you are about to experience, you find the urology department. An extremely large first resident with no name plate on the pocket of his white coat extends his extremely large hand of extremely large fingers and mumbles his name. His first name. Surnames here, you will learn, are not offered, delivered only begrudgingly upon explicit request.

With a file under his arm, Dr. Mumble leads you into an examination room, has you remove your pants and perch on your knees on a metal, paper-decked table. Without prelude or warning, he rams a long fat finger up your kazoo.

You bellow, then croak, "Is that supposed to hurt so much."

"It varies," he says absently, his back to you, washing his fingers at a sink, and continues, "There is a certain enlargement, but not more than might be expected for your age." You wonder what it is that has a certain enlargement. You finally, some years ago, learned about the existence of the clitoris, but still know nothing of the prostate. Dr. Mumble looks in the file—*your* file, instructs you to go to the nurses' station for further instructions. There you are given a large glass of colored water to drink and directed by a woman in white into a long narrow room where you are further instructed to micturate into an odd-looking steel vase with a slanted, recessed lid. Kindly, the woman in white steps out and shuts the door. You understand intuitively what micturate means, recognize it as the word of choice here in the land of white and yellow.

The odd-looking steel vase, however, does not look like something you would *want* to micturate in. Nonetheless, you do so. The slanted recessed lid flutters like a butterfly under your stream, causing a kind of needle on a machine you only just noticed to zigzag along a moving belt of graph paper. When the last few drops have dripped, causing the needle to twitch and fall still, you zip away that of you which most rarely sees the light of day and wonder what to do. You have no further instructions. Perhaps you should just go home. Yes, perhaps that is what you should do.

But the woman in white is waiting outside the door for you. You notice that she has beautiful eyes and sensuous lips. You caution yourself not to occupy your imagination with such details in your current situation, and the woman in white with sensuous lips turns you over to another of her sort, though larger of build and darker of complexion. She leads you into another room and instructs you to undress. You never have been naked in front of a strange woman unless the object was hanky-panky.

Everything? you wonder, but trust she will say stop at the appropriate moment.

"You can leave your shirt on," she says with a smile, and you think of Joe Cocker and wonder if she is teasing you. There is no name tag at her breast pocket, and she has mumbled neither her name nor her rank. She pats an examination table, indicating that you are to lie there. Face up, you presume. You do as you are told, noting distantly how passive you have become.

She takes your penis in her fingers. *Your penis!* She sprays something into it. "*Ow!*" you say.

"Yes," she whispers and begins to stuff some manner of wire down your penis. You are rather amazed that such things go on so close to the civilized streets on which you until today so innocently dwelt. It reminds you of a scene in an Alfred Hitchcock film. *Frenzy.* It occurs to you that some men would no doubt pay a great deal of money to have a woman perform this kind of act and curse your imagination, turn your eyes away from her lips, which are also sensual. You concentrate on not noticing the sensation of her fingers touching you, but anyway there seems no real danger that the jaunty head of Eros will poke up here.

She says, "Tell me when you feel the urge to micturate."

You felt the urge to micturate the instant she started stuffing that wire into you. Now you notice that the remainder of the wire is attached to another machine, the nature or function of which you are not destined to come to know.

You say, "Now, please."

She encourages you to stand before another metal vase and says, "You may micturate now."

Nothing happens.

She taps her foot.

Nothing happens.

She says, "Would you like me to wait outside?"

"Yes, please."

She withdraws. Still nothing happens.

When she returns she looks into the empty vase and sighs. "It would seem you didn't really have to micturate," she says.

"I thought I did."

She hums. "Well, we'll just have to try again."

It seems to you this would be an appropriate moment for her to stroke your hair and say, "You poor guy, you, it will all be over shortly, I promise," but instead she says, "Back on the table."

Having finally successfully micturated to her satisfaction, you anticipate release back into the world of clothing where private parts are truly private. Indeed, you are allowed to dress, but are then led into yet another room, instructed to lie on yet another table and left alone for a bit, perhaps to examine your conscience and feel guilty about the fact that you didn't really have to micturate before, but only said so to make her stop shoving that wire in. At length, two women come in, and you are instructed to open your pants. Why does this not surprise you? Why are you not surprised not to know their names or professions? You might ask, but there have been so many nameless people by now that it hardly seems to matter.

The taller, dark-haired of the two women seems to be in charge. She tugs your pants down to your pubis, applies some oil and lays a flat round metal thing the size of a small saucer on your pubic hair. She slides it around a bit. You notice she is looking not at you but at a screen alongside.

"Excellent," she says. "Your bladder is completely empty. Nothing is left. Excellent."

You ask, "May I go home now then?"

"Won't be long," she says. "Please wait here."

Presently another woman in white enters. "You'll have to take off all your clothes except your shirt," she says.

You wonder about your socks, but think, *Fuck it!* Back on the table, naked but for your unbuttoned shirt, and suddenly half a dozen people, men and women, tramp in and surround the table you are on. No one is identified, but a familiar face appears amidst them—that of the very large first resident with very large fingers. All things considered, you are glad that you are lying on your back. To put you at ease, he peers down into your face with a terrifying smile and says, "I bet this won't be nearly as bad as you fear."

Then he is inserting a wand the thickness of three or four pencils into Private Johnson while he and the other unidentified people peer alternately at you, at a screen, at you, at a screen.

The wand seems to have been plunged into the very pit of your soul where it is being stirred around. You groan, but it elicits no attention or relief. You cross your arms and groan louder. Someone, a woman, tries to uncross your arms to pin your hands down, which seems to you an odd thing for her to want to do. You decide to make a stand. Your arms are crossed and will stay that way, and you set free all the groans within you, listening with some obtuse comfort to their melody, flooding from your chest in a minor key.

The very large first resident peers unsympathetically into your face and snaps, "Would you please *stop that!*"

But you and your groans are working together now. At last you have a partner, and you will not let him go until that wand is removed from your inner sanctum.

When the thing is out, you lay groggily on the table. A woman in white hands you a pail. "You may have to micturate," she says.

How can I micturate when my bladder has just been pronounced excellently empty? you wonder, but micturate you do. It comes in pints and quarts. You note the level of micturition rising toward the lip of the pail and croak, "Nurse! Another bucket, *hurry*, please!"

At last, dressed again, dazed, you sit in a chair alongside a desk in an empty room, waiting. You do not know what you are waiting for. No doubt you have been told to wait. Thoughts of escape no longer find refuge in your consciousness. You wait. The door opens. The large first resident appears with the same thin folder under his arm. *Your* folder.

He smiles at you. "Did you have a bad time of it?" he asks.

"It was no picnic lunch in the Tivoli Gardens," you say, but your bravado rings lame even in your own ears.

He sits, opens the file. "Okay," he says. "We can offer two forms of treatment. Surgical or pharmaceutical."

You don't even think to ask treatment for what. Instantly, you yelp, "Pharmaceutical, please." *No incisions.*

"Don't dismiss the surgical possibility," he says earnestly. "It is by far the fastest and most effective." He looks at you expectantly.

"I think I should prefer the pharmaceutical," you say.

"*Pre-cision*," he says, making a ring of finger and thumb and jolting it. "With surgical precision we can take the thinnest slice or two, thin as the thinnest salami slices, thinner. I urge you to consider it. It's safe and precise. I'm required to tell you about the possibility of side effects but the chances are *extremely* slight."

"Of . . . ?"

"Uh, impotence. And incontinence. I am required to tell you that. But it is highly unlikely. Unlikely. With this procedure you won't have to be getting up two or three times in the middle of the night to urinate any more."

You say, "I don't get up in the middle of the night to urinate. Only like if I drink a bottle of beer at bedtime."

He furrows his brow, looks at the folder on his desk. "Here it says that you do."

"Well," you hear yourself say, "I am sitting right here and telling you that I don't. So what it says there is not correct."

The very large first resident juts out his lower lip. He looks very sad. For reasons unknown, you thank him as you slip out the door.

The thirty-minute bicycle ride to your office is not the most pleasant you have ever experienced. Each of the morning's invasions is echoed in every bump and pothole and curbstone that the rims of your Raleigh strike. At the office, your wife phones to ask how things went.

"Everything's fine," you say. "There was nothing wrong with me."

Epilogue

A dozen years, two domiciles, one wife, and no medical problems later, a routine blood test teaches you a new scrap of scientific terminology: PSA. The letters stand for Prostate Specific Antigen, but that sounds even more cruelly clinical than the simple, jaunty "PSA." You learn that PSA should not be higher than 4, but yours is 6.9. A follow-up sample shows it to be 12. By now you know what that very large first resident was talking about slicing like a salami—your prostate. You might have known this sooner if only the *Reader's Digest* had included an article entitled "I Am Joe's Prostate" in its talking organ series back in the '50s. But you know now how good your little walnut-sized prostate has been to you all these years, with what joy it has assisted.

Although you have no symptoms—no prostate enlargement, no urinary difficulties, no pain—the elevated PSA alarms your GP sufficiently to send you once again for tests—this time to F—— Hospital. Here the personnel seem considerably more like human beings than they did at G—— Hospital. They have names and identify themselves as doctors or nurses, and this time you are equipped with questions and a pad and pen. You write everything down. You are alert to the possibility that they may endeavor to insert foreign objects into narrow hypersensitive places, and you are determined not to allow them to do so. So determined are you that they measure your blood pressure at 160 over 120. But this time, they navigate another canal, through the backdoor with ultrasound needles. You are told that there will be some discomfort but no real pain.

There is terrific discomfort and real pain as well. Each time the doctor positions the needle and aims, watching the ultrasound screen, he says by way of warning, "And . . . *now!*" and something painfully uncomfortable happens somewhere you have never felt anything but pleasure before. You engage in a philosophical discourse with yourself as to the differentiation between discomfort and pain.

First, they take six biopsies. No cancer. Then they take thirteen more biopsies. No cancer. But your PSA has now risen to 15. They take twelve more biopsies. By now, after thirty-one biopsies, you are urinating and ejaculating blood, but still no cancer is found. Your PSA drops to 9, hops back to 12, up to 19, back down to 14, up to 18, down to 13. Once your prostate has recovered from all the probing and sticking, you have no further signs of blood in your urine or seed.

But there is a tall, slender long-faced chief physician there at F—— Hospital who knows, who *intuits*, that the cancer is there. He reminds you of the policeman Porfiry Petrovitch in *Crime and Punishment*. Or a taller, morose version of Lt. Colombo of the LAPD. They have not yet found it but it *is* there he assures you. He is, in fact, 80 percent sure it is there and 15 percent sure that it has already spread. But he can do nothing until he has the hard evidence: a cancer cell. He wants to take a scrape of your prostate. He wants to put you into full narcosis (where they stop your heart and lungs for a while and keep you alive by the grace of a machine) and scrape the tiny 5 percent portion of your prostate where the ultrasound needles can't reach. Then you will come out of narcosis, and he will send the tissue sample to the pathologists for determination of whether there are malignant cells present.

Your ex-wife was a pathologist. She once revealed to you how difficult it is to determine malignancy. Sometimes healthy cells are falsely identified as malignant. Sometimes malignant cells are falsely identified as healthy. She quit practicing because the hospital administration was pressuring her to make too many fast decisions about what was and was not malignant.

This long-faced morose physician who is convinced that cancer is present in your prostate, which has otherwise been so good to you for half a century, will then, once he has found the cancer, be able to make a diagnosis and offer treatment. The treatment he urges will be removal of the prostate. All of it.

"You're fortunate," he tells you. "You're still young, and the cancer is very early. You can be completely cured."

Of the cancer that might not be there. Any possible side effects?

"There is a risk, I am obliged to tell you, that the scrape could result in impotence and/or incontinence."

And removal of the prostate?

"That *will* lead to impotence and incontinence. But the worst likely side-effect of the scrape, which is not very likely to occur at all, although I am obliged to inform you of the slight possibility, would be a modest leakage and a possible reversal of your ejaculatory trajectory."

You stare at his long, morose face, his protruding eyes, and you are aware that your own face radiates the meaning of the word *aghast*. "*What, exactly*," you whisper, "does that mean?"

"Well, when you have sex, which you could continue to have quite satisfactorily by the way, you might be likely to ejaculate into your bladder instead of, well . . . outward. But the pleasure would be precisely the same, the sensation."

Incredulously, you tell him, "The pleasure would *not* be the same at all. The whole point of ejaculating is to do it into someone else! You think I'd be happy fucking my own bladder!" For one disoriented moment, you picture *impregnating* your own bladder.

"No need to be facetious," he quietly advises you. "Besides this is all quite hypothetical." His expression clearly is one he learned in a patient-management course: Deactivating the Prostate-Protection Reflex in the Recalcitrant Aging Male Patient.

You are invited into another room to watch a video entitled, *Grand Dad's Prostate Cancer.* In it, a man who has had his prostate removed plays with his two very cute grandchildren, a boy and a girl, twins of about four. He sports a wispy gray beard and has tiny teeth; he looks into the camera and smiles a rather silly smile with his tiny white teeth. "My grandchildren think it is very funny that they have just stopped wearing diapers and Grand Dad has to start wearing them again." He chuckles.

You are not amused. You definitely do not want to wear diapers. And not that you're such a stud or anything, but you do greatly enjoy waking each morning with some lead in your pencil as indeed you cherish the occasional two-backed beast with your beloved or even the good old honeymoon of the hand. You definitely do not wish to take a permanent vacation to the land where even Viagra offers no hope. You will never willingly ejaculate into your own bladder—which seems to you of a magnitude of strangeness equal to the man in the *Ripley's Believe It Or Not, Volume 2, Sexual Aberrations,* who inserted a seventy-five-watt lightbulb into his own colon.

·   ·   ·

You develop your own future plan of treatment. You will return to the lake. On the east side of Copenhagen there is a lake you love. You love this lake because it is a street lake, in the midst of the bustling city. You have loved this lake from the moment you first spied it, thirty-four years ago. It is called Black Dam Lake, and there is an old Copenhagen proverb: *I'll go out to Black Dam Lake.*

If and when it should become necessary, on a fair and sunny day, you will rent a row boat from the rental wharf on Black

Dam Lake. You will paddle out to the center of the lake, and there you will drop anchor. You will unpack the picnic lunch you will have brought with you in a wicker basket. You will dine on smoked eel and dark rye bread spread with raw fat. Lots of it. And because fish must swim, you will drink cold bottles of beer. Many of them. And iced snaps in your favorite Holmgaard aquavit glass, many of them. While you dine, you will watch the swans float past like beautiful white question marks. You will watch the ducks and glebes paddle along the surface, and to encourage the seagulls—for they are an important part of your plan—you will fling bits of bread and eel up into the air to get them hovering overhead in an excited, crying cluster.

And then, when you are sufficiently satisfied, sufficiently besotted but not yet incapacitated, you will take the pistol from your belt, place the barrel in your mouth, pointed upward toward your cranial cavity and pull the trigger. It will be a high-caliber pistol and will tear a broad path through your brain, spraying bits and clumps of gray matter upward, which the seagulls will catch in their beaks and gobble down, wheeling over the lake, their gullets full of morsels of your thought and personality so that you will sweep across the lake like a great pointillist consciousness on your way to forever.

Where will you get a pistol?

Oh, you'll get one. By Charlton Heston's eyes, you will!

And how can you be sure you'll be strong and deliberate enough to carry all this through when that day comes.

Well, isn't it pretty to think you might?

Coda

Nonetheless, once again, you sit in a chair before the desk of Porfiry Petrovitch.

"You must choose now," he says. "The number is very high. The disease is present. It may already have spread. I *know* this."

His protruding eyes make you think of the face in an ancient ikon.

You say, "Well, I had a second opinion from . . ."

"I *know* the source of your second opinion," says Porfiry Petrovitch, "both professionally and socially. He is a nice fellow and a good internist, but he is *not* a urological surgeon, and he knows *nothing* of this."

Porfiry Petrovitch is younger than you, but his eyes are stronger, his protruding eyes. You turn your own gaze from them, look out the window behind him at the slate gray sky, toward the door which is shut and unpromising. His protruding eyes never waver from your face. They contain the words that he has spoken, that he need not repeat: "You must choose now." But he already has chosen.

. . .

So you nod. The procedure is scheduled. For three weeks you watch its inexorable approach. Then, finally, in the ward, you are dressed in a flimsy gown, being measured for support stockings, checked over like an old car, stuck with needles, thermometers, fed a pill and told it is best you get into bed because you might get woozy.

You note that you feel pretty good. Feisty even. Planning some havoc as a silent orderly rolls your bed out into the hall, the elevator up to the OR where the anesthesiologist looks soberly into your eyes and says, "We have to ask your name, standard procedure."

"My name," you say, "is Porfiry Petrovitch," giving the name of the head of the urology unit. The surgeon, alongside, laughs. "Then we'll cut right in!"

A nurse adjusts the valve set into the vein on back of your hand and the anesthesiologist does something to it, and now you are feeling *very good*. You cannot believe it is possible to feel this good.

"Think about something nice now," the anesthesiologist says.

You say, "I feel pretty damn good," and he whispers at your ear, "Men pay lots of money to feel the way you're feeling right now."

You do not reply. You are completely absorbed thinking about your wife, about how she looked in her aquamarine two-piece swim suit last summer on the beach at Skorpios, the surf frothing around her beautiful legs, blond, tan, smiling. She is smiling for you with her blue, blue eyes, drawing you forward into her gaze, her gorgeous body . . .

Suddenly they're rolling you out again.

"Say, where are you taking me?" Your voice sounds slurry.

"It's over," says a nurse. "We want you down in the wake-up room for a while, where we can keep an eye on you."

You open your mouth and hear yourself say, "Dr. No. Ursula Andress." This seems hilarious to you, but no one even smiles. Can they even hear you? Are you dead? Is this death? You want to explain your words but you notice a fly on the sheet, just sitting there, so still.

A while later you notice that you are hooked up to some contraption on which hangs a clear plastic bag of blood. From the bag runs a tube which disappears under your sheet. You become aware of an annoying discomfort in the worst of places. The blood, you understand then, is your own micturition. You have been fitted with a catheter. You are given permission to get out of bed. You do so carefully, supporting yourself on the contraption from which your bag of blood hangs and to which you are connected by a long flexible tube. The contraption looks like some kind of garment rack, and you discover that it is on wheels.

For want of anything better to do, you shuffle out of the room and along the ward corridor, rolling the rattling contraption alongside you, your bag of blood swaying there. You do not like looking at the bag of blood, but it seems wherever you send your eyes, they wander back to it, recoiling from it again, wandering back. You shuffle the length of the hall, learn how to turn your contraption without causing the connecting tube to tug at your exhausted tugger where you least want to be tugged just now. It occurs to you that all the nurses here are good-looking, and you advise yourself not to even think about that for a second lest your tugger begin to get untoward ideas.

You begin to shuffle again, back along the corridor. Three men sit around a table, their contraptions parked alongside them as they play cards with a greasy-looking deck. "How come you don't sit down?" one of them asks as you shuffle past.

"Hurts less when I'm on my feet."

"Hurts less when he's on his feet," another man explains to the first as you proceed to shuffle the night away.

Next morning the surgeon comes in to visit. Not Porfiry Petrovitch but the smiling good-humored fellow who actually did the cutting. "Just to let you know," he says brightly, "I took three good slices and everything looked fine. No enlargement, no irregularity. It is a good-looking prostate I saw."

"Should be," you say. "It's Joe's prostate."

They laugh as though they understand.

The surgeon returns that afternoon, a nurse alongside him, a dark-haired nurse who fills her translucent white uniform so perfectly that you have to avert your eyes for fear of losing your catheter.

"Is there still blood in his urine?" the surgeon asks her.

"The color of rosé wine," she replies.

You thank her for ensuring that you will never again for the remainder of your life drink rosé wine.

"We don't drink rosé wine here either," she says with a twinkle of regret.

"How do you feel about going home now?" the smiling surgeon asks.

Then you are alone with the nurse. You are in bed. She is alongside. She reaches under the covers. Could this be love? you wonder as she whispers, "Take a deep breath now. I'm going to remove the catheter. I'm afraid I'll have to move back your foreskin first."

"If you try to do that," you say, "we'll be here forever because I don't have one."

"Then take a breath."

You do, and you hear a strangling gargling horror-comic groan contract your throat: *Argh!* You consider that the first person who ever thought to write that sound with just those letters had been through this very procedure.

She holds it up for you to see—a thick pencil-like device with a ragged bulb on the end. She points at the bloody bulb. "That's the thing that hurts coming out."

You have just reached an understanding of what the ugliest word in the language is: *Catheter.* Three syllables of misery. Even worse in Danish: *Kateter.*

It will be a fortnight before you have the biopsy results. That, you know, is when the treatment can begin. The aim of this exercise has been to tenderize you for the real cut.

Two weeks ensue with frequent, fiery micturitions. You live in dread of the micturition urge. You have twisted the water pipe alongside your jakes into a pretzel and ground a millimeter off your molars. You sustain yourself by contemplating your hatred of the word catheter. You check its etymology, hoping that it is named for its inventor so that you can put a face on your hatred, but find it is built of Greek and Latin word parts that mean something like "passing through." Every time you grit your teeth and micturate fire you consider the fact that this ugly collection of letters—some of your favorite letters of the alphabet, though here organized in the ugliest possible fashion—represents a device that threatens to become a long-term fixture in your life.

There will be catheters, there will be catheters. . . . In the room the nurses come and go talking of catheters. . . . We have lingered by the catheters of the sea by sea girls wreathed with plastic tubing. . . . I should have been a pair of ragged catheters scuttling across the floors of rosé-colored seas.

On the appointed day, you enter the appointed consultation room and shake the hand of the smiling surgeon as well as the hand of the dark-haired nurse at his side. The dark-haired lady. There is always a dark-haired lady. Saying, "Take a deep breath now . . ."

You are motioned to a chair. The smiling surgeon sits, lays the flat of his palm on a folder before him on the desk top. "Well," he says, and smiles. "Nothing. There is nothing."

"Nothing?"

"No cancer. Not even a single cell. I took samples from every corner where the ultra sound needles can't reach. And there is nothing. You have a healthy prostate."

"What happened?"

"Sometimes the PSA is wrong," he says. The dark-haired nurses nods, smiles reassuringly. "Sometimes the PSA is wrong."

Thus, after two years, twenty blood tests, thirty-four biopsies, the last three of which were surgical, and two weeks of micturating fire, you are sent out into the world, onto the sunny pavement to find your way in a world of health.

What is a man to do? Down the street and on the other side, you see a sign that says BAR. You head for it.

New York

With probing curiosity and a relentlessly honest voice, Kurt Andersen's "The Imperial City" columns deconstruct matters of business, politics, and society, while revealing how he came to what he's arguing and convincing us even as he convinces himself.

Kurt Andersen

American
Roulette

A couple of weeks back, out in Omaha, I happened to share a ride to the airport with a pair of United pilots. Both were classics of the type—trim, square-jawed, silver-haired, twangy-voiced white men, one wearing a leather jacket. Sam Shepard or Paul Newman could've played them. They spent the entire trip sputtering and whining—about being baited and switched when their employee ownership of the airline had been evaporated by its bankruptcy, about the default of their pension plan, about their CEO's 40 percent pay raise, about the company to which they'd devoted their whole careers and now didn't trust a bit, and, in effect, about turning from right-stuff demigods who worked hard and played by the rules into disrespected, sputtering, whining losers. The next morning back in New York, I read the news about the record-setting bonuses on Wall Street, an aggregate amount 1,100 percent higher than in the go-go year of 1986. The 2006 revenues at just one bank, Goldman Sachs, were larger than the GNPs of two-thirds of the countries on Earth—a treasure chest from which the firm was disbursing $53.4 million to its CEO and an average of $623,000 to everybody who works at the place.

Ordinarily, I would shrug and move on with New Yorkerly indifference—the pilots are still flying, their reduced pensions notwithstanding, and I wouldn't trade my life for any banker's.

But I haven't been able to stop thinking about my jump-cut visions of those defeated pilots and the megabonused Wall Street guys shopping for $15 million apartments. And as a result, this holiday fortnight has felt to me fully Dickensian—the jolly bourgeois bustle and glow, as usual, but also in the foreground the conceited, unattractive rich, our Dombeys and Bounderbys and unredeemed Scrooges.

A month ago, I was ragging on CNN for presenting Lou Dobbs's hour of pissed-off populism as if it were a traditional nightly news show, and I still think it has a serious truth-in-packaging problem. But (like Dickens's Mr. Gradgrind, with his epiphany about the poor in *Hard Times*) I now get Dobbs's and his followers' anger and disgust about the ongoing breaches of the social contract, an American economic system that seems more and more rigged in favor of the extremely fortunate.

I know capitalism is all about creative destruction, that the pain of globalization must be endured and flexible labor markets are good; inequality is endemic; life is uncertain and unfair, sure, yeah, of course. We're all Reaganites now—or at least no longer socialists by instinct. But during the past two decades we've not only let economic uncertainty and unfairness grow to grotesque extremes, we've also inured ourselves to the spectacle. As America has become a lot more like Pottersville than Bedford Falls, those of us closer to the top of the heap have shrugged and moved on.

.   .   .

The asymmetry between the Goldman boss's compensation and that of his average employee—eighty-five times as big—is virtually Ben-and-Jerry's-like these days: An average CEO now gets paid several hundred times the salary of his average worker, a gap that's an order of magnitude larger than it was in the seventies. In Japan, the ratio is just eleven to one, and in Britain twenty-two-to-one.

This is not the America in which we grew up.

Back before the Second World War, in the teens and twenties, the richest one-half of 1 percent of Americans received 11 to 15 percent of all income, but from the fifties through the seventies, the income share of the superrich was reasonably cut back, by more than half. The rich were still plenty rich, and American capitalism worked fine.

Starting in the late eighties, however, the piece of the income pie taken each year by the rich has once again become as hugely disproportionate as it was in the twenties. Meanwhile, the median household income has gone up a measly 15 percent during the past quarter-century—and for the last five years it has actually dropped.

It used to be that when the economy thrived and productivity grew, pay for working people rose accordingly. Yet as the *Times* reported this past summer, the first six years of the twenty-first century look to be "the first sustained period of economic growth since World War II that fails to offer a prolonged increase in real wages for most workers."

People have put up with all this because it happened so quickly and for the same reason that the great mass of losers in casinos put up with odds that favor the house: The spectacle of a few ecstatic big winners encourages the losers to believe that, hey, they might get lucky and win, too. We have, in effect, turned the U.S. into a winner-take-all casino economy, substituting the gambling hall for the factory floor as our governing economic metaphor, an assembly of individual strangers whose fortunes depend overwhelmingly on random luck rather than collective hard work. And it's been unwitting synergy, not unrelated coincidence, that actual casino gambling has become ubiquitous in America at the same time.

I don't know about you, but I find casinos, for all their adrenaline and glitz, pretty depressing places.

•   •   •

Risk-taking is fabulous, central to the American ethos—but not when it's involuntary. Too many Americans have been too suddenly herded into our new national economic casino, and without debate turned into the suckers whose losses become the elite's winnings.

That's the central argument of Yale political scientist Jacob Hacker's valuable new book, *The Great Risk Shift*. Beyond our recent reversion to extreme, twenties-style income inequality, he presents data explaining the new sense of economic dread hanging over Americans. We all know that in this globalized, ultracompetitive age, job security has been beggared, but Hacker attaches startling numbers to the national anxiety. In short, people's incomes are swinging wildly—like winnings in a casino. In 1970, a family in any given year had a one-in-fourteen chance of its income dropping by half; today, the chance is one in six. No wonder mortgage foreclosures and personal bankruptcies have quintupled during the same period. Middle-class Americans live more and more with the kind of gnawing existential uncertainty that used to be mainly a problem of the poor.

The Great Society programs of the mid-sixties—Food Stamps, Head Start, Medicaid, Medicare—were the final flowering of a social-welfare era that began with FDR's New Deal thirty years earlier. The countervailing rightward pendulum swing—deregulation and tax cuts under Reagan, welfare reform under Clinton, still more tax cuts under Bush—has dominated our political economy for nearly the past thirty years.

In other words, the time seems to be ripening for a transformative surge of new passion and policy and political traction around the idea of economic fairness. Blaming illegal Mexican immigrants and dollar-an-hour Chinese workers for our troubles is an easy way to vent, but Lou Dobbs's other regular targets are pretty much on the mark: corporate greedheads and their craven enablers in the political class.

For more than a generation, the Republicans have pitched themselves as the good-old-days party, appealing to the nostalgic hunger for the wholesome, coherent society and culture of mid-century, before life went crazy around 1968. What the Democrats can do now is the same thing, only different—that is, appeal to the nostalgic hunger for the sense of basic economic security and fairness that prevailed before life went crazy around 1986.

Just as Republicans depicted Democrats as insanely free-wheeling social experimenters determined to lavish money on the undeserving poor, the caricature can be convincingly reversed: Now the GOP is the party of arrogant, reckless risk-takers—invading Iraq, denying climate change, privatizing Social Security—determined to lavish money on the undeserving rich.

Populism has gotten a bad odor, and not just among plutocrats—for most of the political chattering class, it is at least faintly pejorative. But I think that's about to change: When economic hope shrivels and the rich become cartoons of swinish privilege, why shouldn't the middle class become populists? What Professor Hacker calls "office-park populism" will be a main engine of any new cyclical progressive renaissance. The question is whether we'll elect steady, visionary FDR-like national leaders—Bloomberg? Obama?—who can manage to keep populism's nativist, Luddite tendencies in check.

I think practical-minded political majorities can be brought together to fix the big, important things that have nothing to do with religious faith or sex. In polls, between 60 and 70 percent of people now think "it is the responsibility of the federal government to make sure all Americans have health-care coverage" "even if taxes must be raised." Universal health coverage, protecting everyone against the mammoth downside economic risk of illness, would empower people to take constructive economic risks, freeing them to move to new jobs or start new businesses. We could enact de facto compensation caps for top executives, either by limiting the tax deductibility of CEO pay or, as in Britain, by making CEO pay subject to a shareholder vote every year. We can raise—and certainly not further reduce—taxes on the extremely well-to-do.

We've had a bracing, invigorating run of pedal-to-the-metal hypercapitalism, but now it's time to ease up and share the wealth some. We can afford to make life a little more fair and a lot less scary for most people. It's not only a matter of virtue and national self-image. Because the future that frightens me isn't so much a too-Hispanic U.S. caused by unchecked Mexican immigration, but a Latin Americanized society with a high-living, blithely callous oligarchy gated off from a growing mass of screwed-over peons. I think we need to put up with the Republicans' complaining about "class war!" now in order to avoid a real one later.

Los Angeles

FINALIST—PROFILE WRITING

Chris Leon's death by sniper fire in the Iraqi city of Ramadi might have seemed like just one more casualty of war, but Steve Oney's profile of Chris and his family turns the story into a heart-wrenching tale of childhood, family, and loss.

Steve Oney

Casualties of War

That Tuesday afternoon, as Jim Leon steered his red
Nissan Maxima into his windswept Lancaster neighborhood, he sighed in relief. No government vehicles
were parked in front of his beige clapboard-and-flagstone house.
Which meant there was no bad news from Iraq, where his
twenty-year-old son, Marine Corps corporal Christopher Leon,
was serving in Ramadi, one of the country's most violent cities.
During the four months since Chris deployed, this had become
Jim's ritual. Because his job as a lab technician at Quest Diagnostics in Tarzana required him to be at work by 6:30 A.M., he
always arrived home early. If anything was wrong, he would at
least find out before his wife, Kathi, who kept normal business
hours in the billing office of an Antelope Valley urologist.

Like so many streets in Lancaster, Avenue K-9, where the Leons live, is a link in a vast grid of alphabetized avenues running
east to west and numbered thoroughfares laid out north to
south. An unincorporated desert community just thirty years
ago, Lancaster now has a population of 130,000 and sprawls
across the top of Los Angeles County. From its chain restaurants
to its proliferating subdivisions, it exudes newness and unifor-
mity. The big residential developers are KB, Beazer, Pulte, and
Heritage, and the interchangeable versions of paradise they've
created are advertised on fluttering banners proclaiming 7 FLOOR

PLANS, YOU'LL LOVE IT HERE, or NO PAYMENTS UNTIL 2008. The Leons own a three-bedroom house in Harris Homes, one of the earlier neighborhoods on the desirable west side. The living room, all green and white with a faceted mirror over the fireplace, is dominated by a fabric-and-rope tree for their five cats. A Sony big-screen TV fronts one wall of the den. Plates adorned by Norman Rockwell paintings are mounted to another. But photographs of Chris are the interior's most distinctive element. A shot of him as a towheaded three-month-old hangs near his parents' bed. Pictures of him on a recent Easter and on his prom night top the mantelpiece. The first thing visible on entering the front door is a formal portrait of him in his Marine Corps dress blues. Blond haired and hazel eyed with a square jaw, he radiates self-assurance.

The Leons adopted Chris at birth, making him not less than flesh and blood to them but something more. At the time, they'd been together twelve years and were living in a tiny condo in Agoura. Tall with a thin gray mustache, Jim, who moved to Los Angeles from the Midwest in the 1960s, is urbane, deliberate, and at seventy-two, his wife's elder by sixteen years. Dark haired and exuberant, Kathi grew up in the North Valley, and most of her family still lives in the area. Each went through troubled early marriages, and both are deeply religious, regarding faith as a bulwark against an uncertain world. Indeed, Jim—who was raised Jewish—converted to Catholicism shortly after marrying Kathi. For a long time they saw themselves as liberals, but eventually they drifted to the right. Not that they were doctrinaire about it. They opposed abortion and felt that the Republican Party offered the best hope for a culture that fostered life. Jim, who's estranged from a son and daughter by his first wife, especially wanted a child, a he and Kathi tried hard to have one, invoking the Lord—they prayed constantly—and science. Despite side effects that made her hands ache so badly she had to bandage them, Kathi took the fertility drug Danazol. Nothing worked. Then in the fall of 1985, Kathi's obstetrician phoned with wonderful news. A thirteen-year-old patient named Nikki Ruhl was putting her child up for adoption. Were they interested? On November 5, the day Nikki gave birth, Jim and Kathi were at Thousand Oaks' Los Robles Hospital. After the papers were signed and Nikki was granted a few hours to hold her son, the couple took the infant home. They called him Christopher David, but Baby, Kathi's pet name for him—which even after he joined the marines she continued to use—emphasized his status in their family as a fragile and precious gift. "It was such a God thing," she says. "He gave us this blessing. You think you're in control, but God is."

Jim and Kathi moved to Lancaster in 1988 because it was a part of Los Angeles where they could afford a new house with a big yard. It took time for Jim to adjust to the one-hour commute to and from work in Tarzana, but soon enough the two were using the same expression used by others in the Antelope Valley for the more urban Southern California they'd left behind: Down Below. Down Below was crime and congestion. But here, especially in Harris Homes, which had materialized overnight, was a community of like-minded people seeking something better. In its orderliness, Lancaster offered a place of greater safety.

For Jim and Kathi, Chris's childhood was a happy blur. They ferried him to T-ball games, bought him *Star Wars* toys and skateboards, and enrolled him in one of the Antelope Valley's most elite elementary schools, Desert Christian. Chris and his best friend since second grade, David Meade, played on various roller hockey teams—the Sabres, the Hawks, and the Rangers—at an indoor rink. The only trouble anyone remembered Chris getting into as a boy occurred at the age of seven or eight when he and David set some sagebrush at the end of Avenue K-9 on fire while fooling with matches. They tried to put out the flames with Super Soakers, but when that failed they did the right thing, telling Kathi, who called the fire department, which extinguished the blaze.

Since Chris departed for Iraq, Jim and Kathi had thought back often on those days. They'd also thought back on more recent, harder times. Like many young marines, Chris had gone through a period in his teens when he'd behaved heedlessly. He had nearly destroyed himself with alcohol and drugs. There was a long stretch during which Jim and Kathi despaired of ever reaching him. But Chris fought his way clear, the battle largely taking place in his room. Painted electric blue, it is plastered with posters of Eminem and 50 Cent. A hockey stick autographed by the Kings looks down from one side, a row of Dodger caps from another. Here Chris sought meaning in his life and forgiveness for his trespasses, at eighteen scrawling a plea for divine intervention on the closet wall with a Magic Marker:

> I feel like I serve no purpose
> Strivin ta succeed but always
> Fallin ta my knees,
> Please God please
> Let my thoughts guide me
> Light my path
> Don't hide me
> I'll change the world you provided me.

Jim and Kathi were thankful the Marine Corps had given their son a sense of purpose, but they were terrified because it had placed him in danger. Jim was particularly fearful, as he viewed the world so differently from his son. Where Chris was vigorous and confrontational, he was bookish and reserved. He spent his days in a lab coat performing repetitive tasks with names like "enzyme-linked immunosorbent assay." Neither had much patience for the other's interests. The gap had been the source of much tension during Chris's adolescence, but they had gotten through it.

All of this was in the back of Jim's mind on Tuesday, June 20, 2006, when he saw the Father's Day card from Iraq. Greetings for specific occasions are hard to come by in Ramadi. Chris was forced to select one that read "Happy Birthday Dad" and displayed a lighthouse. Inside, he'd written a note that from its spotty spelling to its assessment of past failings was a synopsis of his life:

> Sorry they didn't have any fathers day cards. I know the light house is really gay. I hope you know how thankful I am for having a great man and father in my life. You've done more than youre share of hard work raising me and I know it wasn't easy. Now I'm all grown up and reflecting youre teachings and dissapline on the world. You've made me into a man and I thank you with all my heart for youre sacrifices and determination. Thanks for never giving up on me even threw all the shame I brought upon myself. Thank you for all you've done for me. I couldn't ask for a better father. Happy fathers day. I love you dad. Love, Chris

Jim's eyes filled with tears. Chris had never told him that he looked up to him or regarded him as a source of strength. Maybe he had been a better father than he imagined. Maybe their life in the Antelope Valley had worked out according to plan. When he finally composed himself, Jim called Kathi to tell her everything was okay and that he'd received an amazing card from their son that he couldn't wait for her to read. Ten minutes later, the doorbell rang.

·　　　·　　　·

One day during his sophomore year, Chris was standing on the grounds of Lancaster's Paraclete High handing out sticks of gum to some friends when a classmate approached and demanded a piece. Chris refused, and the boy grabbed him by the hair. Chris retaliated with a vicious punch to the mouth. He mostly ended up hurting himself, though, opening a jagged gash across his knuckles. The cut became infected, and the next morning he awakened with a hand as big as a balloon. He missed half a week of classes, but the worst thing was that he didn't care. In fact, he took pride in the entire episode, regarding it as a defining moment.

Paraclete High is on the northwest side of Lancaster, just below Quartz Hill, the area's wealthiest enclave, home to physicians, lawyers, and aerospace engineers employed by the giant Boeing and Northrop Grumman factories that dominate the Antelope Valley's economy. Although affiliated with the Catholic Church, the school draws students of all religions to its yucca-studded campus. Ninety percent of the graduates attend college, and as a freshman Chris had given every indication that he would be one of them, earning mostly As and Bs. The next year had begun just as promisingly, with Chris playing cornerback on the varsity football Spirits, getting into enough games to feel that he contributed to the team's 2001 California Interscholastic Federation Southern Section Championship.

Then the bottom fell out. In his second sophomore semester, Chris received a C in English, Ds in French, biology, and religion, and an F in algebra. Never again would he walk onto the football field. His new sport was paintball, which had him running through the desert blasting away with a $1,300 Angel gun his parents dutifully helped him buy. He'd taken up drinking and smoking, choosing brands—potent King Cobra 40s and nicotine-rich Camel Wides—that he believed gave him gangster credibility. Many weekend nights he stayed out until dawn without calling home. He also started stealing money from Jim and Kathi, even taking Christmas presents intended for his grandparents, returning them to the store where they were purchased, and pocketing the refund.

Jim and Kathi racked their brains to understand what was going on. How could their baby have so quickly become a demon? What had they missed? There had, of course, been signs. When Chris was at Desert Christian, he'd been diagnosed with attention deficit disorder, and his doctor had prescribed Ritalin, then Dexedrine. During his teens, though, he stopped taking the drugs. They made him feel dull. Without them, he was prone to rogue bursts of energy. There was also something else: By the time Chris turned fifteen, Jim was sixty-six, far older than other boys' dads. Jim lived for baroque music, believing that in the intricacy of a Bach mass he could hear the truth in all its nuances. Chris loved rap, especially anything by Dr. Dre, finding authenticity in its discordant rhythms and harsh lyrics—to him the truth was a blunt object. They quarreled over control of the CD player. "I'm gonna put you down, old man," Chris would growl, to which his father would retort, "That's very mature." The relationship degenerated. "I felt inadequate," Jim says. "I didn't know what to do for him." Hoping to pick up the slack, Kathi often assumed the paternal role, going camping with her son while Jim stayed at home. In an extreme gesture of solidarity for a fifty-year-old mom, when Chris got his ears and tongue pierced, she got a diamond nose stud.

At the heart of it all was a riddle that Jim and Kathi couldn't solve: It was one thing for Chris to accept intellectually that he'd been given up for adoption, but emotionally it was another story. No matter how hard Jim and Kathi tried, he felt detached and betrayed. He didn't know who he was, which meant that the battle to forge an identity fought by every teen was for him doubly intense.

On top of all this, Chris was plainly using drugs. What Jim and Kathi lacked was evidence. Shortly after Paraclete let out for summer 2002 vacation, they found it—a bag of marijuana in their son's things. The discovery produced a moment of clarity for Kathi. "I thought, 'All right, it's time to put the screws to him,'" she says. "I thought, 'I'm gonna show him.'" She phoned the Los Angeles County Sheriff's Department. On a June Sunday as Chris was sleeping, two deputies appeared at the door. After awakening and cuffing him, they put him in the back of a squad car. Since he was a minor and in possession of less than an ounce, they charged him with a misdemeanor and did not transport him to the Lancaster substation. He would be required to attend several Narcotics Anonymous sessions and pay a $400 fine, but ultimately his record would be wiped clean. Chris was devastated and furious. "Fuck you, Mom," he screamed when he stormed back into the house. "Fuck you. Fuck you. Fuck you." He then stomped off to his room, slamming the door behind him.

During this period, Jim and Kathi sought consolation and guidance at the 5,000-member Desert Vineyard Fellowship. Wearying of Catholicism's rigidity and seeking a form of worship that was at once less dogmatic and more vibrantly rooted in Scripture, they had joined in 1999. The Vineyard movement, which grew out of the countercultural Jesus craze, began on Santa Monica Beach during the early 1970s. Preachers wear jeans, sermons are conversational, and the music is guitar-driven soft rock to which parishioners stand and sway with hands uplifted to the Lord. Desert Vineyard, which is presided over by the Reverend David Parker—known to everyone as Pastor Dave—is the second oldest of the denomination's 1,500 churches. The congregation includes Northrop Grumman engineers and businesspeople. But many who attend are troubled—35 percent have experienced substance-abuse problems. Desert Vineyard offers a variety of prayer-based support programs, and Jim and Kathi enrolled in one composed of other parents of children using drugs. "They let us know we weren't alone and weren't failures," says Kathi. "They'd say, 'We've been there. Don't give up.'"

Still, Jim and Kathi were at a loss about what to do. One minute Kathi would announce that they were kicking Chris out, but Jim wouldn't hear of it. The next, Jim would declare that he'd lost patience, and Kathi would say that they had to keep trying. They agreed on one matter, though: They were through paying thousands of dollars for private schooling. Their son's days at Paraclete were over.

Chris's junior year at Lancaster High started off disastrously. Forging notes from Jim and Kathi, he skipped classes and attracted the attention of truant officers. His grades dropped even lower: Fs in Spanish, English, algebra, history, and science. Affecting hip-hop style in Enyce sweaters and cargo pants from Shady Ltd., he spent afternoons racing his mom's navy blue Saturn along secluded streets. His favorite was Bulldog Avenue near Quartz Hill, where a tight four-lane turn provides an ideal spot for drifting . To give the car a high-performance roar, he removed its air filter, ignoring warnings that this was a surefire way to burn out the engine, which he did. At night Chris was often at a party house owned by an older guy who kept crack in the refrigerator and loved to brag about the life. Strange girls and ex-cons were always passing through, and four or five people would still be awake at sunrise. Before long, Chris was smoking and dealing methamphetamine, the Antelope Valley's hardcore drug of choice.

"He was a classic Lancaster kid," says David Meade, who stayed on at Paraclete but remained Chris's closest friend. "He screwed around in high school because there's nothing to do here but drink and smoke. You get sucked into it, and it's a nasty cycle. You get your girlfriend pregnant, and you end up in a crappy job to pay the bills. And crystal meth is always a danger. It's the largest problem in our town. There are lots of meth labs on the east side, where people's houses blow up in the middle of the night. This was the road Chris was on."

Jim and Kathi didn't know everything, but they knew enough. During talks with a Lancaster High guidance counselor, they were given two choices: Chris could either attend Desert Winds, a separate campus for delinquent students, or he could enroll in Independent Study. Just two months into his new school, their son was running out of options.

On the periphery of the Lancaster High campus, far from the school's busy quads, is room 306, home of the Independent Study program.

The location is intentional and symbolic. Here, students who have rebelled against order being imposed on them are expected to impose it on themselves. Rather than meet in class for lectures and instruction, they work on their own schedules. Whether they read textbooks at home or study online at a cybercafé is immaterial. They're only required to appear in room 306 to submit papers and take tests.

One morning in November 2002, Chris walked through the drab blue door for the first time. Instead of desks lined up in neat rows, there were casually arranged round tables. At the entrance was an area reminiscent of a library checkout counter. In a cubicle formed from tall black filing cabinets sat Cheryl Holland. A fifty-eight-year-old mother of two and a teacher in the Antelope Valley School District since 1974, Holland projects empathy and toughness. Almost every inch of her work area is covered with photographs of kittens, singer Céline Dion, and former NFL quarterback John Elway. She loves nothing more than to talk about making a difference in children's lives. Then she'll square her jaw and declare that if a student ever hit her she'd deck him.

"When Chris's parents decided it was time to put the brakes on his tailspin," Holland says, "it was the luck of the draw that he was assigned to me. I took one look at him and realized he just needed a little time to get his head out of his ass. He thought he could continue to be a slacker. He thought he could just go through the motions. I told him that wasn't going to fly here. I told him I'd be nice if he did his work, but if he didn't I'd get down and dirty."

Chris told David Meade that Holland was a bitch and complained to Jim and Kathi that he hated her. "She was in his face," says Kathi, "and he didn't like it. But she got his attention." To

Jim and Kathi's relief, Chris responded to Independent Study's unstructured environment, in part because it allowed him to call his own shots, a privilege he had never before been accorded. "The program required him to become accountable," says Holland. "After a while I no longer had to tell him to do his work," adds Kathi. "He just did it." In his first grading period, he earned two Bs and a C.

Shortly before Chris enrolled in Independent Study, he fell in with several boys who'd recently formed a crew whose name could not have been more purposeful: Insanely Determined to Succeed. Aside from Chris, IDS had four other members: Jon Sherman, Sonny Huerta, Alan Iosue, and his old friend David Meade. "We started it for protection," says Jon. "We were kind of crazy and got into a lot of fights. It got dangerous out here." This was one reason Jon recruited Chris. "He just had this strength about him. I wanted him on my side."

The first months Chris was at Lancaster High, the boys of IDS spent the bulk of their time driving the Antelope Valley's backstreets or hanging out in an isolated cul-de-sac near Alan's house known as "the spot." There they drank, talked, and when the testosterone was running high, squabbled. "We didn't do shit," says Jon, "and that's where we did it." Their regimented desert city felt stultifying. Too much conformity. Too many naysayers. Too few outlets for creativity. They were always up for anything unsanctioned, even if it took them to the party house. "It was a fucked-up time," says Jon. "There were days we'd have $1,000 in our pockets."

All the members of Insanely Determined to Succeed came from middle-class or privileged backgrounds (David's dad was an astronaut who flew on three shuttle missions), and each possessed intrinsic skills or qualities. Sonny could cook so well, people thought he could be a chef. Jon could paint. Alan loved architecture. David followed politics and read voraciously. Chris was different. He didn't pursue an obvious passion, but he was the most alive, the most resilient, the one the others turned to. "My mom died, and afterward I was pretty messed up and got into some trouble," says Alan. "I spent nineteen days at juvenile hall. Chris was the first person I saw when I got out. He came over to see how I was doing and talked to my dad. I was having difficulty in school, and he told me to stick with it." While none of the group's members was headed to Harvard, and all except David were going to have difficulty graduating from high school, they were to a one idealistic—which had always been part of the attraction. "When I first got to know Chris," says Jon, "he was hanging around with guys who were much lower in intelligence. He just needed help. He needed brothers."

By the start of their senior year, the boys of IDS had begun to follow their own code. "We had too much respect for ourselves to go on the way we had been," says Jon. "I feel like we ultimately became a reincarnation of King Arthur's knights. If someone fell down, we picked him up. We sought knowledge. We told one another the truth. We pushed ourselves to lead lives of valor."

As Chris started to feel better about himself, two good things happened. First, he found a girlfriend. Analyse Reaves, a Paraclete student from an academic family (her father administers the UCLA physics lab), had long resisted his approaches. During his sophomore year, she'd outright rejected him. "That Valentine's Day she broke his heart," says David. Yet Chris persisted, and when he asked her to go to Disneyland in March 2003, she said yes. Soon the two were inseparable. Not only did she boost Chris's ego and improve his manners ("He was very rough around the edges," says David), she got him to swear off meth. "Until then he didn't have a reason to stop," she says. "I think I helped him find one."

Chris also landed a job, taking the position of stock boy at PetSmart in Lancaster's Valley Central Mall. Initially, he put in just a few hours after school unloading merchandise and helping customers carry purchases to their cars. Eventually, the manager came to trust him, assigning him the task of opening the place on Sunday mornings.

PetSmart is next door to the city's Armed Forces Career Center. All the major branches of the military have offices there, and on breaks Chris would wander down to see what was going on. He gravitated to the space occupied by the United States Marine Corps. Decorated by posters bearing slogans like PAIN IS TEMPORARY PRIDE IS FOREVER and a wall plaque displaying the corps' eagle, globe, and anchor seal, the office was run by Gunnery Sergeant Larry Watts and Staff Sergeant Leann Elizabeth Dixon. Watts is a stern, black Chicagoan, Dixon a white Floridian known to pick up stray animals and nurse them at home. Chris liked them both, but he was even more taken by the Marine Corps itself. As he saw it, the service could provide him a chance to excel as an individual while becoming part of something bigger. The romance, the call to duty, the machismo—the corps was Insanely Determined to Succeed writ large. Here, at last, was an opportunity for Chris to merge the warring parts of his soul. He was so gung ho that he told his parents he was quitting school and joining immediately. Kathi objected, insisting that he get his diploma. As it turned out, the Marine Corps offers a Delayed Entry Program designed for those in his position. On July 22, 2003, with Sergeant Dixon bearing witness, Chris signed up.

"This was Chris's way of redeeming himself," says Jim. "He wanted to do something difficult. I think he was a little elitist about it." David believes Chris saw the marines as a calling: "He told me God wanted him to do it, that it was a vocation." Jon puts it more enthusiastically: "It was fucking cool."

Chris immersed himself in the Delayed Entry Program. "He was one of my faithful fellows," says Sergeant Watts. "Each Saturday we'd run, do pull-ups and push-ups, and every week I'd go by Lancaster High to see how he was doing with his studies."

Chris stopped eating fast food and began downing protein shakes and vitamin supplements. "He started drinking this green goop," says David. "It was awful." He also applied himself to Independent Study. "During his junior year I had to push him," says Cheryl Holland. "But during his senior year all I had to do was guide him. He became a pleasure to have in my life. It was hard for him—he never did learn to spell—but in fact he was smart, a deep thinker." To graduate on time, Chris needed to make up all the classes he'd failed. During his last semester he took seven courses, receiving Bs in six. The sole blemish was a C in food. He also undertook a senior project titled "Becoming a U.S. Marine." Chris accompanied his six-page essay with a cover letter that opened, "For the past four years I have gone through more struggles than the average high school student. . . . I never really thought I was going to graduate high school. That was until I started really getting involved in the Marines. My whole outlook on life has changed. . . . I look forward to becoming a Marine. I will do everything possible in my position to make this country a better place for everyone." The project received the Independent Study Program's highest mark—a 4, for "Distinguished." On June 10, 2004, Chris graduated from Lancaster High with his class. Several weeks later Jim and Kathi drove him to the Armed Forces Career Center, where a van was waiting to transport him to Los Angeles. From there, it would be on to the Marine Corps Recruit Depot in San Diego, and then Camp Pendleton.

The war in Iraq had entered its second year, but just a few months before, President George W. Bush—whom Jim and Kathi had supported in 2000 and would vote for again in November—had proclaimed, "Mission accomplished." Says Kathi, "It never crossed our minds that Chris would see combat. Our goal had been to get him through school. The marines helped us achieve it. Iraq felt very far away."

●　　　●　　　●

The Leons' living room door opens onto a metal security screen, and through it Jim could see a Marine Corps staff sergeant, a chief warrant officer, and an air force chaplain. Jim made no move to unlock the screen, convinced that if he kept his visitors at bay, what they had come to tell him could not be true. He said nothing. He stared at the men, his hands at his sides. The stand-off lasted only a minute, but it felt longer. Finally, Sergeant Jeff Brown, who'd never before had to perform this duty, asked, "Can we come in?"

"I don't know how you guys do this," Jim said after stepping aside.

"Your son, Christopher Leon, has been killed in action," Brown began. As the casualty assist calls officer (CACO, in marine argot), Brown was in charge, but there was no prescribed protocol. All he had to go on was his memory of what it had been like for his parents when he was a boy and his brother died. He knew he couldn't protect the Leons from pain, but he could at least assure them that the Marine Corps would take care of the myriad details. As he started to explain, however, he saw that Jim had turned white, becoming at once agitated and withdrawn. Brown thought he must be recalling memories of Chris. That was only partly right.

The image Jim could not get out of his mind was of Chris's dead body. His facial features were unchanged, but the animating force—the spirit that had made him Chris—had been extinguished. Eyes gone vacant, mouth slack, he was pasty, cold, rigid, inert. Oddly, he was not in uniform but in street clothes, yet maybe that was fitting. Before he was a marine, he was the son whose Father's Day card was lying open on the den table. Jim fought hard to dislodge the vision. Once he did, though, he felt the first flush of a familiar toxic glow. In 2002, while commuting to Tarzana, he'd suffered a mild heart attack. In 2003, he underwent triple bypass surgery. He was later diagnosed with congestive heart failure. Now he was experiencing the same sensation. Pressure surged in his chest. Sweat beaded on his forehead.

"Would you like me to call an ambulance?" the chaplain asked.

"You'd better."

While the paramedics were en route, Jim phoned Kathi. She was at her desk near the refrigerator in the back of the urology clinic, entering charges into a computer and sending claims to insurance companies, when she picked up. "We've lost Chris," Jim said, his voice breaking. She screamed, "No" and continued screaming until her boss's wife took the receiver from her hand. One of her coworkers attempted to reassure her, saying there had to be a mistake, but Kathi knew better, and as she walked through the crowded reception area she kept screaming. She screamed all the way home and was still doing so when the emergency technicians arrived: "No. No. No." Finally, one of the men said, "You have to stop," but she wouldn't. The advice was an affront from someone who couldn't possibly comprehend what she was feeling. Her baby, the unexpected miracle in her life, was gone.

The EMTs raced Jim to Antelope Valley Hospital, where he was diagnosed as having suffered another mild heart attack and placed in the intensive care unit. Kathi stayed behind and began notifying friends and family members, among them her sister, LoriAnn, and her mother, who because of a bad connection couldn't hear what her daughter was saying, forcing her to repeat, "Chris was killed. Chris was killed." All the while, Sergeant Brown and the other servicemen stood at the edge of the room at parade rest. They would do whatever they were asked, but they would not infringe.

By eight o'clock the Leons' house had filled with people—most from Desert Vineyard. Among them were Dana and Dawn Stewart, whose son, Marine Corps lance corporal Ian Stewart, had been killed in Iraq two years before. "I never wanted to walk in your shoes," Kathi burst out on seeing Dawn, and they embraced. Associate Pastor Paul Lopiccolo led the group in prayer, kneeling in Kathi's living room and assuring her that her fellow church members would keep vigil. That night, after everyone departed, Kathi took strength from the knowledge that others would be beseeching the Lord in her name. "I was too devastated," she says, "to pray for myself."

Of the boys in Insanely Determined to Succeed, Jon heard first. He had just come home from his job at T-Mobile, where he was working to put himself through Antelope Valley College. He called the others. Sonny was attending the California School of Culinary Arts in Pasadena by day while grilling steaks at a Claim Jumpers by night. Alan was selling electronics components in Las Vegas to pay for classes at the Community College of Southern Nevada. David was studying at Pepperdine University while employed in a Santa Monica law firm's collections office. He was the last to learn. He'd turned off his cell phone Tuesday night and didn't find out until the next morning when he picked up a text message from Jon as he was walking to the corner of Wilshire Boulevard and Third Street. Suddenly, the palm trees and the Pacific dissolved in a blur of tears. After crying for fifteen minutes, David told one of the partners that his friend had been killed in Iraq. He then headed to Lancaster. Up the Antelope Valley Freeway, out of the green basin, and into the dry mountains that rim Los Angeles County he drove. Eventually, he found himself at Jon's apartment. Both of them wanted to visit the Leons, but neither could muster the courage that night.

Over the next several days, as Jim lay in a hospital bed, Kathi leaned heavily on LoriAnn, who'd come from Westlake Village to stay with her. The house was filled with flowers, but Kathi could barely see them, having ruptured blood vessels in her eyes during her screaming. Nor could she eat any of the casseroles and sandwiches members of Desert Vineyard kept dropping off. She had no appetite. "I was just broken down," she says. "My mind had become mush. I couldn't reason." Her biggest concern was the return of Chris's remains. The bodies of fallen American servicemen are initially flown to the Charles C. Carson Center for Mortuary Affairs in Dover, Delaware. The length of time they are kept there can vary widely. Each morning Kathi called Sergeant Brown to see where things stood, but he couldn't get an answer. The only information he could provide was that Chris's remains were viewable. Unlike many servicemen killed in Iraq, he had not been torn apart by an improvised explosive device. A sniper had shot him. "I never thought I'd want to see a body, especially my son's," says Kathi, "but I was comforted by the fact that I'd be able to."

At eleven P.M. on June 29, a week and a half after Chris was killed, a Delta flight carrying his remains landed at Ontario International Airport and taxied to the gate. Jim had been released from the hospital, and he and Kathi, her parents, and her sister and brother-in-law were standing on the tarmac alongside a marine honor guard commanded by Jeff Brown. After the passengers disembarked, Chris's casket appeared in the mouth of the cargo hold. Encased in Styrofoam and shrink-wrap, it looked like an appliance carton. The marines needed ten minutes to rip away the packing material. They then draped the coffin with an American flag and carried it to a waiting hearse. "It's such a horrible car to see your baby go in," says Kathi. "But at least we got to touch the casket and kiss the flag. We were in such a state of shock. A woman in a ground-level shipping office saw us standing there and opened a locked door and said that if we needed to use the bathroom to come in. It was a tiny thing, but it showed real kindness. We were so grateful." As the hearse pulled away, Jim saluted. Behind the glass wall of a busy concourse, people standing in line were saluting, too.

The next day Kathi and her family went to Lancaster's Joshua Memorial Park to view the body. Jim, in his mind having already seen Chris dead, didn't go. "I just can't take it," he told Kathi. After the family filed out, David Meade and Jon Sherman entered. "I was so glad to see him," says Jon. "I was so glad he was home."

That evening, family members gathered at the Leons' to make memory boards to display at the funeral. Jim and Kathi had assembled a stack of photographs from different periods in Chris's life. As the group began to cut and paste, something unexpected happened—the sadness lifted. Grief, unbearable as it is, offers moments of euphoria, and they were experiencing one, so much so that around ten o'clock Jim rushed out to a Marie Callender's and bought pies. Everyone stayed up late eating and passing around pictures. There was Chris at two with a baseball cap on sideways and a plastic bat in his hands. Here he was at four in a bathing pool filled with frogs he'd collected. A shot of him at ten riding on his skateboard conjured memories of his frequent falls and how he always jumped back up. They laughed at these images, but one taken of Chris in Iraq elicited a different emotion. He's wearing a desert camouflage uniform, with his helmet pulled down low. Eyes wary, lips set in a straight line, he looks fierce yet mindful. For years his parents had worried that Chris wouldn't find himself, but here was evidence that he had, and it made them proud. "I wouldn't want to tangle with that guy," Jim thought.

•   •   •

The most daunting part of marine boot camp is the Crucible. A fifty-four-hour training mission during which sleep-deprived recruits each carrying seventy-five pounds of gear march, crawl, and run more than fifty miles through mock battlefields, the drill amounts to a final exam. It concludes with a ten-mile climb known as the Reaper. Characterized by rocky terrain and nearly vertical ascents, it is Camp Pendleton's most formidable challenge. Shortly before Chris started, he bent over to adjust his boots and heard a loud crack, then felt pain. He'd broken his left foot . For a second, he contemplated what to do. Yet as he looked back on what he'd already been through during the eight weeks since he'd left Lancaster—the loneliness and the exhaustion—he decided to push forward. Every inch of the Reaper was excruciating, as was every inch of a six-mile run that followed, but Chris finished. Boot camp was essentially behind him. The life he'd aspired to since he walked into the recruiting station next to PetSmart lay ahead.

Chris's injury, although not severe, required him to wear a walking cast, and he did not graduate with his class. Accompanying Jim and Kathi to the December graduation ceremony were Analyse and three members of Insanely Determined to Succeed—David, Jon, and Alan. Chris, they all agreed, seemed older, more polite, and for someone who'd been immersed in a culture that prizes toughness, surprisingly more loving. Afterward, everyone went to lunch at the San Diego Yacht Club, snapping pictures of Chris in his uniform with its eagle, globe, and anchor pin as he stood before the sparkling water. He was now a marine. Two days later he walked into a tattoo parlor and had USMC inked onto his right triceps and his last name inked onto his left.

Chris returned to Camp Pendleton for six weeks of infantry training, then reported to Twentynine Palms, home of the Marine Corps Communications School. He wanted to become a radio operator and spent hours learning how to operate the PRC-117 and PRC-119, each about the size and weight of a VCR. Along with bulletproof steel plates, a flak jacket, ammunition magazines, and an M-16 A4 rifle, these machines would become part of the 120 pounds of equipment he would carry in the field. During downtime, he began working out obsessively. At first he just wanted to be strong enough to do his job, but he found he loved physical training. Within months he was bench-pressing 300 pounds and on his way to a green belt in karate.

Because he was close to the Antelope Valley, Chris could go home on weekends. Jim and Kathi's hope that the Iraq war would be over by the time their son finished training had been a delusion. In boot camp, Chris had told them as much. In one of the weekly letters he sent them, many of which were simply addressed "Mom and Dad, Avenue K-9, Lancaster, Ca.," he'd written:

> I'm getting kinda scared. . . . The DIs keep telling us that most of us will go to Iraq for sure, including all infintry. But its OK if I go. I'll come back walking and talking, that is. I don't want you to tell Analyse this. Okay.

Now deployment was drawing nearer. One night Chris and David Meade were hanging out. "Why are you going?" David asked. "So you don't have to," Chris responded. Around this time, Chris attended the funeral of a marine killed in Iraq. Afterward, he dropped in on David at his mom's house, which offers a view of the entire Antelope Valley. The two boys were standing outside looking down on the lights of the town where they'd grown up when Chris said, "The funeral I was at—only one person spoke. If anything happens to me . . ."

David refused to let Chris finish. "If you're predisposed to it, it'll happen."

But Chris wouldn't be silenced. "If anything happens to me and only one person gets to speak, I want it to be you."

The night before Chris left for Okinawa for final training, Jim and Kathi threw a going-away party. About halfway through the evening, with no explanation or tenderness, Chris told Analyse that he was breaking up with her. They had been together for two years. She was devastated. "He did it in a very cold, very fucked-up way," says David. "She sat outside in her car for two hours. He knew he was going to die and didn't want any attachments." Chris's other friends felt that his motivation had more to do with the deteriorating nature of the relationship. All agree that his behavior was cruel. "He felt he should just break things off," says Analyse. "I never saw him again."

In Okinawa, Chris was assigned to the highly regarded Air Naval Gunfire Liaison Company. Although not as elite as Force Recon, ANGLICO is among the marines' most demanding outfits. Working in small groups usually no larger than four and typically commanded by a high-ranking fighter pilot, ANGLICO teams are the communications link between ground combat missions and air support, which can come in the form of everything from helicopter gunships to F-18s. It's ANGLICO's job to call in bomb and missile strikes, and since the missions require precision, units are frequently within one hundred yards of their targets. The radio operator must maintain contact between the foot soldiers and the forces aloft. "At first he wasn't proficient with the radios, not that this was surprising," says Captain Adam Blanton of Fifth ANGLICO. A twenty-nine-year-old Boise State English graduate who grew up in Riverside County, he was Chris's team leader. "We have the most complicated equipment out there. But he picked things up quickly."

In November 2005, Chris phoned Kathi. He knew that within a couple months he would be in Iraq, and he wanted to meet his birth mom before leaving. "At first my heart sank," says Kathi. "I thought I was going to lose him. But I realized that was my own insecurity, my own problem. I needed to do what was best for Chris. So I dug up the paperwork from the adoption. There was a phone number for Nikki Ruhl's mother. When I called it, I got a forwarding number—and here's the remarkable part. When I reached Nikki's mom, who'd moved to Nevada, she told me the forwarding number was due to be disconnected that very day. If I hadn't called when I did, who knows if we'd ever have found her?"

Nikki was thirty-three, living in Simi Valley and training to be a veterinary technician. Each November 5, ever since that day twenty years earlier at Los Robles Hospital, she'd quietly celebrated Chris's birthday. When he turned eighteen, she'd begun hoping he'd call. Now, here was Kathi on the phone saying Chris was leaving for Iraq and wanted to meet her. Nikki couldn't hold back the tears. "I was so happy," she says. "Kathi and I talked for two hours. Then I drove to Lancaster a couple of weeks later and spent the afternoon with Jim and Kathi. We looked at pictures and talked about the good and the bad. They made me feel like family." Jim and Kathi were taken with Nikki, and at the end of the visit, Kathi said Chris would be home for the holidays and she'd make the arrangements.

Everything about Chris's 2005 Christmas leave, indeed everything about the weeks before he deployed for Iraq, seemed touched by the miraculous. The day after he got back to Lancaster, he went on a date with Aimey Vaccaro. The two had known each other in grade school at Desert Christian, but they'd lost touch. Just five feet two inches tall and 105 pounds, with straight brown hair with red highlights, Aimey is tiny and saucy. She favors faded jeans and Dooney & Burke bags and drives a white Toyota with the vanity tag AIMEY V. She was attending Antelope Valley College and working at a local clothing store. Chris, who Aimey remembered as "a little pip-squeak," had metamorphosed into a five-feet-ten-inch, 175-pound marine. He liked to show off his ripped upper body and his tattoos, which now included a rosary on one arm and a dragon on his back that he'd acquired in Okinawa. Yet for all his toughness, Aimey found him dear. By night's end, both were smitten. "I liked him," she says, "but I told myself, 'I'm not going to be a nineteen-year-old girl tied down to a boyfriend in Iraq.'" Still, in the coming days the two spent hours together around a giant Christmas tree at Jim and Kathi's house, wrapping presents and watching DVDs (Jim Carrey's *The Grinch*, an entire season of Fox's rude *Family Guy*). "He was addictive," Aimey says. "It was impossible not to be with him. I gave in."

Chris attended a candlelight Christmas Eve service with Jim and Kathi at Desert Vineyard, then the next morning rode with them to Westlake Village for dinner at his aunt and uncle's home. He supervised the distribution of presents and taught his four-year-old niece how to ride the new bicycle she'd received.

The following day, Chris drove to Simi Valley to meet Nikki Ruhl. He was so nervous that he phoned Aimey three times before he arrived. Nikki was equally flustered, calling Kathi three times as well. Like Chris, Nikki is blond with hazel eyes. "You're so pretty," he said when she came to the door. The two spent the morning together, with Nikki doing most of the talking. She told Chris she had gotten pregnant the first time she'd ever had sex. The reason she'd put him up for adoption was that she'd been so young and scared. If only she hadn't been thirteen, she added, asking if he could understand. He said he did. She offered to tell him about the seventeen-year-old boy who was his father. But he didn't want to hear about him. He was just interested in her. Chris spoke of the difficulties he'd caused Jim and Kathi, but he stressed that it was all in the past. He went on about the marines. Nikki thought he was earnest and cocky, an impressive combination.

In the early afternoon, the two drove to a T.G.I. Friday's, which made the occasion feel like a first date—in many ways it was. Over lunch they discovered all they had in common. Each had found school difficult. Both loved animals. Neither possessed a good sense of direction. Near the meal's end, Chris told Nikki that meeting her had made his life complete. Then he pulled out a picture of Nikki taken the year she'd given birth to him. Jim and Kathi had given it to him when he entered high school. He told her he'd been carrying it ever since and would carry it with him in Iraq.

Chris spent January at Camp Lejeune in North Carolina, perfecting his radio skills. "He went from being merely proficient to being one of the best I've seen," says Captain Blanton. It was also during this period that Chris and Aimey fell in love. Maybe it was the war, maybe it was just luck, but they were open to each other in ways neither had been to anyone before. Despite his rejection of Analyse, Chris realized he needed someone now more than ever, and he was astonished that Aimey was willing to be that person. On January 8, he e-mailed her:

I just wanted to say thank you. Thank you for being there for me (for us) for what I'm about to go threw 'what we're about to go threw.' You have a lot of courage and strength for what you're taking on. A lot of women in your position can't handle what you're about to go threw. I admire you so much for you're strength.

In February, Chris flew back home for a last few days' leave before deployment. His grandparents hosted a party, and he took Aimey out for a Valentine's Day dinner at Café del Rey overlooking the Pacific in the Marina. The next day he phoned David Meade and suggested a double date. That night, Chris and Aimey and David and his girlfriend, Anna, met at an Islands restaurant. Everyone had hamburgers except Chris, who true to his new obsession with fitness ordered a chicken and lettuce combination. The four then drove to the Sunset Strip, where David had purchased tickets for a Louis C.K. show at the Laugh Factory. After his set, the emcee announced a surprise guest—Dave Chappelle, whose midseason defection from his Comedy Central series had sparked headlines. To Chris, Chappelle was a giant, the stand-up equivalent of Dr. Dre. He loved a sketch called "Black Bush," in which the comedian, playing the president, takes the country to war in Iraq because he doesn't understand the meaning of yellow cake, confusing the weapons-grade uranium his advisers claimed Saddam Hussein possessed for a piece of Duncan Hines. The absurdity of the notion broke Chris up. Seeing Chappelle in person was just the right send-off.

Two days later at 5:45 A.M., Kathi and Jim climbed into the front seat of the family car and an exhausted Chris and Aimey fell into the back for the mad dash down the Antelope Valley Freeway to make an 8:50 flight from LAX to Charlotte, North Carolina. There Chris would change planes for Camp Lejeune and departure for Iraq. Chris slept for the trip's first hour, but by the time they hit the 405 freeway he was awake and furious. Traffic was barely moving—they were never going to make it. "I can't miss this flight," he hissed at Kathi. Around 8:30, they arrived at the US Air terminal, and Chris leaped out. He was too late. An attendant told him he'd have to wait for the next departure at one P.M. At first Chris was angry, but when he returned to the car, he smiled. Instead of having to say good-bye in a rush, he could spend the morning with his parents and Aimey. After breakfast at an International House of Pancakes, where they talked about everything and nothing, they drove to a bookstore, where Chris bought copies of *Playboy*, *Maxim*, and *Vibe*. They then stopped at a Starbucks and lingered over coffee. Finally, it came time to head back to LAX. The line for security snaked outside onto the sidewalk, allowing them a luxurious few more minutes together. As they inched along, Aimey held one of Chris's hands and Kathi the other. They took every opportunity to say, "I love you," or exchange kisses with him, not caring if strangers saw them hugging and crying and holding on until they reached the point beyond which only passengers could continue. "You're the best," Jim shouted after his son, and Kathi called out, "Baby." On hearing her pet name for him, Chris turned and smiled. In time, Jim and Kathi would regard these four extra hours as the most valuable gift they had ever received.

· · ·

The only thing Chris told Jim and Kathi about Iraq was that he could "feel the evil." Ramadi, where he was stationed, was christened "the most dangerous place in the world" by *Time* shortly after Fifth ANGLICO arrived. The city of 400,000 just west of Baghdad was the center of both the Sunni insurgency and Al Qaeda. Block after block had been reduced to rubble.

Fifth ANGLICO found itself in regular daily combat. Chris's four-man unit was part of a larger thirteen-man squad that reported to Major David Berke, an F-18 pilot. Sometimes they went out with 1,000-man army battalions, other times with

Iraqi forces, and occasionally with small detachments of Navy SEALs. "We were mortared, hit by IEDs, fired on constantly—everything," says Sergeant Jerred Speller, who was part of Chris's team. "We went on the worst of the worst missions, and the most dangerous aspect was that when we received contact, we ran toward it. We have to see the enemy before we can order planes to drop 500-pound bombs. If we don't, there's too much chance for innocent people to get injured."

One day early on, when Fifth ANGLICO was returning from a rural section of Ramadi, Chris was nearly killed. They'd been out with the Delta 149th Infantry in an area riddled with IEDs and were on their way to their vehicles when someone started shooting at them. Speller and the captain managed to dive into a ditch, but Chris took cover behind a haystack, which provided no cover at all. His comrades yelled at Chris to get out of there. When a lull came, he bolted toward them, firing his M-16 over his shoulder.

This was what Ramadi was like in the spring of 2006. "We'd be out all day on some brutal, ridiculously painful mission," says Major Berke, "and we'd get back to base and all I could do was crawl off to my quarters. Chris, on the other hand, would go straight to a pull-up bar and do a set of chin-ups—while still wearing his gear. Then he'd get to work on his radios."

Chris sought support in daily phone calls and e-mails to Aimey. Several weeks after reaching Iraq, he wrote:

hello my love!

One more mission down, I miss you so much Aimey! Im so thankful I have you to appreciate and love. Everyday my love for you gets stronger, my heart and soul needs you. Everyday I think of youre touch and how I cant wait to have you in my arms again! I LOVE you so much! You give me strength and confidence in everything I do. Knowing there's someone behind me 100 % is breath taking! . . . I love you with all my heart, soul, body and mind and don't ever forget that.

Everything about their exchanges was heightened, the urgency amplified by the inability to see or hold each other. All told, they had been in each other's presence for less than a month. "When someone isn't there physically," she says, "you have to ask a lot of questions and you begin to know them on a profound level. I could talk to him for hours. Being in Iraq, he'd learned not to take life for granted." It wasn't always easy for her to convey the certitude that he was seeking, but she tried:

My love, my strength, my faith— I miss you so much. Even though I'm having a hard day I know you have it much worse. . . . You said today—"I sometimes think, 'How can someone be waiting for me? How can she make that commitment and take such a big risk?'" My reason: YOU. We have such a special connection that is accompanied by complete honesty— and trust. . . . I read that once in a great while one person comes across another person who is the perfect companion to accompany us in our travels through life. . . . You're mine. Even though you're far away, miles are just location. I will always act in your absence as I would in your presence. I love you with all my heart Chris.

In May, Chris asked Aimey to marry him. She said yes. They set December 30 as the date. Aimey and her mother found a church in Valencia, contracted a caterer, sent out "Save the Date" notices, and at David's Bridal Shop in Northridge bought a gown.

On June 2, Chris e-mailed David Meade with the news:

What's up bro, not much here we've had a lot of time off lately because the army unit we work with is packing up to leave and a new one is settling in. But things are going to pick up soon enough. . . . I'm getting married in December and I would be honored if you would be my best man. So how is everything going back in Cali. Man I cant wait to get home. It was 114 today you can't even walk outside without sweating you're ass off. And wearing all you're gear and going on foot patrol. Holy shit! Allright Dave I'm gonna get going take care Chris

On June 11, American and Iraqi troops launched yet another campaign to pacify Ramadi. The plan was to establish fortified outposts in a number of contested sections of the city and use them to create safety zones in the hope that stable social and economic life would follow. "Our objective," says Berke, "was a house on the high ground in southern Ramadi that looked out over a train track and a large neighborhood."

Unlike its surrounding structures, the house that became known as Command Post Iron—or COP Iron—was in excellent shape. Two stories in height and built of stucco-covered stone, it was the perfect location from which to project order onto chaos. By June 20, the building had been in U.S. possession for six days. Parked in front were several Abrams tanks and a number of Bradley fighting vehicles. Spread out on the grounds, twenty or thirty GIs were building sandbag parapets. On the rooftop, which was surrounded by a thick masonry wall, Chris and the marines of Fifth ANGLICO provided cover for the grunts working below. "It was still a very hot area of Ramadi," says Speller. Yet compared with the spots he and Chris had been during previous weeks, this one felt secure, so much so that Speller curled up with a book.

"The thing about Iraq," says Blanton, who was inside the building at the time, "is that you can go forever without anything happening, and then in an instant your life is hanging by a thread." All day the men of Fifth ANGLICO stood watch. When Berke radioed to order Blanton's team to remain in place a few extra hours, no one expressed the least concern. Then the unit came under fire. "Sniper," screamed Speller. He and Lance Corporal Matthew Odom popped their heads up over the wall to scan for signs of the shooter. Chris raced into the house to alert Blanton, then returned to the roof. The fire was coming from the east, not the north, he told Speller. Thirty seconds later, Chris went down. Speller, who was at his side in an instant, saw blood pouring from a wound behind Chris's right temple. "I tried to put a bandage on his head, but the blood was coming out so fast I couldn't make it hold," he says. "He was still breathing, so I kept working. I finally got one wrapped all the way around, and a couple of army medics helped me get him on a litter and downstairs to one of the Bradleys."

Charlie Med, the hospital at Camp Ramadi—the huge base that houses most American troops in the city—is a ten-minute drive from COP Iron. As the Bradley was on its way, Blanton radioed Berke that Chris had been hit. The major raced to Charlie Med and was there when the Bradley arrived. "When they opened the back of the truck, I looked right at him and I knew in an instant he was dead. He was all gauzed up. There was a big hole in his head. I could see the entrance wound. They took him inside, and two minutes later the surgeon came out and confirmed it."

Around nine P.M., Speller, Odom, and the other men of Fifth ANGLICO carried Chris's body out of Charlie Med, passing through a cordon of marines standing at attention. They then loaded him onto a CH-46 helicopter for what is known as an Angel Flight. As the chopper lifted off, the group on the ground saluted. Several days later there was a service at Camp Ramadi. Blanton maintained his composure until it was over, then walked off by himself and broke into sobs. Afterward, he posted his thoughts on his Web site:

> The loss of Chris hit everyone in the unit pretty hard. I don't think it hit me hardest, but it has affected me greatly and changed the way I do business. I experience a sense of fear I never had before Chris was killed. . . . I still can't believe he's gone. In time I will find my way home from this awful place.

Chris's homecoming came at Desert Vineyard Fellowship a week after the ceremony at Camp Ramadi. The day before, a fringe group had sent a threat over the Internet, vowing to protest the services. As a consequence, a contingent of sheriff's deputies greeted the Reverend David Parker when he arrived at the church. The lawmen were later reinforced by about a hundred members of the Patriot Guards—a motorcycle-riding contingent of veterans and supporters of American troops. But no demonstration ever materialized.

A thousand mourners packed the vast sanctuary. Sitting in front were Jim and Kathi, Nikki Ruhl, and Aimey Vaccaro and her mother. In the middle of the hall sat Chris's Independent Study teacher, Cheryl Holland; his old girlfriend, Analyse Reaves; and the clerks and managers from PetSmart. Captain Blanton's mother had driven over from Riverside County, and Lieutenant Colonel Joseph Shrader, ANGLICO's commanding officer, had flown in from Okinawa. The boys of Insanely Determined to Succeed—except for one—were there, too. Against the urgings of David, Jon, and Alan, Sonny had decided to go on a long-scheduled family vacation to Mexico. "It was the hardest decision I ever made," he says. Not everyone understood or quickly forgave.

The services began with the old hymn "On Christ the Solid Rock I Stand." Then Reverend Parker delivered a sermon in which he alluded to Chris's troubled teens ("After losing his way, he graduated from Lancaster High") and applauded his service to his country ("He willingly and proudly defended America"). Fulfilling his friend's request, David gave the eulogy. In it he sought to exalt the fraternal ideals of IDS. "I believe that imagination is stronger than knowledge," he said. "Myth is more potent than history. Dreams are more powerful than facts. Love is stronger than death. The way we remember Chris is the way he becomes immortal."

Aimey Vaccaro followed David. She spoke of her love for Chris, calling herself "the luckiest girl there is," but as she looked out on a room filled by their contemporaries, her tone changed.

"Not only did Chris die for his country," she said, "but for his friends. I hope that's really a wake-up call. It's up to you to know what life is all about. It's not about the parties and the things we get so worked up about." The lesson of Chris's death, she was saying, was that one's time on earth is finite. Only dedication and accomplishments, not myths and dreams, would properly commemorate him.

The funeral procession then drove to Joshua Memorial Park, where Jim and Kathi received the flag from Chris's casket and a marine honor guard delivered a twenty-one-gun salute. Several weeks later Jim and Kathi picked up a bronze box adorned with an eagle, globe, and anchor seal containing Chris's ashes and brought it home. They placed it on a granite-topped buffet in the den, where they would see it every day. Their son, Christopher David Leon, was the 2,509th American service member killed in the Iraq war.

· · ·

A month or so after Chris's funeral, Kathi Leon, accompanied by her sister, Nikki Ruhl, and Aimey Vaccaro, found herself climbing a flight of stairs in a down-at-the-heels minimall in east Lancaster. At the top, beneath a sign reading THIS FACILITY IS UNDER VIDEO SURVEILLANCE AT ALL TIMES, was Sanitarium Tattoos, a cramped room dominated by drawings of skulls and crossbones and a table holding needles and inks. Ever since Chris got his first tattoo after boot camp, Kathi had chided him. "Why would you make yourself look so ugly?" she'd ask. "Why have you done something so revolting?" Yet just as she'd at times tried to reach Chris by following his lead in life, now she would do so in death. Proprietor Rick Labosh inscribed a red heart, Chris's birth and death dates, and the words A GIFT FROM GOD onto her right calf. She later returned and had Labosh etch Chris's face onto her shoulder. Even as she was doing these things, Kathi was slightly appalled, but she had passed into a stage of grief where, as she puts it, "nothing is too weird."

In the weeks before and after Kathi's trip to Sanitarium Tattoos, many of those who were closest to Chris also visited Rick Labosh's shop, turning over legs and arms to his needles. Nikki, who felt like she'd now lost Chris twice, had his dates and the words REST PEACEFULLY MY SWEET ANGEL tattooed in a garland of ivy leaves on her left calf. Three of the boys from Insanely Determined to Succeed—David, Jon, and Alan—had their biceps tattooed with jeweled crosses surrounded by the epitaph REST PEACEFULLY CPL. CHRIS LEON. Aimey went to Buzz Bomb, a tattoo parlor on the Venice Beach boardwalk she and Chris had visited together, and had his dog tag and the words A TRUE HERO NEVER FORGOTTEN inked onto her left shoulder blade. En masse, it seemed, those who'd loved Chris were trying, as David had urged in his eulogy, to immortalize him.

By autumn Kathi had gone back to work at the urology clinic, but Jim never returned to Quest Diagnostics. The treatment for his congestive heart failure had adversely affected his kidneys, and he was weak and disoriented. He felt Chris's absence keenly, yet he couldn't cry. Numbness had set in. On many days he never got up from the sofa. Aimey dropped out of college for the semester—holding down her job was triumph enough during a period when she often had to take Ativan to fend off panic attacks and Ambien to sleep—and David entered therapy with an Encino psychiatrist. He blamed himself for Chris's death, believing that if he and the others in IDS had forced him to study harder and avoid drugs he would have joined them in college rather than gone to war. As for Jon, he downed a six-pack of beer many nights to turn out the lights.

The place where the opposing opinions of how to face Chris's death met was his MySpace page. Chris had started the page—which he topped with the motto "My sacrifice is your comfort"—shortly before leaving for Iraq. Now that he was gone, his friends refreshed the site with postings that reflected their conflicted feelings. David championed the view that Chris's good deeds would give him eternal life. "Chris protected our freedoms," he wrote. "He protected our right to know the truth about what's happening in this country." Aimey, however, often despaired. In an early fall note addressed directly to Chris, she wrote, "I miss you so much baby. It hurts every day. I keep wishing that this wasn't real and that my phone would ring again. I still sign onto MySpace hoping that my new message is from you—but I know that will never happen again." On September 17, the day Fifth ANGLICO returned from its tour of duty in Iraq, Kathi added her voice. "Baby, I can't believe today is going to come and go and we won't have had you home to celebrate. This is really too hard for words." Several weeks later David also came around to this view. "I never knew it took so long to come to terms with something like this. I thought someone died, you mourned for a while, and you moved on. On the contrary, it takes time to accept that a person you love isn't coming home."

Surprisingly, those close to Chris felt their moods lift on November 5—his twenty-first birthday. Everyone congregated at Jim and Kathi's for cake and margaritas. Nikki, Aimey and her mother, David, Jon, and Alan, and Chris's grandparents and aunts and uncles sat around talking about him. Jim, who on previous visits by his son's friends hadn't been well enough to say hello, joined the party. They passed around Chris's medals, among them the Purple Heart, the Combat Action Ribbon, and the Navy and Marine Corps Commendation Medal. Late in the afternoon, David and Jon walked into the front yard and in a private ritual that they knew would have delighted their friend poured two King Cobra 40s into Avenue K-9. "That day," says David, "marked the first time I could breathe."

On December 30, which should have been her wedding day, Aimey donned a white button-down shirt and white jeans and went to dinner at an Italian restaurant in Lancaster with her mom, sister, and several of the girls who would have been her bridesmaids all dressed in red—the color she'd picked for the big event. The previous night, as she'd reflected on what it would have been like to oversee the final details—the seating, the music, and the flowers—she'd cried. But as she and her friends enjoyed a long evening, she felt peace. "A few weeks earlier, I was a disaster," she says. "But I'm starting to feel okay. I thought, 'A new year is coming. I can carry over the crippling emotion or I can start in a different way.' I've decided to start in a different way."

The next night, New Year's Eve, David's girlfriend threw a party at her Sherman Oaks apartment. The twenty guests ate sushi and drank vodka while listening to rap and rock. Everyone laughed and gossiped until shortly before midnight, when four of the revelers disappeared into a bedroom, closing the door behind them. It was the first time the members of Insanely Determined to Succeed had all been together since Chris's death. Before anyone could speak, Sonny, who after skipping the funeral had avoided the group, broke down. "I've missed you guys," he said. They agreed that Chris would want them all to go on with their lives. Jon then draped a dog tag bearing their friend's likeness around Sonny's neck, and he and the others, each of whom wore similar tags, were back at the party before 2007 began.

Looking forward wasn't going to be as easy for Jim and Kathi. They decided to forgo a massive Christmas tree, opting instead for a tiny artificial one that Kathi decorated with cards bearing handwritten remembrances of Chris. "A son who loved deeply," said one. "A son who was deeply loved," said another. On Christmas Eve, they and other church members who'd experienced loss during 2006 attended a "Blue Christmas" service at Desert Vineyard. As always, on Christmas morning they drove to LoriAnn's house in Westlake Village, where they were joined not just by Kathi's family but by Nikki and her mother. Kathi, dressed in a bright purple sweater and black slacks, and Jim, in a red-checked shirt and khakis, tried to be festive. They looked on as their niece opened her Disney Tea Party Play Set, and they talked about a holiday care package they'd sent to the men of Fifth ANGLICO, who were in Okinawa preparing to redeploy. But after presents were exchanged, their spirits darkened. When LoriAnn pulled out a photo album from the previous Christmas in which she'd pasted pictures of Chris and written a holiday prayer—"For everyone to be together again next year—safe and healthy (Chris home from Iraq)"—they began to cry, and while Jim noted that his newfound ability to shed tears was a step forward, he didn't sound convincing.

"This is our first Christmas without Chris," he said, "and I don't like the fact that there are now 3,000 families that have gotten the same news we got. I resent it. I wish we would get out of Iraq. What we're doing there doesn't make sense."

"But he was a marine," said Kathi. "He was doing what he wanted to do. He was doing his job."

At that, LoriAnn announced lunch, and Jim and Kathi, carrying a box of Kleenex, walked into the dining room.

New Year's was, if anything, even harder. Where Chris's friends saw a beginning, his parents saw an end. On her son's MySpace page Kathi wrote:

Chris there is no happy to this new year. Only the knowledge that we are further apart than ever. It's hard enough that the day changes but we are already into another year. I can't bear the thought of having time continue and making the distance even greater. How do I get past this?

In stronger moments, Jim and Kathi can both dimly perceive happier times ahead. Kathi has joined a gym in the hope of getting into good enough shape to run in the annual Marine Corps Marathon honoring war dead. Jim has rallied sufficiently to volunteer several days a week at Desert Vineyard. Yet they remain inconsolable. On days when he's not at the church, Jim finds himself sinking deeper into depression. Although he's taking

Prozac, the drug can't keep him from fixating on Chris. He frequently pops a DVD of the funeral into the machine in the den, watching it over and over, the images serving as a narcotic. "Kathi doesn't like me immersing myself in it," he says, "but I find it comforting." Kathi's grief reveals itself differently. "I'm flatlining," she says. "I try not to show any feelings at all." But she's only partially successful. Whenever President Bush, someone she once trusted, appears on TV, she changes the channel. Then there are times she picks up one of their many pictures of Chris, presses her lips against it, and whispers, "Baby."

Chris's bedroom is as it was when he last slept there. The Dodger caps still stare down, and the handwritten plea for guidance is on the closet wall. Even little things—a bottle of Calvin Klein Truth Cologne for Men on the chest of drawers and a can of Bud Lite on the television cart—are unchanged. To be surrounded by their son's possessions gives Jim and Kathi a sense of security. Yet they now know there really is no such thing. Chris went out from Lancaster with its symmetrical streets and identical subdivisions into anarchy. That anarchy has come back to Avenue K-9, shattering the Leons' lives and filling them with doubt. If their son died in an unjust war, they wonder, can there be a just God? Jim and Kathi remain believers, seeing the Lord's hand in Chris's emergence from his difficult adolescence and keeping faith they'll meet him in a better world. But this one holds few allures. They are grateful for Pastor Dave and the others at Desert Vineyard, who regularly check in on them. They are thankful for family members who do the same. They are indebted to the many neighbors who've hung blue-and-gold banners declaring SUPPORT OUR TROOPS from trees and roofs. Their home, though, is as much a prison as a refuge. "We've lost not just Chris but our future," Jim says one late winter afternoon sitting in the den. "There will be no wedding, no grandchildren, no one to leave any of our possessions to. Ahead for us is nothing. It's just a hole."

Slate

FINALIST—COLUMNS AND
COMMENTARY

In his reliably unpredictable and bracing columns for Slate, *Christopher Hitchens leaves readers better informed, challenged to think anew about the issues of the day, and a bit staggered by his command of fact and reference. His columns are the best kind of strong medicine.*

Christopher Hitchens

So Many Men's Rooms, So Little Time

I knew it was all over for Sen. Larry Craig when he appeared with his long-suffering wife to say that he wasn't gay. Such moments are now steppingstones on the way to apology, counseling, and rehab, and a case could be made for cutting out the spousal stage of the ritual altogether. Along with a string of votes to establish "don't ask, don't tell" and to prohibit homosexual marriage, Craig leaves as his political legacy the telling phrase "wide stance," which may or may not join "big tent" and "broad church" as an attempt to make the Republican Party seem more "inclusive" than it really is.

But there's actually a chance—a 38 percent chance, to be more precise—that the senator can cop a plea on the charge of hypocrisy. In his study of men who frequent public restrooms in search of sex, Laud Humphreys discovered that 54 percent were married and living with their wives, 38 percent did not consider themselves homosexual or bisexual, and only 14 percent identified themselves as openly gay. *Tearoom Trade: Impersonal Sex in Personal Places*, a doctoral thesis which was published in 1970, detailed exactly the pattern—of foot-tapping in code, hand-gestures, and other tactics—which has lately been garishly publicized at a Minneapolis–St. Paul airport men's room. The word *tearoom* seems to have become archaic, but in all other respects the fidelity to tradition is impressive.

The men interviewed by Humphreys wanted what many men want: a sexual encounter that was quick and easy and didn't involve any wining and dining. Some of the heterosexuals among them had also evolved a tactic for dealing with the cognitive dissonance that was involved. They compensated for their conduct by adopting extreme conservative postures in public. Humphreys, a former Episcopalian priest, came up with the phrase "breastplate of righteousness" to describe this mixture of repression and denial. So, it is quite thinkable that when Sen. Craig claims not to be gay, he is telling what he honestly believes to be the truth.

However, this still leaves a slight mystery. In the 1960s, homosexuality was illegal in general, and gay men were forced to cruise in places where (if I can phrase it like this) every man and boy in the world has to come sometime. Today, anyone wanting a swift male caress can book it online or go to a discreet resort. Yet people still persist in haunting the tearoom, where they risk arrest not for their sexuality but for "disorderly conduct." Why should this be?

In my youth, I was a friend of a man named Tom Driberg, a British politician who set the bar very high in these matters. In his memoir, *Ruling Passions*, he described his "chronic, lifelong, love-hate relationship with lavatories." He could talk by the hour about the variety and marvel of these "public conveniences," as Victorian euphemism had dubbed them. In Britain, they were called "cottages" in gay argot, instead of "tearooms," and an experienced "cottager" knew all the ins and outs, if you will pardon the expression. There was the commodious underground loo in Leicester Square that specialized in those whose passion was for members of the armed forces. There was the one at the Institute of Contemporary Arts, much favored by aesthetes, where on the very foot of the partition, above the six-inch space, someone had scribbled "beware of limbo dancers." (The graffiti in cottages was all part of the fun: On the toilet wall at Paddington Station was written: "I am 9 inches long and two inches thick. Interested?" Underneath, in different handwriting: "Fascinated, dear, but how big is your dick?") On Clapham Common, the men's toilet had acquired such a lavish reputation for the variety of lurid actions performed within its precincts that, as I once heard it said: "If someone comes in there for a good honest shit, it's like a breath of fresh air."

Perhaps I digress. What Driberg told me was this. The thrills were twofold. First came the exhilaration of danger: the permanent risk of being caught and exposed. Second was the sense of superiority that a double life could give. What bliss it was to enter the House of Commons, bow to the speaker, and take your seat amid the trappings of lawmaking, having five minutes earlier fellated a guardsman (and on one unforgettable occasion, a policeman) in the crapper in St. James' Park. Assuming the story about the men's room in Union Station to be true, Sen. Craig could have gone straight from that encounter to the Senate floor in about the same amount of time.

Driberg was a public campaigner for gay rights and carried on as such even after being elevated to the House of Lords (where I am pretty sure he told me there was more going on in the lavatory than most people would guess). But it was with a distinct hint of melancholy that he voted for the successful repeal of the laws criminalizing homosexuality. "I rather miss the old days," he would say, wistfully. Well, the law legalized homosexual behavior only "in private," so he could (and did) continue to court danger in public places. The House of Lords actually debated the question of whether a stall in a public lavatory constituted "privacy," the reason being that in Britain you have to put money in a slot in order to enter such a place, and this could be held to constitute rent. *Private Eye* printed a poem about the learned exchange on this between two elderly peers of the realm: "Said Lord Arran to Lord Dilhorne, a penny / should entitle me to any / thing I may choose privately to do. Except you."

Thus, without overthinking it or attempting too much by way of amateur psychiatry, I think it's safe to assume that many tearoom traders have a need, which they only imperfectly understand, to get caught. And this may be truest of all of those who are armored with "the breastplate of righteousness." Next time you hear some particularly moralizing speech, set your watch. You won't have to wait long before the man who made it is found, crouched awkwardly yet ecstatically while the cistern drips and the roar of the flush maddens him like wine.

GQ

Tom Carson's columns regularly deliver audacious, surprising, occasionally infuriating film and television criticism. He provides both the energy of headlong commitment and the strength of complex, passionate, highly nuanced responses to the subjects under consideration.

Tom Carson

Don't Cry For Me, Iwo Jima

Six years in production and as mournfully patriotic as a coffin made of apple pie, Ken Burns's mammoth seven-part, fourteen-and-a-half-hour documentary on America in World War II, grandly titled just *The War*, is definitely the TV event of the fall. It deserves to be. As memorials go, what Burns has wrought is a thousand times more heartfelt and affecting than the ugly, Teutonic thingamabob now potholing the Mall in Washington, D.C. Even so, I do wonder whether, nearly a decade after Steven Spielberg and Tom Brokaw started the flood, we've already gone as far as a country can go in drowning its current-events sorrows in adulatory nostalgia.

Burns's own view of his intentions is very different. Yet he wouldn't draw such a large audience if he didn't conceive his epics about our past as immense cathartic emotional experiences. Impressive as his gifts are, they aren't analytical—and they're certainly not caustic. Even when the grim combat clips he's dug up speak for themselves, he can't quit gilding the lily, with Yo-Yo Ma sawing pensively at his cello as men fight and die and Tom Hanks overdoing the plumy-voiced Thornton Wilder bit in his readings of a small-town newspaper editor's reports from Heartland, U.S.A. Did I mention that Norah Jones occasionally croons something called "American Anthem" over the credits? If Burns weren't so good at leaving viewers awed and weepy at our mighty history—and if I didn't know full well that that's the only way of getting most of them to give a damn—people like me would feel less rotten about asking whether being moved is enough.

That doesn't mean I'm immune. While you have to go to the series' tie-in book to find out, the unidentified GI in its valedictory image is Ken's father, and what can I say? A similar picture of Jim Carson, Burns senior's U.S. Navy equivalent, is beaming at me as I tap away. And sure, even from Burns, a title as overweeningly simple as *The War* is pushing it. (Don't tell my eighty-year-old mom, though: Without mentioning the documentary's name, I describe it to her on the phone. "You know," she says, "it drives me crazy when I hear people say 'World War II.' We always called it 'the War.'") But after he'd followed *The Civil War* with *Baseball* and then *Jazz*, what did you expect him to call his Pearl Harbor-to-VJ Day opus—*Ken Burns and the Deathly Hallows*?

The truth is, if PBS had been less eager over the years to peddle him as public broadcasting's answer to Harry Potter—a part he even looks, including hair management that makes John Edwards seem as unkempt as a Bowery bum—then people who kvetch about his taste for grandiosity might have an easier time admitting he's a master at his craft. However ripe for parody, his style is as unmistakable as Martin Scorsese's. Though I'm not altogether sure what he does—he seems to rely on more assistants than Jeff Koons—nobody tops him at making yesteryear haunting.

Even History Channel devotees who think they've seen it all will be sobered by the battle footage, a lot of it in literally bloody color, that floods the screen here. Harrowing in its own right, it's also superbly edited to mesh with the testimony of a well-chosen batch of elderly survivors while conveying—and this is the hard part—the conflict's unimaginable dimension. Compared with the random way most war docs ram in handy battle clips, the attention to place—muddy Italy, pulverized Iwo Jima, creepy Huertgen Forest—is phenomenal. Especially if you know how little real visual documentation exists of the chaos and misery at Omaha Beach (sorry, but I've been hung up on D-Day my whole life), the power of Burns's use of it is unprecedented.

All the same, when he says he's refuting the war's "bloodless, gallant myth," I wonder what time capsule he's been living in. Ever since *Saving Private Ryan*, horror at the ordeal Dad or Grandpa went through has been the new piety. Making us gape at the carnage is how every film pays tribute and by implication reproaches us for our own petty lives—the point of Brokaw's hack "Greatest Generation" coinage. Burns's leg up on Hollywood is that his materials are authentic, and *The War* does a magnificent job of shoving the war's costs in our faces. But it's still an overembellished, not infrequently syrupy serenade.

•   •   •

Given Burns's track record, it's no surprise his take is unabashedly America-centric. (The Russians, with their 20 million dead—that's fifty for every one of ours—might be forgiven for rolling their eyes.) Localizing things more, he frames *The War* as a tale of four communities: Dixie-fried, shipbuilding Mobile, Alabama; plucky, ethnic Waterbury, Connecticut; charming, tiny Luverne, Minnesota; and Sacramento, California, home to a sizable—c'mon, guess—Japanese-American population. Still, Burns knows how to modulate from micro to macro, and the individual story lines are woven into the big picture with uncommon artfulness. Because the ancient footage we're seeing dovetails in such detail with the memories of his dozen or so main talking heads—and because viewers can't help realizing that not many future Second World War documentaries will feature firsthand witnesses—watching these placid octogenarians reminisce about long ago and far away feels like sorcery.

The most likable is Mobile's Katharine Phillips, who put her love life on hold until her brother Sid—also spryly and engagingly on hand—got back from the Pacific. The most touching is Sascha Weinzheimer, who was interned as a girl in Manila and seems to have her eleven-year-old self (and voice) permanently petrified inside her. The gentlest is Minnesota fighter pilot Quentin Aanenson, whose wartime marriage to his home-front sweetheart, Jackie Greer, gives Burns his central love story; they're still together, and she's in *The War*, too. The most incredible—just seeing him alive, robust, and chatting away on-camera six and a half decades later is mind-boggling—is Glenn Frazier, who survived the Bataan Death March in 1942. The story of his first phone call home after three years as a POW is also a moment of sitcom slapstick I won't spoil, especially since Burns is so short on humor that the only one of Bill Mauldin's famous Willie & Joe cartoons he shows us omits the caption.

Holding down Shelby Foote's job as *The War*'s voice of reflection are two veterans who became men of letters: Paul Fussell, author of *Wartime* and *Doing Battle*, and Samuel Hynes. The difference is that while Foote's Methuselan charm created a pleasant illusion he'd been there at Gettysburg, Fussell and Hynes really were in Europe and the Pacific. "Our two ringers," Burns calls them, and I've got my own confession: Back when *The Gong Show* roamed the earth, Hynes was my favorite college professor. I've loved *Ulysses* ever since, so he's naturally the one I'm rooting for to achieve Foote-like stardom. But it's Fussell who owns the series' most vulnerable moment, breaking down as he describes how discovering the Nazi death camps made our GIs realize they'd been fighting the good fight.

If you know his crusty rep, seeing him in tears is jolting. Yet his presence is also a reminder of some hornets' nests Burns doesn't stir up. A notable contrarian, Fussell has written at length about his abomination of the wartime propaganda that helped spawn the huckster United States of today, his loathing of military chickenshit, and so on. Even when he's on-camera, these are topics *The War* skirts or omits. For instance, a segment on rationing briefly mentions black markets, including the statistic that an estimated one out of four retail transactions here at home was illegal. But you have to go to Fussell's *The Boys' Crusade* to learn that the black market in liberated Paris was merrily run by over 2,000 American deserters. That's more than the number of extras in *Saving Private Ryan*, isn't it?

Burns does let Fussell talk about our troops' ineptitude in their early tests against the Germans. But what's unmentioned is his heretical belief that the U.S. Army didn't get much better with practice. In fact, with a beefy assist from Detroit and Boeing, the glum, unaggressive soldiers we shipped off to fight Hitler were just barely good enough to prevail—and that's not to their discredit. I don't know about Ken's father, who looks like a sweet man. Mine taught me to be fonder of a country that's just martial enough to win its wars than one that thinks it's great at them.

Every warrior Burns shows us is reluctant, and that's admirable. But there isn't a shirker or an operator out for private gain in the bunch, and even if those guys didn't care to be interviewed, it's a valorizing falsification to imply none existed.

· · ·

The same goes for a seamy, liberating underside to America's experience of World War II that Burns is too dainty to touch. Most people first heard of *The War* when Latinos complained about their invisibility in his American tapestry, and the final broadcast version has been augmented to make amends. But maybe ACT UP should have protested, too; as delightful as the Frank Capra lyricism of Quentin Aanenson's marriage to his Jackie is, it is trite as the series' *only* portrait of the cataclysm's effect on private lives across the social and sexual spectrum. About the closest the series comes to evoking the carousing new freedoms Pearl Harbor unleashed is Sam Hynes's description of the selfish side of signing up: "It is the opportunity to be somebody more exciting than the kid you are."

On the flip side, the irony of this filmmaker being attacked for racial insensitivity is that he's usually at his toughest and best when race is the topic. It's always the grenade in his patriotic birthday cakes, and some viewers may be surprised by how much *The War* dwells on not only the Japanese internment but on African America's World War II. What's wrenching is how both groups' patriotism was thwarted: black soldiers' frustration at not getting into combat, images of Nisei kids playing baseball and, in Boy Scout uniforms, raising the Stars and Stripes in the camps. Famously, the segregated Nisei unit that served in Europe, the 442nd Regimental Combat Team, ended up as the most decorated U.S. outfit of the war. Burns tells their story well.

That's why it's even more impressive that *The War* makes the best case for dropping the atom bomb on Japan of any doc I know. The reason couldn't be more basic; we've been made vividly aware that invasion is the only other option, and we've watched our soldiers, sailors, and marines go through so many meat grinders from Guadalcanal on that we revolt at the idea of putting them through another. And yes, we quail at sitting through two more hours of *The War*, too. But that's not meant to be a joke: It's a compliment.

Sorry, but size does matter. Over these fourteen hours, Burns does every saccharine, sonorous thing that drives his naysayers up the wall, avoiding hard inquiry in favor of summoning memory's mystic chords and splurging on emotion. I think *The War* is simpleminded. I think it's unduly obsessed with slaughter—not the fact of it, but the mystique, fetishizing combat as the ultimate crucible when only a cruelly punished fraction of the American military went through anything of the kind. I dread the perfect storm of national self-love it's likely to provoke, especially at a time when clear thinking about our no-longer-so-Manifest Destiny wouldn't come amiss. But by the end, you know you've seen a monument.

If you can stay dry-eyed or less than spellbound, more power to you: You'll make a better historian than Burns one day. But while people can and should argue with his Hallmark-card notion of history, even a grumpy-guts like me can't gainsay his achievement in expressing—and for better and worse, helping to shape—how later generations feel about it. In a perfect world, "Too much and not enough" would be my verdict on *The War*. But I'm only human, and something in me can't help adding, "Hell, that must mean it's just right." My main regret is that only one of my parents is still alive to see it.

2008 National Magazine Award Finalists

NOTE: All nominated issues are dated 2007 unless otherwise specified. The editor whose name appears in connection with finalists for 2008 held that position, or was listed on the masthead, at the time the issue was published in 2007. In some cases, another editor is now in that position.

General Excellence

This category recognizes overall excellence in magazines in six circulation categories. It honors the effectiveness with which writing, reporting, editing, and design all come together to command readers' attention and fulfill the magazine's unique editorial mission.

Under 100,000 circulation

Aperture: Melissa Harris, editor-in-chief, for Summer, Fall, Winter issues.
The Georgia Review: Stephen Corey, editor, for Spring, Fall, Winter issues.
Metropolis: Susan S. Szenasy, editor-in-chief, for May, June, November issues.
Print: Joyce Rutter Kaye, editor-in-chief, for March/April, July/August, September/October issues.
The Virginia Quarterly Review: Ted Genoways, editor, for Spring, Summer issues; Daniel Alarcón and Ted Genoways, co-editors, for Fall issue.

100,000 to 250,000 circulation

Foreign Policy: Moisés Naím, editor-in-chief, for March/April, July/August, September/October issues.
Mother Jones: Monika Bauerlein and Clara Jeffery, editors-in-chief, for March/April, May/June, September/October issues.
Paste: Josh Jackson, editor-in-chief, for April, July, August issues.
Philadelphia: Larry Platt, editor-in-chief, for September, October, December issues.
Radar: Maer Roshan, editor-in-chief, for March/April, June/July, November issues.

250,000 to 500,000 circulation

Backpacker: Jonathan Dorn, editor-in-chief, for April, May, September issues.

Cookie: Pilar Guzmán, editor-in-chief, for July/August, September, December/January issues.

New York: Adam Moss, editor-in-chief, for February 12, July 16, November 19 issues.

W: Patrick McCarthy, chairman and editorial director, for March, October, December issues.

Wondertime: Lisa Stiepock, editor, for February/March, September/October, November issues.

500,000 to 1,000,000 circulation

Budget Travel: Erik Torkells, editor, for July/August, September, November issues.

The Economist: John Micklethwait, editor-in-chief, for August 25–31, November 3–9, December 22–January 4 issues.

GQ: Jim Nelson, editor-in-chief, for March, September, October issues.

National Geographic Adventure: John Rasmus, editor-in-chief, for June/July, November, December/January issues.

Wired: Chris Anderson, editor-in-chief, for February, October, November issues.

1,000,000 to 2,000,000 circulation

Men's Health: David Zinczenko, senior vice president and editor-in-chief, for September, October, December issues.

The New Yorker: David Remnick, editor, for February 19 & 26, August 13, October 8 issues.

Play: The New York Times Sports Magazine: Mark Bryant, editor, for March, June, November issues.

Popular Mechanics: James B. Meigs, editor-in-chief, for May, August, September issues.

Vanity Fair: Graydon Carter, editor, for March, August, December issues.

Over 2,000,000 circulation

Glamour: Cynthia Leive, editor-in-chief, for June, September, December issues.

Martha Stewart Living: Martha Stewart, founder; Margaret Roach, editorial director, for March, October, December issues; Michael Boodro, editor-in-chief, for October, December issues.

National Geographic: Chris Johns, editor-in-chief, for June, August, December issues.

People: Larry Hackett, managing editor, for February 5, March 12, May 7 issues.

Time: Richard Stengel, managing editor, for April 9, June 18, July 9 issues.

Personal Service

This category recognizes excellence in service journalism. The advice or instruction presented should help readers improve the quality of their personal lives.

Field & Stream: Sid Evans, editor-in-chief, for a two-part package, "F&S Survival Guide: Survivor" and "F&S Survival Guide: Never Get Lost Again," by Keith McCafferty, February.

Good Housekeeping: Rosemary Ellis, editor-in-chief, for "Passport to Cheaper Health Care?" by Jennifer Wolff, October.

O, The Oprah Magazine: Oprah Winfrey, founder and editorial director; Amy Gross, editor-in-chief, for "O's Be-Prepared, You're-Tougher-Than-You-Thought, We've-Got-You-Covered Guide to Saving Yourself from Every Imaginable Disaster. And Then Some," April.

Popular Mechanics: James B. Meigs, editor-in-chief, for "Facing Down Disaster," by Logan Ward, August.

Popular Mechanics: James B. Meigs, editor-in-chief, for a three-part series by Alex Hutchinson, "Know Your Footprint: Energy," June; "Know Your Footprint: Water," September; "Know Your Footprint: Waste," December.

Leisure Interests

This category recognizes excellent service journalism about leisure-time pursuits. The practical advice or instruction presented should help readers enjoy hobbies or other recreational interests.

Domino: Deborah Needleman, editor-in-chief, for a three part series, "Domino's Big Black Book: Decorating," August; "Renovating," October; "Entertaining," November.

Field & Stream: Sid Evans, editor-in-chief, for a two-part package, "The Rut Calendar '07," by Gerald Almy; "Huge Successes," as told to Bill Heavey, November.

Men's Health: David Zinczenko, senior vice president and editor-in-chief, for "Women, Money, and Friends Come and Go, But Dogs are Forever," by Jim Thornton, October.

New York: Adam Moss, editor-in-chief, for "Cartography: The Complete Road Map to New York City Street Food," by Michael Idov, Rob Patronite, Robin Raisfeld, and Emma Rosenblum, June 25.

Time Out Chicago: Joel Reese, editor, for "Dive In," July 19–25.

Reporting

This category recognizes excellence in reporting. It honors the enterprise, exclusive reporting and intelligent analysis that a magazine exhibits in covering an event, a situation or a problem of contemporary interest and significance.

National Geographic: Chris Johns, editor-in-chief, for "China's Instant Cities," by Peter Hessler, June.

The New York Times Magazine: Gerald Marzorati, editor-in-chief, for "Where Boys Grow Up to Be Jihadis," by Andrea Elliott, November 25.

The New Yorker: David Remnick, editor, for "The Taliban's Opium War," by Jon Lee Anderson, July 9 & 16.

The New Yorker: David Remnick, editor, for "The Black Sites," by Jane Mayer, August 13.

Vanity Fair: Graydon Carter, editor, for "City of Fear," by William Langewiesche, April.

Public Interest

This category recognizes journalism that sheds new light on an issue of public importance and has the potential to affect national or local debate policy.

5280: Denver's Mile-High Magazine: Daniel Brogan, editor and publisher, for "Out in the Cold," by Mike Kessler, November.

Bloomberg Markets: Ronald Henkoff, editor, for a three-part package, "Toxic Debt: The Subprime Sinkhole," by Seth Lubove and Daniel Taub; "The Ratings Charade," by Richard Tomlinson and David Evans; "The Poison in Your Pension," by David Evans, July; and "Unsafe Havens," by David Evans, October.

BusinessWeek: Stephen J. Adler, editor-in-chief, for a three-part special report, "The Poverty Business," by Brian Grow and Keith Epstein, May 21; "Prisoners of Debt," by Robert Berner and Brian Grow, November 12; "Fresh Pain for the Uninsured," by Brian Grow and Robert Berner, December 3.

The Nation: Katrina vanden Heuvel, editor and publisher, for a two-part series by Joshua Kors, "How Specialist Town Lost His Benefits," April 9; "Specialist Town Takes His Case to Washington," October 15.

The New Yorker: David Remnick, editor, for "Betrayed," by George Packer, March 26.

Feature Writing

This category recognizes excellence in feature writing. It honors the stylishness and originality with which the author treats his or her subject.

Atlanta: Rebecca Burns, editor-in-chief, for "You Have Thousands of Angels Around You," by Paige Williams, October.

GQ: Jim Nelson, editor-in-chief, for "Underworld," by Jeanne Marie Laskas, May.

New York: Adam Moss, editor-in-chief, for "Everybody Sucks," by Vanessa Grigoriadis, October 22.

The New Yorker: David Remnick, editor, for "Swingers," by Ian Parker, July 30.

Vanity Fair: Graydon Carter, editor, for "Gone Like the Wind," by Buzz Bissinger, August.

Profile Writing

This category recognizes excellence in profile writing. It honors the vividness and perceptiveness with which the writer brings his or her subject to life.

The Atlantic: James Bennet, editor, for "Present at the Creation," by Matthew Scully, September.

Los Angeles: Kit Rachlis, editor-in-chief, for "Casualties of War," by Steve Oney, June.

The New Yorker: David Remnick, editor, for "Azzam the American," by Raffi Khatchadourian, January 22.

The New York Times Magazine: Gerald Marzorati, editor-in-chief, for "The Huckabee Factor," by Zev Chafets, December 16.

Vanity Fair: Graydon Carter, editor, for "Pat Dollard's War on Hollywood," by Evan Wright, March.

Essays

This category recognizes excellence in essay writing on topics ranging from the personal to the political. Whatever the subject, emphasis should be placed on the author's eloquence, perspective, fresh thinking and unique voice.

The Atlantic: James Bennet, editor, for "The Autumn of the Multitaskers," by Walter Kirn, November.

Elle: Roberta Myers, vice president and editor-in-chief, for "My Year of Living Dangerously," by Katrina Onstad, August.

Entertainment Weekly: Rick Tetzeli, managing editor, for "J. K. Rowling's Ministry of Magic," by Stephen King, August 17.

Harper's Magazine: Roger D. Hodge, editor, for "Chemo World," by Sallie Tisdale, June.

New Letters: Robert Stewart, editor-in-chief, for "I Am Joe's Prostate," by Thomas E. Kennedy, Volume 73, Number 4, Summer 2007.

The New Yorker: David Remnick, editor, for "Parallel Play," by Tim Page, August 20.

Columns and Commentary

This category recognizes excellence in short-form political, social, economic or humorous commentary. It honors the eloquence, force of argument and succinctness with which the writer presents his or her views.

Inc.: Jane Berentson, editor, for three columns by Norm Brodsky and Bo Burlingham, "The Offer, Part Three: But Then Who Will I Be?" January; "The Offer, Part Eight: You Have Got to Be Kidding Me," June; "The Offer, Part Nine: What I Learned From My Fiasco," July.

New York: Adam Moss, editor-in-chief, for three columns by Kurt Andersen, "American Roulette," January 8; "Greed Is Good and Ugly," July 30–August 6; "The Age of Apoplexy," October 15.

The New Yorker: David Remnick, editor, for three columns by Hendrik Hertzberg, "Desolation Rows," January 15; "Offenses," September 17; "Brouhahaha," October 15.

Rolling Stone: Jann S. Wenner, editor and publisher; Will Dana, managing editor, for three columns by Matt Taibbi, "Worse Than Bush," June 14; "My Favorite Nut Job," November 29; "Obama's Moment," December 27.

Slate: Jacob Weisberg, editor-in-chief, for three columns by Christopher Hitchens, "Lynching the Dictator," January 2; "Suck It Up," April 24; "So Many Men's Rooms, So Little Time," September 3.

Reviews and Criticism

This category recognizes excellence in criticism of art, books, movies, television, theater, music, dance, food, dining, fashion, products and the like. It honors the knowledge, persuasiveness, and original voice that the critic brings to his or her reviews.

The Atlantic: James Bennet, editor, for three columns by Caitlin Flanagan, "The Sanguine Sex," May; "Babes in the Woods," July/August; "No Girlfriend of Mine," November.

GQ: Jim Nelson, editor-in-chief, for three columns by Tom Carson, "You Actin' Like Me?" February; "Don't Cry For Me, Iwo Jima," September; "Strong, Silent, Ultraviolent," December.

The Nation: Katrina vanden Heuvel, editor and publisher, for three reviews by William Deresiewicz, "Cafe Society," May 14; "The Imaginary Jew," May 28; "Fukú Americanus," November 26.

New York: Adam Moss, editor-in-chief, for three columns by David Edelstein, "See Sickness," August 13; "Coen Heads," October 1; "Savage Grace," December 3.

The New Yorker: David Remnick, editor, for three columns by Louis Menand, "Notable Quotables," February 19 & 26; "Drive, He Wrote," October 1; "Woke Up This Morning," December 10.

Magazine Section

This category recognizes excellence of a regular, cohesive section of a magazine, either front- or back-of-book and composed of a variety of elements, both text and visual. Finalists are selected based on the section's voice, originality, and unified design and packaging.

Condé Nast Portfolio: Joanne Lipman, editor-in-chief, for its "Brief" section, September, November, December.

Esquire: David Granger, editor-in-chief, for its "Man at His Best" section, April, September, December.

Good: Zach Frechette, editor-in-chief, for its "Transparency" section, January/February, July/August, September/October.

O, The Oprah Magazine: Oprah Winfrey, founder and editorial director; Amy Gross, editor-in-chief, for its "Reading Room" section, March, August, October.

Wired: Chris Anderson, editor-in-chief, for its "Start" section, October, November, December.

Single-Topic Issue

This category recognizes magazines that have devoted an issue to an in-depth examination of one topic. It honors the ambition, comprehensiveness and imagination with which a magazine treats its subject.

Departures: Richard David Story, editor-in-chief, for "Russia Now 2007," October.

Domino: Deborah Needleman, editor-in-chief, for "The Green Issue," March.

Gourmet: Ruth Reichl, editor-in-chief, for its special "Latino American" issue, September.

IEEE Spectrum: Susan Hassler, editor-in-chief, for "Engineering the Megacity," June.

The Virginia Quarterly Review: Ted Genoways and Daniel Alarcón, coeditors, for "South America in the 21st Century," Fall.

Design

This category recognizes excellence in magazine design. It honors the effectiveness of overall design, artwork, graphics, and typography in enhancing a magazine's unique mission and personality.

Good: Zach Frechette, editor-in-chief; Scott Stowell, design director, for July/August, September/October, November/December issues.

GQ: Jim Nelson, editor-in-chief; Fred Woodward, design director; Jim Moore, creative director, for January, September, October issues.

New York: Adam Moss, editor-in-chief; Chris Dixon, design director, for March 26, June 25, December 17 issues.

T: The New York Times Style Magazine: Stefano Tonchi, editor; Janet Froelich, creative director; David Sebbah, senior art director; Christopher Martinez, art director, for September 16, August 26, December 2 issues.

Vanity Fair: Graydon Carter, editor; David Harris, design director, for March, September, November issues.

Wired: Chris Anderson, editor-in-chief; Scott Dadich, creative director, for August, October, November issues; Wyatt Mitchell, design director, for November issue.

Photography

This category recognizes excellence in magazine photography. It honors the effectiveness of photography, photojournalism, and photo illustration in enhancing a magazine's unique mission and personality.

Gourmet: Ruth Reichl, editor-in-chief; Richard Ferretti, creative director; Erika Oliveira, art director; Amy Koblenzer, photo editor, for September, October, December issues.

GQ: Jim Nelson, editor-in-chief; Fred Woodward, design director; Jim Moore, creative director; Anton Ioukhnovets, art director; Dora Somosi, director of photography, for September, October, December issues.

Martha Stewart Living: Martha Stewart, founder; Gael Towey, chief creative officer; Margaret Roach, editorial director; Michael Boodro, editor-in-chief; Eric A. Pike, creative director; James Dunlinson, design director; Heloise Goodman, director of photography and illustration, for May, October, November issues.

National Geographic: Chris Johns, editor-in-chief; David Griffin, director of photography; Susan A. Smith, deputy director, photography, for March, April, June issues.

New York: Adam Moss, editor-in-chief; Jody Quon, photography director; Leana Alagia, senior photo editor; Chris Dixon, design director; for January 15, October 29, November 12 issues.

W: Patrick McCarthy, chairman and editorial director; Dennis Freedman, creative director; Edward Leida, group design director; Nathalie Kirsheh, art director; Nadia Vellam, photo editor, for March, September, November issues.

Photojournalism

This category recognizes the informative photographic documentation of an event or subject in real time. Although photo essays accompanied by text will be eligible, they will be judged primarily on the strength of the photographs.

Aperture: Melissa Harris, editor-in-chief; Yolanda Cuomo, art director, for "Mikhael Subotzky: Inside South Africa's Prisons," by Michael Godby; photographs by Mikhael Subotzky, Fall.

Mother Jones: Monika Bauerlein and Clara Jeffery, editors-in-chief; Susan Scandrett, creative director; Tim J. Luddy, art director; Sarah Kehoe, photo director, for "The Hidden Half," by Elizabeth Gettelman; photographs by Lana Šlezić, July/August.

National Geographic: Chris Johns, editor-in-chief; David Griffin, director of photography; David C. Whitmore, design director; Susan A. Smith, photography deputy director; Sarah Leen, senior photo editor, for "Bedlam in the Blood: Malaria," by Michael Finkel; photographs by John Stanmeyer, July.

The New Yorker: David Remnick, editor; Elisabeth Biondi, photo director, for "The Interpreter," by John Colapinto; photographs by Martin Schoeller, April 16.

The Virginia Quarterly Review: Ted Genoways, editor, for "A Window on Baghdad," photographs and text by Chris Hondros, Summer.

Photo Portfolio

This category honors creative photography and photo illustration. Although photo essays accompanied by text will be eligible, they will be judged primarily on the strength of the photographs.

New York: Adam Moss, editor-in-chief; Jody Quon, photography director; Leana Alagia, senior photo editor; Chris Dixon, design director; for "Leaps and Bounds," photographs by Rodney Smith; styling by Harriet Mays Powell, August 27.

Newsweek: Jon Meacham, editor; Amid Capeci, assistant managing editor, design; Simon Barnett, director of photography, for "Faces of a Fiery Year," photographs by Nigel Parry, November 19.

T: The New York Times Style Magazine: Stefano Tonchi, editor; Janet Froelich, creative director; David Sebbah, senior art director; Christopher Martinez, art director; Kathy Ryan, photography director; Judith Puckett-Rinella, senior photography editor, for "A Cultivated Eye," photographs by Fabrizio Coppi and Lucilla Barbieri, April 15.

T: The New York Times Style Magazine: Stefano Tonchi, editor; Janet Froelich, creative director; David Sebbah, senior art director; Christopher Martinez, art director; Kathy Ryan, photography director; Judith Puckett-Rinella, senior photography editor, for "Snow Bound," by Jeffries Blackerby; photographs by Raymond Meier, November 18.

Vanity Fair: Graydon Carter, editor; David Harris, design director; Susan White, photography director, for "Killers Kill, Dead Men Die: A 2007 Hollywood Portfolio," Michael Roberts, fashion and style director; photographs by Annie Leibovitz, in collaboration with Vilmos Zsigmond, cinematographer, March.

Fiction

This category recognizes excellence in magazine fiction writing. It honors the quality of a publication's literary selections.

Harper's Magazine: Roger D. Hodge, editor, for "Death of the Pugilist," by Daniel Mason, July; "Fiction," by Alice Munro, August; "A Report on Our Recent Troubles," by Steven Millhauser, November.

McSweeney's: Dave Eggers, editor and founder, for "Retreat," by Wells Tower, May; "How To Sell," by Clancy Martin, May; "How to Make Millions in the Oil Market," by Christopher R. Howard, September.

The New Yorker: David Remnick, editor, for "Good People," by David Foster Wallace, February 5; "The Insufferable Gaucho," by Roberto Bolaño, October 1; "Or Else," by Antonya Nelson, November 19.

The Paris Review: Philip Gourevitch, editor, for "Monsieur Kalashnikov," by André Aciman, Summer; "Speak No Evil," by Uzodinma Iweala, Summer; "Icebergs," by Alistair Morgan, Winter.

Zoetrope: All-Story: Adrienne Brodeur, Francis Ford Coppola, founding editors; Michael Ray, editor, for "The Burning of Lawrence," by Andrew Malan Milward, Fall; "Those Americans Falling from the Sky," by Fiona McFarlane, Winter; "Methane and Politic," by Anya Ulinich, Winter.

General Excellence Online

This category recognizes outstanding magazine Web sites, as well as online-only magazines that feature original content. The site must convey a distinct editorial identity and create a unique magazine environment on the web.

Babble.com (www.babble.com): Ada Calhoun, editor-in-chief.

Chow.com (www.chow.com): Jane Goldman, editor-in-chief.

NewYorker.com (www.newyorker.com): Blake Eskin, editor.

RunnersWorld.com (www.runnersworld.com): David Willey, editor-in-chief; Mark Remy, executive editor; George Vlahogiannis, executive producer.

Slate (www.slate.com): Jacob Weisberg, editor-in-chief.

Personal Service Online

This category recognizes an outstanding service feature on the web. The practical advice or instruction presented should help readers either improve the quality of their personal lives or enjoy recreational interests. The category honors a site's creative use of multimedia technology, user involvement and community tools, and/or exceptional work in the blog form.

BusinessWeek.com: "B-Schools" (www.businessweek.com/bschools): Stephen J. Adler, editor-in-chief.

NYMag.com: "Grub Street" (http://nymag.com/daily/food): Adam Moss, editor-in-chief; Kelly Maloni and Ben Williams, coeditors.

People.com: "StyleWatch" (www.people.com/stylewatch): Mark Golin, editor.

Self.com: "The Self Challenge" (www.self.com/challenge): Lucy Danziger, editor-in-chief.

SI.com: "mySI" (www.si.com/mysi): Paul Fichtenbaum, managing editor.

Interactive Feature

This category recognizes an outstanding interactive section of the Web site, featuring news, entertainment, and other subjects that do not offer practical instruction or advice. The category honors a site's creative use of multimedia technology, user involvement and community tools, and exceptional work in the blog form.

Bicycling.com: "GPS Rides Tool" (http://bicycling.allsportgps.com): Stephen Madden, vice president/editor-in-chief; David L'Heureux, Web editor.

Economist.com: "Debate Series" (www.economist.com): John Micklethwait, editor-in-chief.

ESPN.com: "NBA Section" (www.sports.espn.go.com/nba/index): Rob King, vice president, editor-in-chief; Patrick Stiegman, vice president, executive editor and producer; John Kosner, senior vice president, ESPN Digital Media; John Zehr, senior vice president, digital media production, ESPN Digital.

Essence.com: "30 Dates in 30 Days" (www.essence.com/essence/30datesin30days): Angela Burt Murray, editor-in-chief; Lynya Floyd, senior editor; Jen M.R. Doman, multimedia development director; Nazenet Habtezghi, assistant editor; Shelly Jones, senior Web developer.

National Geographic Online (www.ngm.com): Chris Johns, editor-in-chief; Rob Covey, ngm.com.

Judges, 2008

Patrice G. Adcroft	*Discover*
Stephen J. Adler	*BusinessWeek*
Chris Anderson	*Wired*
Tim Appenzeller	*National Geographic*
Amy Astley	*Teen Vogue*
John Atwood	*Travel+*Leisure Golf
Florian Bachleda	FB Design
Laura Baer	Studio LB
Glenda Bailey	*Harper's Bazaar*
Lisa Bain	*Parenting*
Jenny Barnett	*Harper's Bazaar*
Jennifer Barr	*Travel+Leisure*
Deborah Barrow	TheDailyGreen.com
Sylvia Barsotti	About.com
Maria Baugh	
Keith Bellows	*National Geographic Traveler*
Melina Gerosa Bellows	*National Geographic Kids*
Gary Belsky	*ESPN The Magazine*
Lisa R. Benenson	*Hallmark Magazine*
Dorian Benkoil	Teeming Media
James Bennet	*The Atlantic*
Jane Berentson	*Inc.*
Debra Birnbaum	*TV Guide*
Deb Bishop	*Martha Stewart Living Omnimedia*
Matthew Bishop	*The Economist*
Kent Black	*Outside's Go*
Arabella Bowen	*Sherman's Travel Media*
Richard Bradley	*02138 Magazine*
Nicola Bridges	Prevention.com
Denise Brodey	*Fitness*
Daniel Brogan	*5280 Magazine*
Peter G. Brown*	*Scientific American*
Donna Bulseco	*InStyle*
James Burnett	*Boston Magazine*

Angela Burt-Murray*	*Essence*
Roberta Caploe	*Ladies' Home Journal*
Michael Carroll	*Institutional Investor*
Jeanne Carstensen	Salon.com
Michael Caruso	TheDailyTube
Janice Castro	Northwestern University
Andrea L. Chambers	New York University
Janet Chan	*The Parenting Group*
Timothy B. Clark	*Government Executive*
Bob Cohn	*Wired*
Roger Cohn	*Yale Environment Online*
Joanna Coles	*Marie Claire*
Corynne L. Corbett	*Real Simple*
Evan Cornog*	Columbia University
Dana Cowin	*Food & Wine*
Judith Coyne	*More*
Jennifer Crandall	*O, The Oprah Magazine*
Charity Curley	Martha Stewart Living Omnimedia
Scott Dadich	*Wired*
James Daly	*Edutopia*
Will Dana	*Rolling Stone*
Hope M. Daniels	*American Style, Niche Magazine*
Lucy Danziger*	*Self*
Maxine Davidowitz	*More*
Hugh Delehanty*	*AARP the Magazine*
Suzanne Donaldson	*Glamour*
Stephen Drucker	*House Beautiful*
Arem Duplessis	*The New York Times Magazine*
Alfred A. Edmond Jr. *	*Black Enterprise*
Jim Ellis	*BusinessWeek*
Rosemary Ellis*	*Good Housekeeping*
Sid Evans	*Garden & Gun*
Maryjane Fahey	*Better Homes and Gardens*
Barbara Fairchild	*Bon Appétit*
Michael Famighetti	*Aperture Magazine*
Thomas P. Farley	*Town & Country*
Brian Farnham	*Polar News*
Jay Fielden*	*Men's Vogue*
Neil Fine	*ESPN the Magazine*
Peter Flax	*Runner's World Magazine*

Franklin Foer	*The New Republic*
Fred Frailey	*Kiplinger's Personal Finance*
Lisa Lee Freeman	*ShopSmart Magazine*
Michael Freidson	*Time Out New York*
Anne Fulenwider	*Vanity Fair*
Nancy Gagliardi	Weight Watchers Publishing Group
Ted Genoways	*Virginia Quarterly Review*
Pilar Gerasimo	*Experience Life Magazine*
Paul Glastris	*Washington Monthly*
Klara Glowczewska	*Condé Nast Traveler*
Jon Gluck	*New York Magazine*
Judy Goldberg	*Parents*
Jane Goldman	*Chow & Urban Baby*
Susan Goodall	*Glamour*
Dan Goodgame	*Fortune Small Business*
Kellie Gould	
Nancy Perry Graham	*AARP the Magazine*
David Granger	*Esquire*
Sam Grawe	*Dwell Magazine*
Charles A. Green	*National Journal*
Freddi Greenberg	New York University
Edward Grinnan	*Guideposts*
Michael Grossman	Michael Grossman Consulting
Pilar Guzmán	*Cookie*
Larry Hackett	*People*
Rachel Hager	*Gilda's Club Worldwide*
Kendall Hamilton	*Ski Magazine*
Tish Hamilton	*Runner's World Magazine*
Douglas Harbrecht	*Kiplinger's Personal Finance*
Peter A. Harkness	*Governing*
Susan Hassler	*IEEE Spectrum*
James Heidenry	
Roseann Henry	*Waterfront Media*
Jill Herzig	*Glamour*
Aaron Hicklin	*Out*
Roger D. Hodge	*Harper's Magazine*
Regan Hofmann	*Poz Magazine*
Brandon Holley	*Yahoo Lifestyles*
Andrew J. Horton	*BusinessWeek*
Gail Horwood	*InStyle*

John House	
Sarah Humphreys	*Real Simple*
Adi Ignatius	*Time*
Robert Ivy	*Architectural Record*
Josh Jackson	*Paste Magazine*
Andrzej Janerka	*AARP the Magazine*
Mark Jannot	*Popular Science*
Clara Jeffery	*Mother Jones*
Roy S. Johnson	*Men's Fitness*
Tina Johnson	*Women's Health*
Radhika Jones	*The Paris Review*
Sandeep JunnarkarCity	University of New York
James Kaminsky	*Maxim*/Alpha Media Group
Jurriaan Kamp	*Ode*
Susan Kane	*BabyTalk*
Eliot Kaplan	Hearst Magazines
Joyce Rutter Kaye	*Print*
Kathryn Keller	*This Old House*
Bruce Kelley	*San Francisco Magazine*
Catherine Kelley	*O, The Oprah Magazine*
Susan Kittenplan	*Allure*
Kimberly D. Kleman	*Consumer Reports*
Laurie Kratochvil	
Ellen Kunes	*Health*
Diana La Guardia	
Steven Lagerfeld	*The Wilson Quarterly*
Yanick Rice Lamb	*Heart & Soul*
Valerie Latona	*Shape*
Kate Lawler	*Parents*
Jacqueline Leo	Chloe Consulting
Dennis Lewon	*Backpacker*
Lisl Liang	*SRQ Magazine*
John A. Limpert	*The Washingtonian*
Emily Listfield	
Robert Love	*Best Life*
Abbie Lundberg	*CIO Magazine*
Stephen Madden	*Bicycling/Mountain Bike Magazine*
Paul Maidment	Forbes.com
Michael Martin	Nerve.com
Paul Martinez	*Men's Journal*

Gerald Marzorati	*The New York Times Magazine*
Valerie May	*AARP the Magazine*
Pamela Maffei McCarthy*	*The New Yorker*
Harry McCracken	*PC World*
Louisa McCune-Elmore	*Oklahoma Today*
Terry McDonell	*Sports Illustrated*
Kevin S. McKean	*Consumer Reports*
Jon Meacham	*Newsweek*
James B. Meigs	*Popular Mechanics*
Mary Melton	*Los Angeles Magazine*
Peg Moline	*Fit Pregnancy*
Terence Monmaney	*Smithsonian*
Kitty Morgan	*Better Homes and Gardens*
Don Morris	Don Morris Design
Stacy Morrison	*Redbook*
Adam Moss*	*New York Magazine*
Marcy O'Koon Moss	*Arthritis Today*
Scott Mowbray	Health.com
Cullen Murphy	*Vanity Fair*
Roberta Myers	*Elle*
Moisés Naím	*Foreign Policy*
Christopher Napolitano	*Playboy*
Silvana Nardone	*Every Day with Rachael Ray*
Victor Navasky	*Columbia Journalism Review*
Jim Nelson	*GQ*
Martha Nelson	People Group
Robert Newman	
Terrance Noland	*Men's Journal*
Judith Nolte	*American Baby*
Peggy Northrop*	*Reader's Digest*
Ethan Nosowsky	Graywolf Press
Bernard Ohanian	*AARP Publications*
James Oseland	*Saveur*
Jack Otter	*Best Life*
Deborah Paul	Emmis Communications
Chee Pearlman	Chee Company
Abe Peck	Northwestern University
Jodi Peckman	*Rolling Stone*
Daniel Peres	*Details*
Robert Perino	*Fortune*

Stephen Perrine	*Best Life*
Stephen L. Petranek	Weider History Group
Steven Petrow*	Waterfront Media
George E. Pitts	*Latina*
Larry Platt	*Philadelphia Magazine*
Sean Plottner	*Dartmouth Alumni Magazine*
Jason Pontin	*Technology Review*
Tom Post	*Forbes*
Alexandra Postman	*Elle*
Robert Priest	*Condé Nast Portfolio*
Joshua Quittner	*Fortune*
Angelo Ragaza	
John Rasmus	*National Geographic Adventure*
Audrey Razgaitis	*Guideposts*
Susan K. Reed	*Golf for Women*
Ruth Reichl	*Gourmet*
John Rennie	*Scientific American*
Evelyn Renold	
Laura Rich	*Condé Nast Portfolio*
Susan Strecker Richard	*Caring Today*
Paul Ritter	*Elle*
Michael Roberts	*Outside*
Meredith Kahn Rollins	*Lucky*
Maer Roshan	*Radar*
Margaret Russell	*Elle Decor*
Robert Safian	*Fast Company*
Ina Saltz	Saltz Design
Diane Salvatore*	*Ladies' Home Journal*
David G. Schonauer*	*American Photo*
Eric Schurenberg*	*Money*
Cynthia Hall Searight	*Self*
David Seideman*	*Audubon Magazine*
Ellen Seidman	*Glamour*
Philip W. Semas	*The Chronicle of Higher Education*
Andrew Serwer	*Fortune*
Lesley Jane Seymour	*More*
James Shaheen	*Tricycle: The Buddhist Review*
Bill Shapiro	Time Inc.
Michael Shapiro	Columbia University

Stephen B. Shepard	City University of New York
Ann Shoket	*Seventeen*
Mitch Shostak	Shostak Studios, Inc.
Steve Slon	*AARP The Magazine*
Gretchen Smelter	*Brides*
Evan Smith*	*Texas Monthly*
Nancy Soriano*	*Country Living*
Robin Sparkman	*The American Lawyer*
Sreenath Sreenivasan*	Columbia University
Mike Steele	*Us Weekly*
Thomas A. Stewart	*Harvard Business Review*
Lisa Stiepock	*Wondertime*
Cyndi Stivers*	Consultant
Jay Stowe	*Cincinnati Magazine*
Scott S. Stuckcy	*National Geographic Traveler*
Bill Stump*	MensHealth.com
Katie Tamony	*Sunset*
Jerry Tarde	*Golf Digest*
Rick Tetzeli	*Entertainment Weekly*
Casey Tierney	*Real Simple*
Stefano Tonchi	*T: The New York Times Style Magazine*
Holland Utley	*Glamour*
Mimi Valdes Ryan	*Latina*
Norman Vanamee	*Sherman's Travel*
Antonia van der Meer	*Modern Bride, Elegant Bride, Your Prom*
Kristin van Ogtrop*	*Real Simple*
Victoria von Biel	*Bon Appétit*
Steven Waldman	*Beliefnet*
Donna Warner	*Metropolitan Home*
Jacob Weisberg	*Slate*
Matt Welch	*Reason*
Linda Wells	*Allure*
Charles Whitaker	Northwestern University
Mark Whitaker*	NBC News
Kate White	*Cosmopolitan*
Slaton White	*SHOTBusiness*
Brad Wieners	*Men's Journal*
David Willey*	*Runner's World*
Paige Williams	*Atlanta Magazine*

Robert S. Wilson	*The American Scholar*
Ellene Wundrok	*Real Simple*
Scott Yardley	*Ladies' Home Journal*
David Zinczenko*	*Men's Health*
David Zivan	*Indianapolis Monthly*

National Magazine Award Winners, 1966–2008

Best Interactive Design

2001   *SmartMoney.com*

Columns and Commentary

2002   *New York*
2003   *The Nation*
2004   *New York*
2005   *National Journal*
2006   *The New Yorker*
2007   *Vanity Fair*
2008   *Rolling Stone*

Design

1980   *Geo*
1981   *Attenzione*
1982   *Nautical Quarterly*
1983   *New York*
1984   *House & Garden*
1985   *Forbes*
1986   *Time*
1987   *Elle*
1988   *Life*
1989   *Rolling Stone*
1990   *Esquire*
1991   *Condé Nast Traveler*
1992   *Vanity Fair*
1993   *Harper's Bazaar*
1994   *Allure*
1995   *Martha Stewart Living*
1996   *Wired*
1997   *I.D.*
1998   *Entertainment Weekly*
1999   *ESPN The Magazine*

2000   *Fast Company*
2001   *Nest*
2002   *Details*
2003   *Details*
2004   *Esquire*
2005   *Kids: Fun Stuff to Do
        Together*
2006   *New York*
2007   *New York*
2008   *Wired*

Essays

2000   *The Sciences*
2001   *The New Yorker*
2002   *The New Yorker*
2003   *The American Scholar*
2004   *The New Yorker*
2005   *National Geographic*
2006   *Vanity Fair*
2007   *The Georgia Review*
2008   *New Letters*

Essays and Criticism

1978   *Esquire*
1979   *Life*
1980   *Natural History*
1981   *Time*
1982   *The Atlantic*
1983   *The American Lawyer*
1984   *The New Republic*
1985   *Boston Magazine*
1986   *The Sciences*
1987   *Outside*

1988	*Harper's Magazine*
1989	*Harper's Magazine*
1990	*Vanity Fair*
1991	*The Sciences*
1992	*The Nation*
1993	*The American Lawyer*
1994	*Harper's Magazine*
1995	*Harper's Magazine*
1996	*The New Yorker*
1997	*The New Yorker*
1998	*The New Yorker*
1999	*The Atlantic Monthly*

Feature Writing

1988	*The Atlantic*
1989	*Esquire*
1990	*The Washingtonian*
1991	*U.S. News & World Report*
1992	*Sports Illustrated*
1993	*The New Yorker*
1994	*Harper's Magazine*
1995	*GQ*
1996	*GQ*
1997	*Sports Illustrated*
1998	*Harper's Magazine*
1999	*The American Scholar*
2000	*Sports Illustrated*
2001	*Rolling Stone*
2002	*The Atlantic Monthly*
2003	*Harper's Magazine*
2004	*The New Yorker*
2005	*Esquire*
2006	*The American Scholar*
2007	*GQ*
2008	*Atlanta*

Fiction

1978	*The New Yorker*
1979	*The Atlantic Monthly*

1980	*Antaeus*
1981	*The North American Review*
1982	*The New Yorker*
1983	*The North American Review*
1984	*Seventeen*
1985	*Playboy*
1986	*The Georgia Review*
1987	*Esquire*
1988	*The Atlantic*
1989	*The New Yorker*
1990	*The New Yorker*
1991	*Esquire*
1992	*Story*
1993	*The New Yorker*
1994	*Harper's Magazine*
1995	*Story*
1996	*Harper's Magazine*
1997	*The New Yorker*
1998	*The New Yorker*
1999	*Harper's Magazine*
2000	*The New Yorker*
2001	*Zoetrope: All-Story*
2002	*The New Yorker*
2003	*The New Yorker*
2004	*Esquire*
2005	*The Atlantic Monthly*
2006	*The Virginia Quarterly Review*
2007	*McSweeney's*
2008	*Harper's Magazine*

Fiction and Belles Lettres

1970	*Redbook*
1971	*Esquire*
1972	*Mademoiselle*
1973	*The Atlantic Monthly*
1974	*The New Yorker*

1975	*Redbook*
1976	*Essence*
1977	*Mother Jones*

General Excellence

1973	*BusinessWeek*
1981	*ARTnews*
	Audubon
	BusinessWeek
	Glamour
1982	*Camera Arts*
	Newsweek
	Rocky Mountain
	Magazine
	Science81
1983	*Harper's Magazine*
	Life
	Louisiana Life
	Science82
1984	*The American Lawyer*
	House & Garden
	National Geographic
	Outside
1985	*American Health*
	American Heritage
	Manhattan, inc.
	Time
1986	*Discover*
	Money
	New England Monthly
	3–2–1-Contact
1987	*Common Cause*
	Elle
	New England Monthly
	People Weekly
1988	*Fortune*
	Hippocrates
	Parents
	The Sciences

1989	*American Heritage*
	Sports Illustrated
	The Sciences
	Vanity Fair
1990	*Metropolitan Home*
	7 Days
	Sports Illustrated
	Texas Monthly
1991	*Condé Nast Traveler*
	Glamour
	Interview
	The New Republic
1992	*Mirabella*
	National Geographic
	The New Republic
	Texas Monthly
1993	*American Photo*
	The Atlantic Monthly
	Lingua Franca
	Newsweek
1994	*BusinessWeek*
	Health
	Print
	Wired
1995	*Entertainment Weekly*
	I.D. Magazine
	Men's Journal
	The New Yorker
1996	*BusinessWeek*
	Civilization
	Outside
	The Sciences
1997	*I.D. Magazine*
	Outside
	Vanity Fair
	Wired
1998	*DoubleTake*
	Outside
	Preservation
	Rolling Stone

1999	Condé Nast Traveler		New York
	Fast Company		Time
	I.D. Magazine		The Virginia Quarterly
	Vanity Fair		Review
2000	National Geographic	2007	Bulletin of the Atomic
	Nest		Scientists
	The New Yorker		Foreign Policy
	Saveur		National Geographic
2001	The American Scholar		New York
	Mother Jones		Rolling Stone
	The New Yorker		Wired
	Teen People	2008	Backpacker
2002	Entertainment Weekly		GQ
	National Geographic		Mother Jones
	Adventure		National Geographic
	Newsweek		The New Yorker
	Print		Print
	Vibe		

1999   Condé Nast Traveler
      Fast Company
      I.D. Magazine
      Vanity Fair

2000   National Geographic
      Nest
      The New Yorker
      Saveur

2001   The American Scholar
      Mother Jones
      The New Yorker
      Teen People

2002   Entertainment Weekly
      National Geographic
      Adventure
      Newsweek
      Print
      Vibe

2003   Architectural Record
      The Atlantic Monthly
      ESPN The Magazine
      Foreign Policy
      Parenting
      Texas Monthly

2004   Aperture
      Budget Living
      Chicago Magazine
      Gourmet
      Newsweek
      Popular Science

2005   Dwell
      Glamour
      Martha Stewart Weddings
      The New Yorker
      Print
      Wired

2006   ESPN The Magazine
      Esquire
      Harper's Magazine

General Excellence in New Media

1997   Money
1998   The Sporting News
      Online
1999   Cigar Aficionado
2000   BusinessWeek Online

General Excellence Online (formerly General Excellence in New Media)

2001   U.S. News Online
2002   National Geographic
      Magazine Online
2003   Slate
2004   CNET News.com
2005   Style.com
2006   National Geographic Online
2007   Beliefnet.com
2008   RunnersWorld.com

Interactive Feature

2007   *nymag.com*
2008   *Bicycling.com*

Interactive Service

2007   *BusinessWeek.com*

Personal Service Online (formerly Interactive Service)

2008   *BusinessWeek.com*

Leisure Interests (formerly Special Interests)

2002   *Vogue*
2003   *National Geographic Adventure*
2004   *Consumer Reports*
2005   *Sports Illustrated*
2006   *Golf*
2007   *O, The Oprah Magazine*
2008   *New York*

Magazine Section

2005   *Popular Science*
2006   *Backpacker*
2007   *New York*
2008   *Condé Nast Portfolio*

Personal Service

1986   *Farm Journal*
1987   *Consumer Reports*
1988   *Money*
1989   *Good Housekeeping*
1990   *Consumer Reports*
1991   *New York*
1992   *Creative Classroom*
1993   *Good Housekeeping*
1994   *Fortune*
1995   *SmartMoney*
1996   *SmartMoney*
1997   *Glamour*
1998   *Men's Journal*
1999   *Good Housekeeping*
2000   *PC Computing*
2001   *National Geographic Adventure*
2002   *National Geographic Adventure*
2003   *Outside*
2004   *Men's Health*
2005   *BabyTalk*
2006   *Self*
2007   *Glamour*
2008   *Popular Mechanics*

Photography

1985   *Life*
1986   *Vogue*
1987   *National Geographic*
1988   *Rolling Stone*
1989   *National Geographic*
1990   *Texas Monthly*
1991   *National Geographic*
1992   *National Geographic*
1993   *Harper's Bazaar*
1994   *Martha Stewart Living*
1995   *Rolling Stone*
1996   *Saveur*
1997   *National Geographic*

1998	*W*
1999	*Martha Stewart Living*
2000	*Vanity Fair*
2001	*National Geographic*
2002	*Vanity Fair*
2003	*Condé Nast Traveler*
2004	*City*
2005	*Gourmet*
2006	*W*
2007	*National Geographic*
2008	*Gourmet*

Photojournalism

2007	*The Paris Review*
2008	*National Geographic*

Photo Portfolio

2007	*City*
2008	*Vanity Fair*

Photo Portfolio/Photo Essay

2004	*W*
2005	*Time*
2006	*Rolling Stone*

Profile Writing

2000	*Sports Illustrated*
2001	*The New Yorker*
2002	*The New Yorker*
2003	*Sports Illustrated*
2004	*Esquire*
2005	*The New Yorker*
2006	*Esquire*
2007	*New York*
2008	*Vanity Fair*

Public Interest
(formerly Public Service)

1986	*Science85*
1987	*Money*
1988	*The Atlantic*
1989	*California*
1990	*Southern Exposure*
1991	*Family Circle*
1992	*Glamour*
1993	*The Family Therapy Networker*
1994	*Philadelphia*
1995	*The New Republic*
1996	*Texas Monthly*
1997	*Fortune*
1998	*The Atlantic Monthly*
1999	*Time*
2000	*The New Yorker*
2001	*Time*
2002	*The Atlantic Monthly*
2003	*The Atlantic Monthly*
2004	*The New Yorker*
2005	*The New Yorker*
2006	*The New Yorker*
2007	*Vanity Fair*
2008	*The Nation*

Public Service

1970	*Life*
1971	*The Nation*
1972	*Philadelphia*
1974	*Scientific American*
1975	*Consumer Reports*
1976	*BusinessWeek*
1977	*Philadelphia*
1978	*Mother Jones*
1979	*New West*
1980	*Texas Monthly*

1981	Reader's Digest
1982	The Atlantic
1983	Foreign Affairs
1984	The New Yorker
1985	The Washingtonian

Reporting

1970	The New Yorker
1971	The Atlantic Monthly
1972	The Atlantic Monthly
1973	New York
1974	The New Yorker
1975	The New Yorker
1976	Audubon
1977	Audubon
1978	The New Yorker
1979	Texas Monthly
1980	Mother Jones
1981	National Journal
1982	The Washingtonian
1983	Institutional Investor
1984	Vanity Fair
1985	Texas Monthly
1986	Rolling Stone
1987	Life
1988	The Washingtonian and Baltimore Magazine
1989	The New Yorker
1990	The New Yorker
1991	The New Yorker
1992	The New Republic
1993	IEEE Spectrum
1994	The New Yorker
1995	The Atlantic Monthly
1996	The New Yorker
1997	Outside
1998	Rolling Stone
1999	Newsweek
2000	Vanity Fair
2001	Esquire
2002	The Atlantic Monthly
2003	The New Yorker
2004	Rolling Stone
2005	The New Yorker
2006	Rolling Stone
2007	Esquire
2008	National Geographic

Reviews and Criticism

2000	Esquire
2001	The New Yorker
2002	Harper's Magazine
2003	Vanity Fair
2004	Esquire
2005	The New Yorker
2006	Harper's Magazine
2007	The Nation
2008	The Atlantic

Service to the Individual

1974	Sports Illustrated
1975	Esquire
1976	Modern Medicine
1977	Harper's Magazine
1978	Newsweek
1979	The American Journal of Nursing
1980	Saturday Review
1982	Philadelphia
1983	Sunset
1984	New York
1985	The Washingtonian

Single Awards

1966	Look
1967	Life

| 1968 | *Newsweek* |
| 1969 | *American Machinist* |

Single-Topic Issue

1979	*Progressive Architecture*
1980	*Scientific American*
1981	*BusinessWeek*
1982	*Newsweek*
1983	*IEEE Spectrum*
1984	*Esquire*
1985	*American Heritage*
1986	*IEEE Spectrum*
1987	*Bulletin of the Atomic Scientists*
1988	*Life*
1989	*Hippocrates*
1990	*National Geographic*
1991	*The American Lawyer*
1992	*BusinessWeek*
1993	*Newsweek*
1994	*Health*
1995	*Discover*
1996	*Bon Appétit*
1997	*Scientific American*
1998	*The Sciences*
1999	*The Oxford American*
2002	*Time*
2003	*Scientific American*
2004	*The Oxford American*
2005	*Newsweek*
2006	*Time*
2007	*Departures*
2008	*The Virginia Quarterly Review*

Special Awards

| 1976 | *Time* |
| 1989 | Robert E. Kenyon Jr. |

Special Interests

1986	*Popular Mechanics*
1987	*Sports Afield*
1988	*Condé Nast Traveler*
1989	*Condé Nast Traveler*
1990	*Art & Antiques*
1991	*New York*
1992	*Sports Afield*
1993	*Philadelphia*
1994	*Outside*
1995	*GQ*
1996	*Saveur*
1997	*Smithsonian*
1998	*Entertainment Weekly*
1999	*PC Computing*
2000	*I.D. Magazine*
2001	*The New Yorker*

Specialized Journalism

1970	*Philadelphia*
1971	*Rolling Stone*
1972	*Architectural Record*
1973	*Psychology Today*
1974	*Texas Monthly*
1975	*Medical Economics*
1976	*United Mine Workers Journal*
1977	*Architectural Record*
1978	*Scientific American*
1979	*National Journal*
1980	*IEEE Spectrum*

Visual Excellence

1970	*Look*
1971	*Vogue*
1972	*Esquire*
1973	*Horizon*

1974	*Newsweek*	1977	*Rolling Stone*
1975	*Country Journal*	1978	*Architectural Digest*
	National Lampoon	1979	*Audubon*
1976	*Horticulture*		

Permissions

Contributors

KURT ANDERSEN is the author of the novels *Heyday* and *Turn of the Century*. The former was a *New York Times* best-seller that the *Los Angeles Times* called "a major work." He has also written for film, television, and the stage. During the 1990s Andersen was executive producer and head writer of two prime-time specials for NBC, *How to Be Famous* and *Hit List*, starring Jerry Seinfeld and Julia Louis-Dreyfus, and a creator of three pilots for ABC and NBC. He writes a column called "The Imperial City" for *New York* magazine, and contributes to *Vanity Fair*. Andersen has previously been a columnist for the *New Yorker* and *Time*. He began his career in journalism at *Time*.

TOM CARSON is currently a columnist at *GQ* and a regular book reviewer for *Los Angeles* magazine, where his work has won the CRMA award for criticism. He was a two-time National Magazine Award winner during his stint as *Esquire*'s "Screen" columnist. Carson is also among the contributors to *Stranded*, Greil Marcus's anthology of rock writing, and the author of *Gilligan's Wake* (2003), a novel.

CAITLIN FLANAGAN began her magazine-writing career in 2001 with a series of extended book reviews about the conflicts at the heart of modern life. She has quickly established herself as a highly entertaining social critic unafraid to take on self-indulgence and political correctness. Flanagan's *Atlantic* articles have been named as finalists for the National Magazine Award five times, and her essay "Confessions of a Prep School College Counselor," was included in the 2002 compilation of *Best American Magazine Writing*. Her work has also been included in *Best American Essays 2003* and *Best American Magazine Writing 2003*. She is the author of the book *To Hell with All That*.

VANESSA GRIGORIADIS is a contributing editor at *New York* magazine and *Rolling Stone*. She has been with *New York* on and off since she graduated from Wesleyan University in 1995, first as an editorial assistant, then promoted to contributing editor in 1998. She was also a writer on the Style desk at the *New York Times* in 2003. Prior to that, she spent a year studying the sociology of religion at Harvard University. She has been a contributing editor at *Rolling Stone* since 2004, and has written twenty stories in her four years at the publication, ranging from profiles of Paris Hilton, Jessica Simpson, and Jenna Jameson to investigatory pieces on medical marijuana, and a twelve-page breaking-news story of the country's largest eco-terrorist ring, which was nominated by *Rolling Stone* for a National Magazine Award in Reporting.

HENDRIK HERTZBERG is a staff writer and senior editor at the *New Yorker*. He has also been an officer in the navy, a reporter for *Newsweek*, President Carter's chief speech writer, and editor of the *New Republic*. He is the author of *Politics: Observations and Arguments*, a *New York Times* Notable Book of the Year and a *Washington Post* and *Los Angeles Times* Best Book of the Year for 2004. Under his editorship, the *New Republic* was nominated for ten National Magazine Awards and won three, including two for General Excellence. His *New Yorker* columns have been nominated four times and have won once, in 2006.

PETER HESSLER is the Beijing correspondent for the *New Yorker* and a contributor to *National Geographic*. He is the author of *River Town* and *Oracle Bones*.

CHRISTOPHER HITCHENS is one of the best known and most controversial writers and critics in the media. He has been a columnist for *Vanity Fair*, *The Nation*, and *Slate*. He is also a frequent contributor to the *New York Review of Books*, the *London Review of Books*, the *New York Times Book Review*, the *Los Angeles Times*

Book Review, and the *Atlantic Monthly*, among other publications. As foreign correspondent and travel writer, Hitchens has written from more than sixty countries on five continents—from Afghanistan, Albania, and Angola, through Ireland, India, Iran, and Iraq, to Japan, Vietnam, Western Sahara, Xylophagou, and Zimbabwe. He is the only writer to have written, since 2000, from Iran, Iraq, and North Korea. Hitchens's essays and articles have been collected or anthologized in *The Penguin Book of Twentieth-Century Essays*, *Best American Essays of 2001*, *Best American Travel Writing of 2002*, *Best American Political Writing of 2004*, and the "best of" collections published by the *London Review of Books*, *The Spectator*, *The Nation*, *The New Statesman*, *The Weekly Standard*, and the *Atlantic Monthly*. He is the author of many books, including: *God Is Not Great*; *Class and Nostalgia: Anglo-American Ironies*; *Karl Marx and The Paris Commune*; *The Monarchy: A Critique of Britain's Favorite Fetish*; *International Territory: The UN After Fifty Years*; *The Palestine Question*; *The Trial of Henry Kissinger*; and *A Long Short War: The Postponed Liberation of Iraq*.

THOMAS E. KENNEDY has published eleven books of fiction, including two volumes in 2007—the novel *A Passion in the Desert* and a story collection, *Cast Upon the Day*. Other recent fiction includes The Copenhagen Quartet, his novel series about which Harper College produced a DVD documentary in 2004. In 2007, the AWP annual conference dedicated a panel to his work. He lives in Denmark.

MIKE KESSLER was articles editor and editor-at-large of *5280*, Denver's monthly city magazine, from 2006 through 2008. His first feature for *5280* (December 2007's "A Leg to Stand On") was a finalist for a City and Regional Magazine Award in the profile-writing category. He has previously worked as executive editor at *Skiing Magazine* (where he wrote a story that made the

Notable list of *Best American Sports Writing 2006*); editor-in-chief of *No Boundaries*, an adventure-travel quarterly; cowriter and producer of the Fox Network documentary series *No Boundaries*; and a junior staffer at *Outside* magazine. Kessler currently lives in Los Angeles, where he writes full time for such publications as *Details*, *Men's Journal*, and *Backpacker*.

WALTER KIRN is a novelist, essayist, and critic who lives in Livingston, Montana. His works of fiction include *Up in the Air*, *Thumbsucker*, and *Mission to America*, two of which have been turned into feature films. A frequent contributor to the *New York Times Book Review*, he has served as a contributing editor to *Time* magazine and as the literary editor of *GQ*. His nonfiction articles and essays have appeared in the *Atlantic*, the *New Yorker*, the *New York Times Magazine*, and *Esquire*. His next book, *Lost in the Meritocracy*, a scathing memoir of his years at Princeton and Oxford, first appeared in the *Atlantic* and will be published by Doubleday in expanded form in the spring of 2009. Kirn will be the nonfiction writer-in-residence at the University of Chicago in the fall of 2008.

JOSHUA KORS is an investigative reporter for *The Nation*, where he covers military and veterans' issues. He is the winner of a number of awards, including the National Magazine Award for Public Interest (for a two-part series that showed how military doctors are purposely misdiagnosing soldiers wounded in Iraq and labeling them mentally ill in order to deny them medical care and disability pay), the George Polk Award, and a National Headliner Award. He was also a finalist for the Michael Kelly Award and the American Bar Association's Silver Gavel Award.

WILLIAM LANGEWIESCHE is an international correspondent for *Vanity Fair*. Before that, he was a national correspondent at the

Atlantic. During his tenure there, he was nominated for eight consecutive National Magazine Awards and won in 2002 for reporting. Langewiesche is the author of numerous books, among them *Cutting for Sign*, about the complex reality of the U.S.-Mexican border; *Inside the Sky: A Meditation on Flight*; *American Ground: Unbuilding the World Trade Center*, an insider's account of the cleanup of the Twin Towers; and *The Outlaw Sea: A World of Freedom, Chaos, and Crime*. Before joining the *Atlantic*, Langewiesche had been a professional pilot.

JEANNE MARIE Laskas is the author of five books, including the newly released *Growing Girls*, *The Exact Same Moon*, and *Fifty Acres and a Poodle*. Since 1994 she has been a regular, syndicated columnist for the *Washington Post Magazine*, where her "Significant Others" essays appear weekly. Most of her magazine feature stories now appear in *GQ*, where she is a correspondent writing on everything from Iraq to plastic surgery to coal miners. Formerly a contributing editor at *Esquire*, her stories have appeared in numerous anthologies. Laskas is the voice behind "Ask Laskas" in *Reader's Digest*. She also writes the "My Life as a Mom" column for *Ladies' Home Journal*.

JANE MAYER joined the *New Yorker* as a staff writer in March 1995. Based in Washington, D.C., she writes about politics for the magazine and has been covering the war on terror. Before joining the *New Yorker*, Mayer was a reporter at the *Wall Street Journal* for twelve years. In 1984, she became the *Journal*'s first female White House correspondent. She was nominated twice by the *Journal* for a Pulitzer Prize in the feature-writing category. Before joining the *Journal* in 1982, Mayer worked as a metropolitan reporter for the *Washington Star*. She began her career in journalism as a stringer for *Time* magazine while still a student in college.

STEVE ONEY is a senior writer for *Los Angeles* magazine. His work has also appeared in *Esquire*, *GQ*, *Playboy*, and a number of now-defunct publications, among them *Atlanta Weekly*, *California*, and *Premiere*. *And The Dead Shall Rise*, Oney's 2003 book on the lynching of Leo Frank, won the Southern Book Critics Circle Award for best nonfiction book about the South.

GEORGE PACKER became a staff writer for the *New Yorker* in 2003 and has covered the Iraq War for the magazine. His book *The Assassins' Gate: America in Iraq* was named one of the ten best books of 2005 by the *New York Times* and won the New York Public Library's Helen Bernstein Book Award and an Overseas Press Club book award. Packer is also the author of *The Village of Waiting*, about his experience in Africa. His book *Blood of the Liberals*, a three-generational nonfiction history of his family and American liberalism in the twentieth century, won the Robert F. Kennedy Book Award. Packer has served in the Peace Corps and was a 2001–02 Guggenheim Fellow.

MATTHEW SCULLY, currently a speechwriter for Republican presidential candidate John McCain, served for five years as a senior speechwriter for President George W. Bush. He has also written for vice presidents Dick Cheney and Dan Quayle, presidential candidate Robert Dole, and the late Pennsylvania Gov. Robert P. Casey. A former literary editor of the *National Review*, his work has appeared in the *New York Times*, the *Wall Street Journal*, the *Washington Post*, and the *Los Angeles Times*, among other newspapers and magazines. He is the author of *Dominion: The Power of Man, the Suffering of Animals, and the Call to Mercy.*

MATT TAIBBI is a contributing editor for *Rolling Stone*. He graduated from Bard College in New York in 1991 and finished his studies at Leningrad Polytechnical University in Russia. Taibbi worked as a freelance reporter in the former Soviet Union and returned to the United States in 1994, working as an investigator in a Boston-based private detective agency. In 2002 he founded the Buffalo-based newspaper *The Beast*, which he left after a year to work as a columnist for the *New York Press* and eventually as a contributing editor for *Rolling Stone*. His *Press* column on George Bush's prewar press conference, "Cleaning the Pool," was included in the *Best Political Writing 2003* anthology, and a year later, he was named one of the thirty-five most influential New Yorkers under thirty-five by the *New York Observer*.

PAIGE WILLIAMS is deputy editor of *Atlanta* magazine. Williams has written for magazines including *Men's Journal*, *GQ*, *New York*, the *Financial Times* magazine, *Playboy*, and *More*, and for newspapers including the *New York Times*, the *Charlotte Observer*, and the *Washington Post*. Williams's stories have been anthologized in *The Best American Crime Writing* (2002 and 2006), *The Best American Legal Commentary* (2005), and in *The User's Guide to College Writing*. She has taught journalism at the University of Mississippi, New York University, and Emory University, and fiction workshops at Columbia University, where she recently earned her MFA.

EVAN WRIGHT began at *Vanity Fair* in 2007. He previously wrote for *Rolling Stone*, where he served as "Unofficial Ambassador to the Underbelly," reporting on subcultures ranging from radical environmentalist groups to Hollywood's runaway skateboarders to Russian gangs in the Southwest. Wright also has written extensively from combat zones in the Middle East. His "Killer Elite" series about a marine reconnaissance unit in Iraq won the National Magazine Award for Reporting. His book *Generation*

Kill was honored by the Marine Corps Heritage Foundation as the "Best History" of the Marine Corps in 2005. Wright also works as a book reviewer for the *Los Angeles Times* and has contributed to the *New York Times* and *Time* magazine. His first job was for Larry Flynt, for whom he worked as *Hustler*'s adult film critic and editor of *Barely Legal* magazine.